PRAISE FOR PHILIP FURIA'S *SKYLARK*, THE FIRST BIOGRAPHY OF AMERICA'S MOST POPULAR LYRICIST.

"As the years go by, certain songs become an indelible part of our collective memory. The songs themselves may be unforgettable, but alas, not so the names of the men and women who created them. Johnny Mercer, one of America's finest lyricists, deserves to be memorialized and, happily, he has been brought vividly to life in this fascinating and illuminating biography. Philip Furia's full-length portrait, sympathetic yet candid, is an overdue tribute to the accomplishments of this extraordinarily gifted songwriter-poet. As an ardent admirer of Mercer's work, I am deeply grateful."   —Sheldon Harnick

"*Skylark* explains Johnny Mercer so well. Furia's book helped me understand a man who was like a father to me, but many of whose complexities remained well hidden. It also establishes a rich connection between Mercer's life and lyrics. *Skylark* is a brilliant and thoughtful book that everyone interested in popular American music will be enriched by. It is also a delicious read."
—Margaret Whiting

"In this sensitive and wonderfully in-depth work on the lyricist of classics like 'One for the Road' and 'Moon River,' Furia displays his talent for writing about the giants in American popular song."   —*Publishers Weekly*

"Furia brings an encyclopedic knowledge of American pop songs and show tunes to *Skylark*. [It] reveals the joys and anguish that fueled Johnny Mercer's graceful, seemingly heaven-sent prose."   —*Boston Herald*

"Mercer was an absurdly talented, enormously complex man, and Philip Furia's new biography does justice to both parts of the equation."   —*Palm Beach Post*

"Furia has come out with a fine biography—even the chapter titles should set off some great tunes in your head: 'Jeepers Creepers,' 'Hooray for Hollywood,' 'Blues in the Night,' 'Ac-cent-tchu-ate the Positive,' 'I'm Old Fashioned.'"
—*San Jose Mercury News*

"Johnny Mercer . . . could be a charmer. He could be a swine. We see both sides in *Skylark*, Furia's impressive biography of the . . . lyricist . . . Furia sensitively captures his subject's maddening contradictions."   —*Savannah Morning News*

"*Skylark* makes a fascinating read. A novelistic narrative of a sadly tortured soul, a useful guide to the history of American music, and a closely argued case for what made Mercer lyrics not just good, but great."   —*Wilmington Star-News*

"*Skylark* will be revelatory to some, long overdue to others, and a lasting pleasure to anyone with an interest in American popular music."
—*New Orleans Times-Picayune*

Also by Philip Furia

The Poets of Tin Pan Alley: A History of America's Great Lyricists

Irving Berlin: A Life in Song (The Companion Series)

Ira Gershwin: The Art of the Lyricist

Skylark

The Life and Times of
Johnny Mercer

PHILIP FURIA

St. Martin's Griffin ✺ New York

www.stmartins.com

The author is grateful for permission to reprint excerpts from copyrighted material. These permissions appear on pages 307–313, which constitute a continuation of this copyright page.

Library of Congress Cataloging-in-Publication Data

Furia, Philip, 1943–
  Skylark : the life and times of Johnny Mercer / Philip Furia.
    p. cm.
  Includes bibliographical references (p. 305) and index (p. 317)
  ISBN 0-312-28720-8 (hc)
  ISBN 0-312-33099-5 (pbk)
  EAN 978-0312-33099-6
  1. Mercer, Johnny, 1909– 2. Lyricists—United States—Biography. I. Title.

ML423.M446F87 2003

782.42164'092—dc21
[B]
                                                          2003043161

First Edition December 2004

10 9 8 7 6 5 4 3 2 1

To Laurie,
who, as promised,
has loved me "Come Rain or Come Shine"

Contents

Moon River

During what has been called the golden age of American popular song, most of the great songwriters were Jews, immigrants or the children of immigrants, who grew up in New York City in the early twentieth century. One of the greatest of them, however, came from a prominent family in Savannah, Georgia, that could trace its ancestry back to distinguished Scottish forebears. When Irving Berlin was a singing waiter in a Chinatown saloon, inventing risqué parodies to popular tunes of the day and carefully kicking the coins customers tossed at him into a pile behind the bar, Johnny Mercer was cradled by his black nanny. When George Gershwin quit high school to play piano on the stretch of West Twenty-eighth Street known as Tin Pan Alley because it housed the cacophonous offices of many sheet-music publishing firms, Johnny Mercer was a choirboy at Christ Episcopal Church. When Richard Rodgers and Lorenz Hart were struggling to place their urbanely witty songs in Broadway musicals and getting so many rebuffs that Rodgers contemplated giving up music for the children's underwear business, Johnny Mercer was playing pranks at a fashionable Virginia prep school.

Although Mercer would move among such New York songwriters for much of his life, his genteel southern background would always set him apart. Berlin, the Gershwins, even Cole Porter, another well-to-do Episcopalian who hailed from Peru (pronounced *Pee*-ru), Indiana, were "indoor" writers, whose songs radiated the rhythm, energy, and cosmopolitan verve of New York. Mercer, by contrast, was an "outdoor" writer, whose lyrics drew their imagery from the world of nature and from the American landscape. Consequently, his songs had a greater range and took in more of America than those of any other songwriter. He could be hiply urbane in "Satin Doll," elegantly sensuous in "That Old Black Magic," down-home folksy in "In the Cool, Cool, Cool of the Evening," excitedly childlike in "Jeepers Creepers," achingly nostalgic in "Days of Wine and Roses."

To Oscar Hammerstein, Johnny Mercer was "the most perfect American lyricist alive. American. Pure American." To Yip Harburg, who grew up in wretched poverty on the Lower East Side but went on to write "Over the Rainbow," Johnny Mercer was "one of our great folk poets," whose lyrics had their roots in the prose of Mark Twain and the songs of Stephen Foster. "Mercer had an ability to write from roots different from mine," said Hal David. Even though David has penned such folksy lyrics as "Raindrops Keep Falling on My Head" and "Do You Know the Way to San Jose?" he envied Mercer's regional roots: "He was southern. I am Brooklyn. And he created the most wonderful images. He wrote lyrics I wish I could write, but I knew I couldn't because I came from a different base." Another New York writer, Alec Wilder, once visited Mercer at his home in the Bel Air section of Los Angeles. As Wilder got out of his cab, he saw Mercer in the backyard, feeding the birds. "Good God," Wilder thought, "the man who wrote 'Mr. Meadowlark,' 'Bob White,' and 'Skylark' really *does* love birds."

What also set Mercer apart from his fellow songwriters was his successful career as a singer, a harbinger of songwriters, such as Paul Simon and Bob Dylan, who perform their own songs. While Mercer was a consummate interpreter of his own works, however, he preferred to sing the songs of Irving Berlin, Jerome Kern, and others he had loved as a boy. He sang with Paul Whiteman, Benny Goodman, and other big bands on numerous radio programs (including some of his own shows) and, in later years, on television. As a singer, he could interact with performers as other songwriters could not, and he recorded songs with singers as varied as Judy Garland, Nat King Cole, Bing Crosby, and Bobby Darin. As a radio singer in the 1940s, Johnny Mercer became a household name, and that saved him from the relative oblivion to which most lyricists are consigned by a public that usually associates a song with its composer. "Gershwin," to most people, means George Gershwin, even though it was his brother Ira's lyrics that made many a "Gershwin tune" memorable. Mrs. Oscar Hammerstein, so the story goes, grew so tired of composers overshadowing lyricists that when she heard someone refer to "Ol' Man River" as a great "Kern" song, she said, "Jerome Kern did not write 'Ol' Man River.' Mr. Kern wrote *'dum dum dum da.'* My husband wrote *'Ol' Man River.'* "

While people never refer to a "Hammerstein" song or a "Harburg" song, they do speak of a "Johnny Mercer song," making Mercer the only lyricist from a generation of brilliant wordsmiths to identify himself with his songs in the public imagination. When Ella Fitzgerald made her classic series of songwriter albums for Verve Records in the 1950s, virtually every album was based on a composer: *The Duke Ellington Song Book, The Harold Arlen Song*

Book . . . The sole exception was *The Johnny Mercer Song Book*, an album of songs by a single *lyricist*.

For twenty years, from the mid-1930s to the mid-1950s, Mercer dominated the popular song charts. During that era, he had at least one song in the Top Ten for 221 weeks; for 55 weeks he had two songs in the Top Ten; for 6 weeks he had three songs in that circle; during 2 weeks in 1942, he had four songs there—virtually half the *Hit Parade*. In some years, he had a song in the Top Ten during every week of the year, the songwriter's equivalent of Joe DiMaggio's hitting streak, and his songs were number one a record thirteen times. In the course of his career he would write the lyrics, and sometimes the music as well, for 1,088 songs; of these, 18 would be nominated for the Academy Award for Best Song, and four would win the Oscar.

Not only were these songs popular in his lifetime; they have endured as standards, songs that remain as fresh today as when they were first heard, fifty, sixty, seventy years ago. Recorded by such artists as Frank Sinatra and Tony Bennett, heard in jazz clubs and cabarets, in Broadway revivals and on film sound tracks such as *Midnight in the Garden of Good and Evil*, even on television commercials, such songs constitute the closest thing America has to a body of classical music. If there were a Louvre Museum for popular song, Johnny Mercer would have a wing all his own.

Some of his songs have so steeped themselves into the American sensibility, they have assumed the status of folk songs. The annual Academy Award celebration opens with "Hooray for Hollywood." Parents look at their newborn and break into "You Must Have Been a Beautiful Baby." A kid climbs on a horse for the first time, and a father sings, "I'm an old cowhand from the Rio Grande." A castoff lover orders a drink in bar, drops a coin in a jukebox, and listens for "It's quarter to three, / There's no one in the place except you and me, / Set 'em up, Joe." Johnny Mercer's most famous song touched the American landscape when Chatham County renamed the Back River, where the Mercer family had a summer home, "Moon River."

Moon River is one of several rivulets—the Burnside, the Skidaway, the Little Ogeechee—that the Vernon River breaks up into just before it flows into the Atlantic below Savannah, creating a filigree of islands covered in golden grass, stretches of white sand, and green clumps of cypress, live oak, and magnolia. Johnny Mercer spent his childhood summers here, on the water, fishing, swimming, sailing, and sometimes just lying still and watching pheasants, egrets, and herons soar over the marshland. On my first trip to Savannah, as I drove over one of the bridges that stitch these islands together, I saw the sign "Moon River" and stopped. (Locals told me I was lucky; usually, soon after the sign is put up, somebody steals it.) Even I, a city kid who thinks nature is best encountered from behind the windshield of a moving car, was stunned by the beauty of the landscape. I got out and stood looking over the water. Like Wordsworth's Lake District, this shimmering landscape must have been a source of Mercer's artistry, but it also must have shaped "that best portion of a good man's life, / His little, nameless, unremembered, acts / Of kindness and of love."

It certainly nurtured his imagination at the lowest point in his career, when the rise of rock and roll in the 1950s shoved songwriters such as Cole Porter and Irving Berlin to the sidelines, and Johnny Mercer was no exception. But Berlin and Porter were at the ends of their careers and could look back on their great Broadway musicals, assured that regular revivals of such classic shows as *Annie Get Your Gun* and *Kiss Me, Kate* would keep their songs fresh for generations to come. Mercer, however, still in his forties, at the full force of his creative powers, but with fewer and fewer outlets for them. Although he had had many individual hit songs, he had not yet managed to create a classic Broadway score. Musical films, a form in which he had flourished for decades, were disappearing in the face of the popularity of the new medium of television.

All that was left for him in Hollywood was the piecework of writing a single theme song for a dramatic motion picture. But, as Mercer accepted the lowly assignment of writing a lyric for a melody by Henry Mancini that would figure in *Breakfast at Tiffany's*, his imagination went back to his childhood and the Vernon River spreading out "wider than a mile." He also remembered how he and his friends, on the "sandy spit called the hummock, once basked peacefully in the heat of the day," dreaming of going out in the world and coming back with a token of their success: driving a Packard ("the best in those days") with a sign, "Who's Sorry Now?" painted on the big spare tire. Out of that memory came another line: "I'm crossing you in style some day."

But his most telling memory came near the end of the song as he thought of his closest childhood friend, his cousin Walter Rivers, playing along the river and gathering huckleberries to make ice cream:

We're after the same rainbow's end,
Waitin' round the bend,
My huckleberry friend.

The phrase became the signature piece of a song that pulled Mercer out of his creative torpor and earned him his third Academy Award. Irving Berlin predicted, accurately, that "Moon River" would achieve the stature of an American folk song.

This shimmering coastal waterway had supplied Johnny Mercer with "beauteous forms" and "sensations sweet, / Felt in the blood, and felt along the heart." But where, I wondered as I took in the glorious scene, did the horrifying side of this avuncular southern gentleman have its roots? The side that came out when he drank—bitterly frustrated, deeply despondent, overcome by a sense of failure. The side that would turn on friends and strangers in bars, in restaurants, and at parties, insulting them with vitriolic abuse, then send a dozen roses the next morning with a wrenching note of apology. "He could seek out your weak spot," a friend said, "and stick a needle into it." The side that would tell one hostess who wanted to introduce him to her mother, "I don't want to meet your fucking mother," and would prompt him, angry at another hostess, to walk into her bedroom closet and urinate on all of her shoes. The side that turned most often on his wife, Ginger, and made up cutting lyrics about her at parties; then, as he slipped deeper into his cups, simply cursed at her; and finally, when he was too besotted to talk, looked at her, looked at the drink in his hand, and poured it over her head.

I got back into my car and drove farther across the waterway to meet a niece of Mercer's who had been the victim of a particularly painful attack. A lovely, graying woman about my own age let me in. She had on a white blouse and plain gray sweater, and the house was decorated simply, with a country touch of pine-paneled walls and expansive windows covered in blue-and-white checked curtains. She invited me to sit down at the dining-room table where we looked out over the iridescent landscape. "I always felt that Johnny's heart was tied to here," she said, pulling the curtains farther apart. "He was really a man who liked simple pleasures and nature's beauty and clever words and music, and he got thrown into the fast lane with fame and fortune. I just don't think he was ever happy with it. He never said that to me, but I just always felt that about him, that he was out of place, he was not where he belonged, it was not where his heart was. But that's just a feeling. . . . He wanted a place that felt like home. Savannah felt like home, and I don't know but maybe this place was the only other place that felt like home. But I just felt like he didn't have a home. I guess his heart didn't have a home."

His heart didn't have a home. Her phrase echoed so many of Mercer's lyrics that express a longing for a lost world of love and peace and beauty:

Skylark,
Have you seen a valley green with Spring?
Where my heart can go a journeying,
Over the shadows and the rain, to a blossom covered lane?
And in your lonely flight,
Haven't you heard the music in the night,
Wonderful music,
Faint as a "will o' the wisp,"
Crazy as a loon,
Sad as a gypsy serenading the moon,
Oh, Skylark,
I don't know if you can find these things,
But my heart is riding on your wings,
So, if you see them anywhere,
Won't you lead me there?

"The sadness and lostness of him," she said, "when you hear the lyrics to his songs, almost all of them have that quality."

The niece could speak so insightfully and poetically about a man who had betrayed her brutally. She had grown up close to Amanda, Johnny's adopted daughter. "I just remember feeling—I don't know—I always felt bonded with Johnny somehow—there was something 'lonely' about him that just attracted me, you know. I just felt a lot of compassion for him, I always did." She had stayed with the Mercers as a teenager, gone to Broadway shows with them as a college student, and, despite the vicious arguments she would hear between Johnny and Ginger, felt like their daughter. Then, when she was a grown woman, suffering from a recent divorce, she went to a party in Savannah, where Uncle Johnny, as usual, got drunk. She offered to drive him home. Once in her car, however, this man she had adored as a father turned and, as she put it with southern delicacy, made a "pass" at her.

"I never had any respect for him after that," she said, her mouth in a tight line that reflected the pain the memory still brought her, in juxtaposition to the bucolic landscape beyond the window. "He may have felt like he was losing his grip. I mean, a lot of men go after younger women when they get to that stage in life, but it was a real bitter disappointment to me. . . . I certainly didn't expect it. It was the last thing I expected." She paused and looked out the window to where the wind was blowing the golden marsh grass in long waves. "Our relationship was ended," she added. "I never saw him again after that. I didn't really care to."

Then, a grim afterthought: "I don't think he was ever happy."

Awkwardly, I said that I had interviewed people, actresses and chorus girls, who had witnessed his sexual advances. "They said that he made his passes with charm, that he was always a gentleman, that there was never anything threatening to it."

She looked at me as if I were the biggest fool in Chatham County: "It was shabby."

As I drove back to Savannah across the waterway, I thought of the eight-month-old girl my wife and I had just adopted from Guatemala. The thought of making a sexual overture to anyone even remotely like a daughter was utterly repugnant. Yet I wondered if I was being prudish. When I told an old college friend, who'd been raised in the South, about Mercer's behavior, he cackled and said, "So Johnny Mercer tried to boink his own niece. Welcome to Southern Gothic."

At a family gathering, I told my brother-in-law about it. An Ivy League professor who counsels presidents, he asked, "Was Mercer's niece an adult when he did this?" When I assured him she was, he said, "Well, then there's nothing wrong with that." Like Robert Frost, I know how it feels to think of the right thing to say too late. The family gathering we were at was our niece's wedding. "Oh, really?" I should have said. "So it would be all right for you to make a pass at Rebecca?"

Yet as I talked with more and more people who knew Johnny Mercer, people who had stories of his drunken behavior and had been victims of his vicious insults, I found no one who did not adore him—not merely like him or feel fondness toward him but *adore* him—even, so far as I could gather, his wife, Ginger, the target of his worst abuse. When pressed about why he behaved as he did when he drank, people offered every excuse from the chemical imbalance brought on by alcohol to the possibility that such vicious insults reflected a twisted sense of humor. Always, the love that people bore him overrode even their worst memories of his attacks.

André Previn recalled being warned by Mercer, "I can get kind of nasty when I drink, but it doesn't mean anything." Mercer had no "governor," as Previn elegantly put it, and would lash out at the simplest of questions, such as someone asking what time it was. "'What time is it?' 'What time is it?' 'What time is it?' Mercer would mimic. 'Can't you think of anything else, for Christ's sake?'" Yet, as Previn spoke of Mercer, absolute warmth and love came through, leading him to say he considered Johnny Mercer the greatest of all song lyricists and that writing a song with Johnny Mercer, even after working with such distinguished writers as Alan Jay Lerner and Stephen Sondheim, was the thing he was most proud of.

As appalled as I was by the stories people told me, I found that I could not imagine a man more, to borrow one of his own song titles, "Dearly Beloved."

One

You Must Have Been a Beautiful Baby: 1909–1927

I suppose the reason for my being a songwriter is largely due to my childhood in Savannah. . . . Savannah was smaller then and sleepy, full of trees and azaleas that filled the parks which make it so beautiful. . . . I can remember so many things about it, all connected with music in various ways. . . . Although I have never written a song directly about Savannah, so many of my lyrics are filled with boyhood images that you might say they all sprang from there.

On September 12, 1884, Johnny Mercer's grandfather wrote a letter to his son George, who had just gone off to boarding school, stipulating what his prominent family expected of him. First, however, the elder Mercer tries to comfort the homesick boy: "In sending you away from home to prosecute your studies in a distant state, your father is actuated only by an earnest desire to prosper you physically and intellectually." For his own part, he says, "It is extremely painful to me to part with you," but he then displaces his own emotions onto his wife: "Your tender-hearted, loving mother will grieve over your absence." With Victorian solemnity, the father stresses the need for self-reliance, effort, and progress, reminding George that "this course will cost me a good deal, and that every dollar expended for your benefit, my son, is the fruit of your father's hard labor."

After placing all of these great expectations on his son's shoulders, he adds one more demanding standard: forbearance. "Avoid, my dear son, as you would the plague, that terrible habit of self-abuse, to which so many boys are addicted." Without using the word "masturbation," he warns that it drove one of Savannah's most brilliant young men to an insane asylum and calls it the first challenge to a young man's self-control. "By his power to resist this, he may judge it his ability to resist the appetites and passions that will assail him in future life." If the urge grows "too powerful to be mastered," he counsels, "intercourse with a woman, wicked and forbidden though it be, is more decent and in every way better than self abuse." After inviting his son to discuss such "private matters" as "emissions that occur in dreams at night," he adds the strongest of deterrents: "When you are tempted to do wrong, think of your dear mother, of her pure love, imagine she sees you and ask yourself what she will think."

George Armstrong Mercer had inherited his father's stern Victorian fiber, and he passed it on to his sons, whom he also held to the very highest standards. His expected them to follow his model as one of Savannah's most respected citizens, an attorney and real estate developer, a man known for his generosity and integrity, who prided himself on doing "good deeds in the dark of the night" and shunning public recognition. The one public gesture he allowed himself was on behalf of the Bethesda Orphanage, the oldest existing orphanage in America. "Mr. Mercer Sr. was president of the Union Society which ran the orphanage," a business associate explained, "and periodically, he would run ads at his expense that said, 'If you will leave something in your will to Bethesda, I'll draw your will up without charge.'" At a time when it was considered unprofessional for attorneys to advertise their services, George Mercer's beneficence outweighed propriety, and he always included an inspirational poem or quotation in the ads.

Yet while George Mercer's heart could embrace the orphans of Savannah, it could shun one of his own sons when the son failed, even in infancy, to live up to his rigorous expectations. His wife, Mary Walter Mercer, bore him two sons, George junior and Walter, but died, just shortly before Christmas on December 19, 1900, at the age of twenty-nine, while giving birth to Hugh Mercer. "His father was a pretty severe person," said a niece, noting that he blamed his wife's death on the baby. "He destroyed that child's life," she said. Hugh Mercer "always felt that he was a nobody in that family." George Mercer banished the baby from his home, and Hugh had to be raised by his aunt Katherine.

Eight years later, George Mercer married his secretary, Lillian Ciucevich. Her father, Giovanni Ciucevich, had emigrated from the Austrian-Hungarian Empire in the 1850s and ran the Yankee blockade during the Civil War, his sloop slipping under the noses of the Union forces to bring supplies into Savannah. After the war, he married a Georgia girl, Julia Ann Merritt, and "prospered like Rhett Butler in *Gone With the Wind*." His daughter Lillian had a sensitive, melancholy disposition, and once she married George Mercer in 1906, her heart went out to his banished child. After Hugh was permitted to visit his family, Lillian described the time when he had to be returned to his aunt: "We had to take Hugh back to Katherine, and he didn't want to go and cried bitterly." Ultimately, she prevailed upon her husband to bring the child into their home.

As if in compensation for Hugh, on November 18, 1909, Lillian bore George Mercer a fourth son, John Herndon Mercer, who would absorb his father's highest standards of behavior and fulfill his greatest expectations. From his mother, however, he inherited a dark, melancholy temperament that always lay beneath the surface of his jubilant, pixyish personality. "Miss Lillian" had "that kind of melancholia," a niece said. "I'm not saying she was depressed. That's not what I'm saying. Not a clinical depression, but that sort of quality that he had . . . Some of us in the family have it."

Lillian Ciucevich had grown up on a farm south of Savannah, on the Augusta road, which used to be called the Five Mile Bend because that was where trains, having hit the end of the line in coastal Savannah, would turn around to go back into the Savannah station. Her granddaughter said Lillian "always thought that the sound of the train whistle was so lonesome and so mournful, and would say to me—she would tell me this story. She rocked me a lot, and she would say how the whistle went: 'Whoo-oo—whoo! Whoo-oo—whoo!' And I can still hear her saying it. I know she told the same stories to him. She had to have. And I think that's where 'Blues in the Night' came from":

Hear dat lonesome whistle
Blowin' 'cross the trestle,
Whoo-ee,
(My mama done tol' me)
A whoo-ee-duh-whoo-ee.

Johnny Mercer would have heard those same whistles, a little fainter, from his home at 226 East Gwinnett Street.

While Mercer attributed his dark temperament to his mother's "Dalmatian side," he also credited her with his musical talent. When he was asked about the source of his songwriting genius, he would simply say, "My mother." His aunt Hattie said that when he was only six months old, she hummed a song to him, and he hummed it right back to her. His earliest memory was of hearing a band play in a gazebo in Forsyth Park, around the corner from his home. He could recall his mother singing to him as an infant, songs "of the most mournful outlook," such as "I Don't Want to Play in Your Yard," "After the Ball," and other sentimental sob ballads of the turn of the century that bewailed tragic romantic misunderstandings, children who pined for dead mothers, and young girls from small towns who went astray in the big city. Her granddaughter said that Lillian was "very sensitive and loved music to the point of the emotional love that people have for music, and I believe that was the kind of intensity that Uncle Bubba had." Mercer, whose family nickname was "Bubba" (southern dialect for "brother"), sometimes burst into tears when he heard a song he loved.

More genial but still melancholy musical influences came from his father, who would hold his tiny son in a rocking chair in front of the fireplace and sing "In the Gloaming," "When You and I Were Young, Maggie," and other songs from the nineteenth century. "I know that a lot of songs that I have written over the intervening years were probably due to those peaceful moments in his arms. Secure and warm, I would drift off to dreams." Mercer was born into an age that didn't *consume* music by listening to it on the radio or phonograph but *produced* music on parlor pianos or in group sings with guitars and banjos. But soon the twentieth century entered their home. The Mercers bought what their black servants called a "graffola," and Johnny grew up listening to the cylindrical records of Harry Lauder and other British music hall singers until he knew them by heart. Such songs offset the lugubrious ballads he heard from his parents and the mournful songs of World War I, such as "Keep the Home Fires Burning," which tugged at the dark, melancholy depths of his spirit.

He heard more contemporary music when his aunt Hattie took him to minstrel shows. After ragtime was introduced to the general public at the World's Columbian Exposition in Chicago in 1893, the popular music industry, just getting established in New York as sheet-music publishers congregated on Tin Pan Alley, began producing "coon songs." These were slightly syncopated, rhythmic melodies set to slangy, colloquial lyrics that depicted blacks in comic caricatures. "Hello, Ma Baby," "Bill Bailey, Won't You Please Come Home?" and other coon songs—written by whites and performed in blackface—proffered racist stereotypes but were a further, vernacular antidote to the mournful Victorian ballads of his mother and father. So powerful was music's draw on him that at the age of six he wandered away from home, lured by a local band. "He disappeared one morning and was gone all day," his mother said. "I looked all over town for him. When he finally got home late in the evening I found out that he had followed a town band, the Irish Jasper Greens, out to a picnic and stayed with them all day. He just couldn't resist the music." That love of music held Mercer for all of his life. "Songs," he said, "always fascinated me more than anything."

He had other musical influences as a child. From the age of six he sang in the choir at Christ Episcopal Church, and he went to vaudeville shows that included Savannah in their touring circuits where he heard such sprightly songs as "Who Threw the Overalls in Mrs. Murphy's Chowder?" But the one musical tradition Mercer did not have in Savannah was the Broadway musical. He did not, like Lorenz Hart, Ira Gershwin, and other New York kids, go to the theater to see the operettas of Victor Herbert and Rudolf Friml, the lavish *Ziegfeld Follies*, or the urbane musical comedies of Guy Bolton, P. G. Wodehouse, and Jerome Kern. He caught a snatch of that world on recordings but later reflected that the "rarified airs of the theatre seldom swept the South like certain popular songs. I don't know what Cole Porter and Larry Hart were listening to to become so sophisticated and glib, but as I look back on my musical education I can see it was quite meager . . . consisting mainly of Tin Pan Alley song hits during and after the war, with a sprinkling of campfire and mountaineer folk songs." That lack of early exposure to the Broadway musical would always haunt Mercer in his quest to write the kind of blockbuster musical show his friends Frank Loesser and Alan Jay Lerner had with *Guys and Dolls* and *My Fair Lady*.

But while he did not grow up with musical theater, Johnny Mercer, alone among the great songwriters of his generation, was, from the day he was born, influenced by the music of blacks. As a baby, he had a black nurse, Susie Lokie, whom he called "Soapy," who would sing lullabies and spirituals to him. One family story is about Susie and Johnny when he was five, and his mother had to go into town and told Susie to watch him. But when she returned, she found Susie walking alone on the road. "I'se headed for home, Miss Lillie," she explained. "Johnny done fired me." Many years later, Mercer would pay for a new roof for her church. He also remembered their cook Rachel, who would fix him a quail he had "swiped" and entertain him in her "'news-wall-papered' shanty." He would visit her when she was an "'ageable' lady" in a nursing home, where she told him the only thing she missed was "walking on the big road."

"About the time Johnny was born," a friend recalled, his father "bought the wooded island of Vernon View, about 15 miles from Savannah. They built a causeway across the water and marsh and sold waterfront lots. The Mercers were the first to build." Vernon View was one of the loveliest islands on the Vernon River and until then had been inhabited by blacks "whose forebears had been slaves on the plantation there 'befo' the War.'" The clan was headed by "a tall, dignified fellow, Prophet Barnes, who ruled his people and settled all differences lone-handedly." Once the Mercers built their summer home and other white families followed, these blacks "were hired as yard boys, cooks, and nursemaids."

Mercer loved the summers he spent at Vernon View. He looked forward to the drive out there from Savannah: "The roads were still unpaved, made of crushed oyster shell, and as they wound their way under the trees covered with Spanish moss there was hardly a view without vistas of marsh grass and long stretches of salt water." The Mercers hired black servants from the "back island" to stay in a small cottage behind their house and take care of the cooking, cleaning, and baby-sitting. The children of these black servants played with Johnny and his white friends. Having been almost completely cut off from civilization for so long, they spoke a Creole dialect called

"Geechee." It was, a family friend explained, one of two West Indies island dialects that were predominant in South Carolina and Georgia. "They called it in South Carolina the Gullah, and down here we call it the Geechee. That's from the Ogeechee River." Gullah, the South Carolina dialect that was spoken by blacks around Charleston, became the idiom of *Porgy and Bess*. Geechee became a source for Mercer's most richly vernacular lyrics. Always intrigued by language, he became fluent in Geechee by contact with these island blacks, as did his mother, and for the rest of their lives Johnny and "Miss Lillian" would converse with each other in their private idiom. A grandson recalls how bewildered he was when "Beebah," the grandchildren's nickname for Mercer, would launch into Geechee with their great-grandmother: "He'd just be going 'Ga-Ga-Ga' and that used to blow me away."

Johnny's black playmates at Vernon View had colorful Geechee names: "Buh Dayday (Brother David)" and "Maybud (Maybird) and Ol' Year (Old Year—born on December 31st)." "It was quite an adventure," he recalled, "to walk over to the hummock on the Back River. There were no homes there then, just marsh grass and cattails surrounded by pines and live oaks. Sand-pipers were abundant, and if we were looking for bird eggs, cootuhs or squirrel nests, it was a thrill to see the gannets flying south in the lazy afternoon." Black servants were always there to watch over the boys. "Manuel or Eli were usually along to take care of us and see that we got home safely, always on the lookout for the deadly moccasin or rattlesnake. They knew the Back River well because all the colored people lived there further toward the causeway." On summer nights, "out on the starlit veranda, I would lie in the hammock and, lulled by the night sounds, the cricket sounds, safe in the buzz of grown-up talk and laughter, or the sounds of far-off singing in the distance my eyelids would grow heavy."

Mercer's childhood memories conjure up an idyllic image, which he once compared to the boyhood world portrayed in the "barefoot boy with cheek of tan" poems of James Whitcomb Riley. In the country in the summers, it was warm days filled with fishing in the rivers, swimming off the jetties and piers, sitting in an inner tube and drifting in and out with the tide. Boyhood friends recalled how Johnny would pick out a bird in a nearby tree and begin to whistle to him. The bird would whistle back and sometimes fly down to the ground near Johnny—never close enough for Johnny to put the proverbial salt on its tail but near enough to establish a rapport with him. His cousin, Walter Rivers, recalled how "John and I and three black boys, Caesar, Eli and Tommie," would go "huckleberrying." Johnny, he said, relished these trips. "The black boys knew mainly the best places for finding the berries, and I think now of the brambles, briers and *snakes* which we encountered. I wouldn't dare go into some of the places now! We would spend several hours to fill our pails and trudge homeward on the oyster shell roads of Vernon

View." Rivers recalled that Walter Mercer, John's half-brother, made ice cream for Sunday dinner—"Huckleberry Ice Cream—It turned out pretty bad and no one would eat it."

Growing up so close to nature taught Mercer some lessons for life. One day when he and his friends were walking on the oyster shell road, they came across a partridge with a broken wing. They scrambled to catch her, but Johnny, who lagged behind the bigger kids, saw a brood of her baby chicks scramble into the tall grass after the boys ran after the mother bird, who then, seeing her chicks were safe, flew into the air, leaving the boys behind. The incident deepened Mercer's lifelong fascination with birds, and taught him a lesson he remembered when he entered the no-holds-barred world of songwriting: "A country boy can learn a lot if he keeps his eyes open."

Near the Mercer summer home at Vernon View, a family friend and business associate recalled, "there was a colony of blacks who lived on the river—they crabbed and shrimped and fished—really a fine colony. And from that colony came the present justice of the Supreme Court, Justice Thomas. That was a place they called Pinpoint. . . . Johnny would go over sometimes buying wares, and when he went visiting he would stay visiting. He would—he liked to chat with them, and talk to them. And you feel that in his lyrics when you hear him say, 'My mama done tol' me,' you know, where did he get that from? And 'Lazybones, sleepin' in the sun, how you 'spec' to get your day's work done?' All of these expressions come out of his dialogue with the black colony of Pinpoint." As black women sat at long tables shelling crabs, they would sing hymns, and Johnny would absorb their sounds, as he would the chants of the scissors grinder, the ice man, and other wandering vendors who peddled their wares up and down the streets of Savannah. He could even enter the homes of blacks he knew. "A little boy who mainly used the back door might have to help shell butterbeans, but he could absorb all the beautiful Negro hymns and discussions of the Sunday evening sermons."

In Pinpoint and Savannah were black churches, and Johnny would go to listen to the "singing and gospel and loud clapping and stuff like that. And sometimes they'd be so loaded with congregation that Johnny and them couldn't get in, so they'd sit outside the window because the windows would be open—be no air conditioning. And he'd listen to the singing along. If there was a seat available, they'd go inside the church." "On what is now Ogeechee Road," a friend recalled, there was "a very big popular Afro-American congregation headed by a Bishop Grace, they called him 'Daddy Grace,' and they used to have services; oh, several nights a week. And there was a lot of singing and clapping, and I think that Johnny would also venture down there with some friends and just listen to it because they really had a traditional black songfest in their churches, besides the oratory, but they did a lot of singing, and Johnny would sneak down there too." It was fascinating to listen to Daddy Grace, another of the boys recalled. "He didn't object to your coming, but I don't imagine the congregation liked to be an obvious object of—I don't know what they thought we were there for. I suppose they thought we were just there to laugh at them, but we weren't. We were there to enjoy him." Years later, on one of Mercer's many trips back home to Savannah, he would revisit the church and hear Daddy Grace exhort his congregation to "ac-cent-tchu-ate the positive."

Walter Rivers also recalled the black Easter Day celebrations that he and Johnny loved: "The Easter parade on West Broad Street . . . Black ladies dressed in evening gowns, triple high heels, and big flowered hats. Men in everything—tuxedos, tails, morning formal wear, most with *orange* shoes, strolling musicians—it seemed that every man in the crowd had a trumpet, banjo, or clarinet. On this day, Easter, the curb was filled with white people with ancient cars, buggies, and wagons, watching the spectacle and it was almost Mardi Gras. I didn't miss one for years and usually went with my mother and some disapproving aunts. John was there with his father." At the center of these "colorful and noisy parades" would be Daddy Grace, leading the "Colored Elks" or overseeing street dances in front of the grand DeSoto Hotel.

"Music was always a huge part of his life," a niece said. "And there are many, many stories of him chasing down the Daddy Grace parades, going over to the black churches and the black movie theaters and Pinpoint where the oysters would be shucked and the black people who at that time were working the oyster-shucking place would sing as they did it, and he and Walter Rivers, his cousin, would go over there and listen. You know, they'd be gone for hours. Johnny grew up with a lot of black playmates. In those days, it was perfectly acceptable for black and white children to play together until they got to be about thirteen or fourteen."

This direct exposure to black music gave Johnny Mercer a background that other American popular songwriters of his era lacked. George Gershwin could go up to Harlem to hear jazz and blues, but Mercer had been absorbing black music since infancy. And as he was growing up, he was becoming more interested in commercial popular music, which also was increasingly absorbing black musical influences. Irving Berlin's spectacularly successful song of 1911, "Alexander's Ragtime Band," was rooted in the ragtime coon song. The name Alexander was a comically pretentious name for blacks in such songs as "Alexander, Don't You Love Your Black Baby No More?" But while ragtime had been associated with the deterioration of morality and the corruption of youth, Berlin's lilting invitation—"C'mon and hear, C'mon and hear"—made ragtime seem safe for middle-class consumption. In 1914, W. C. Handy would have another enormous hit with "St. Louis Blues," and by 1920 jazz and blues had filtered into the mainstream of American popular music.

By the age of eleven, Johnny Mercer wanted to know who wrote the songs he listened to on the Victrola, and when his brother told him Irving Berlin was a big songwriter, Mercer began to associate songs with their composers and lyricists. "By the time I was twelve," he recalled, "I knew about Walter Donaldson and Victor Herbert," two diametrically opposed songwriters—Donaldson the Tin Pan Alley tunesmith who concocted such catchy melodies as "Carolina in the Morning" and "How're You Gonna Keep 'Em Down on the Farm (After They've Seen Paree)?"; Herbert the master of such soaring operetta airs as "Ah! Sweet Mystery of Life." Popular songs of the widest variety were fixing themselves in his memory, creating a storehouse of sentiments, images, and phrases that would serve him well when he turned to writing songs himself.

The first glimmer of interest Mercer showed in writing songs instead of merely listening to them came at a carnival in Savannah where he encountered a professional song plugger. Pluggers, who preferred being known as "professional music men," were hired by music-publishing firms to "plug" and promote the company's latest songs to stimulate sheet-music sales. In the tradition of "buskers outside of London theatres" who "try to get the public to buy or sing the song they were promoting," pluggers were adept at "putting over" a song. Mercer always remembered the way this plugger put over his song. First the initial phrase:

I'm gonna steal a million dollars, I'm gonna settle down

Then the same idea repeated, with variation, to drive it into the listener's memory:

I'm gonna steal an automobile and the sweetest little girl in town

Then the build to the climax:

I'm gonna steal a wedding ring, dear, and I'll steal a preacher too

And finally the "pitch" that wrapped the song up and drew the listener in with its vaudeville finish:

And when I've stolen everything, then I'LL STEAL YOU!

A song was not just something to listen to. It was a crafted creation with a structure, a pattern of repetition and variation; it *worked*. For the first time it occurred to him that he would like to *make* the kind of song he loved; but then he wanted to be a composer rather than a lyricist.

Although Johnny may have wanted to compose, apart from singing in the boys' choir at Christ Episcopal Church, he showed no interest in learning music. His parents tried to get him to play the piano, but he gave up after a few lessons because he feared other boys would call him a sissy. "I was sent to have piano lessons," he recalled. "And it bored me so and the kids were out playing ball, I couldn't sit there and take it. Then I had a trumpet, and I was impatient because I had to get an embouchure. I had to form my lip, and I didn't have time. Well, if I had a little tin whistle, that was great because I could do it immediately, you see."

While he didn't want to study music, Johnny Mercer did love to read. His grandfather had been a book collector and had left the family a host of first editions of Guy de Maupassant, William Makepeace Thackeray, Charles Dickens, and Samuel Taylor Coleridge, but Johnny also read classic boys' books series such as Tom Swift and the Rover Boys. He read every night until he fell asleep, and by the time he was eight years old he developed eyestrain and had to wear glasses. But after a few weeks of staying away from books, he threw the glasses away and returned to reading.

A revelation that he might become a writer came in the form of a visit by a friend of his aunt Katherine's to Vernon View in 1919. The woman wanted to publish a book of stories made up by children, and she had Johnny, his cousin Walter Rivers, and several black children write short stories and illustrate them with drawings. Johnny, at age nine, was clearly the most prolific of the group, writing four stories, each longer, more complex, and more suspenseful than the two stories written by his cousin Walter Rivers, who was three years older. Both boys' stories are typical adventure tales of fighting sharks, bears, rattlesnakes, and robbers, but Johnny's sentences have a drive and rhythm to them that reflect the action depicted. In "The Shark and the Fisherman," for example, he concludes the story with "And, as the shark came towards him, he dived, with the knife in his hand, and just as the shark came towards him to cut him with his fin, he stuck the knife in him, and killed him."

The stories by the two black boys sound like animal fables, but the short story by the seven-year-old black girl, Anna Sands, is really the most charming of the group, reflecting, as it probably did, her own real slice of life:

Once upon a time I had a little chicken named Sukey. I loved the chicken so. I call it and feed it. The preacher man come, and the chicken had to die. The Preacher Man so loved chicken, till mother had to kill the chicken for the Preacher.

Johnny was so into the spirit of the enterprise that he illustrated not only his own stories but those of Walter and the other children with stick-figure drawings. In his large, youthful scrawl he would put captions on his drawings, and some of these contain his childhood slang, such as a picture of a man riding a horse under the caption "And went home as fast as he could bust it." For Anna's story, Johnny drew a picture of a preacher sitting alone at the table and dining on chicken over the caption "And Sukey had to die." A slight incident out of childhood, yet Mercer said it "gave me the confidence to perform without fear and trembling and to begin to write." He saved the typed versions of the stories, along with his illustrations, for the rest of his life. A childhood friend recalled that Johnny always had a flair for the limelight. "He was in our house frequently. . . . In fact, we have some family pictures with two boys and two girls taken at the house, and I thought for a long time that maybe I had an older brother that had died or something. But Johnny was a ham even in those days, and when he heard a photographer was coming, he'd dress up and come over and get in the pictures."

Mercer hated to leave Vernon View at the end of the summer and return to Savannah for the start of the school year. At the Mercer household, the day would start with a breakfast of oatmeal and bacon with grits or sausage and hotcakes; then his father would drive him and his brothers to school along the dirt streets, which, with the increase of automobile traffic, were rapidly becoming paved, or a black servant would walk them to school. Massie School, four blocks from his home, still stands and has been turned into a museum. There is one large schoolroom on the second floor with the old desks lined up in rows, and, set apart from them, a stool with a dunce cap on it, waiting to humiliate a slow student. Like most little boys, Johnny dipped the pigtails of the girl sitting in front of him into his inkwell; the girl became a nun (not, of course, because of Johnny's prank) and remembered him fondly. At recess the children would play in the tiny schoolyard or go over to the tree-lined park at the center of the square, where they had to be careful not to run into trees as they played football or tag.

After school the boys roamed the streets in gangs, such as the Red Hussahs and Confederate Grays, tunneling under fences and roads, a practice that was becoming increasingly dangerous with the increase of motor traffic. They liked to hop on horse-drawn ice wagons and "snitch" a piece of ice, but this could throw you off at a sharp turn and leave you with skinned elbows. They played "roly-poly" (marbles), "one-o-cat" (softball), street football, and "half rubber," a baseball game played with broom handles and Coca-Cola and Orange Crush bottle caps. You learned to "shim" the bottle cap in a curve. One strike made a batter out (if it was caught by the catcher), but a good batter could stay at the plate for a long time, swatting singles of twenty yards doubles of thirty, triples of fifty, and hundred-yard home runs. Later, when half of a rubber ball was used instead of a bottle cap (giving the game its name of half rubber), boys learned to increase the speed and the English curves of the ball, but it was still a long, drawn-out game that could entertain three or four boys for hours on end. While Johnny played sports, however, he never excelled. "Big boys inspire respect," he reflected. "Jolly boys, fun. If you are next to smallest, as I was, you may be cute, like a pet, but you are also too small to participate equally in almost any competitive sports."

While he might have been too slight to excel at sports, Johnny acquired a tough resiliency from a childhood fraught with accidents. At the age of three, he was riding his tricycle in the park when he went over a curb and bit clear through his tongue. Susie swept him up, grabbed the severed tongue, and rushed him to the hospital, where doctors managed to sew the tongue back together. At four, he pulled a boiling ham off the stove, and it scalded the skin off his feet. At six, he cracked his head open as he tried to crank the family car, leaving a scar that grew larger as he got older. At seven, a friend pushed him off a wall, and he broke his elbow. Then at eight, playing softball out at Vernon View, Walter Rivers slid into him and broke his leg. Johnny had to wait until his father got home from work in the evening with the car and rode with him all the way back to town to the hospital. He recalled sitting in the backseat with his father holding his leg and telling the black servant who was driving over the bumpy country roads that it was all right to speed up to fifteen miles an hour. Johnny spent the next six weeks in a wheelchair, missing the best part of the summer. He was so miserable and petulant that his mother hired Caesar, one of his black friends, to play with him for a quarter a day, only to find Caesar, like Susie, become a victim of Johnny's wrath. Miss Lillian saw him walking away from the house where he was to entertain Johnny, and asked him why he was not there.

"Mistuh Jawnny done fire me"

"Why would he do that, Caesar?"

"I ain't know, Ms' Mercer, but we duh play fish, and I holluh Fish and Mistuh Jawnny holluh 'E ain't fish,' and I holluh 'e is fish,' and 'e fire me!"

When the cast finally came off, the doctors found the leg had healed crookedly, so they had to break it again and put him in another cast for six more weeks. It came off just in time for the start of school, leaving Johnny with a lifelong fear of doctors.

Because he grew up during World War I, his own childhood injuries felt "rather like a purple heart or medal gotten by a veteran," and he acquired "a certain devil-may-care attitude and reputation. . . . I can't say it made me glamorous like a sword-scarred, Heidelberg student, but it made me feel more grown up and my attitude was slightly that of the yokel who has gone two rounds with Jack Johnson; only I had gone 10 years with fate and had the scars and the casts to prove it."

As the school year wore on, the children's routine fell into ritual patterns. At Thanksgiving time, they would start "borrowing" wooden crates from neighborhood backyards and garbage areas behind stores and around factories. Week after week, the boys would gather boxes, storing them away in secret hiding places until New Year's Eve, when they would build huge bonfires on the city squares, kids on each square vying to create the biggest bonfire. To spice up the festivities, boys would throw blank cartridges onto the fires and occasionally even live bullets that, amazingly, never hit anyone.

Even more spectacular than these annual celebrations were those that followed the armistice that marked the end of World War I on November 11, 1918. But Johnny also remembered the gold stars on the doors and in the windows of homes that had lost sons in the war. There were horrible losses on the home front as well. The influenza epidemic of 1918 killed 20 million people worldwide and 548,000 in the United States. The Mercer family had its own loss as well. A baby girl, Nancy, born two years after Johnny in 1911, died of diphtheria in 1914, at the age of three. However, he had another little sister, Juliana, by the time he was eight. Family tragedy, national tragedy, deepened his emotional attachment to songs. By the time he was ten, he was listening to songs on the new half-inch-thick Edison flat records, which were more durable than cylindrical discs. But his heart would still break and make him burst into tears when he listened to a melancholy song such as "When It's Apple Blossom Time in Normandy."

With the war over and Prohibition going into effect in January of 1920, Johnny Mercer plunged into adolescence at the same time America did. The age was so marked by its music that it was dubbed the Jazz Age. "My father never understood how I became interested in jazz or in writing songs," Mercer recalled. "And he called me 'a product of the age.'" In January of 1917, the Original Dixieland Jazz Band, a small all-white orchestra, began playing at Reisenweber's restaurant in New York, and the sensational public response soon led to recordings that established the popularity of jazz. While much of what passed for jazz was really just energetic Tin Pan Alley fare, one could hear authentic jazz, by such performers as Bessie Smith, Ma Rainey, and Louis Armstrong, on what were called "race records," records marketed to blacks in urban neighborhoods and in the South. In Savannah, these records were sold in white-owned record stores, furniture stores, and other businesses in the black part of town. As a teenager, Johnny Mercer would haunt these stores, at a time when a white boy in a black neighborhood would be as safe as he would be in any part of town. "He would go to a lot of the music shops on West Broad Street, which is now Martin Luther King Boulevard," a friend recalled, "and they would have records on sale which was appealing to the black music lover." Mercer himself recalled the stores and the "No Free Rider" signs (which meant "Buy or Don't Listen") that owners put up to discourage customers from simply listening to the records in the store. As a well-to-do white boy, Johnny always felt compelled to buy at least one record on every visit, particularly at one "dusky emporium" that sold records so marked by racial character that you could not find them in any other store in town.

His cousin Walter Rivers remembered "West Broad Street in Savannah" as "totally *black*. Stores, houses, R. R. station, churches, everything for blacks. Just like old time Harlem! John and I frequently slipped off from our families and went over to the record shops." There they would listen for hours to black artists or to the white performers of such "hot" music—Bix Beiderbecke, Red Nichols, and Frankie Trumbauer. "John loved to imitate Bessie Smith's record 'Go Back Where You Stayed Last Night.' We were good customers so we were allowed to listen for hours." In such stores, Rivers believed, Johnny Mercer "picked up his beat and phrasing." As they listened to records in the shops, Johnny would talk to the black customers, swapping stories and refining his Geechee dialect.

American popular music changed dramatically after World War I as jazzier songs took inspiration from such race records. "Red Hot Mama" and "Flamin' Mamie, the Sure Fire Vamp" caught the spirit of the Roaring Twenties. But the frenetic dances like the Charleston and Black Bottom, the flappers with their bobbed hair and short skirts, their dates with raccoon coats and hip flasks of bootleg hooch, also moved at a heady speed set by the omnipresent automobile. The automobile would, more than anything else, ring down the curtain on the Victorian era and usher in the modern age. Barely 10 percent of cars produced in 1919 were closed cars, but by 1927, when Johnny Mercer turned eighteen, more than 80 percent of cars were closed. The closed car, observed Frederick Lewis Allen in *Only Yesterday*, was "in effect a room protected from the weather which could be occupied at any time of the day or night and could be moved at will into a darkened byway or a country lane. . . . The automobile offered an almost universally available means of escaping temporarily from the supervision of parents and chaperones, or from the influence of neighborhood opinion." Moreover, the cars themselves were becoming objects of sensuous desire. In 1925, with the invention of pyroxylin finishes, the somber-colored cars of the beginning of the decade were displaced by vehicles in a rainbow of colors "from Florentine cream to Versailles violet. Bodies were swung lower, expert designers sought new harmonies of line, and balloon tires came in." Along with beauty came more mechanical precision and reliability, so that from 6,771,000 automobiles in America in 1919, by 1929 the number had increased to 23,121,000.

George Mercer was the first in Savannah to buy an automobile, and Johnny remembered a succession of cars—a Mitchell, a Mercer Race-About (purchased, sentimentally, because of its name, just as Johnny Mercer years later would buy a Buick Skylark because of his song), then finally a Model T Ford. He also remembered taking Sunday afternoon drives with his father, who, in a practice always indulged by car drivers, would sing as he drove. Johnny himself was driving at the age of eleven, and because he could usually get access to a car, he became the linchpin of his group of friends. Here, too, singing and driving went together. With his friends he would drive around the countryside singing, and when the ukulele craze took hold, a spin-off from the fashion that produced so many Hawaiian songs, Johnny and his friends would accompany themselves on "It Ain't Gonna Rain No More" and "Somebody Stole My Gal."

The automobile brought new wonders. The early days of auto racing drew the first daredevils to makeshift racetracks. Johnny and his friends would pack a picnic lunch, pile into the back of a Ford pickup, and watch in awe as Ralph DePalmo, Louis Chevrolet, and Barney Oldfield would "careen around the steeply banked, but imperfectly engineered, turns at the unheard of speed of 60 miles an hour—a mile a minute!—and down the straightaways in clouds of swirling brown dust or the dry fine powder stirred up from the oyster shell road until they had covered the spectators and themselves from head to foot."

But the automobile brought its horrors as well. Even though cars were slow and cumbersome, Johnny Mercer recalled coming home from a dance to learn that friends had "piled up" and either died or been "disfigured for life." Even worse, to a southern boy raised in "the good Samaritan tradition," were stories of hitchhikers who had turned upon and murdered the kindly driver who'd stopped to give them a lift. "Retribution here," Mercer wrote, still seething years later, "should have been as swift and sure as the terrible swift sword."

The automobile also gave middle-class families the chance to take vacations a considerable distance from their homes. From the time he was eleven, Johnny's family began escaping the humid summers of Savannah in the mountains of North Carolina. George Mercer developed property in the mountains where the Vanderbilts had built their Biltmore Mansion. The Mercers would stay at the Manor Resort or the Princess Hotel in Asheville, where George Mercer found relief from his asthma and Johnny built up his leg muscles walking and riding his bicycle up the mountains. With other boys he would look for buckeyes, shiny chestnut tree pods, but he also began to pay attention to girls, particularly when they enhanced his primary love for music. One girl played "Georgette," "Leave Me with a Smile," and other post–World War I hits on the piano. Two other girls, visiting from New York, brought even more up-to-date sheet music such as "When My Baby Smiles at Me" and persuaded Johnny to join them in singing. He especially loved such songs as "Avalon" and "California, Here I Come," which conjured up a world of orange groves and sunshine that held his imagination in a way all of Tin Pan Alley's confected visions of the South, from "Swanee" to "Alabamy Bound," could not; written by first- or second-generation Jewish immigrants who had never been farther south than Atlantic City, such "mammy" songs could never fool a boy who'd grown up in the most southern of cities.

In Asheville, Mercer encountered an itinerant black piano player who went to the piano in the deserted bowling gallery in the Manor Resort and played "Bee's Knees" over and over again by ear, ragging and jazzing the instrumental so brilliantly that it almost inspired Johnny to return to his piano lessons. But, as part of the new consumer culture, he found it much easier to buy records and play them on a phonograph than learn to play the piano himself.

One thing he did learn to do in Asheville was dance. Arthur Murray came to Asheville to teach its young debutantes how to dance the fox-trot and other new dances that had been toned down from the wild dance craze that began before World War I. That craze, fueled by ragtime music, had been breaking down class lines and standards of gentility that, among proper people, had traditionally precluded dancing in public. But by the 1920s, jazz and dancing no longer seem to spell the doom of Western civilization. Mercer recalled going to his first dance in his Boy Scout uniform, but by his second dance he was joining the boys outside the gym to talk about girls who could be kissed and one who went even further, though to his eyes she looked angelic. "I suppose today's readers would be surprised to learn that I didn't smoke and really didn't want to know if the girl in question was that much of a woman of the world or not. I thought she was too pretty that night, looking all gossamer and spun sugar in her voile or gauze or whatever girls wear."

With the daredevil determination born of his many childhood injuries, he went back into the dance "determined to get in on the fun." He went up to the prettiest girl, who was also the best dancer, and plunged in. She encouraged him to keep trying, and he kept at it with her until he'd mastered a few steps. The extraordinary sense of rhythm that Mercer would display as a singer was already there. In *Jazz Singing*, Will Friedwald called Mercer "one of the greatest rhythm singers of all time," the only songwriter of his generation who could have "made it had he never written a single song, so catchy was his Southern accent and so sure was his command of the beat." On the night of his second dance, however, Johnny Mercer was content to have mastered a few tricky steps. "I can remember the feeling of elation as I lay in bed that night, feeling that I had really accomplished something. I had learned to dance." He had also learned something about women: "Southern girls are terrible flirts with that 'Hi 'ya, sugar! Come back soon, y'hear?' and all that old-time antebellum jazz, but they're the greatest dancers in the world, bar none. Talk about feeling like a feather in the breeze! You hardly know you've got one in your arms, unless she wants you to know she's there."

One partner he remembered in particular was a buxom beauty named Fanny who asked him to be her partner in a Charleston contest at the old DeSoto Hotel in Savannah. "As we really got into the rhythm of the dance, she would swirl her semi-minis, which they wore in those days also, and giggle disarmingly at our ineptness and our courage for attempting such intricate steps and her bounteous feminine goodies would bounce in such a delightful fashion, that we had everyone entranced." They won the contest in the "bantamweight" division, and in old age Mercer still recalled the prizes of a scarf and a bottle of perfume. "Ah, Fanny, merci, mademoiselle, for an evening to remember as Ginger Rogers to my bumbling Fred Astaire! If I was not becoming famous musically I was becoming notorious as a fellow who would try anything."

Mercer felt he had truly come of age when he went off to prep school. His brothers had gone to Woodberry Forest, a fashionable boys school in Virginia, and Johnny looked forward to enrolling there. Once again, however, his health plagued him: he came down with diphtheria. After several months of recuperation, he headed off to school in the fall of 1922. He would attend Woodberry Forest for five years, completing his education in 1927. While he did not excel academically, he received a rigorous education and, for what seems to have been the first time in his years of schooling, had fun. Even today, Woodberry Forest, larger and more elegantly laid out than many private colleges, quietly exudes an atmosphere of privilege and class, where boys in small groups of ten or twelve imbibe their lessons seated around a table with a "master."

Johnny Mercer studied Caesar and Cicero in Latin; took ancient, Western, and English history; read Shakespeare, Milton, Macaulay, Emerson, Tennyson, and other classic English and American authors; and had three grueling years of grammar and two of "frequent compositions" where "Mr. Pritchett and Mr. Dick saw to it that he would grow up to be the most punctiliously punctuated of all our lyricists." He loved poetry and would copy out poems and send them home to his parents. Eventually, he tried writing his own verses in the metrical, rhymed style of Edgar Guest. He was a member of the Madison Society, one of two literary clubs where boys recited poetry, debated, and gave orations, all of which fueled Johnny Mercer's growing literary and dramatic talents. More fun came from singing in the choir—though according to one account, the choir director, Mrs. Walker, kicked him out because of his poor singing (possibly because his voice was changing). Another report, however, suggests the expulsion might have been for his prankish behavior. One classmate recalls a party for the choir where, from a balcony overhead, some boys doused the choir mistress, who was also the wife of the headmaster, with a bucket of water. Eventually Mrs. Walker reinstated him, and Johnny sang in the chapel choir for the remainder of his five years at Woodberry Forest.

Mercer was something of a class clown, and his yearbook epithet was "Wit is thy attribute." A roommate recalled the practical jokes they would play, such as finding a way to get inside a dormitory wall and place an alarm clock there that went off in the middle of the night while boys groggily searched for the source of the ringing. He continued to read omnivorously—novels such as *The Pickwick Papers*, *Treasure Island*, and *Robinson Crusoe*, and such magazines as *College Humor*, *American Mercury*, and *Smart Set*, in which H. L. Mencken and other writers fueled the Roaring Twenties with jibes at Victorian morality and Puritan prejudices that appealed to a collegiate audience bent on flouting propriety and acquiring sophistication.

Emulating such wits, Johnny became the humor editor for two Woodberry publications: *The Fir Tree*, the school yearbook, for which he wrote a column called "The Daily Dope," and *The Oracle*, the campus newspaper. The humor he wrote was typical of student humor—silly puns ("U. R. Goofey"), in-jokes about classmates ("Why did Gibson cut his hair? To make a mattress? To get a load off his mind?"), and mock ads in a mildly anti-Semitic vein not unusual for exclusive prep schools ("Oi . . . Oi . . . Oi Ve buy used toothbrushes, gold teeth, diamonds, listerine, soap, shoit-tails, socks, vigs, toenails, and vat haf yous . . . Pawn Breakers vit an instinct"). The only flashes of distinctive humor came when he used the black dialect he had learned so well growing up in Savannah, as in the "Sorrycycle" column of "Advice to the Lovelorn":

Dear Mother Motley:
Ma man done done me wrong and I'se gwine to see de pawnbreaker an' git a razor fo' dat black debbil if he doan come back. But Ah loves him. What mus' Ah do? Ah needs yo' ad-vice like you needs Mista' McIlhenny.
Black Betty Beury

Ans. Go sit on a tack, you charcoal camel.

As crude as the racist humor is, the style reflects Mercer's command of vernacular speech.

Given Woodberry Forest's location in Virginia's rolling Piedmont region, Johnny's love of nature could only have deepened during his prep school years. Each day the boys played outdoors—football, tennis, and other sports, swimming and boating in the nearby Rapidan River, or in winter, skating on the campus pond. During Mercer's time there the school built a nine-hole golf course to keep up with the popularity of that sport during the 1920s, and Johnny acquired a lifelong pastime.

Johnny Mercer's main distinction at Woodberry Forest, however, was his thoroughgoing knowledge of popular music, particularly the hottest jazz that emanated from black artists and their white imitators. In his yearbook entry for 1927, where his nickname is given as "Doo," the following description of him focuses on his musical expertise:

Among Doo's hobbies and accomplishments there is one which eclipses all others, his love for music. The symphony of Johnny's fancy can best be described with his own adjective "hot." No orchestra or new production can be authoritatively termed as "good" until Johnny's stamp of approval has been placed upon it. His ability to "get hot" under all conditions and at all times is uncanny.

He served on the hop committee that brought bands, such as that of Kay Kyser (then known as "Kike Kyser"), to campus for dances. America was rife with bands in the Jazz Age. Hotels, tearooms, even radio stations had their own bands, which also played for dances at local schools. Classmates regarded him as the authority on "hot" music, and they recalled how, at school dances, he would borrow the baton from the conductor and lead the orchestra. A fellow member of the hop committee recalls that "at Woodberry Johnny was an extrovert of the first order. . . . Johnny would get up in front of the orchestra and jiggle around—like this—'Get hot!' he'd say, 'Get hot! Get hot! Get hot!'

"Everybody had a Victrola," the classmate recalled, "and you got records and you would swap records." He said the boys especially loved the Gershwins' "Fascinating Rhythm," from 1924, and from 1925, Kern and Hammerstein's "Who?" Johnny Mercer listed some of his favorites as the songs of Jerome Kern, Victor Herbert, and Irving Berlin's "What'll I Do?," "All Alone," "Remember," and other great waltzes of the mid-1920s. He would always consider Gus Kahn and Isham Jones's 1924 hit "It Had to Be You" the greatest pop song ever written, though he himself would write far greater ones. "My youth was filled with great songs—both from shows, movies and Tin Pan Alley," he said. "To grow up with these tunes coloring your youth is one of the greatest gifts anyone could have. To go to high school dances to 'Who?' and 'Make Believe' and have all those tasteful melodies spread across those beautiful, formative years is a gift I will be grateful for until I die," he said, "and perhaps longer."

One friend recalled how "many times, rather than dancing, he'd be sitting on the edge of the bandstand, and he would be beating his feet to the tunes and just doing all kinds of *dah-da-dah-da-dah-da-dah-da*—following everything and adding crazy stuff to it, you know. But he was a music man from the word 'Go.' It was in his blood." Mercer himself admitted in later years that when a new band came to Woodberry Forest he could not contain himself. He compared himself to the screaming young fans at 1960s rock concerts. He would stand before the orchestra and play along with an imaginary trumpet in his hands. "I must have looked idiotic standing up in front of the orchestra," he reflected, "with my trumpet made of air held in front of my face. . . . I see the same rapt look on little girls' faces who are actually carried away by their favorite male groups."

Although Mercer might politely define the energy as "youthful," his later mortification at his behavior suggests that he knew it was sexually charged energy. By fifteen, Johnny Mercer hungered for sexual contact, but he found that in his social circle proper girls "husbanded" (in every sense of the word) their virginity like a "rare jewel." "My relationships were as innocent as could be, though I, of course, longed for them to be more exciting. From the time I first knew the female was different from the male, I longed to be close to them, and indeed, tried constantly to achieve the supreme bliss of lovemaking. Unfortunately, they hardly ever took me seriously and my experiences were pretty much confined to necking on sofas, in corners and car seats, or surreptitious games of post-office."

Recalling that one of the popular songs of the day was "Girl of My

Dreams," he said he was always searching for a girl who would grant him the ultimate sexual favor. "I can't remember when I didn't try to get a girl or when I didn't get turned down." It was the days before the pill, he later reflected. "Anne would no more think of letting you kiss her than Helen would let you go 'all the way.'" Still, the automobile provided a setting for partial fulfillment. "Necking was different and almost every other night both the boy and girl would go home exhausted from all the wrestle holds they had struggled so hard to establish or to break. Most of my sexual education came from books but it wasn't from a lack of trying."

The outlet he found for that sexual drive was music.

After years of merely listening to music, at the age of fifteen Mercer began to write it. He later said that in those days it was rare for a teenager to write such derivative little ditties; "now"—in the age of rock—"everybody does it." At prep school he worked a song out on his ukulele that he called "Sister Susie, Strut Your Stuff." Although the music is lost, Mercer wrote down the lyric, which clearly resonates with the songs by Ma Rainey and Bessie Smith that he'd been absorbing from race records:

Sister Susie, strut your stuff,
Show those babies you're no bluff.
Let those fellows see you step,
Do that dance with lots of pep.
Toss your toe—and kick your heel;
This ain't no Virginia reel.
Do your walk—and strut your strut.
Shake that thing—you know what.
Ain't she hot, boys?
That's my gal!
Sister Susie Brown.

Compared to the earliest efforts of lyricists such as Irving Berlin and Ira Gershwin, Mercer's maiden voyage is surprisingly good, with its idiomatic phrasing, clever lines such as "This ain't no Virginia reel," and daringly suggestive phrases such as "Shake that thing—you know what." The sexual associations of the hot dancing reflect the way music provided Mercer an outlet for his pent-up desires.

When the fledgling songwriter sang "Sister Susie" to a classmate, however, the boy "walked away in disgust," saying "the whole thing had been pilfered." For one thing, it sounded too much like two popular race-record hits of the day, "Red Hot Mama" and "Flamin' Mamie." Even the name "Susie Brown" seemed derivative: two popular Tin Pan Alley hits of the day were "If You Knew Susie" and "Sweet Georgia Brown." On top of that, the friend complained, Johnny had just taken current slang expressions, such as "Ain't she hot" and "shake that thing," and built a lyric out of them.

Neither Johnny nor his friend realized it at the time, but Mercer had subconsciously done what all songwriters do—reweave existing vernacular expressions and lyrical and melodic phrases from older songs into new ones. Just looking at the titles of some of the great pop standards shows them to be built up from idiomatic catchphrases—"Say It Isn't So," "Just One of Those Things," "How Long Has This Been Going On?," "I Can't Get Started," "I Didn't Know What Time It Was," "I'm in the Mood for Love," "You Took Advantage of Me," "What'll I Do?," "I'm Beginning to See the Light." As Ira Gershwin pointed out, such phrases may seem clichéd in a poem, but when mated with the right musical phrase, "can sound like a million." Later, Mercer reflected that "all creative artists begin by 'stealing' from others, possibly even Mozart did. But it's how fast you develop, how high your standards are and how quickly you find your OWN style that sets you above and apart from your contemporaries."

Although that first friend denounced Mercer's effort, others loved it, and "having tasted the heady brew of applause and surprise from all my friends except the one, I was never to be either the same again or without a song, to drop a title." He took his second step as a songwriter that summer when a girl he had met at prep school came down to Savannah. She joined their group rambles in rumble-seated cars, canoes, and motorboats. "I just had to write a song for her." Dick Hancock, a musically gifted friend, learned the music from Mercer's "dubious singing" and, on a double date, accompanied Johnny on a guitar as he serenaded his inamorata. "Talk about wet-palm time. My hands were perspiring, my voice was shaking and I know I sang in the wrong key—but she liked it—or said she did." A song had gotten him closer to a girl than all of his frustrated "tusseling." Music became "my sun on a dark day, my solace in time of pain and disappointment, and if not my life, my best friend. . . . It still is," he said many years later. "I know of no joy like it, outside of sex."

Two

When the World Was Young: 1927–1930

Seventeen was a beautiful age. . . . That summer was an important one for me.
I learned the important things you don't always learn in school and had a mar-
velous time doing it. How to avoid a fight or win one. How to compete for girls.
How not to be a horse's ass. How to get along with guys and how to sing harmony.

Mercer family tradition was that its young men attended Princeton University. Their ancestor, Hugh Mercer, had been one of Washington's most trusted generals in the American Revolution. He had helped plan the surprise attack on Hessian forces in Trenton by crossing the Delaware River, but he was killed weeks later at the Battle of Princeton. Mercer's troops stumbled upon a much larger British force, and as his own soldiers retreated, Mercer was shot, then surrounded by British troops and ordered to surrender. When he struck out with his sword, they stabbed him with their bayonets, "seven times to the body, twice to the head." But Mercer lived to see the tide of battle turn as Washington himself, astride a white horse, rallied the fleeing colonials. Thirty thousand mourners attended his funeral in Philadelphia.

In honor of his sacrifice to his country, a statue was erected on the grounds of Princeton University, and Mercer's son, by an act of Congress, was educated at Princeton at no charge. Johnny Mercer's grandfather had attended Princeton, and family plans called for Johnny to enroll there after he graduated from Woodberry Forest. But in the spring of 1927, a letter arrived from his mother that made the question of going on to Princeton purely academic. She broke the news to Johnny that his father's real-estate business was more than a million dollars in debt. He would be able to finish his final year at

Woodberry Forest, but the family could not afford to send him to college. The prosperity of the 1920s had fueled real-estate speculation, particularly in Florida, where property changed hands in dizzying spirals that sent prices soaring until a devastating hurricane and investor panic burst the bubble. The George A. Mercer Company had made solid investments in Florida property, as well as in mountain property in North Carolina, but it could not meet investors' demands to cash in their certificates of deposit, which had promised a return of 6 percent at a time when banks were offering only 2.5 percent on savings.

"His company never went bad," said a business associate. "The truth is that it was on solid grounds. Mr. Mercer saw what was happening in the way of mountain areas, and he would invest the certificate money into mountain areas and then into Florida areas and into commercial ventures. . . . Now, Mr. Mercer says, 'Hey, we don't have the money to pay our certificate holders, but we've got good hard investments, mountain areas, Florida areas, commercial areas. We are not going to go bankrupt." Going bankrupt would have saved him. "He could've made a ton of money if he had bankrupt and then bought it back and wiped them all out for twenty cents on the dollar." But George Mercer had seen bankruptcy ruin people, paying them back twenty, fifteen, even ten cents on the dollars they had invested. It sickened him, and he would not take that course with people in Savannah who had trusted him. "This is not the way to go," he announced. "I'm going to put this corporation into an orderly liquidation, and as the market rises and revenues come in, we'll be able to systematically pay off, but we can't pay them off on demand today." At the time, there were three thousand creditors who held certificates of deposit ranging from a few hundred to tens of thousands of dollars. George Mercer could not foresee the stock market crash of 1929 or the long-lingering depression of the 1930s, but his decision to liquidate rather than declare bankruptcy was an act of steely southern honor.

Even though it meant his son would not be able to go to Princeton, George Mercer made yet another honorable decision. Before putting his company into liquidation, he put his own savings of $73,500 into the empty company coffers, then turned the company over to the Chatham Savings Bank to handle the liquidation. The banker, George Hunt, was astounded that Mercer not only would not declare bankruptcy, save himself, and even turn a profit but would pour his personal savings into his company's black hole. "George Mercer," he said, "are you crazy!" "Listen," Mercer replied, "when I'm walking along Bull Street and I see one of my certificate holders, and he says, 'George Mercer— you have my money,' I want to be able to say, 'Your money is where mine is.'"

Johnny wrote back to his mother that he cared only about what the business failure meant to his father and that he wanted only to help his family. In the envelope he placed two one-dollar bills to help repay his father's debt. His mother kept them in an old wallet, together with a note—"Johnny's two dollars he gave Pop after the liquidation"—until the day she died.

On the day the liquidation papers were to be executed, a member of the firm recalled, Johnny "dropped by Pop's office to 'bum' Pop out of money to go to the movies.

" 'What time does the movie start?' asked 'Mr. G. A.'

" 'One o'clock,' replied Johnny.

" 'Walk with me to the bank to sign some papers. You have plenty of time, and I'll give you the money.'

"At the Chatham Bank, Johnny was wandering around, occasionally listening to the conversation between his father and Mr. Hunt. He was hearing big figures like 'a million and three-quarters.' This kind of money was unimaginable to Johnny, but he moved closer to the conference.

" 'How much will it take to keep father's company going?'

"Mr. Hunt replied, 'Can you get me a quick million and ¾?'

" 'Not today, Mr. Hunt, but some day I hope to make it big, and then I'll see that everyone who bet on my father will not lose a dime.' " While George A. Mercer would not be able to continue the family tradition of sending his son to Princeton, the nobility of their ancestor Hugh Mercer lived on in father and son.

Putting his prestigious prep school background behind him, Johnny Mercer enrolled in a typing course in night school to make himself more employable. George Mercer's reputation was solid enough that he could borrow thirty thousand dollars to open another real-estate business and begin the long, slow process of trying to repay his certificate holders. The loss of family money and position, as hard as it was on him and his family, had a liberating effect on Johnny. He was finished with school, had a job collecting rents for his father's new firm, and could break out of the confines of his patrician upbringing. At nights he would pile friends into his car and go to dances. It was at a country-club dance, at intermission, that he took his first drink, breaking all of his promises to his father. "I had resisted temptation before, but this night, after all the fellows had taken a drink from the bottle, a GIRL took one too, and what could a respectable young man do?" Soon he was including a trip to the local bootlegger among his preparations for a dance, along with picking up his linen suit from the cleaners.

The dances he remembered most vividly were those out on the ocean at Tybee Island. The center of Savannah's musical world in the summer was the open-air Tybrisa pavilion. "They had a big pavilion, and they used to have a dance there every weekend and the big bands would come," one childhood friend recalled. "It was a wonderful old thing," another said, still enthralled after seventy years, "built way up, a big square, rectangle, longer than it was wide, railings all around and a roof, and it was all open, and in the middle they put iron railings to make a dance floor, and over here was the bandstand, and we used to have big bands come down—Guy Lombardo and some of those well-known bands . . . and they had those great big crystal balls up there—two of them—up in the middle of the dance floor that went around and had colored lights shining on them so that those things were sparkling."

One of the big hits of 1927 was Irving Caesar and Vincent Youmans's "Sometimes I'm Happy," which played the first night Johnny Mercer danced at Tybresa. As an older man he said, "Every time I hear . . . 'Sometimes I'm Happy,' I think of myself as about seventeen years old. First time I ever went dancing on a pavilion over the ocean and everybody was young and the band was great. And I'll always see that whenever I hear that song. And I'll be about that age." But if music and drinking could elate him, they could also drown him in sorrow. At one dance while his "pretty little date" flirted and danced with every boy there, Johnny stood outside, drinking peach brandy and weeping as the orchestra played "Coquette."

After the dances, he and his friends would climb into his car and go cruising around, singing and playing ukuleles. They knew nothing about harmony, and Johnny would strain his voice trying to reach for high notes on such barbershop quartet classics as "You Tell Me Your Dream." They might wind up at a railroad station or a roadhouse for some food, then go to somebody's house to play hot records by Red Nichols or Louis Armstrong.

But as that wonderful summer passed and he settled into the routine of work, Johnny Mercer felt increasingly suffocated by the world he had grown up in. When his family had wealth and prominence, his pampered existence was delightful, but now he found working for his father a dull routine of running errands, collecting rents, and answering the phone. "The firm was months recovering from the effect of his services," said a fellow worker. "We'd give him things to deliver," his brother Walter recalled, "letters, checks, deeds and things like that—and learn days later that he'd absent-mindedly stuffed them in his pocket. There they stayed." Such absentmind-edness would persist throughout his life, as he evinced a gentlemanly disregard for things monetary. His wife would come across checks, months old, for thousands of dollars, uncashed, sitting among the socks in his dresser.

The Mercers had two interrelated businesses: the Mercer Realty Company, which was run by Johnny's father, and the Mercer Insurance Company, which was under the direction of Johnny's brother Walter. Walter Mercer, a business associate explained, "was one of the few agents in the insurance business who would dare insure properties owned by the Afro-Americans. And so he had cultivated all of this little colony." Johnny's business errands strengthened his ties to Savannah's black culture, particularly to the colony of Pinpoint. "He would stroll down there on company business," a fellow worker said, "and he would engage in conversation with them. And of course they would use this Gullah language and expressions, you know, and he would be fascinated by it."

While Johnny did what he could for his father's business, his friend Dick

Hancock, with his musical skills, got a job playing on boats that ran to and from New York. Dick would return from New York to report he had been at the Paramount Theatre when Bing Crosby and Al Rinker sang "Mississippi Mud" to the driving accompaniment of Bix Beiderbecke and Paul Whiteman's orchestra. Such stories fired Johnny Mercer's desire to get out of Savannah, so when a girl he had danced with told him her family was returning to New York, he went to see her off. As she was boarding the boat, Johnny impulsively promised he would come to visit her in New York.

It was a double dare he had given himself. His family had no money for a ticket to New York; indeed, a friend remembers nights when Johnny couldn't even afford the twenty-five-cent admission to the Tybresa pavilion and had to stand on the beach below to listen to the band. With Dick Hancock he worked out a plan to stow away aboard the SS *Savannah* and hide in Dick's cabin. But when it came time to put the plan into action, Johnny Mercer proved to be more like Tom Sawyer than Huck Finn: he told his mother where he was going. He later learned that she, in turn, told his uncle, who was the purser on the ship, to watch out for Johnny. Mercer speculated that his uncle must have told his mother he couldn't risk his job by helping conceal Johnny for the voyage but assured her "I wouldn't be thrown to the sharks."

On the day of departure, Johnny casually sauntered aboard the ship, then hid in Dick Hancock's cabin as the calls went out—"All ashore . . . all ashore that's going ashore"—music played, whistles blew, and the SS *Savannah* pulled out into the ocean and headed north. Thinking he was safely stowed away, Johnny strolled out on deck. No sooner had he lighted what might have been his first cigarette—a prop to look like an older, paying passenger—than an officer asked to see his ticket.

He spent the rest of the voyage working belowdecks amid the filthiest conditions he had ever seen. "No bed was ever made, the toilet too filthy to touch skin to, so consequently for the three-day trip I didn't use it once." The crew, which to this scion of Savannah society consisted of "Polacks, Canucks, Swedes, and a Fat Greek or two," was allowed on the passenger decks only to wash them down, then had to return to its lowly quarters in the forecastle. Yet all of his self-pitying misery evaporated when he caught his first glimpse of the Manhattan skyline: "It was about five in the morning, the sun coming up behind the skyscrapers and a cold wind whipping my grey flannel shirt as I stood at the railing taking it all in."

Johnny's mother had also made arrangements for him to stay with relatives who were in Europe for the summer and were letting his cousin Joseph Mercer stay in their apartment in midtown Manhattan. Joe was studying with Daniel Chester French, the renowned sculptor who had created such works as the statue of Abraham Lincoln in the Lincoln Memorial, so Johnny had plenty of time to explore New York City on his own. "The steam coming up out of the sidewalks, the noise of the traffic and the subways, the kaleidoscopic anonymity of the faces in the crowd more than fulfilled any ideas I had had of it, and I wandered around for the first few days like a kid in a candy store, or a peasant in Baghdad."

Although the Paul Whiteman orchestra was out of town, Johnny went to hear the Williams Sisters at the Paramount, where they sang their new hit, "Sweet Sue," and after the show he walked down Broadway and into a music store to buy his first copy of sheet music. Although he had very little money, he managed to see Vincent Youmans's smash musical *Hit the Deck* and Louise Grody in *Rio Rita*, a show that made him "more enchanted and enraptured than ever with the make-believe of the theater." Although he had seen minstrel shows and vaudeville in Savannah, this trip gave him his first real taste of the Broadway musical.

When he called the girl he had promised to visit in New York, however, he was told she was not at home. In retrospect, he realized she was probably frightened by his impetuosity, but at the time her refusal punctured his self-confidence. Gathering himself together, he called another New York girl he'd known from prep school, and she invited him to spend the weekend with her family in New Jersey. When he got there, however, he sensed that she wanted to pair him with her younger sister. Although nothing romantic ensued, he had an elegant weekend that soothed his bruised ego. Besides, he later reflected, "I found another girl I was really stuck on . . . New York City!"

Although he returned to Savannah and found a better-paying job putting up stock quotations with the Hentz and Company brokerage firm, his trip to New York had fired him with a desire to return. One day two older girls drove up to his house, "honked their automobile horn 'AAAooogah-aahoogah'—as they used to sound in those days," and one of them, whom Mercer secretly adored, asked him if he would play the role of her little brother in a play Savannah's little theater group, the Town Theatre, was putting on. The little-theater movement was sweeping America in the 1920s, as small towns and cities across the country emulated the success of the Provincetown Players, which had mounted plays by Eugene O'Neill, Susan Glaspell, and Edna St. Vincent Millay in Greenwich Village. Although he was eighteen, Mercer agreed to play the role of a fifteen-year-old and found he was able to bring the part off, enduring the tedium of rehearsals and overcoming stage fright on opening night.

He did well enough that he was given a part in the group's next production, *Hero Worship*, a one-act play that was entered into the Belasco Cup contest, a national competition named after the great director David Belasco. Little theater companies across America and Great Britain performed one-act plays in regional competitions, and the Savannah troupe was selected as a semi-finalist and traveled to the finals in New York. They presented their offering at the Frolic Theatre on Friday night, May 11, 1928. Returning to a city he'd fallen in love with so soon after his first trip there was a heady experience for

Mercer. James McIntire, whose mother was in the play, recalled their perfor-mance from his days in prep school. "I went down from Exeter to New York to see it. And, of course, they were very good. And mother was an old lady in it. I hadn't seen her in about three months, and she had hair that was absolutely white, and I thought, 'Oh, my Lord, my mother has aged so!' and burst into tears." Lucy McIntire was singled out by the *New York Times*, along with Johnny Mercer, for praise: "The sketch contained some amusing detail and was well played by Lucy McIntire as the elderly woman and John Mercer as the grandson." The reviewer also noted that "attendance at the tournament this year was the best" in the contest's six-year history, and the final perfor-mance "was completely sold out, with a row of standees in addition."

The Town Theatre's performance impressed the judges as well: the Savan-nah production was chosen to be a finalist and reprised its production on Sat-urday afternoon, only to lose out to a company from Scotland that, some believed, was more professional than amateur. Johnny recalled coming out after the performance with his makeup still on and being kissed by Elsie Fer-gusson, a noted actress of the day. Then Tony Brown, another professional actor, who sported a regimental mustache and spoke with an English accent, complimented his performance and offered to help him if he ever needed it. Another actor, Ralph Bellamy, who would go on to success on Broadway, in movies, and on television, singled out Johnny for praise. Mercer took the train back home, but after that dizzying success he was determined to become an actor in New York. While the other actors in his company "combed star-dust out of their hair and went back to their honest livings," he said, "nothing was to hold me in Savannah from then on." In retrospect, he could see that his acting ambitions were doomed: "I thought acting was easy," he reflected. "You just walked on stage and played yourself—it worked for a while."

According to a childhood friend, his parents were opposed to Johnny's ambitions. When he went to Lucy McIntire, however, she encouraged him. "Mother is the one that advised Johnny to give songwriting and acting a try," said James McIntire. "His parents were very much *against* it. . . . 'Johnny, you want to do it so badly,' she advised. 'You ought to just go ahead and try it. You are young enough to start over again if it doesn't work out.' So he was always very grateful to Mother for that." The very opposition of his family might have sharpened Mercer's acting ambitions. The Mercers were a patrician clan that prided itself on its high standards, one of which was never to seek public notice. Now out of a line of prominent doctors and lawyers, a Mercer wanted to pursue a career on the New York stage. But if they opposed his going to New York, the Mercers never let their opposition show to the public. When a Savannah friend was asked how the family felt about Johnny's pursuit of a career in show business, he said, "They were very proud of his attachment to the amusement industry. . . . There was nothing but pride evidenced in what he was doing. There was no stigma to the fact that he was on Broadway or trying to make it on Broadway."

The final straw came when somebody at the brokerage firm said something insulting to him. While Mercer might have been looking for an excuse to quit, he also had received an invitation to visit with some friends in Lake Mahopac, in Putnam County, New York, about twenty miles outside of Manhattan. He made a deal with his father that, after the visit, he would spend two weeks in New York to see if he had any success as an actor. When his visit at Lake Mahopac ended, Johnny Mercer went into the city with his friends, bought cut-rate tickets to the show *Rain or Shine* (a phrase he would later use in three different lyrics), and delighted in Ethel Norris singing the jazzy "Oh, Baby." By a stroke of luck, they ran into Tony Brown, the actor who had encouraged him after the Belasco contest. When Johnny told him he had come to New York to try to make it as an actor, Brown offered to show him the ropes. They next day Johnny saw his friends off at the train station, checked into a boarding house recommended by his uncle, and girded himself for his assault on Broadway.

It was a propitious moment, for the Jazz Age was riding to its climax on a wave of unparalleled prosperity. The Harlem Renaissance had brought the kind of music Johnny had listened to in the black record stores of Savannah into the mainstream of American popular music, and whites were trekking up to Harlem to hear Louis Armstrong, Bessie Smith, and Duke Ellington. Blues and jazz also flavored such Tin Pan Alley songs as "Am I Blue?" and "The Birth of the Blues." On Broadway, the songs of George and Ira Gershwin and Rodgers and Hart set a new standard for sophistication with shows that featured such witty songs as "'S Wonderful" and "Thou Swell." Their lyrics bristled with cosmopolitan elegance and vernacular ease; and in 1928, after many years of being dismissed as a wealthy dilettante, Cole Porter finally found acceptance on Broadway with the urbanely risqué "Let's Do It."

Along with the flourishing musical comedy, there were sumptuous revues that featured songs, comic sketches, and dances. At his own Music Box Theatre, Irving Berlin mounted shows built around his songs, from dreamy ballads such as "All Alone" to rhythmic numbers such as "Pack Up Your Sins and Go to the Devil." George White's annual *Scandals* relied upon the trio of DeSylva, Brown, and Henderson to supply such period pieces as "Button Up Your Overcoat" and "You're the Cream in My Coffee." The master impresario of Broadway revues, however, was Florenz Ziegfeld, whose spectacles grew more lavish every year to keep pace with the dizzying spiral of hilarity in the Roaring Twenties. Stars such as Eddie Cantor, Fanny Brice, and Bill "Bojangles" Robinson performed "If You Knew Susie," "My Man," and other song classics in the annual *Ziegfeld Follies*. Ziegfeld, however, also recognized that a new form of musical theater was emerging, a musical drama that could carry tragic themes, where songs were not performed as free-standing "numbers" but grew integrally out of character and dramatic situation. At the same time that he was mounting his frothy revues, Ziegfeld also produced *Show Boat*, in which Oscar Hammerstein took Edna Ferber's novel about racism and miscegenation and transformed it into a libretto that flowered into such songs as "Ol' Man River" and "Can't Help Lovin' Dat Man."

At the opposite end from such elevated productions was vaudeville, still going strong despite the rise of musical comedy. At the Palace, where Johnny would climb to the very highest (and cheapest) gallery seats, he could still catch his favorite act, Clayton, Jackson, and Durante, as well as George Burns and Gracie Allen, Ted Healy and the Stooges, Van & Schenck, the McCarthy Sisters, and many of the other great vaudevillians. "The last gasp of vaudeville," he recalled, "was like a fireworks display, most dazzling just before the end."

Stepping into this musical world in 1928, Johnny Mercer would have heard the richest mix of popular music in American history: Louis Armstrong singing "I Can't Give You Anything but Love"; Paul Robeson booming out "Ol' Man River"; Ethel Waters, then known as "Sweet Mama Stringbean," doing "Am I Blue?"; Duke Ellington's orchestra playing "Basin Street Blues"; Bing Crosby and the Rhythm Boys jazzing "Mississippi Mud"; Helen Kane, the "Boop-Boop-Be-Doop Girl," cooing "I Wanna Be Loved by You"; Eddie Cantor rolling his eyes suggestively to "Makin' Whoopee"; and any number of cabaret singers calling the tune for "Doin' the Racoon," the raucous Charleston, and the even more shocking Black Bottom. "To come from a small town and hear the best in the world is quite exciting," Mercer later reflected. "What a thrill it was for us to see these famous stars in person."

Tony Brown gave Mercer the names of two little old ladies who had a "sleazy" booking office above the National Theater. They got him bit parts in two Theatre Guild touring productions: Eugene O'Neill's *Marco Millions* and Stefan Zweig's updated version of Ben Jonson's *Volpone*. Both plays had run on Broadway earlier in the year with such soon-to-be-major theatrical figures as Alfred Lunt and Morris Carnovsky, and by the fall of 1928 they were ready to go on the road. Mercer received a salary of thirty dollars a week for playing a "Chinese coolie" in the O'Neill play and a Venetian policeman in *Volpone*, out of which he paid his landladies a commission of three dollars each week. When he got back to the boarding house that night, he shared his good fortune with Mrs. Drake, his landlady, and her daughter, who were obviously relieved that their boarder had found a job. Mrs. Drake gave him some pithy advice that he tried to follow for the rest of his life: "Always pay your bills, keep your collar and wristbands clean, and buy your clothes at Brooks Brothers." Her daughter's advice was even more laconic: "Go back home."

Theatre Guild productions toured for six months on their subscription circuit, so Mercer traveled from town to town with the company. At times it was grueling. In particular, he recalled the severe winter of 1929 when they played Chicago. "Walking the lake front in Chicago that year was like walking to the North Pole." He was an "atmosphere" player—an actor who subsisted on bit parts on the fringes of the theatrical profession—and he was learning about life in the wings. Although he adored the beautiful actresses in the company, they only confirmed his belief that girls his age wanted older men. He worried that he was "too gauche, naive, or plain-looking to attract them" and even feared they assumed he was gay since many of the atmosphere players were homosexual. He was at once fascinated and terrified by the homosexuals in the company. "It was like throwing me to the wolves and in this case, the fags," he recalled. "It was a footrace to get back to the dressing room after curtain calls." Yet the "queens" intrigued him. "They are so funny, and quick and bitchy, and they had the girls laughing all the time—as well as me—and it was really fun being around them if you could go to bed by yourself. I was homely enough so it was no problem." He even perfected his own gay impersonation: "Sweetie, I can still flutter a pretty good punch line—if the mascara doesn't run!" Later, he observed that "most of us had a little of both sexes going for us, and just to be away from a small town and on one's own in New York was like being freed from slavery."

When he returned to New York, he learned that his landlady's daughter had died of pneumonia in the bitter winter and that Mrs. Drake was closing her boarding house to marry "a very old admirer." A member of his touring company, who had also gone to prep school in the South, invited Johnny to look for an apartment they could share. They found a basement apartment farther uptown, but soon after they moved in, someone broke in and stole all of Johnny's clothes. In typical New York fashion, a few days later a man with a trunk stopped him on the street and offered to sell his clothes back to him. On another night he returned to the room to find his roommate in bed "with a boy. Now, I'm not a prude," he later reflected, "and I wasn't a prude then, but I couldn't see living in a ménage à trois unless the third member were a girl, so as pleasantly as I could, I packed up, left and went to live with three other guys in a five-story walk-up behind a big electric sign that flashed 'Coca-Cola' in big red neon letters all night long." Years later, he recalled hearing that his first roommate was beaten to death on an army post. "What he was doing there is questionable as he was a civilian. I guess he always did pick the wrong people. But what a tragedy. To be sensitive and to like the wrong sex."

In his new quarters one roommate had a piano, and as acting opportunities dwindled, Mercer turned to his other interests—picking out tunes on the piano, toying with song lyrics, drawing cartoons, and writing poems, short stories, and plays. His mother took the train up from Savannah to visit him. "He and three other boys were holed up in a terrible one-room apartment," she said, "four flights up, someplace in Greenwich Village. The place had no sink or washbasin, only a bathtub. Johnny insisted on cooking a chicken dinner in my honor—he's always been a good cook—and I'll never forget him cleaning the chicken in the tub."

As acting jobs proved harder and harder to come by, Mercer fell back on his singing abilities, taking jobs with orchestras in nightclubs and restaurants for ten dollars a night. As times got even tougher, he took a day job with a brokerage firm on Wall Street. "I did everything again but sweep up, as I punched holes in the stock certificates, ran between banks, gulped down a sandwich, and spent a nickel on the subway to climb those five long flights to a bath and a drink of bath-tub gin." Even though he was doing the same kind of work in New York that he had hated doing in Savannah, he was confident that he was going to make it as an actor and not have to go back home.

Yet that confidence began to wane as more weeks went by and no acting jobs turned up. Two of his roommates got parts in another Guild production, but Mercer and the other roommate couldn't afford the rent, so they parted ways. Another role came up for him in the revival of an old melodrama in Hoboken, New Jersey, *Stepping Out*, which opened on May 29, 1929, but closed in two weeks. In the company, however, he met Charles "Buddy" Dill, a good-looking actor who shared Johnny's love of S. J. Perelman. Dill "could do more with a dollar than anyone I ever knew, but he always insisted on having a good address." He and Johnny moved into the Whitby Hotel, where many vaudeville performers stayed, but to economize they ate oatmeal—"No milk, just sugar and oatmeal"—and washed their own shirts, ironing the collars and cuffs with the bottom of a pot they heated on their electric grill.

Just when Johnny feared they were going to starve, he and Buddy got roles in *Houseparty*, a collegiate murder mystery, which opened on September 9, 1929, and ran for one hundred seventy-seven performances. Dill had a substantial part, but Mercer got only another walk-on role. "All I did was run around the fraternity house with tennis rackets." But he was working and getting paid $55 a week. Even in these flusher times, however, Dill was penurious. He took Johnny to Ye Eat Shoppe, a restaurant on Eighth Avenue where dinner, including a piece of cake or pie, cost only thirty-five cents. Their good fortune did not last, as *Houseparty* played to smaller and smaller audiences over its six-month run, and Mercer's salary was cut from $55 to $35 to $25 and finally to $15 a week before the show finally closed.

During the run, however, the assistant stage manager, Everett Miller, played Johnny part of a song he was working on. The two young men had found a mutual interest in music, and Miller wanted Mercer to set a lyric to his melody. Johnny promised to work on it. After the show closed, Miller went back to school at Syracuse University, and Mercer and Dill moved to a cheaper, but still "good" address at another hotel "fallen on poorer days." Mercer might have devoted himself more assiduously to Miller's lyric had he known Everett's father worked as an arranger for the great sheet-music publishing company T.B. Harms, which specialized in publishing songs from Broadway musicals. Harms was headed by Max Dreyfus, who for years had nurtured such talented writers for the theater as George Gershwin and Cole Porter.

But while Mercer kept up his work in songwriting, an actor was what he burned to be. According to one account, to impress producers and casting directors, he took to wearing a monocle. One day, as he was having a drink, he put the monocle on the bar and a friend accidentally set his beer mug on it. The friend insisted upon buying him a new monocle, but, when he presented it, Mercer noted that it was square rather than round. "Anyone who would wear a square monocle," he sniffed, "is affected."

As fewer and fewer roles came his way, he began to devote more time to writing songs. One night when he and Buddy were, as out-of-work actors put it, "between assignment," they passed the New Amsterdam Theatre, where Eddie Cantor was starring in *Whoopee*. With that impulsive daring Mercer had manifested since childhood, he told Buddy, "I think I'll go in and play him some of my comedy songs." "Why not?" Buddy said encouragingly. Mercer went back to their hotel room, spent a few days neatly writing out his lyrics, and then walked to the stage door and asked to see Mr. Cantor. To his amazement, the doorman let him in. At the time, Johnny thought the kindly old man had mistaken him for one of Cantor's relatives, but in later years it occurred to him that Buddy Dill, who knew a lot of people in the theater, might have put in a word for him.

He got on an elevator just as several chorus girls, skimpily dressed as Indians, were going up to their dressing rooms after the show. To the nineteen-year-old boy from Savannah, they "looked like Aphrodite and were just as naked." As he rode up in the tiny elevator, his shocked ears took in the language used by these voluptuously ethereal creatures. Still gawking at the girls and with his heart thumping, he knocked on Eddie Cantor's dressing-room door and walked in. Cantor was sitting in a flannel dressing gown, talking with his wife, Ida, and some friends. "His big eyes opened even wider," Mercer recalled, "as he found out that I had simply made my way past the doorman and up in the elevator with all the beautiful redskins."

Instead of having Mercer thrown out, Cantor was magnanimous. Maybe he saw in the nervous kid a reflection of himself as he had clawed his way up out of the hideous poverty of New York's Lower East Side. Now Cantor was at the peak of his career, starring in Ziegfeld's *Whoopee*, one of the last glorious musical extravaganzas of the 1920s. *Whoopee* might have been short on plot and characters, but it was a fast-paced, frothy, and opulent production that featured songs by Gus Kahn and Walter Donaldson that have become classics, such as "Love Me or Leave Me" and "Makin' Whoopee." It was also peppered with snappy gags, such as Cantor's noting that Pocahontas saved John Smith's life but then, in a reference to New York mayor Al Smith's loss of the presidential nomination because of his Catholicism, asking, "Why didn't she do something for his brother Al?"

At the time, Cantor was building a Tudor mansion for his family in Great Neck, Long Island, with a ballroom, servants' quarters, and Aubusson rugs hand-woven in France. As they were getting rubdowns at a health club,

Ziegfeld told Cantor he had "everything—a family, money, success, fame." But Cantor said he still lacked the Rolls-Royce he had seen millionaires ride in when they came to his first successful shows for Ziegfeld in 1916. A week later, Ziegfeld met him for dinner at Dinty Moore's restaurant on Forty-sixth Street. Waiting for Cantor was a Rolls-Royce convertible with an orchid on the handle and a card from Ziegfeld saying, "Dear Eddie. Now you have everything."

Cantor's wealth came not only from his show business earnings but from his successful stock investments. Like many Americans, he profited enormously from the big bull market of the late 1920s. In September of 1929, he took his fourteen-year-old daughter Margie to a restaurant for lunch. She wanted the chocolate cream pot for dessert, but despite her father's urgings, would not order it because it cost an entire dollar. After lunch, father and daughter went for a walk, and Cantor checked in at a brokerage house where he learned he had earned fifty thousand dollars in the stock market during the course of the lunch. When he told Margie, she "led her father back to the dining room and ordered dessert."

A month later, "Black Tuesday," October 29, 1929, reduced him, on paper, to the poverty of his childhood. Despite the stock-market crash, Cantor continued playing in *Whoopee* until it closed in November of 1929, but he also reverted to something he had not done in years—playing private parties. For example, he would sing songs for guests at a cocktail party thrown by Walter Chrysler. Because he needed comic songs to perform at these occasions, he welcomed Mercer's intrusion. When he listened to Johnny Mercer sing "Every Time I Shave I Cut My Adam's Apple" (whose title, Mercer winced, was suggested by a friend—"Some friend!"), Cantor seemed grave but amused. He told Johnny he was soon going on the road with *Whoopee* but asked him if he could write six or seven extra choruses of the song and send them to him. Within a week, Mercer polished off twenty choruses and put them in the mail. Even as Cantor was doing everything to keep his head above water, he took the time to answer Mercer's letters, telling him he hoped to work his song into the show. "These letters actually sustained my determination to be a writer," Mercer recalled. "Because weren't they from Eddie Cantor? He never used the song, of course, but I never stopped writing songs, largely due to his encouragement and kindness."

The Crash also hit back home in Savannah, but even with the onset of the depression, George Mercer sent his son money whenever he could. "Mr. Mercer would write to Johnny from time to time and would try to slip in some greenbacks," a friend recalled. "Johnny used to kid when he would come to Savannah, he says, well, many times the mailman would come just as he was leaving, and he didn't have time to read the letter, so he would rip it open on the end and blow, and if there was anything green in there, he would then open the mail. Otherwise, he would wait until he returned before he started reading his daddy's letter. But, if there was a greenback in there, he would immediately read it."

As Johnny grew homesick with Christmas nearing, his mother sent him a train ticket. Over the holidays, he agreed to an interview for a Savannah newspaper and put on a good face so his hometown press could write about how well the Mercer boy's acting career was developing in the big city. "He is extremely enthusiastic over his new vocation and has optimistic things to say about the theater world, which he says recently reached the peak of the season." "While the home-town talk was undoubtedly about how well young Mercer is doing on the stage," Johnny said later, "I was just about to go back on oatmeal."

When he returned to New York, ready for another assault on Broadway, he moved into his own apartment, one room on the third floor of a walk-up on Jones Street in Greenwich Village. Living alone had its advantages. He could have his phonograph going any time of the day or night, listening to Whiteman's band play a Gus Kahn and Walter Donaldson song such as "Yes, Sir! That's My Baby" or Ruth Etting singing "Mean to Me." But it also made him feel his poverty and the hopelessness of his ambition all the more keenly. The apartment itself was tiny even by New York standards. The bathtub served as his kitchen sink and a hinge lowered a stove over the top of it, so when he cooked he could not use the sink. When he put up the kitchen table to eat dinner, he had to place it over the toilet. By no means, by Buddy Dill's standards, a "good address."

Two of his boyhood friends, Walter Rivers and Buford Smith, had found Johnny's stories of life in New York enchanting, and they took the boat up to try their luck in the city. Johnny met them at the dock "needing a shave and wearing a shirt that had been turned inside out on about the fourth day of its wearing." When he escorted them to his apartment, Buford took one look at the dishes piled in the bathtub, another at the pile of dirty clothes in the corner, and then went out to book passage home. Walter Rivers stayed on to room with Johnny for a while and got a bit part in the 1930 production of *Schoolgirl*, but he too eventually "decided to call it quits and go home and marry his local debutante."

One oasis in Mercer's bleak landscape was Mrs. Willingham's apartment in Greenwich Village. She had been his dramatic coach back in Savannah, and after the triumph of their amateur company she had decided, like Johnny, to move to New York. She lived with her son and two daughters, all of whom were working, so she could usually give Johnny a sardine sandwich, mix him a Tom Collins with bathtub gin, and put on a Louis Armstrong record. "On warm nights," he recalled, "we'd go up on the roof and in the winter go out to one of those little Italian bistros so numerous in Greenwich Village in those days."

Except for these times, however, Mercer's days and nights were bleak. "No one really knew what it felt like or how low I felt at this point," which he later described as "the most Stygian point of my life professionally." A boy who had grown up in a house attended by servants, he had nothing to show after nearly two years in New York but his cramped, dirty apartment. Jones Street, only one block long, would be the dead end of his acting career in New York.

Fortunately, he had kept at songwriting, filling up notebooks with song titles and ideas, since his failure to secure acting jobs left him with considerable time on his hands. It was a lucky break, therefore, when, acting on a tip from a friend that the Theatre Guild was mounting a new show, he went over to their theater on Fifty-second Street only to be told no actors were wanted—"only songs and pretty girls." Mercer called the prettiest girl he knew, Cynthia Rogers, who had been in *Houseparty* with him, then set to work on the melody Everett Miller had given him. "I had half a song," he said, meaning that Miller had given him an eight-bar melody. Most popular songs of the time were thirty-two bars long and divided into four eight-bar sections, usually in an AABA pattern so that the same eight-bar A melody was repeated three times. What Mercer had to come up with was the B melody, often called the "bridge" or "release" because it served as a transition away from and then back to the A melody. For someone who could not play the piano or even read music this was quite a challenge, but it foreshadowed the substantial number of songs Mercer would compose, as well as write lyrics for, over the course of his career.

Once Mercer completed the music of the chorus, he started working on the lyric. It would always be his normal way of working; he wrote *to* music. The first—and hardest—part of the process was finding the title of the song. Mercer picked a short, syncopated phrase near the end of the first eight measures of the melody. With his singing experience, he instinctively knew how to make a lyric singable by matching consonant and vowel sounds to musical notes. His ear picked up the aptness of using crisp consonants and short vowels for rhythmic musical phrases, so he took as his title "Out of Breath," a common vernacular expression that, when wedded to music, took on new currency. He then paired it with another vernacular phrase, "scared to death," which had the same breathless immediacy, with its short vowels and dental consonants, and, nicely, rhymed with his title. To round out his first lyrical line he went to the long note that concluded the musical phrase, and, again with his singing instincts, knew he needed a long vowel:

Out of breath and scared to death of *you*

From all of his years of listening to popular songs, he knew that a title phrase needed to be repeated throughout the lyric so that a listener would know what song to ask for at a sheet-music or record store. Mercer used his title phrase to conclude each of the A sections of the song and, most effectively, at the end of the chorus where he used the music's abruptness to curtail his long vowel sound in "Boo" so that, for an instant, music and lyrics are cleverly mismatched:

> All you have to do is say "Boo!"

In that line as well, he demonstrated an instinctive understanding of another rule of lyric writing that Yip Harburg called "memorability"—using subtle interior rhymes to impress a lyric on the listener's subconscious. In the line "All you have to do is say 'Boo!'" there are four barely heard rhymes, *you, to, do,* and *Boo,* that stitch the lyric together.

With the chorus completed, Mercer worked on the music and lyric for the introductory verse, and here he invoked the witty patter of Gilbert and Sullivan:

> When tasks superhuman
> Demand such acumen
> That only a few men
> Possess

"Out of Breath" was, if not masterly lyric writing, strong apprentice work, and it was accepted into *The Garrick Gaieties.* The song was featured near the end of the revue, with multiple choruses and lots of lyric patter in between. The number begins with the male and female leads hiding from each other behind a couch. They then come out and confess their mutual fears:

> Love was first divined
> Then explored and defined,
> Still the old sensation is new.
> Out of breath
> And scared to death of you.

The boy then got down on his knees to propose:

> I would love to roam
> Through an old ladies home
> Give the girls a new thrill
> But I'm out of breath and scared to death of you.

The girl responded:

> Should old massa loose the hounds upon my fleeting tail,
> I would not quail

And the boy, galloping after her, sang:

I'd arrive in time to save what honor I could save

Then, in a comic finale, he put his hands on her throat and began choking her as they sang, "Out of breath . . ." Corny as it was, "Out of Breath" became one of the show's biggest production numbers—quite an auspicious debut for a young actor turned songwriter.

Five years earlier, the first *Garrick Gaieties* had been a fund-raiser by the Theatre Guild and had featured "Manhattan," the first hit song by the young team of Rodgers and Hart. When sung by Sterling Holloway and June Cochrane, "Manhattan" turned *The Garrick Gaieties*, originally planned for only two benefit performances, into a long-running Broadway hit. The second *Garrick Gaieties* was mounted in 1926 and featured another Rodgers and Hart hit, "Mountain Greenery," again sung by Sterling Holloway. Rodgers and Hart then moved on to big-time Broadway musicals, and the Theatre Guild revues stopped; but with the onset of the depression, big Broadway productions, such as the *Ziegfeld Follies*, fell on hard times, and the smart "little" revue came back in vogue. Thus when Johnny Mercer placed "Out of Breath" in the 1930 edition of *The Garrick Gaieties*, he was continuing a tradition of lyric writing that had begun with Lorenz Hart, whom he always considered, along with Irving Berlin and Cole Porter, one of the three greatest lyricists in American popular song. In fact, the continuity was made even stronger by the fact that Sterling Holloway, along with Cynthia Rogers, sang "Out of Breath" in the 1930 version of the show. Holloway, by then an established figure on Broadway, heard the song and claimed the right to do it in the show.

The 1930 edition of *The Garrick Gaieties* opened on June 4, 1930, ran for a respectable 158 performances, then reopened on October 16 for another 12 performances that included a newcomer to Broadway, Rosalind Russell. Songs in the show had music by such soon-to-be-auspicious composers as Aaron Copland, Vernon Duke, and Marc Blitzstein and lyrics by the likes of Yip Harburg and Ira Gershwin. Savannah newspapers reported the success of "Out of Breath" by hometown boy Johnny Mercer: "The New York papers have been lavish in their praise of the popular air and critics have put it at the top of selections singled out for favorable mention." The song was recorded by Joe Venuti and his New Yorkers with a jazzy vocal by Scrappy Lambert.

"The *Garrick Gaieties* had been a fork in the road for me and had pointed me in the direction I suppose I had to go," Mercer later reflected, "towards Tin Pan Alley."

Three

Jeepers Creepers: 1930–1931

During all this time, I was an assiduous and avid student of the popular song.
No school boy lover ever swooned over nor courted his beloved more passionately
than I did the songs of the day. I knew every one that came out, the verses, as
well as the prominent writers and usually all record versions, no matter what
label. I didn't make a fetish of it. I just liked them.

In the chorus line of *The Garrick Gaieties* was a beautiful young dancer whose
stage name was Ginger Meehan. Her mother, Anna Meltzer, had at the age
of eighteen walked from Russia across Europe with only "a great big bag of
sugar cookies, and she had what would be equal to, like, a nickel a day for milk
and a quarter that she had to save to send a telegram" to her husband, Joseph,
who had already immigrated to America with his family, telling him when she
would arrive. When she reached New York, Anna moved in with Joseph's
family in a large house in Brooklyn, where she bore him three daughters.
After Joseph committed suicide, however, she was left alone to raise them.
Anna fell back on the one thing she knew. In Russia she had worked in a ribbon shop as a child, so she started sewing children's clothes. "She did very
exclusive, elegant children's clothes," a granddaughter recalled. She hired several people to work for her and, in the depression, advertised dresses for little
girls that cost forty-five dollars. "So she was an early businesswoman," her
granddaughter said. "And that's how she raised her three daughters."

In immigrant families, studying music was regarded as one way to success.
Learning to play a musical instrument was a relatively easy and affordable
skill for children, and immigrant parents, whose command of the English

language usually was far weaker than their children's, could recognize a child's progress at the piano. In the Meltzer home, music lessons were regarded even more highly, if more selectively. The middle daughter, Rose Elizabeth, was the only one who studied piano, but she studied it seriously, for Anna was determined that she would become a concert pianist. "We all thought it was a shame that she didn't bother with her music because she just wasn't an ordinary player," a sister said. "We all thought she'd be a concert pianist." But Elizabeth evidently resented the rigors of her training, such as having to get up before school every morning to practice. Anna had also paid for acrobatic dancing lessons for Elizabeth and her older sister Claire, and Elizabeth used that training to thwart her mother's plan by going on stage in another fashion— as a chorus girl in Broadway musicals.

While it would be unimaginable today for a girl to walk into a Broadway theater and get a part in the chorus line, in the mid-1920s prosperity was so high that the theater flourished, and talented and comely young women were welcome. During Christmas week of 1927 alone, twenty new musicals opened on Broadway, eleven of them on the night of December 26. Successful productions would then go on the road, usually with new casts, while the original cast remained on Broadway to do new shows. Elizabeth's first show was with the touring company of *Honeymoon Lane*. "She was performing with this Mary Meehan," her sister recalled, "whose father was a director, and they got on the stage together. . . . They said that they were sisters." Taking the stage name of Ginger Meehan, Elizabeth roomed with Dolores Reade, who would later marry Bob Hope and remain a lifelong friend.

While they were performing in Philadelphia, Paul Whiteman's band came to town. It featured Bing Crosby and the Rhythm Boys, a trio of white men who sang songs like "Mississippi Mud" in a laid-back but rhythmic black style that enthralled Jazz Age audiences. Crosby roomed with Bix Beiderbecke and imitated his mellifluous cornet style as well as his habit of drinking himself into a stupor. "Bing could be cantankerous and was becoming unreliable. Some nights he was so green from drink that he had to be held up at the mike; on other nights he didn't show at all. . . . The women they dated were chorus girls, of which there was a limitless supply." In Philadelphia, Crosby started dating Ginger, and it quickly became serious. When he got back to New York, he sent her a late-night telegram at the Emerson Hotel:

ACCORDING TO US STATISTICS THERE 7 MILLION PEOPLE HERE BUT WITHAL IM A STRANGER AND MISERABLY ALONE BECAUSE YOURE NOT ALONG LOVE UNDYING BEST REGARDS TO DELORES AND STUFF BING

Ginger's next role was in the chorus of *Good News*, one of the frothiest musicals of the Jazz Age. With DeSylva, Brown, and Henderson songs such as "The Best Things in Life Are Free" and "The Varsity Drag," and a gag-filled story about college life, *Good News*, called by Walter Winchell "flip, fast, furious, free, and flaming festive," ran for 557 performances on Broadway. Anna Meltzer was concerned enough about her daughter that she sent her older sister Claire to meet her after the show each night and bring her home. When *Good News* went on the road, Ginger was again in the chorus, and Bing Crosby was still pursuing her. The show was playing at the Selwyn Theater in Chicago in July when Whiteman's band came to town and Bing wired her:

WOULD LIKE TO SAY HELLO THIS EVE AFTER YOUR
PERFORMANCE SAY AT ELEVEN FIFTEEN BING

Within a week came another telegram:

WOULD LIKE TO CALL YOU TONIGHT IF BUSY SUE ME BING

"The story in the family," according to Ginger's niece, "was—she dated him, and he wanted to marry her. . . . I don't know whether it reached an engagement part or not, but it was . . . pretty serious."

A Crosby biographer speculates that Bing shifted his attention to the star of *Good News*, Peggy Bernier, a beauty who could also hold her own with him on a night of saloon hopping. "To Bing, the *Good News* cast was a chicken coop and he was the fox." But it is equally possible that Ginger cooled things down. Another cast member, seventeen-year-old Dixie Carroll, refused to even talk to Bing when he called for a date, having heard enough about him, presumably from Ginger, to be wary. A year later, in Hollywood, Dixie, who had by then changed her name to Dixie Lee, would date and eventually marry the crooner. Dixie, Dolores, and Ginger would remain lifelong friends from their days on the road, and so would the men they married—Bing Crosby, Bob Hope, and Johnny Mercer.

Ginger's next role was in the chorus of the 1930 edition of *The Garrick Gaieties*, and it was here that she met Johnny Mercer. He thought she assumed he was a producer of the show because he watched rehearsals from the wings; she simply found him charmingly innocent of the ways of the theater. Anna Meltzer would invite cast members and their friends to parties at her house so that she could keep an eye on her daughter's social relationships. As Claire, the oldest of Anna's daughters, recalled, "My mother liked him. . . . We all liked him. Everybody liked him. My girlfriends used to get crushes on him." Mercer helped his cause by giving Ginger a copy of J. B. Priestley's novel *The Good Companions*. He had bought the book when it came out in 1929 and loved its story of the adventures of a British acting troupe. "Her uncle told her it was safe to go out with a man who liked a book like that," Mercer later recalled. "I owe a lot to Jack Priestley."

Although she later said Mercer "was interested in every girl in the show *but* me," Ginger welcomed the attentiveness of the young man with the incomprehensible southern accent. "I still don't know what attracted her interest in me," he later said, "except that possibly I was so ingenuous and naive, wearing Panama hats, walking up to the dressing room to bring her ice cream or buying her cokes and hot dogs, and taking her to movies in her time off." . . . "We didn't have much to talk about at first, except Bing Crosby, whom she had known and whom I admired." The Crosby connection was vital, for Mercer adored Crosby and the Rhythm Boys. "All the kids were hungry for the music that the trio was putting down," he reflected, "but . . . only a few seemed to understand it." Mercer numbered himself among the aficionados. "I knew their records by heart but wasn't interested in 'I Surrender, Dear.' I wanted to hear more 'Wistful and Blue's'—more 'Old Man River's'—more 'Because My Baby Don't Mean Maybe Now,' " singling out early Crosby hits with a jazzy, laid-back style. "It seemed to me he employed a completely new and different style which sounded more natural and effortless than any I'd ever heard."

But while Crosby was their first main topic of conversation, Johnny and Ginger soon began to have the experiences that draw people closer together. One night riding the subway back to Brooklyn, they noticed a black man asleep in the car when they boarded at Times Square station. As they arrived in their Borough Hall station in Brooklyn, he awoke, looked around disgustedly, and said, "Borough Hall! Ain't dat a pain in de ass!" "For years," Mercer said, "anytime anything went wrong, Ging and I would just look at each other and say 'Borough Hall!' and think of that poor man who thought he was on his way to Harlem."

Another experience that drew them closer was their cab rides with a driver named Ruby, who, when Johnny could afford cab fare, took them to Brooklyn after the show. One night Ruby said, "Hey, how about you folks comin' along with me and my girlfriend this Sunday afternoon out on the Island?" "We tactfully begged off due to business engagements," Mercer said, "but we hailed other cabs after that, feeling Ruby was taking a little too much for granted and getting a little too close for comfort." Class lines may have frayed in New York, but they still held tight when it came to double-dating with a cabbie and his girlfriend.

Their relationship grew more intense. Ginger's sister Claire recalled that Mercer "used to come over lots of times and stay," and one particular time, "when my sister Debbie was very sick with pneumonia, and Johnny used to come at night and stay with Ginger and Ginger would stay up with her." The deepening relationship with Ginger strengthened Mercer's resolve to make a solid career for himself as a songwriter. Acting would always be the youthful dream that would never let go of him, but it was as a songwriter that his career advanced—a published songwriter, thanks to the help of Everett Miller. Miller had finally told Johnny that his father was an arranger for the prestigious T. B. Harms music publishing company, which published "Out of Breath." "This was again destiny taking a hand in my life," Mercer said, "though I had no inkling of it at the time."

Mercer began to hang out at music publishers' offices, as well as at songwriter meeting places such as Walgreen's and the English Tea Room. The mild success of "Out of Breath" gave him an entrée with publishers and songwriters, and his obvious love of popular songs opened up opportunities to collaborate. He got to know some of the great songwriters whose work he'd admired since childhood: "If we were lucky, we might bump into Jerome Kern or Otto Harbach in the lobby, or get a nod from Sigmund Romberg or Rudolf Friml while Oscar Hammerstein, that tall shy Abe Lincoln of a librettist, was quietly padding around the corridors, working out his assignments with most of the great composers then under contract to Harms." He would hear about someone who was looking for material for a revue or someone else looking for nightclub material—songs as well as jokes. He was willing to work at all hours and travel far into the suburbs to meet with a collaborator. "We'd leave no stone unturned and covered all fields, picking up experience and learning all the while."

One day as he was walking along Broadway he noticed a sign on a second-story window that read "Charles K. Harris Music Co." Mercer knew that Harris's "After the Ball" had galvanized Tin Pan Alley back in 1893 when it was the first song to sell a million copies of sheet music. "I timidly climbed the stairs to see what a music company looked like, and perhaps a real live songwriter as well. To my surprise, there was no secretary and I was greeted by a little old, gray-haired cat in his seventies, or perhaps even older, with a cordial:

" 'What can I do for you, young man?' "

Mercer said he was a fan of Harris's songs, and the composer began to regale him with stories of his triumphs, which included going "down the line" in Chicago (meaning visiting all the high-priced bordellos on State Street). Mercer grew bored, realized Harris had no secretary, but "being a polite Southern lad," sat through more stories, including the fact that Harris had recently written a book about his career.

" 'Indeed?' I inquired politely.

" 'Oh, yes. Would you like an autographed copy?'

" 'I'd be honored,' I replied.

"Whereupon, with much flourish and in an elegant Spencerian hand, he wrote extravagantly upon the flyleaf: 'To my good and dear friend, Johnny Mercer, with the best wishes of the Author, Charles K. Harris.' "

As Harris escorted Johnny to the door, he said "quite clearly, 'That'll be two dollars!' "

At the time, Mercer recalled, "I had only about three dollars to my name."

He hung out with other fledgling songwriters, trying out their latest work and swapping show business gossip but then suddenly falling silent if a more famous songwriter joined them for a few minutes. One day, Herman Hupfeld played them his new song of 1931, "As Time Goes By," which went nowhere beyond a few recordings by Rudy Vallee and other singers and only became a hit when, more than ten years later, Dooley Wilson sang it in *Casablanca*. Mercer was learning the vicissitudes of a fickle marketplace that could turn a nearly forgotten number into a hit. At the end of the workday, the young songwriters would go off together for a few drinks and bemoan their luck, swearing that they were every bit as good as George or Ira Gershwin.

He was intrigued by the established songwriters who would collaborate with various partners, a practice Mercer himself would adopt, looking for a song that "sounded 'hitty,' " which they then pitched to all the music publishers along Tin Pan Alley. Once they found a publisher, they would ask for a cash advance against their song's future royalty payments, then go off to a bar to celebrate or to the racetrack. They were characters right out of Damon Runyon, and Mercer relished the stories that circulated about them, such as the one about two songwriters who dashed into a publisher's office and pitched their latest creation:

> With a C and an O
> And an L and an O
> And an R and an O
> And a D and an O
> That's how you spell Colorado!

The publisher was so impressed that he issued them an advance check for five hundred dollars, which the writers cashed and took to Belmont just in time for the first race. When the pleased publisher sang the song to his partner, however, he was told, "Unless you change that next to last O to an A, you won't sell many copies in Colorado."

Some of these men, such as composer Arthur Schwartz, who was enjoying his first big hit with "I Guess I'll Have to Change My Plan," took the time to advise and even tutor Mercer as he worked on songs. Phil Charig, who had written songs with George Gershwin, invited Mercer to write songs with him and Richard Meyers for a show called *Pajama Lady*. In the course of their collaboration, Charig took Mercer for a weekend at Freeport on Long Island, "a popular resort for vaudevillians then, telling me I'd have to do my share of bed-making and dish-washing. That was okay with me, but I must have been a little dilatory about it, as I remember the person who shared the cottage with us losing his cool because I was so slow in doing my share. How did I know he was going to turn out to be Cary Grant? His name was Archie Leach then—

and I recall he had a most attractive blonde Mehitabel as his week-end companion!" *Pajama Lady* played in Philadelphia in October of 1930 but never made it to New York. Still, it gave Mercer three more published lyrics, along with another song he wrote with Charig and Harris, "Another Case of Blues," which was interpolated into the score for *Tattle Tales*.

As Johnny Mercer was gradually establishing himself as a lyricist, producer Louis Macloon and his wife, Lillian Albertson, walked into the Harms offices one day. They had just returned from Europe, where they had purchased the rights to an operetta by Emmerich Kalman that they were going to turn into a musical called *Paris in the Spring*. A sentimental story of young artists and musicians struggling for success in Montmarte, the operetta had played well in Europe, and the Macloons planned to produce it on the West Coast, then bring it to New York. What they wanted was someone to write English lyrics to Kalman's songs. "And work cheap," Mercer recalled. "That last qualification is probably what got me the job." On the strength of a few published songs, fledging lyricist Johnny Mercer had been given the challenging opportunity to write English lyrics to an operetta score by one of Europe's most popular composers.

Just before he left for California in September of 1930, and perhaps because of his imminent departure, his relationship with Ginger took an intimate turn. Ginger's "head shots," glossy photos taken by professional photographers that she could give to agents and casting directors, show her to have been a strikingly lovely, sultry beauty. She was also a voluptuous woman with large breasts that, in photographs taken throughout her life, are apparent beneath blouses, dresses, and sweaters. Johnny Mercer, always enamored of well-endowed women, admitted that what attracted him to her was the fact that her charms were "amply apparent." One afternoon she told him that while riding on the subway she had been approached by a man who exposed himself to her, and she'd hit him with her umbrella. "I told her she should have undone her bra at him. That would have made him seem small." Mercer's remark suggests that there had been a certain level of sexual intimacy between them, but letters that he wrote to her from California indicate that Ginger and Johnny had sexual intercourse before they parted. The letters also suggest that it was Johnny Mercer's first sexual experience.

From the rattling Pullman car of the Santa Fe Chief as it sped him westward across the plains, he wrote to Ginger that he was not at all awed by the landscape unrolling before his eastern eyes because "the only thing I can think about, Ginger, I never will forget Wednesday. I have never had anything so sweet happen to me before. I'm sure it never will or could with anyone else. Someday, I hope you find out how real and sincere my love is for you—you can't possibly know by anything I say, because if I try to, I could never approach the real feeling." The politely chosen adjective "sweet" to describe what happened on the previous Wednesday, his insistence on the singularity of the experience, and his affirmations of absolute and inexpressible love all intimate that Ginger was his first sexual conquest.

In letters he sent her from California, he reaffirms his ardency. "Ginger," he pleads, "don't ever worry about Johnny being your own. As long as you want him he can't help himself. I adore you, my precious, and always will as long as you'll let me." He goes on to some veiled sexual boasting: "I've been around a bit," then backpedals, "although not as much as most," but then hints again at his prowess: "but I've had the experiences that everyone has, and maybe I know the facts—maybe not." But then, after assuring her that "there's never been anyone who's meant as much to me as you," he nearly makes a direct confession that he was a virgin: "You see, precious, you're 'my first love' in the real meaning of the word—and no one else can hardly be that, can they?"

While he might have told Ginger he was too much in love with her to notice the prairie, Johnny Mercer, with his abiding love of the natural world, was in awe of the California landscape. "It really was a 'Rose Room,'" he said, "as you looked at the gardens filled with big cabbage roses and chugged along through the orange groves on either side. Coming into San Bernardino, Monrovia, and Pomona in those days, I'm sure the poor traveler thought he was really in heaven as he looked out of his train window to see the palms of Arcadia and the green rolling hills filled with orange blossoms and topped by purple mountains with snowy peaks. The only smog then was made occasionally by the smudge pots lit to fire and warm the orange trees to keep the frosty mornings down to a respectable temperature."

The Macloons rented a house in Beverly Hills that had once belonged to Greta Garbo. "A favorite joke," Mercer said, "was that they hadn't even taken the ring from the bathtub." They took Johnny around Los Angeles, where *Paris in the Spring* would hold its tryout performances before opening in San Francisco. "They showed me around the miniature golf courses, Aimee Semple MacPherson's Temple, the Brown Derby, shaped like a hat, and took me to other places I was longing to go. To the Cocoanut Grove where the Rhythm Boys, now with Gus Arnheim, were playing—and to the Cotton Club, which boasted Louis Armstrong as the main attraction."

Perhaps bolstered by the fact that Ginger had dated Crosby, Mercer went backstage at the Cocoanut Grove and introduced himself. "He was very nice, and I was impressed, as everybody is, by those opaque, China blue eyes, and by his manner and talk, at once warm and hip but with a touch of aloofness that was always there." Mercer, the suitor, also took in another detail of his former rival: "his lack of hair. He was only a few years older than I, who wasn't bald yet, but he was practically bald." At the Cotton Club, he saw Louis Armstrong at "his youthful peak—his prime—but those dumb customers at the Cotton Club didn't want to hear 'Struttin' with Some Barbecue' or the 'Heebie Jeebies' nor 'Knockin' a Jug,' not 'Monday Date.' What they loved and drooled salaciously over was 'Golfin' Papa, You Got the Nicest Niblick in Town.' Honestly, it was enough to drive you up the wall." Hearing Crosby and Armstrong also provided welcome relief from the music of Emmerich Kalman that Mercer was setting lyrics to—"perfect to these old ears, jaded by Dutch music for the last four weeks."

But except for a few nights out on the town, Mercer found that while undergoing the rigors of writing a score for a musical he was "under house arrest, writing, and like a student or inmate only was let out occasionally." In the course of working on songs for *Paris in the Spring*, Mercer wrote a series of love letters to Ginger that reveal what a volatile and mercurial person he was beneath his avuncular southern surface. The slightest developments in his work on the show or in his relationship with Ginger could launch him on a roller coaster of emotional swings. At times he felt he was doing a respectable job on *Paris in the Spring*. "Although I don't think I've done any Hammerstein or DeSylva job on it," he wrote Ginger, "there's talk of doing another in a couple of months." Always a slow worker, Mercer was anxious when the Macloons brought in their son, a songwriter who collaborated with Mercer's friend Len Levinson on additional songs for the Kalman score. "But," Mercer tells Ginger with renewed self-confidence, "I'm slowly writing better ones to keep my self-respect and to replace his." To move from writing pop songs and revue numbers to a full-fledged operetta was a trial by fire for a twenty-year-old novice lyricist, and, as he put it in a letter to Ginger, "Old Madame Mercer isn't used to operettas."

As his confidence waned, he grew despondent and clung to her. "I must sound like a baby in these maudlin letters I've been writing, but, my darling, I'm so crazy about you. I don't believe you know how much (for the 50th time)." In some letters, he starts off jauntily, mimicking the tone of her letters to him, which clearly were more guarded accounts of her daily goings-on: "We must be off and away and return the lady's letter in the casual mien in which she writes it. Not criticism, fair one, but a mere change in tactics to try and please you. For, naturally, if you are given to what I may term narrative letter writing you should rather receive yours in the same vein—with the intimate touch dropped." But a page later he breaks down: "It's pretty awful to let myself be so dependent on one person for every mood I have. I'm afraid you've got me entirely at your mercy—do what you will, Lady Godiva, I'll tag along behind you." By the end of October, he is still complaining about the lack of emotion in her letters to him: "You couldn't manage to struggle out one 'I love you,' could you? I'm such a baby that I still like to hear it—from you." Although none of Ginger's letters to him survives, it seems clear from his constant begging for a letter that she was far less regular a correspondent. When she did write, however, she could inflame his ardor, and he would plead for another of her " 'hair-sing[e]ing' letters—Hotcha."

One can only speculate about Ginger's reaction to this emotional downpour from Johnny Mercer. Surely it must have given her a sense, perhaps for the first time, of how much power she could exercise over a man. Even without his jaunty telegrams that she saved, it is unlikely that Bing Crosby would have so writhed and moaned over her as Mercer did in almost every letter. Such consciousness of her power might have prompted her to strike a more distant and arch pose even as the heady sensation of controlling him proved increasingly seductive to her.

As work on the operetta dragged on, the loveliness of California faded for him. "The trip has been lousy so far," he complains. "So damned hot that I yearn for the Paramount balcony" in New York. "The land of sunshine! Praise God! I'll soon be leaving it. I've never seen a bigger hick town than this one. And the blondes—I've never seen as many and hope I never see another one. It would be all right if they were naturals but they haven't even that excuse." But by mid-October, the show was being pulled into shape, and his spirits were upbeat again. "The music is pretty," he writes. "Most of the corny things having been kicked out—after I had written lyrics, of course." As rehearsals began, he found that the choreographer had "done a swell job on the dances . . . and he's added plenty to the comedy." As opening night approached, he was expansive: "The story and voices and costuming are grand."

At this same time, Ginger went on tour with the road edition of *The Garrick Gaieties*, which opened at the Blackstone Theatre in Chicago on October 27 for a three-week run. Once *Paris in the Spring* opened, Johnny had assumed, his work would be over, and he could see Ginger in Chicago on his way back to New York. "Ginger, won't it be marvellous (the dictionary gives two spellings so I may as well use both) if we can be with each other in Chicago? Darling, will you stay by yourself there so I can have you all for my own?" As he planned their reunion, his fervor mounted: "I have longed for this—to be able to leave and spend a week with you in Chicago—Ginger, my darling, I'm yours—now and always—since I saw you—and I've kept myself yours all this time—because I know how marvellous (cut out one 'l') it will be to see you again. I adore you."

Soon he had more good news to report: "I got a wire from Harms—telling me to report in immediately as soon as I got back—so maybe it means a job and some more money towards our yacht." The prospect of a job with Harms, the premier publisher of popular songs, would put him on the same payroll as Jerome Kern and George Gershwin—heady prospects for an apprentice lyricist just approaching his twenty-first birthday. But he is most thrilled not by his show's prospects for success or even his possible new job back in New York but by the rendezvous with Ginger in Chicago. He writes that he will leave for Chicago the next day: "So if you've got any dates for next week, break them—from Saturday on—and keep every minute open for

The Colonel," invoking a nickname he'd acquired from walking around New York in a white linen suit and a floppy Panama hat.

But the very next day the Macloons insisted that he stay in California and work on a revision of the finale of the second act. One of the reasons for opening a musical on the road, Mercer learned, was that out-of-town audience reactions helped a producer and director see where a show needed to be doctored. The Los Angeles audiences for *Paris in the Spring* clearly showed the Macloons that the production needed some revisions. "Everything seems to happen to keep you away from me—I had my reservation to leave tonight and these bastards decide to rewrite the second act finale—my heart is about to break, Ginger. Sometimes I wish I'd never even met you if I must be away from you so long." Contemplating murder "or something equally as bad," he feels "too badly to write anymore" and closes abruptly with "I adore you—more than anything else in this whole lousy world." As he travels with the show to San Francisco, his melancholy underside surfaces. "I've gotten to the state where I've just given up to circumstances—whatever happens is okay—I can't prevent it—which is a safe although somewhat cowardly philosophy—if it can be called a philosophy."

Contributing to his despair was a newspaper clipping a friend sent him from the *Savannah Morning News*. While Mercer was passionately courting Ginger Meehan by mail, there was another girl, back in Savannah, that he had hoped to marry. Ever since he had attended the coming-out party of Elizabeth Cummins at Savannah's DeSoto Hotel on New Year's Day of 1930, he had adored her. "Although I had left Savannah, I really liked one there a lot. I liked a couple, but it was a natural time to select the one we liked the most and all of us were always looking. But this one, she was by far the prettiest girl I had ever dated, and it just happened that I must have had a good night when we met, because she really liked me too—a little. I felt she did and I still think if we'd both had the chance we wanted something might have 'taken.' But it was the oldest story ever—she wanted to get married—to be sure of me—and I wanted to write songs—and I had to go to New York to do it. I believed in early marriage, but I wasn't giving up my songs for anything, so I went back to New York always thinking I'd come back to her."

The clipping showed an extraordinarily beautiful girl whose eyes glowed even from newsprint. *Those eyes—how familiar they seem.* It announced that Asneath Elizabeth Cummins was engaged to Edward Bubier Wulbern of Charleston. While Mercer was devastated by the news at the time, he later reflected, "Even though we work fast and get lucky early, we can't hold back that swift old runner—Old Father Time. She must have met many others in the year or two I was trying to get it all together, but that never occurred to me. So it was after I had met Ginger and had gone out to California that the blow fell. We men are so conceited I suppose we always think there'll be plenty of time to make our choice. But if the girls don't wait, why should we keep falling for *that* illusion?"

Elizabeth Cummins might have wanted to wait for Johnny Mercer, but circumstances seem to have militated against that. Barely a month after the announcement of her engagement, the *Savannah Morning News* carried the notice of her marriage, adding, "The announcement of the marriage will come as a great surprise to the friends of the couple, for although the engagement was announced several weeks ago no date had been set for the marriage. Immediately after the marriage Mr. and Mrs. Wulbern left for New York where they will spend their honeymoon."

In a fit of pique Johnny sent the clipping to Ginger, "to make her jealous really," presumably by showing her how beautiful a woman had been in love with him. In the letter that accompanied the clipping, he cavalierly noted, "The picture is one of the Savannah belle I have so jokingly referred to. I thought you might like to see what she looked like. I say looked because, what the hell, she's getting married." Always cool, Ginger remarked upon the beauty of Miss Cummins, prompting Johnny to scramble: "About Miss Cummins—she *is* good-looking—I'll have to hand her that, but she can't hold a candle to you." It was at that point, Mercer said, that he "subconsciously made up my mind that it had to be Ginger. It probably had anyway. . . . Both of them were probably miles ahead of me and each knew what they wanted. Anyway, I'm sure it worked out right for all concerned. But some things you never forget, do you? . . . Why do we men think there may be a chance to pick up where we left off and that they'll be waiting for us; that all we have to do is say the word?"

While he had failed to make Ginger jealous with the newspaper clipping, she could plunge Johnny into jealousy without lifting a finger. One of the members of the *Paris in the Spring* company, a boy who had been in *Good News* with Ginger, showed Johnny a photograph he had received from her. "Always be good because your sins will find you out," he writes Ginger in anguish. "Can you imagine how I felt when he showed me a picture of you? I guess I'm not the highest rating boy in the world with you after all." Then he adds to his own pain by alluding to what might have been the scene of their sexual tryst: "I'll certainly have to eat those words I spoke to you by the old pagoda in Brooklyn that night, won't I?" But then he flagellates himself for baring his feelings: "That, of course, stamps me as quite a schoolboy but I won't pretend to be anything I'm not . . . because if I were only treating this as a new experience I couldn't do so quite as vociferously or importantly. If I were thirty-five or fifty-five it would still mean a lot because it's the sweetest thing that's ever happened to me." Even as he derides his compulsion to talk about his emotions, he suspects that what for him was an overwhelming experience was not so for Ginger. "You're probably a little bored with the life or death manner in which I speak of it, because perhaps it doesn't mean quite as much to you as it does to me—I've felt that all along."

But even as he was in despair over Ginger, *Paris in the Spring* had a successful opening in San Francisco on November 3, 1930, at the Curran Theatre. Reviewers stressed the lush beauty of Kalman's melodies but also noted that "John Mercer has done a workmanlike job in fitting the melodies with American lyrics." Suddenly, Johnny Mercer was ecstatic, expressing his amazement in a letter to Ginger: "The fanfare of trumpets have ended, the grief is over, and out of the dust strode—who do you think—a fair-sized hit—not a smash and not for New York—but a hit just the same." But after that heady relief, another downturn. As Mercer watched the show during its three-week run, its many flaws grew increasingly apparent. "I'm so anxious for this show to close and for everyone to forget I ever wrote it," he writes to Ginger. "It will never be in condition to reach New York—if it does, God help it." Adding to his disappointment was the fact that Len Levinson had written "the best song in the show—a comedy song called 'Not Tonight, Josephine!'" Mercer later admitted to "knowing I had a lot to learn and wondering if I would ever learn it."

Paris in the Spring left him with a distaste for writing for the theater that would dog him for the rest of his career. Writing lyrics for a musical where the show was constantly being doctored through rehearsals, with new numbers shunted in and out, songs dropped because of tepid audience reaction, and new lyrics constantly in demand meant writing and rewriting on a very tight schedule. Such frenetic doctoring might have suited the New York sensibilities of a Lorenz Hart or Oscar Hammerstein, but for Mercer's laid-back, easygoing Savannah style it was too pressured, frenzied, too much like *work*. Whereas Hart and Hammerstein wrote *to* dramatic character and situation in a musical, Johnny Mercer was more comfortable writing out of his own emotional state. Just as he had poured out his feelings in letter upon letter to Ginger during their separation, so he would best craft lyrics out of his own emotions—not to express what a particular character was feeling at a dramatic moment in a musical. His theory of lyric writing, like that of acting, seemed to be "play yourself."

In one letter, in fact, he conflates the anguish he pours out to her with the lyrics he's been working on for his operetta. "As you see," he laments, "at this writing I suffer from a most depressing mood." But then he wryly pleads for her to answer his question, which may have been a proposal of marriage, since he later remarks that he has begged her for a year to marry him: "Your answer will be of tremendous importance to me—if you won't think it's from a lyric, I'll say, 'I idolize you.'"

Just before leaving San Francisco after *Paris in the Spring* closed on November 22, he told Ginger that, in addition to the T. B. Harms Company's interest in having him be a staff lyricist, Charlie Miller, the father of his collaborator on "Out of Breath," had wired him and asked him to get in touch when he got back to New York. "I saw in *Variety* that he is opening a publishing house of his own—so maybe I'll have a decent job when I get back—up the stairs to fame and fortune for my Ginger." But then he adds a telling qualifier: "even though the medium is that of a lyricist (a lonely profession—really)." Clearly, his recent experience with *Paris in the Spring* had shown him what a solitary profession it was to write lyrics. Part of that loneliness must have appealed to him. A Savannah friend once described Mercer as an extrovert when he was performing, an introvert when he was not. As his acting career faded, he confronted the prospect of the lonely trade of writing, which seemed to fulfill the introvert in him but offered little for his extroverted performing self.

When he finally was able to leave California and see Ginger again, Mercer was determined to marry. With that curious logic of young men in love, the loss of his Savannah "fiancée" made him all the more eager to replace her with Ginger. "I really think that made up my mind for me—if I ever had any doubt—for I stopped by to see Ginger, who was by now touring in Chicago and Detroit, and before two weeks were over, we were really engaged and were married the following spring. Fortunately for me, she had made some changes in her schedule too, sending a few of her old beaux packing, and lessening the competition for me."

They clearly stayed together in her hotel room, for he says in his next letter, "Everything seemed so empty when you left. I remember vaguely riding to the hotel in a taxi. . . . And all the while I wanted to scream—'Ginger's gone!' and to go walking all by myself where I wouldn't meet a soul. The hotel seemed so deserted and so sad. So I cursed myself for being so sentimental and went immediately to pack and leave the place." Mercer goes through a litany of his emotional permutations, then concludes, "I merely feel a very dull ache—and the desire to be held in your arms while I weep which, of course, could never happen—for if I were in your arms I shouldn't care to weep. Everything seems so dead—like the roses in your room." But then a page later he pulls himself out of his melancholy torpor and flippantly teases Ginger that he can't marry her until he takes piano lessons: "Really—I'm tired of not being able to play—And that means you can't marry me until I've finished learning (in ten easy lessons). Another possible song lyric idea there." Such emotional oscillations might have boded well for a career as a lyricist, but they made for a turbulent inner life.

Mercer returned to New York in December of 1930 "in the most terrible mood . . . a 'blue funk'—I imagined all sorts of terrible things about my future." He continued writing with Everett Miller, traveling up to Schenectady, where Miller was working at a locomotive factory, but they published very few songs together. In a letter he wrote Ginger from there, he alludes to Miller's lack of musical inspiration in a poem:

The miller is a wreck today
No breeze blows in Schenec today

"Schenectady does that to one, you know," he tells her. "As I sit here, stogie in hand, I'm half tempted to write you an impassioned letter of jealous rage—or tender love—which would you prefer? However, I shall do neither but remain stoically indifferent, come what may."

Back in New York City, he went to see *Schoolgirl*, where Walter Rivers had a bit part. "All evening I thought of us," he wrote Ginger. "The play dealing with adolescent love is trite, but so many times the girl character reminded me of you. She saw so much more clearly her way about than did the boy, who was rather much of a jellyfish. I'm not that, am I sweet?" While they might have been engaged, Ginger was too practical to marry a man as unsettled, emotionally and financially, as Johnny Mercer was in those depression years. "Do you feel that you'd like to marry me but that it would be unwise and you'd rather wait?" he asks, but then adds, "But that if we wait something will happen and then you won't want to?" After noting that it's "silly to talk of this in a letter because there can be no conversation," Mercer raises an even more worrisome point: "But do you feel I don't want to enough, or that I'm afraid to now?" His reassurance is an understated clincher: "I do really want to— and I'm only afraid I can't make you happy enough."

While that romantic sentiment might not have completely melted Ginger's reserve, soon Mercer had more practical news about his future that made him more economically marriageable: "Charlie Miller wants me to go with him as lyricist (get it?) number one—contract and all." Although he warns, "not a word about this, babe, as I'm under oath not to tell," he can't repress a jaunty "Heigh ho!" and indulge in a bit of career daydreaming: "Anyway, I won't be running around trying to place numbers and keep the wolf from the door."

Miller Music gave him a position as a staff lyricist, with a "drawing account" of twenty-five dollars a week (based on anticipated royalties from sheet-music sales of songs he would write). It was not much money, but at the bottom of the depression, when men were selling apples on street corners, it was a job. Part of the attraction of writing for Miller Music was that he could write independent popular songs as well as songs for the musical theater. His experience with *Paris in the Spring* had indicated that he was much more comfortable with writing free-standing popular songs rather than the full score needed for an operetta. Working with Miller would afford him that opportunity, while the older and larger firm of T. B. Harms specialized in songs for musical theater. Given the tight times, mounting a book show on Broadway was a risky proposition; aiming an individual song for the pop market or for a loosely structured revue stood a better chance of success. Just such a revue came along in *Jazz City*, with sketches by established writers Norman Krasna and Harry Tugend. It "looked the rosiest," Johnny recalled, "so Ging and I got married on the strength of it." He'd had to wait nearly a year for her to agree to marry him, but now he had a job at Miller and the prospect of a new show. The impression in Ginger's family, her sister recalled, was that "Johnny was getting somewhere."

From his letters to Ginger it is clear that his urge to marry reflected his intoxication with his first sexual liaison, his rebound from the loss of his Savannah sweetheart, and his need for some solid basis in his life after three years of a precarious existence in New York. Ginger's motives for accepting his proposal are harder to discern. In part, she may simply have yielded to the ardent pressure of his courtship. "She was such a meek little thing," a friend recalled; if Mercer was as insistent in her presence as he was in his letters to her, he may have worn her down by his devotion. "I'd have another date," she remarked in later years, "but Johnny would appear from nowhere and I'd find myself in a taxi with him starting out for the evening."

Yet for all of her seeming meekness, she had found that she could exercise a kind of power and control over Mercer. "She was very self-centered," as another friend described her, and by marrying Johnny she might have seen a way to be part of the flamboyant world of show business without having to be a chorus girl. "She was, quote, 'Mrs. Johnny Mercer,' unquote. That was very important to her," another friend said. "She loved being who she was." If that was her motivation, she was taking quite a gamble with Johnny Mercer, compared to Bing Crosby, who was already an established singing star when she dated him. That sense of her desire to bask in a husband's reflected glory was confirmed by a grandson: "She was a very polished lady, very cultured, very learned. She really loved her lifestyle and had a type of love, I think, for her husband, a lot of it built on admiration for his skill and status in the industry."

On June 8, 1931, they were married in the small Chantry Chapel of St. Thomas Episcopal Church on Fifth Avenue in New York City. Ginger's sister recalled was that it was a "very, very simple ceremony . . . just had a few people invited." Johnny Mercer's cousin and boyhood friend, Walter Rivers, was his best man. Mercer also asked Charlie Miller to accompany him to the wedding. They walked the few blocks to St. Thomas for the brief service. Afterward, Mercer recalled, "He had tears in his eyes because we were 'so young' . . . both of us being just 21 at the time."

It was a marriage that, judging from a photograph of Johnny and Ginger in Atlantic City, in 1933, started out blissfully. In a few years, however, it would deteriorate so drastically that a rumor would circulate about their courtship. Even though it could not be confirmed, the rumor would be repeated by reliable sources, perhaps because it seemed to explain, if only in a symbolic way, this mysterious union of a Jewish girl from Brooklyn and a scion of Savannah society: "Ginger was in an accident at the time. I think he was driving and when she was lying there, bleeding or whatever, she said to Johnny, 'You have to marry me. I want you to marry me.' And Johnny, typical of him, would take that, absolutely, and he had to do it."

Four

Lazybones: 1931–1934

I was, in a way, too lucky, and ill equipped for the early good fortune that befell me, both in singing and writing at such a tender age.

By the beginning of 1931, industrial production in the United States had fallen off by 28 percent, more than a thousand banks had collapsed, and 6 million people were jobless. The Great Depression had set in. Among its many victims was *Jazz City*, the musical show on whose promise Johnny and Ginger had gotten married. "It never came off," Mercer lamented, "another unproduced smash!" The newlyweds had to move in with Ginger's mother at Sterling Place in Brooklyn. "He had nothing at that time," said a niece. "Ginger was more successful than he was. And they moved in with my grandmother." Giving up her theatrical career, Ginger saw an ad that read "Wanted: Girls to sew buttons on the 2nd floor" and went to work as a seamstress. Mercer made his daily commute to Miller Music in Manhattan. "I had 25 cents a day," he recalled. "I'd take the subway over for a nickel, have two hot dogs and an orange drink (15 cents) and use the last nickel to take the subway back to Brooklyn for supper." One day he set out with an entire dollar, but on the subway he saw a sad-eyed man begging for his kids, so Mercer, who would always be a soft touch, gave half of it to him. When he got back home that night, Ginger was furious when he told her; she had to stretch their one can of salmon into a week of dinners. A few days later, Mercer saw the same guy again and realized he was a professional beggar.

At least he had a steady job and an office at a time when other men were selling apples on the street. "God knows I was trying, writing with any and everybody, writing at night, spending days waiting in offices for appointments, and traveling endless distances on the subway to work with some obscure melodist who lived way the hell and gone in the suburbs, but who had 'a tune' that might be a hit." These were the twilight days of Tin Pan Alley, as Hollywood studios, with the advent of sound films, were buying up the old sheet-music publishing houses and using their songs and songwriters for "talkie" musicals. "Tin Pan Alley in those days," recalled the son of composer Ray Henderson, "was like a vast tangle of spaghetti with songwriters working from one office to another with various collaborators." That pattern of collaboration would mark Mercer for the rest of his career. He would always be the Alley wordsmith, working with any number of collaborators, looking for a hit song. That free and easy style would make it hard for him to succeed on Broadway, where collaborators such as Rodgers and Hammerstein and Lerner and Loewe served a long apprenticeship together writing theatrical scores.

For all his effort, Mercer was a slow worker. In all of 1931 he published only three songs. Still, Charlie Miller kept him on a drawing account and maintained his faith in the young lyricist. At the end of the year, Miller received a letter from Johnny's father about his son's prospects. Miller, himself a father concerned about his own son's musical ambitions, wrote back on January 15, 1932. Revealing his bias toward musical theater, long nurtured by his work at Harms, Miller reassured George Mercer about his son's talent—"John is a literary genius and will some day hit his stride"—but he cautioned that "the writing of lyrics is not in itself a lifetime occupation. . . . I am looking forward to the time when John will write a play or book for a musical comedy. Then, with his knowledge of the technique of lyric writing he will be fully equipped to follow such a career." Miller explained, however, that because of the depression, audiences were not going to see Broadway musicals, so Johnny was currently writing independent songs rather than the book and lyrics for a musical comedy. "This work, such as John does, is rather spasmodic." Still, he urged George Mercer to continue to send his son fifty dollars a month, supplementing the twenty-five dollars a week Miller could provide. "He must be financed and encouraged so that when the time comes he will be ready to use his talents."

The letter reveals one father leveling with another, both men with a strong business sense. Miller cannot pay Johnny more, he says, "because John, up to now, has been unproductive. However, he has a lot of material ready and with the publication of his two recent songs we hope his income will be increased the coming year." On December 5, 1931, Mercer had published "When We Danced at the Mardi Gras" with composer Alfred Opler, and on January 16, 1932, the day after Charlie Miller's letter is dated to George Mercer, Miller Music would bring out a new song, "The Sweet Little Lady Next Door." George Mercer might have said he was considering stopping his monthly support as a way of forcing Johnny to come home and work in the family real-estate firm, for Miller emphatically states, "I don't think John is building up an unhappy and dissatisfied life. A man is only happy when he does the work he likes and from observation I don't think John would be happy in any commercial pursuits." In closing, Miller commiserates with George Mercer: "I am having the same problem with my son Everett. . . . Everett wants to follow along the same lines as John, but I have come to the conclusion that Everett's mind is not an artistic one but rather mathematical with a tendency toward mechanics and invention. That is why I have kept him away from this business all these years. It has been a lot of grief but these are my convictions." While squelching the dreams of his own son, Charlie Miller preserved those of Johnny Mercer.

As he learned more about the music business, Mercer became as fascinated by Tin Pan Alley song pluggers as he was with the men who wrote the songs. The whole premise behind Tin Pan Alley when it was founded by enterprising sheet-music publishers in the 1880s was that a song became a hit not through its inherent quality alone but through "plugging." Plugging was done by men who relentlessly promoted their company's songs by performing them in saloons, on street corners—anywhere there was a crowd. They also plugged a song by bribing a vaudeville star to use it in his or her act. The bribe could range from a good cigar to a "cut-in"—a share of the royalties by listing the star's name as one of the composers or lyricists on the published sheet music. Little did the public, Mercer reflected, "dream of the skullduggery that went on backstage to knock one guy's song out of an act and get your own in; of the payola that those ever sweeter-than-light vaudeville stars got; or of the cut-ins, the kickbacks of the music business where a big entertainer got his or her name on a song and—forever thereafter—a share of the royalties."

Mercer compared the way these pluggers hung around the big vaudeville stars to the birds that ride the backs of elephants and whales. "If Jolie baby sang your song, it was an immediate sensation," he said. "Sophie Tucker or Jimmy Barton could lift one from obscurity to a permanent place in the hearts of an unsuspecting public." He loved to hang around with the pluggers and, with his love of vernacular language, listen to their showbiz slang over a "cup of jav" as they bemoaned their ill luck in promoting a song or dreamed of making it big with their company's latest ditty. Almost as much as they loved talking about songs, they talked horses, and before they went into Little Lindy's restaurant, they made their bets with "Libby the bookie," who stood on a stretch of sidewalk in front of the restaurant known as "Libby's Beach" because sunlight came down on the spot from amid the tall buildings. "Then they'd go in to gossip about the happenings of the night before which might be who won the fight at the Garden, or the 4th at the Aqueduct, or what band leader was making it with what vocalist. Usually female, but not necessarily."

He recalled one plugger who always called everyone "pally" and "because of his false teeth, his wrist bands and knee bands, his double truss and his arch supporters" always seemed to be leaning forward and was nicknamed "the man who walks uphill." Another plugger was such a compulsive "bender of the truth" that his fellow pluggers suggested his tombstone read, "Here Lies." Pluggers who went home early were "hot meat men" because they had to go home to the dinner their wives fixed for them. The others hung out at the Roosevelt Grill, where they could find the Lombardos; the Pennsylvania, where they'd approach the Dorseys and Glenn Miller; and even out-of-town roadhouses, where they spent their nights trying to get other bandleaders to plug their songs.

Getting to know these pluggers sharpened Mercer's sense of what made for a hit as he worked with more and more collaborators. One composer was Peter Tinturin; Ginger and Johnny would visit the Tinturin family on weekends, and Tinturin's mother, "a dark-eyed, raven-haired lady of great beauty," would make "the best borscht and piroshki you ever tasted." Mercer and Tinturin wrote "Little Old Cross-Road Store" and "It's About Time," both of which were published by Miller Music in 1932, but neither became a hit. Another collaborator was composer Carl Sigman. "After playing softball in the Brooklyn school yards, we'd spend long nights writing. . . . his little round attractive mother would fill me up with blintzes or chopped liver on rye bread. I wished I could have laid some turnip greens or artichoke pickles and divinity fudge on her—but I doubt she would have dug my southern reciprocity half as much as I did the smoked sturgeon." But Mercer and Sigman published only a few songs, none of which became successful. Sigman later went on to success, but as a lyricist, with such songs as "Ballerina," "My Heart Cries for You," and "It's All in the Game." "So you see," Mercer remarked, "sometimes we don't know our own talents or our own strengths."

Miller Music was owned by William H. Woodin, who was the president of the American Locomotive Company and became Franklin Roosevelt's first secretary of the treasury. In 1933, Woodin would help stem the rash of "bank holidays" that greeted the new administration by issuing banks Federal Reserve notes as currency ("money that looks like money"). But in his spare time Woodin was a composer and gave the young Mercer some tunes to set lyrics to. Woodin and Miller, Mercer later reflected, "evidently had faith in me, though I doubt if I ever repaid it to them personally, my only successes being a couple of very questionable lyrics to tunes that Woodin and a foreign composer supplied." One of those songs, "Spring Is in My Heart Again," has a lyric that reflects Mercer's continuing apprenticeship on Tin Pan Alley, with such clichéd phrases as "you are here" and "skies are clear."

Although Mercer was committed to songwriting, he had not given up his dream of becoming an actor, and a compromise between acting and songwriting was performing as a singer. At this time, Paul Whiteman was conducting a national talent search for new singers, whom he featured on his weekly radio program, and Ginger, having heard Johnny sing in the shower, and, perhaps pursuing her own dream of being the wife of a star such as Bing Crosby, urged him to enter. Whiteman had been broadcasting "coast to coast" from the Edgewater Beach Hotel in Chicago ever since network radio was established in 1928, and his sponsor, the Pontiac division of General Motors, sent him on a national tour where local stations would hold amateur singing contests and bring their local finalists to Whiteman when he came to their city. In New York, auditions were held at NBC's Times Square Theatre on March 21, and when Mercer and one of his collaborators, Archie Bleyer, walked in they found three hundred hopefuls: "Cab drivers, truck drivers, porters, white, black (though not as many then), maids, waitresses, bus boys, college boys." Mercer and Bleyer, who would go on to a career as an arranger and conductor, watched as one contestant after another launched into "All of Me" or "Just Friends." After a few bars, a voice would come over the intercom: " 'Thank you very much . . . Next contestant, please.' . . . It wasn't that the management was rude, it was just that there were *so many* awful singers trying out for that one air shot on the Pontiac program." When Mercer's turn came, Bleyer sat at the piano, Johnny grabbed the microphone, "and we hit a tempo . . . lickety-split! . . . that would have delighted Little Richard today. I mean, we were going so fast and so rhythmically that no one could have interrupted our chorus! In any event, they didn't and we were held for the finals, which meant the great Paul Whiteman himself would hear us the following day."

As the comparison to Little Richard suggests, Mercer's singing style had strong black inflections, and that was exactly what Whiteman was looking for. The son of a music teacher who hated jazz, Whiteman broke from his father to start playing ragtime in the Barbary Coast of San Francisco and achieved enormous fame when he produced a program of concert jazz at New York's Aeolian Hall in 1924. Although much of the concert was a dreary "jazzing" of classical works and "concertizing" of jazz and pop pieces, things turned electric when young George Gershwin strode to the piano to play his composition *Rhapsody in Blue*. Whiteman was proclaimed the "King of Jazz," but he knew that "the best jazz musicians were black." He tried to sign several blacks, including Eubie Blake, "but his management came down hard: in addition to all the lost bookings in the south and some in the north, he would humiliate black musicians, who would be relegated to separate entrances, dining and boarding facilities, and even toilets." Whiteman compromised by hiring black arrangers and white performers who could play and sing "authentic jazz, the real thing"—cornetist Bix Beiderbecke, saxophonist Frankie Trumbauer, and the hot trio called the Rhythm Boys that featured Bing Crosby.

When Whiteman heard Mercer sing, he proclaimed him the winner not only of the New York contest but of the national one as well. On March 25,

1932, Johnny Mercer got to sing at the Palace Theatre alongside such stars as Russ Columbo. The show was broadcast, and his family in Savannah gathered around the radio. His brother Hugh wrote him an enthusiastic letter, saying they all "heard you tonight at Pop's and boy you were swell. . . . We all know you are going to make a big success."

But nothing more came of the triumph. "I had won a Pontiac Youth of America contest as a New York contestant, but it only gave me one air-shot singing with Whiteman and no money, so what good was it?" Mercer took a characteristically disparaging view of his success. It is probable that winning the contest earned him the opportunity to make a recording with the Dorsey Brothers Orchestra that fall. Shortly after the contest, on April 5, 1932, he made his first recording, with a group called the Nitecaps, backed by Frankie Trumbauer and his orchestra. As part of his "Sizzling One-Step Medley," Mercer sang "My Honey's Lovin' Arms" in the jazzy style of Louie Armstrong, replete with extensive stretches of pure scat.

Mercer and Ginger were so poor during this period that when Mercer wanted to go to a football game between Southern Methodist University and Fordham University (an unusual contest in the days before air travel made it easy for teams from around the country to play one another), Ginger "demurred, hesitating because of the old grey squirrel coat she had had so many years. I hastened to point out that my old coat had a vent up the back." Seeing that, she agreed to go, and they enjoyed the game, particularly the halftime show, where the SMU band played a jazzy rendition of "The Peanut Vendor" instead of the usual college marches. Mercer turned the experience into two songs. One was with Bernie Hanighen, "The Dixieland Band," about a trumpeter who threw off the band: "He hit a figure that was off the chord, / Apoplexy got 'em and they went to the Lord"; the other was "Jamboree Jones," about a jazz clarinetist who inspires his team to a Rose Bowl victory. "It was only as everybody got up to leave," Mercer recalled, "that Ginger noticed that *all* the men's coats had vents up the back. Too late to blame me— she had had too good a time as had I."

Still, no hit songs emerged from Mercer's typewriter. Sorely in need of inspiration, he got a call from Yip Harburg, who was getting a late start on a career as a lyricist after the Crash had ended his business career. The Shubert brothers were backing *Americana*, a small, slick revue typical of the early 1930s but with a satirical edge that reflected the bitter times, and Harburg was responsible for the score. "The theme was the Forgotten Man," Harburg recalled. "The fellow who fights your wars, who works the lathe, and the mills." Vincent Youmans was given a "a ten-thousand-dollar advance, which was terrific at the time," but then, Harburg said, Youmans "took the money and disappeared. . . . all I could get out of him was the opening chorus, and then he disappeared, and nobody ever heard from him. I had to get the show on in two months. It wasn't written. It wasn't anything."

Desperate, Harburg began calling in other composers and lyricists, including Johnny Mercer. Mercer, in turn, said he introduced Harburg to Harold Arlen, a singer and nascent songwriter who had just had a hit with a rhythmic spiritual number called "Get Happy." Arlen would go on to collaborate with Harburg for much of the rest of the decade, culminating with their score for *The Wizard of Oz* in 1939. Steeped in musical theater and thirteen years Mercer's senior, Harburg took Johnny Mercer under his wing. "In making me a kind of assistant during the formation of the *Americana* score, he taught me how to work at lyric-writing," Mercer said. "I had been a dilettante at it, trying hard but most undisciplined, waiting for the muse to strike." Mercer, whose patrician breeding disdained any suggestion that one had to *work* at something, got an important lesson from the Jewish boy who had clawed himself out of the most abject poverty of the Lower East Side. "God, he'll sit in a room all day and he'll dig and he'll dig and he'll dig. . . . sometimes we'd get a rhyming dictionary and a Roget's *Thesaurus* and we'd *sweat*. And that's the first time I ever knew that you had to work that hard."

Americana opened at the Shubert Theatre on October 5, 1932, and ran for seventy-seven performances. The big hit from the show was Harburg and Jay Gorney's "Brother, Can You Spare a Dime?" which soon became an anthem of the depression, but Mercer also contributed a lyric, written with Everett Miller and Henry Souvaine, that took a lighthearted look at the hard times. The sight of men selling apples on street corners deeply affected Mercer as he struggled to avoid hitting that low, but he turned the image into a lover's plea that went all the way back to the Garden of Eden:

> Would'ja for a big red apple,
> Would'ja for my peace of mind,
> Could'ja for a big red apple
> Give me what I'm trying to find.

The "would'ja"s and "could'ja" of the chorus contrast with the elegant diction of the verse, which sounds more like Cole Porter: "You spurn the vermin who offer ermine and just a bit of sin." Mercer was developing a wide-ranging vernacular idiom that would characterize his best lyrics from this point on:

> Cakes and sweets and sugar beets,
> May be what a girl deserves,
> Choc'late drops and lollipops are sweet on the taste
> But "H" on the curves.

"I was trying to be as witty as Larry Hart, as sophisticated as Cole Porter, as simple as Irving Berlin, as poetic as Oscar Hammerstein," he said, "remarkable that Johnny Mercer's style evolved at all from so many outside influences, even though they were the best in the world." He was finding his own distinctive lyrical voice, and it could be heard in his songs for *Americana*, two of which were singled out for praise by Brooks Atkinson in his review in the *New York Times:* "Whistling for a Kiss," which Mercer and Harburg wrote with composer Richard Meyers, and "Satan's Li'l Lamb," which brought Mercer together for the first time with the composer who would elicit his greatest lyrics, Harold Arlen.

But that first big hit song eluded him until Eddie Wood, who worked in the stockroom at Miller Music, told Mercer he thought he could set up a meeting with another songwriter who had come to Tin Pan Alley from the hinterlands—the Indiana-born Hoagland Howard "Hoagy" Carmichael. Mercer jumped at the chance, for he was a tremendous admirer of Carmichael's current hits, "Washboard Blues" and "Riverboat Shuffle." While Mercer loved these bluesy and folksy hits, Carmichael was also enjoying the fruits of success with "Star Dust." Carmichael had written "Star Dust" as a jazzy instrumental, but when a lushly poetic lyric was added by Mitchell Parish, "Star Dust" was on its way to becoming one of the greatest standards of all time.

One obstacle to their collaboration, however, was that Carmichael was under contract to Southern Music. In a gesture of extraordinary generosity, mixed with some paternal affection, Charlie Miller freed Mercer from his contractual obligation to Miller Music so that he could write with Carmichael. When they met, Carmichael found Mercer "a young, bouncy butterball of a man from Georgia. He hadn't had a song hit, but I could tell that he could write." Mercer found Carmichael "an understanding, sympathetic friend and teacher" who "broadened my ability with his knowledge and experience." Carmichael also intimidated Mercer. "He is such a gifted lyric writer on his own," he said, "that I felt intimidated by him much of the time and tightened up too much to do my best work." Their first effort was "After Twelve O'Clock," for which Mercer, probably because of his contractual obligations to Miller Music, used a pseudonym, "Joe Moore," on the printed sheet music.

For their next song, Carmichael recalled, "I gave Johnny a melody called 'Thanksgivin'' and said, 'It goes along for a while, but then it stops.'" In about twenty minutes, however, Carmichael worked out the musical blockage and turned the melody over to Mercer. It was then that he learned of Mercer's dilatory ways. Mercer recalled that Carmichael "suffered through long months of waiting till I came up with the lyrics of 'Thanksgivin'.'" After he finally completed that lyric, Mercer had a suggestion for another three-syllable song title suggested by a musical phrase in one of Carmichael's other songs: "You're Mama's little lazybones." Carmichael liked the title, and together they worked out the first two sections of the chorus, but then they ran into difficulties. "We had the first sixteen bars the first afternoon we worked on it":

> Lazybones, Sleepin' in the sun,
> How you 'spec' to get your day's work done?
> Never get your day's work done,
> Sleepin' in the noonday sun.

> Lazybones, sleepin' in the shade,
> How you 'spec' to get your corn meal made?
> Never get your corn meal made
> Sleepin' in the evenin' shade.

"Then we got . . . oh, it must have been a month later that we got the middle part," by which Mercer meant the eight-bar bridge in an AABA song:

> When 'taters need sprayin',
> I bet you keep prayin' the bugs fall off the vine.
> And when you go fishin' I bet you keep wishin'
> The fish won't grab at your line.

"And then it must have been three months later that I got an ending which I thought was all right and we had it penciled in. And then Hoagy came up with the surprise line—you know, 'You never heared a word I say.'"

> Lazybones, loafin' thru the day,
> How you 'spec' to make a dime that way?
> Never make a dime that way (well looky here)
> He never heared a word I say!

"Well, of course I got the credit for it because my name was on the lyric. But then after that we had the verse":

> Long as there is chicken gravy on your rice,
> Ev'rything is nice.
> Long as there's a watermelon on the vine,
> Ev'rything is fine.
> You got no time to work, you got no time to play,
> Busy doin' nothin' all the live-long day.
> You won't ever change no matter what I say,
> You're just made that way.

"It took about a year," Mercer gasped, astonished at the amount of plebian hard work that went into the crafting of a successful song, "took forever . . . oh God, it took a long time."

Like Yip Harburg, Carmichael was a diligent craftsman, and he passed on his work ethic to Mercer, who could be something of a genteel "lazybones" himself. In advising aspiring lyricists, Mercer would tell them to write about the people and places they knew, citing "Lazybones" as his example: "'Lazybones' is about myself." But Carmichael had kept him on task. "Have you ever had a tough teacher whom you appreciated later?" Mercer asked. "That's how it was to write with Hoagy."

The hard work paid off. Once it was published by Southern Music, Carmichael took "Lazybones" to Mildred Bailey, who had made a hit of his "Rockin' Chair" in 1930. "The Rockin' Chair Lady" introduced "Lazybones" on a nationwide broadcast and it was a hit within a week. Her Brunswick recording topped the charts, and other records followed by Glen Gray and his Casa Loma Orchestra, Irving Aaronson and the Commanders, and even Carmichael himself on the Victor label. By the end of the decade, Louis Armstrong had a hit on Decca with "Lazybones." Mercer suddenly enjoyed the giddiness of a smashing success. He was made a member of the American Society of Composers, Authors and Publishers (ASCAP), and he and Carmichael each got a check from the performance-licensing association for $1,250, checks so large the bank would not cash them for the lean and hungry-looking songwriters, so Mildred Bailey had them cashed at her bank.

Something about the languid melody and colloquial lyric captured the imagination of a nation that was battling the depression. The song conjured up the image of a man blissfully impervious to the frenzied need to work and earn that almighty dime. A Savannah newspaper noted that "Georgians may be surprised to hear 'Lazy Bones, sittin' in the sun' was not a Negro yard man to Westerners or Yankees; they thought he was any shiftless countryman." By writing a regional song in black dialect, Mercer and Carmichael had touched something universal in America. Roosevelt's National Recovery Act had just gone into effect, and while the country rolled up its sleeves to work, it could still indulge a fantasy of idleness. In Savannah, the NRA was celebrated in a festival that featured an arrangement of "Lazybones" that urged everybody to support the new program. While Mercer's hometown could take the Rip Van Winkle sentiments of his lyric to heart, Hitler's Germany banned "Lazybones" as a "Nigger song" that "encourages idleness and does not conform to Nazi ideals."

"Lazybones" was selling fifteen thousand copies of sheet music a day and was being plugged on the radio by Walter Winchell. Everything from sport shoes to patio furniture was advertised as "Lazybones" models, and cartoonists used it to lampoon Washington bureaucrats for "laggardly implementation of various New Deal programs."

The success of "Lazybones" saved Southern Music, which had been on the verge of collapse, and Mercer was always grateful to Charlie Miller for allowing him to work with Carmichael, particularly when he realized how much money Miller had lost by the generous gesture. One day Miller summoned Mercer from his cubicle in the publishing offices. There stood Irving Berlin, who had dropped by to congratulate the young lyricist and encourage him, as he would throughout his career. Also magnanimous was Cole Porter, who invited Mercer to a cocktail party at his suite at the Waldorf Towers; Porter, Mercer recalled, "was kind at first meeting and thoughtful ever after, sending me little encouraging notes and telegrams when he admired something new I had written." "Lazybones" was Mercer's entrée into the fraternity of great songwriters he had admired since childhood. Larry Hart, his "beautiful mind full of lovely rhymes and courageous ideas," drank highballs with Mercer one fall afternoon in Jack Dempsey's restaurant, and Jules Glaezner had the Mercers to one of his regular soirees, where Johnny met Noel Coward. The Carmichaels invited them to a party where George Gershwin played his own songs. These were the heady fruits of hard work at his trade, and Mercer found a charmed circle of extraordinarily talented people who were so devoted to the art of songwriting that they welcomed, rather than savaged, a gifted new arrival.

The most immediate benefit from the success of "Lazybones" was that Mercer heard from Paul Whiteman, long after he had assumed that the "King of Jazz" had forgotten him. Now, a year after the Pontiac contest, Whiteman was in need of a singer. Bing Crosby had left the orchestra to go to Hollywood, where he was rapidly becoming a movie star, a strange turn in the career of a man who had begun as a hip jazz singer. Whiteman wanted Mercer to put together a trio to replace the Rhythm Boys. Mercer, still burning to succeed as a performer, leaped at the opportunity. "In show business you never say 'no' so I scrounged around and found two guys willing to try it with me. All of us were young with nothing to lose and everything to gain." One performer, Jack Thompson, was an excellent pianist, and the other, Jerry Arlen, was, like his brother Harold, an excellent jazz singer. But, Mercer recalled, "We were all baritones and our harmony left a lot to be desired. Before one week was up, we had our two weeks' notice."

But the night Whiteman fired the trio Mercer talked with Dick McDonough, Whiteman's guitarist, and McDonough went to Whiteman with an idea. McDonough remembered that Whiteman's trombonist, Jack Teagarden, used to sing "black" duets in another band, and he suggested that Whiteman team the tall Texan Teagarden with the pixyish Mercer as a kind of musical Amos 'n' Andy act. "Amos and Andy, without knowing I was even alive, did me a disservice," Mercer said. "When Jack and I began to sing with the Whiteman band, Paul insisted that we be a sort of musical Amos and Andy singing duo, and that I be the comic or 'high' voice. This affected me and my reception for years, spilling over into other performances and it wasn't until I was near middle age that I found my true voice, with the accent gone and somewhere near the right key." But Whiteman shrewdly knew when he had a successful act, and Johnny Mercer became a popular radio figure. "He was cute," a woman who had been a teenager at the time recalled. "I had a big crush on him, we all did. . . . Oh, my gosh, we were nuts about that guy, he was so . . . we hadn't even seen him, but we knew he was cute, just from listening to him . . . and then he did all those wonderful duets with Jack Teagarden where he was the little colored boy."

Hoagy Carmichael regretted losing Mercer to Paul Whiteman, where the young lyricist would write songs with various musicians in the orchestra. "It was a disappointment to me because with the proper guidance and diligent work, Johnny and I could have flooded the market with hit songs. We were atune and I knew he 'knew' and he knew I 'knew.' But the chips didn't fall right. Probably my fault because I didn't handle them gently." Carmichael later admitted that, because of his success with "Star Dust," he treated Mercer as "my helper," thinking "that I was more informed and more worldly-wise than Johnny, being older. I don't think he liked or took it in the right spirit."

Whiteman paid Mercer seventy-five dollars a week, enough for him and Ginger to move into an apartment in Manhattan. "Ginger and I moved into New York City and had a decent apartment of our own for the first time—a chance to entertain friends and make lots of new ones going to wherever the music was being played after hours." Mercer's days were spent working in the cubicles of Miller Music; then, "after working all days in these hot little rooms, I'd probably have a drink with a friend or two, go home to the little apartment I shared with Ginger, where I'd be treated to her thoughtful dinners, and then, after working with the band until 9, we'd drop in on some place where the music was good."

At the time Whiteman was broadcasting *The Kraft Music Hall* from the Bowman Room of the Hotel Biltmore in New York. "Most saloons in those days were in the hands of the gangsters," Mercer recalled. "Over at a side table might be Big Frenchy or Chink Sherman or maybe even Owney Madden, all reputed to be wheels in the underworld, waiting to take some of the little dancers over to a Jersey hangout for the weekend." Despite his own outrageous behavior when he drank, Mercer was a conservative, even puritanical, moralist who was appalled at the decline in American mores during his lifetime. "It would hurt me 'to my soul' to see those youngsters come in Mondays hung over and still half drunk, as they seemed little more than babies to me." And it was still only the *1930s*.

Mercer described himself as a "utility fielder" in Whiteman's band, singing, writing songs, and also writing comic skits for what Whiteman called "clambakes," where guest stars such as Al Jolson would do satires and paro-

dies. "Anything for a laugh, no matter how faint!" Mercer recalled. Whiteman would introduce him on the air as "the Personality Kid" or, when Mercer had written a new song, "the well-known composer Johnny Mercer." In
1934, with Bernie Hanighen, Mercer wrote another black dialect number,
"Fare-Thee-Well to Harlem," which he sang, Amos 'n' Andy fashion, with
Teagarden:

> Things is tight in Harlem,
> I know how to fix it.
> Step aside, I'm gonna Mason Dix it. . . .
> All this sin is "frighteous."
> Goin' back where everybody's righteous.
> Fare-thee-well to Harlem!

With Hanighen, Mercer felt a kinship that might have established the pair as
a collaborative team, "one that could have ridden the crest of the 'new' music.
If anybody felt it or understood it, it was we two. I'm sorry we didn't get to
continue it in movies and shows."

But just as he was riding on the crest of success with Paul Whiteman, a
new opportunity surfaced, and Mercer made a daring move. At RKO, a
young assistant director, Sammy White, listened to Mercer on the radio and
suggested to the studio that he could be a triple threat in movies as a songwriter, singer, and actor. When the studio made him an offer, Mercer couldn't
refuse. He had, after all, gone to New York to become an actor, not a songwriter or a singer. Having seen the success Bing Crosby was enjoying in Hollywood, Mercer thought he, too, might become a movie star, fulfilling that
extrovert's need in him beyond even his wildest boyhood dreams. The offer
came while he was on the road in Pittsburgh with Whiteman's band, recovering from a severe attack of jaundice. Ironically, what had sparked White's
interest in Mercer was his singing act with Teagarden, for he was a big fan of
Amos and Andy.

Before Mercer could accept RKO's offer, the studio had to work out an
arrangement with Whiteman, since Mercer was under contract with the
orchestra leader. He rejoined the band in Atlanta though he was "too weak—
and too thin!—to do any singing in front of the public." After extensive
negotiations, RKO agreed to pay Whiteman a minimum of five hundred dollars a week—the same amount it paid Mercer himself—for the use of the
songwriter's exclusive services. Once the arrangements were completed,
Johnny Mercer left behind all the success he had worked so hard to achieve in
New York to try for another chance as an actor in Hollywood. "Unlike 'show
biz' kids like Mickey Rooney and Mel Tormé," he later reflected, "I didn't
really have the background to stand in the company of the illustrious musicians and composers I was lucky enough to collaborate with." What he did

have was enormous self-confidence. A relative recalled hearing a story about Johnny sitting in a restaurant with friends in the 1930s when Mel Allen, broadcaster for the Yankees, walked in. Someone observed that Allen was being paid seventy-five thousand dollars a year. "Pretty soon," Mercer said, without boasting, just determinedly, "I'll be making lots more than that."

With the prospect of film stardom in his eyes, Mercer bade farewell to Paul Whiteman's orchestra and the friends he'd made there in Benny Goodman, Jimmy and Tommy Dorsey, Artie Shaw, Glenn Miller, and other side men who would soon go on to establish their own orchestras in the big band era. It was also good-bye to a lifestyle he loved: "Youth and excitement and the long shadows falling as I'd hurry home from Broadway, stopping to have a drink with some cats on my way to dinner before changing into my band costume for the night shift. Always writing, writing, writing."

Like Bing Crosby, he was leaving this scintillating New York nightlife to "go Hollywood."

Five

Hooray for Hollywood: 1935–1937

I kept my eyes and ears open, and my mouth shut, for Ginger and I were head-ing for a chance of a lifetime, and I wanted to be as big as my modest talent might allow.

On April 3, 1935, Johnny and Ginger Mercer boarded the Santa Fe Chief for California. It was a propitious time for a young man who wanted to attain stardom by writing songs and performing them in films, because the Hollywood musical was enjoying a renaissance. Musical films had been born in 1927, with the advent of sound, in *The Jazz Singer*, which, except for its song sequences, was a silent movie. The Warner brothers had not set out to make "talkies"; as Harry said to Sam, Art, and Jack, "Who the hell wants to hear actors talk?" At the time, "movies" meant *silent* movies, and the Warner brothers were not visionaries who could imagine breaking that convention by making films where dialogue was spoken from the screen. Even if they could conceive of such a medium, it probably immediately occurred to them that a film with dialogue spoken in English would severely cut into profits from overseas distribution. Silent movies, after all, spoke a universal language.

The Warner brothers wanted only to use the new technology of synchro-nized sound to include an orchestral sound track with a silent movie. That meant that Warner Bros. (they always insisted on the abbreviated title for the studio) could charge more for a film because theater owners would not have to hire a pianist to accompany the movie (or, in large cities, a full orchestra). But once Al Jolson launched into an impromptu monologue in the course of singing "Blue Skies," the engaging nature of spoken and sung words on the screen was apparent to everyone—even the Warner brothers. After Jolson finished the song, *The Jazz Singer* reverted to a silent film, but the talkies had been born.

The early rash of Hollywood musicals that followed *The Jazz Singer* also copied its basic pattern. Whereas silent films had transported viewers to another world, the addition of sound made movies far more realistic, and producers feared that audiences would find it artificial if actors suddenly moved from dialogue into song, then back again to dialogue (without even the applause that cushions such transitions in the musical theater). So in the early years of musical films, actors had to have an *excuse* to sing, and the most realistic excuse was that they were playing the role of singers (as Jolson had in *The Jazz Singer*). They sang because they were rehearsing or performing a song, usually for a Broadway show, creating the odd convention that most Hollywood musicals were set in New York. Most early musical films were "backstagers" that traced the behind-the-curtains story of singers and dancers putting on a show, and the songs in them were done as performance numbers before an on-screen audience that was frequently shown on camera to allevi-ate the tedium of filming a stage performance.

This formula soon grew tiresome, and audiences also found the technical limitations of sound films annoying. As *Singin' in the Rain* hilariously revealed about the early days of the talkies, the movie camera had to be enclosed in a crate to muffle its whirr, and actors had to huddle near stationary microphones that were concealed in props such as lamps or flowerpots. With enclosed cam-eras, immobile microphones, and actors standing still to make sure their voices recorded evenly, the "movies" had ceased to *move*. By 1930, *Variety* reported, customers were going to movie box offices, asking, "Is this film a musical?" and walking away if it was. Musical film production was drastically cut back; from fifty-four musical films in 1929, there were only ten produced in 1932.

But by 1933, the movie musical was making a comeback. A silent camera that moved with performers and boom microphones that followed them above the picture frame gave songs a new vitality. At Warner Bros., *42nd Street* enlivened the conventions of the backstager musical with gritty narra-tives set in New York in the depression, jazzy songs by Al Dubin and Harry Warren, and spectacular production numbers staged by Busby Berkeley where the camera moved with dazzling grace. At Paramount, European actors such as Maurice Chevalier and directors such as Ernst Lubitsch and Rouben Mamoulian incorporated operetta into the movie musical and estab-lished the convention that a song need not be done as a performance but could be expressive of what a character was feeling at a particular dramatic moment.

But it was at RKO, Radio-Keith-Orpheum, where the movie musical found its greatest reincarnation. Driven into bankruptcy, RKO had to take chances. To put itself back in the black, the studio banked on what some regarded as a fading Broadway musical star. Fred Astaire had, since childhood, been teamed in vaudeville and musical comedy with his sister Adele, but when Adele married a British peer, Fred Astaire was on his own. The legendary verdict of the studio on Astaire's screen test—"Can't sing. Can't act. Can dance a little. Balding"— is countered by an actual memo written by David O. Selznick, who was then in charge of production, which acknowledges Astaire's "enormous ears and bad chin line" but also affirms the man's "undeniable" charm.

RKO paired Astaire with Ginger Rogers, who had played tough-talking chorus girls in the Warner backstagers ("The only time she said 'No' was when she didn't understand the question"). Their chemistry (as Katharine Hepburn supposedly remarked, "He gave her class, she gave him balls") was immediately apparent in *Flying Down to Rio*, even though they had secondary roles in what was still a backstage saga about a nightclub troupe. In their next film, *The Gay Divorcee* (1934), RKO established the convention that Fred Astaire and Ginger Rogers could move from dialogue into song as easily as they did from walking to dancing. While they sometimes played dancers or singers who did songs as stage performances, Astaire and Rogers also sang expressively, and songwriters were told to write songs that grew out of their characters and dramatic situations. Once RKO had established this convention, actors as different as Bob Hope and Jimmy Stewart could spontaneously burst into song, and with that convention established, the movie musical was reborn.

Another technological development that would give lyricists in Hollywood more creative freedom than they had had on the Broadway stage was the playback system, whereby songs were prerecorded in the studio, then lip-synched by performers during the actual filming. By merely mouthing the words to their prerecorded songs, singers such as Astaire and Rogers appeared even more effortlessly nonchalant. The playback system freed songwriters from the need to provide singers with long notes and open vowels so that they could project the words of a song to the back row of the balcony. So imperative was the need for long vowels and long notes in stage musicals that theater lyricist Oscar Hammerstein fretted about ending a lyric with the line "And all the rest is talk," since "talk," with its closing guttural consonant, was not a word that could be sustained by a singer.

But in Hollywood, with microphones and playbacks, lyricists were at last free to use the short vowels and guttural, dental, and plosive consonants that were more natural to a Germanic language such as English. While Irving Berlin had had to craft a theater song such as "Blue Skies" out of long notes and long vowels, in Hollywood he could write such rhythmical, alliterative numbers as "Puttin' on the Ritz," "Cheek to Cheek," and "Top Hat, White Tie and Tails." No lyricist would benefit more from this technological breakthrough than Johnny Mercer, whose lyrical style was the most colloquially conversational of all his contemporaries. As the Santa Fe Chief carried him westward, the Hollywood musical seemed the perfect vehicle for his kind of song.

Yet Mercer's most vivid memory of the train trip indicated how out of place he would feel in Hollywood. The train was full of celebrities, he recalled, and in the dining car he noticed Al Jolson and legendary producer Joseph Schenck, the crassest of Hollywood moguls. Jolson and Schenck insisted that the waiters "bring in a brace of dressed ducks or pheasants so that they could see them before being cooked." The incident hardly seems significant, let alone offensive, but for Savannah-bred Johnny Mercer, "that was typical of what we were to find in Hollywood, and in nouveaux taste," a revealing indication that the patrician sensitivity that had been bred into him by his family, where one never called attention to oneself, had been offended by their "New York Jewish" vulgarity.

If Mercer had hoped to write lyrics for Astaire and Rogers musicals at RKO, he had arrived too late. The two dancers had become such a success that only the most prestigious songwriters—Irving Berlin, the Gershwin brothers, and Jerome Kern—would score their films. The first film Mercer worked on was one of Hollywood's typical college musicals, *Old Man Rhythm*, in which a father enrolls in college as a freshman in order to keep tabs on his son's extracurricular activities. Zion Myers, the producer who had offered Mercer a contract to act, sing, and write songs for the movies, was clearly disappointed when he met "his triple-threat man weighing in at about 130 soaking wet, and with a pallor if not of the prison type, definitely oriental from the jaundice still evident on my face." Johnny, for his part, was equally disappointed when he learned that Myers was the lowest producer on the totem pole at RKO; he did only B pictures, and those on the lowest of budgets. In those boom years, Mercer recalled, most studios turned out about twenty A films, which featured their major stars and directors, but also some sixty B or "program" films, which movie theaters had to show to get access to the studio's A movies.

Still, *Old Man Rhythm* had impressive people in its cast and crew: Hermes Pan, Astaire's choreographer, staged the dance numbers; musical star Charles "Buddy" Rogers had a principal role; Eric Blore and Eric Rhodes played the same kind of stock comic characters they played in the Astaire-Rogers films; and Lucille Ball and Betty Grable had bit parts. Mercer's collaborator, Lewis Gensler, had written the depression-era hit "Love Is Just Around the Corner" (playing off Herbert Hoover's assurance to the nation that "prosperity was just around the corner") with lyricist Leo Robin, who had gone on to write with Ralph Rainger at Paramount. But Mercer's songs with Gensler, from "Comes the Revolution, Baby" to "There's Nothing Like a College Educa-tion," were as undistinguished as most other aspects of the film. Most disap-pointing, however, was Mercer's acting. While he might have had some success on stage, on the screen he creates no illusion of character; he's simply himself—Johnny Mercer—woodenly looking into the camera rather than reacting to other actors.

Although *Old Man Rhythm* caused little excitement around most of the country, in Savannah it drew crowds with a marquee that read "*Old Man Rhythm*—Starring Johnny Mercer." "I have seen *Old Man Rhythm* four times," his father wrote, "three times at night and once in the day." But, he adds, "Your mother and Julie are camping there most of the time. I even tease them about taking their lunch with them." He tells Johnny that he has photographed the marquee with the "Starring Johnny Mercer" billing and that every evening performance he attended was packed, and the audiences applauded when Mercer sang a song from the upper berth of a train car. "That was a personal tribute to you, I think." Taking a fatherly pride, he says the movie was "snappy, spritely, very witty and not an unclean word in it." George Mercer is also proud that "a great many of the negroes here are very anxious to have it played at the colored theater on West Broad Street or the Bijou" and, with his characteristic kindness toward blacks, "I will try to accomplish it for them." Then, the note of real affection for a son who finally seemed to be succeeding in the entertainment business: "As we never see you only once every three years, we concentrated on the three days to hear those dulcet tones of yours and to see that face of yours."

Despite Mercer's poor performance in the film, he was offered acting, singing, and songwriting roles from other producers at RKO. But, once more, his genteel southern upbringing came out. He had found Zion Myers a kind and generous man, one of the finest people he'd met in Hollywood. "The studio gave him only leftovers and suffering multitudinous setbacks in every department he still kept cheerful while he watched his staff putting together one of the most old-fashioned college movies ever made." When Myers asked Johnny to work with him on another picture, Mercer turned down the offers from other producers to stick with the man who had brought him to RKO. "If he wanted me," Mercer said to himself, "I wouldn't rat on him." As a southern belle is told when she is sent off to a dance with her escort, "You dance with who brung ya."

Mercer's second movie, *To Beat the Band*, was even more dismal than *Old Man Rhythm*. The story line followed a young collegian whose aunt's will stipulates that he must marry a widow to claim his inheritance, so he tries to find a suicidal man to marry his current fiancée in the hope that she will soon be a widow. Mercer appeared with a group called the California Collegians, which had included Fred MacMurray until he was "discovered" and went on to starring roles. Although it boasted Eric Blore and Helen Broderick, character players from Astaire-Rogers films, *To Beat the Band* was another flop for Mercer and further evidence that he had no future in acting. Still, some of the songs Mercer wrote with Matty Malneck caught on, such as "Eenny, Meeny, Miney, Mo," which was recorded by Mercer and Ginger Rogers, with the offensive "nigger" bowdlerized into "catch a trouble by the toe."

During their recording session, Fred Astaire came to the studio, introduced himself, and casually mentioned that he had written a song and wondered if Mercer would like to give it a lyric. The melody had a rising-falling pattern that Mercer fitted out by pairing two colloquial expressions into a single romantic phrase: "I'm building up—to an awful letdown." He also worked in a clever allusion to the Crash:

> My one big love affair—
> Is it just a flash?
> Will it all go smash?
> Like the nineteen twenty-nine market crash!

Although Fred Astaire never sang it in a movie, he made a recording of "I'm Building Up to an Awful Let-Down" that was more successful than any of the songs Mercer had written for *Old Man Rhythm* or *To Beat the Band*.

At RKO, Mercer was clearly starstruck, even though it must have been apparent to him that stardom was not in his own future. On the studio lot, he said, "You could see Carole Lombard or Claudette Colbert, while Sylvia Sidney lived right around the corner, and Ann Sheridan, Martha Raye, and dozens of other beautiful girls could be seen having a drink in Lucy's or going in full make-up to the Vendome, or maybe getting up in some little supper club and singing." At the time, Hollywood was not a single town but a set of interlocking villages—Glendale, Inglewood, Cucamonga, Tarzana—and they would drive from one village theater to another to see sneak previews. "And what a thrill when it was a 'biggie' . . . not just one of the B pictures."

But what he missed was New York nightlife. In Hollywood, most movie people had to get up early, but there were a few places, such as Sebastian's Cotton Club and the Coconut Grove, where musicians hung out, and there Mercer could hear the jazz he craved. There was the "very groovy" Billie Rogers, a girl trumpeter, and Lionel Hampton, who played piano with only two fingers and also played the vibraphone. A "colored tap dancer" performed "while holding a table in his teeth." Another club he loved to visit was run by Ted Snyder, who had been Irving Berlin's publisher, then publishing partner, back in the early days of Tin Pan Alley. "All the great old writers would congregate there to see their friend Ted," Mercer recalled. "And I got to meet them all." He loved meeting such songwriters as Percy Wenrich, who had written "Put on Your Old Gray Bonnet," and Jean Schwartz, composer of "Chinatown, My Chinatown." These were turn-of-the-century songwriters whose hits Mercer had imbibed as a child. "Now I was young and truly ingenuous, and I think it surprised these men that a young man they considered little more than a boy knew all their songs, not only the hits but the obscure ones, including the verses and often second choruses. It was a thing of genuine admiration on my part: I had learned them all from phonograph records and singing around the piano, turning the pages and subconsciously memorizing a lot of the words. At any rate, without trying to ingratiate myself, that is exactly what I did, for when some opportunity would arise I probably got the nod over my own contemporaries due to the impression I might have made on those gentlemen."

While Mercer could be charmingly ingratiating, it is from this period that the first stories surface about how vicious he could be when he drank. A friend recalled that when he was invited out by RKO, "some big wig there" promised "you'll be the toast of Hollywood, as soon as you're out here we'll give you a party. And just say who you want, we'll just have anybody, we'll just ask a lot of stars." "Do you think I can meet Helen Hayes?" he asked, and the bigwig assured him, "No problem, she's out there at the studio, we'll have her." But at the party Mercer got drunk and by the time Helen Hayes arrived and was introduced to him, Mercer told the dignified actress to go fuck herself.

If it had been an isolated incident, the encounter could be dismissed as a combination of inebriation and insecurity, but it typified a pattern of drunken insults that would haunt Mercer for the rest of his life. "He was the kind of person who under the influence of alcohol," a friend said, "would get very manic and have big swings—very big swings. And if he got quite drunk, he could be a mean drunk. You never know where that part of a person's character comes from." "It was just a reaction against people," another friend said. "I don't know what the basis of it was. It had something to do with Johnny Mercer himself—not the people he was addressing. It has nothing to do with the person. The person doesn't set it off. It's set off within Johnny himself." The intensity of the memory of Mercer's virulence made the friend speak of his attacks in the present tense. After a moment, he reverted to the past. "John was never, in my opinion, a happy man. John—he just did not accept his success with great joy or comfort."

Mercer didn't even have the blackouts that mercifully make some people forget what they've said while drinking; he remembered everything the next morning. "Afterward," a friend recalled, "it must have just killed him to realize" what he'd said to Helen Hayes. In later years, he would send people he'd offended a dozen roses in apology. "What's so poignant," the friend said, "is, it's another case where he's being pulled in two directions. So contrite the next day that you couldn't stand it. I mean, he would overdo, send you absolutely the biggest plant, that you'd have to rearrange your living room, with a note that was so abject and touching. And yet when he was on this tear he would ruin your party, by just being rude. You wonder, 'What's going on there?' I couldn't believe that one martini would set you off that way. I guess all creative people have these demons roiling and broiling inside them, and parts of them that are at war with each other, and it probably comes out when they've had a taste of drink."

"The times when they were truly happy," a friend recalls Ginger saying, "was when they were first out in Hollywood, the first few years. Yes, that's when they were truly happy." The friends recalled how Ginger painted the white picket fence on their first home in Hollywood, and Johnny gave her a mink coat. In those years, the friends said, Ginger "leveled him, too. He didn't go crazy. . . . His head didn't explode, like Hoagy Carmichael's did."

But then, "She said they—from there on in, it was not . . . he was the young king." The friend explained that in the 1940s and '50s it was customary to separate couples at dinner parties: "One would be put at one table, and another at another table, and nobody ever wanted to be at Ginger's table because she was not a stunning conversationalist, and Johnny was. And so all the fun and the laughter was coming from one table, and then there was this formal table over here, and that was a very uncomfortable thing for her, because she knew people wanted to be at Johnny's table, and she couldn't hold up that end of the evening socially, and that must have been a very rough thing for her to have to go through."

"He was the star, and she wasn't, and she would have to sit in the background while he did things. . . . She knew a lot of wonderful things, but she had trouble getting them out sometimes, and she was like a little mouse. She was dear and charming, but he had the great personality, so it took a long time to get to know her. . . . She was not a woman's woman. She didn't sit around and play cards. She'd shop, she'd do this, she'd do that, and she found her world, I guess, through the kids and everything, but she was not a woman to go on her own and do many different things. She'd go to the market, she'd be ready to go with him if he needed it, and always, always, when he wrote, the song, even before the composer, she heard it first. He wanted what she knew and what she knew about the songs, and she knew about him, to tell him that it was okay."

Johnny and Ginger fell into a hard-drinking crowd that centered on the Crosbys. Because Ginger had dated Bing before she met Johnny, they became friends with him and his wife, Dixie, who as a southerner enjoyed being with Johnny. "It was my good fortune to know him when he was married to Dixie and his boys were small," Mercer wrote. "They often rode on my back and I enjoyed the happy days around the track and poolside with this most attractive couple. She was very kind to me, as I was in such awe of him and she knew it." What Mercer loved most about Crosby, even more than his singing, was his hipster talk—"his slang, his ad libs." Mercer's awe at Crosby's stardom must have deepened now that he saw how elusive such success was in Hollywood.

After *Old Man Rhythm* and *To Beat the Band*, RKO did not renew Mercer's contract. His dream of becoming a movie star like Bing Crosby had been dashed, and his gamble of leaving a good job with Paul Whiteman had not paid off. Now he was just another flash in the pan in Hollywood. It was the middle of the depression, and Mercer was out of work, this time in Hollywood, which was far less familiar to him than New York.

It was time to return to his roots. He and Ginger drove across the country to Savannah, a drive they would never undertake again. It took six days and—to Mercer's astonishment—*three* just to cross Texas. As they drove on and on, he was amused by the sight of cowboys, with spurs and ten-gallon hats, driving cars and trucks instead of riding horses. With his recent disappointments in Hollywood, he realized that it was the movies that nourished such absurdity.

It was the era of the singing cowboy, and here was life imitating art. In fifteen minutes, writing on the back of an envelope, he worked the image into a song whose satiric underside vented some of Mercer's own bitter frustration with Hollywood:

I'm an old cowhand from the Rio Grande,
But my legs ain't bowed and my cheeks ain't tanned.
I'm a cowboy who never saw a cow,
Never roped a steer 'cause I don't know how,
And I sho' ain't fixin' to start in now, Yippy I O Ki Ay . . .
I'm a ridin' fool who is up to date,
I know ev'ry trail in the Lone Star State,
'Cause I ride the range in a Ford V-Eight. Yippy I O Ki Ay.

Only Mercer's perfect ear for regional idioms would have come up with a line like "I sho' ain't fixin' to start in now." Cole Porter, at about this same time, would write his own cowboy song, "Don't Fence Me In," but his lyric would employ such erudite phrases as "where the West commences."

In the fifteen minutes it took Mercer to write the lyric to "I'm an Old Cowhand," he also wrote a rollicking melody, which sharpened the satire by suggesting the clip-clop of horse hooves. Many people were amazed that someone like Johnny Mercer, who could neither play the piano nor read music, could write a melody for "I'm an Old Cowhand," as well as for "Dream," "Something's Gotta Give," and other successful songs. His former son-in-law Bob Corwin, a jazz pianist who collaborated with Mercer in later years, said there was nothing surprising about Mercer's feat—or that of Irving Berlin, who could only play the piano in one key and did not learn to read music until late in his career. "The one thing people don't understand is songwriters simply are not musicians," he said. "A songwriter has it in their head, but they can't translate it into an instrument." Corwin would sometimes "take down" a melody for Mercer, playing it at the piano and then writing it down in musical notation. Mercer had his idiosyncratic method of musical notation, which he might have developed when he composed "I'm an Old Cowhand," where he would write down musical letters—A, B, C, D, E, F, G; then, if an interval carried the melody into another octave, he put an arrow beside the letter, pointing up if it was in a higher octave, down if in a lower.

"He had every single thing in his head. He knew every note, he knew what the chord sounded like. He couldn't play the chord, but he knew what it sounded like, and he knew the rhythm, and he could sing the melody. . . . You'd play this chord, and he'd go, 'That's not it,' then you'd play another chord and he'd go, 'That's not it,' and then you'd play another chord, and he'd go, 'That's close,' and pretty soon you'd play a chord, and he'd go, 'That's it.' And then you'd tediously—but gloriously—do this until you got a whole song down on paper." While Mercer returned to composing throughout his career, he became leery when rumors spread that it was really his "musical secretaries" who had written the melodies: the patrician Mercer would rather forgo creating music than be the subject of such unseemly gossip.

With "I'm an Old Cowhand" under his belt, Johnny Mercer could feel more secure during his visit to Savannah, where he served as best man at the wedding of Walter Rivers. Walter's marriage to a local southern belle must only have made more pointed the fact that Johnny had married a Jewish girl from Brooklyn—who had been a Broadway chorus girl to boot. His brothers had also married from within their circle. "George chose Bessie Wheelus, who was from an aristocratic Southern family," a niece recalled. "Walter and Hugh each married sisters, Southern sisters. Johnny married a show girl." Outward relations, however, were cordial. "My grandmother, when she met her, my Aunt Ginger said something about she didn't know how to cook, and my grandmother said, 'Well, don't learn.' "

Ginger might have been easier to accept because she did not conform to Jewish stereotypes. "She didn't consider herself Jewish," a Jewish friend explained. "Never." "She always said her mother was an Austrian Christian until I met her," said the friend, laughing. "An old-fashioned Jewish accent!" The friend was one of several who indicated Mercer had an anti-Semitic streak. "I think he used to dig at her every so often. I always thought that was one of the reasons he married her—was to upset his family." Despite Mercer's devotion to his family, marrying a Jewish chorus girl from Brooklyn might have been a rebellion against the expectations of the genteel but demanding Mercers. So, too, his crass behavior when drinking might also have been an escape from the high standards of propriety the family had impressed upon him.

Adhering to those standards, the Mercers never let it be known that they were disappointed in his marriage to Ginger. "I never heard my grandmother ever say anything mean about Ginger. Ever. Never. She wouldn't—my grandmother wouldn't. My grandmother was very generous to a fault. And she expected Johnny to be the same way." Such high expectations of generosity and gracefulness were hard enough to maintain in Savannah, but for Johnny Mercer to hold himself to such standards in Hollywood would have been quixotic. "I never heard anything negative about her from my grandmother, but I do know that there was some sense that Ginger was not comfortable here in Savannah. There may have been some acceptance problems from some other family members or some friends. I'm not sure exactly. There is lore—I remember this—something about a thank-you note not being written in a timely fashion," she said. "I know that if I didn't write my thank-you note to her within a week, I heard about it." How remote a world of writing timely thank-you notes must have been to Ginger's mother as she trekked from Russia across Europe, raised three daughters after her husband's suicide, and started a children's clothing business. How remote, in turn, her values would have been to a genteel Savannah family who had lost its fortune and for whom every public gesture, down to the writing of a thank-you note, was an effort to maintain their position of respectability in the most caste-conscious city in the South.

At the wedding, James McIntire, who gave away his sister to Walter Rivers, had a positive impression of Ginger. "She was so obviously in love with him and he with her, nobody thought there was anything funny about it," he recalled. "She was an attractive person, and she didn't mind being second fiddle to him either. She'd sit back and not do anything unless somebody would—you know, address a remark to her, and she'd answer. But he could grandstand all he wanted to. It didn't bother her. . . . You were never even aware of her doing that—only when you thought back on the day, you'd realize that he'd sort of monopolized everything. I don't mean in a rude way, but he was just such an attractive person that everybody wanted to enjoy his company." Ginger's willingness to let Johnny take center stage in Savannah suggests that she did the same in New York and Hollywood, content in these early years of marriage to move in show business circles as "Mrs. Johnny Mercer."

James McIntire's brother Pope had a more guarded impression of Mrs. Johnny Mercer: "I think that some people didn't like Ginger too much. I never knew why. She was a very, very sweet person. She did not have a very outgoing personality. I don't think she sought people out much, and they may have thought she was aloof or stand-offish, but I think she was more just sort of shy and an inward person. Johnny was the personality in the pair. . . . she had been a chorus girl. I think maybe some of the snobbish folks thought that Johnny had married beneath himself or something like that." He added that such problems were endemic to Savannah. "Savannah is a hard town, or it used to be, to break into. I don't think it's—socially—I don't think it's quite that way any more, but in that period of time, anybody that had a party of any size invited virtually everybody that you knew in town to the party. Society was a fairly small group—debutante parties and weddings and big Christmas parties and that sort of thing. If you were not born in Savannah, you were not considered to be a Savannahian even though you might have lived there for thirty years."

The barest wisp of tension was sounded in a friend's recollection that it was hard for Johnny's mother to accept Ginger. "She would say, 'She can't even join the Oglethorpe,'" indicating Savannah's most exclusive private club, which did not accept Jews. If people in Savannah may have thought she was snobbish, another friend recalled, "It was because she didn't feel at home with the southern people there, because his mother didn't like her because she was Jewish, and neither did they. There was a tremendous thing in Savannah about the Jewish people. . . . So that would make him feel he can't go home as much, because he didn't want to leave Ginger. But he wanted to go home. So then he'd have to go home alone and make up excuses of why she wouldn't come. She didn't like it because they didn't like her. So that was one thing he probably had to consider and think about all his life, ever since he met her." A saving grace was that in a few years one of Ginger's sisters moved to Jacksonville, Florida, so throughout the marriage Ginger could spend a few days in Savannah for form's sake, then travel on to be with her own family.

When they returned to Hollywood, Mercer had "I'm an Old Cowhand," but, as he knew from his days on Tin Pan Alley, a good song didn't make it on its own; it needed a "plug" from a big star. The best plug he could have hoped for came from Bing Crosby, who liked the song and got it into his next movie, *Rhythm on the Range*, where it became a hit in the fall of 1936. "I really think he saved my Hollywood career," Mercer said. "Because I began to get more offers after that." While Mercer was obviously grateful for Crosby's help at this critical time, it might also have gnawed at those inner demons he carried that he was beholden to a man whose success he had recently hoped to emulate and perhaps even surpass.

Another hit in the same year required no help from Crosby. "Goody Goody" was a "trunk" song left over from Mercer's days with Paul Whiteman's orchestra. Supposedly inspired by a Chinese restaurant menu in New York, Mercer had jotted the idea down, put it in a bureau drawer, then found it again in California when he was desperately in need of a hit. The sprightly melody was by Matty Malneck, who had worked with Whiteman, and Mercer set it with a paean to romantic revenge by a scorned lover who exults when another woman takes the heart of her former mate and breaks it into pieces. Mercer and Malneck did their own plugging by getting "Goody Goody" to Benny Goodman, who assigned it to his premier "canary," Helen Ward, despite her pleading not to have to sing "that damn song." It made *Your Hit Parade* and held the number one position for four weeks in March 1936. Mercer always considered "Goody Goody" one of his best lyrics. "It's a phrase that everybody said, but I just, I don't know why I got that particular approach to it." The success of "I'm an Old Cowhand," Mercer said, "saved me from odious failure and complete oblivion," and the success of "Goody Goody" kept his reputation from "evaporating." Then one song after another led to opportunities, "all of which I was eager to chase to the rainbow's end."

One opportunity he coveted was to write lyrics with composer Ray Henderson for the Shirley Temple movie *Curly Top*. Henderson had been part of the great songwriting trio of DeSylva, Brown, and Henderson, but after the team moved to Hollywood, Buddy DeSylva turned to producing films. Lew Brown and Ray Henderson continued to write songs, including the flippant depression-era rumination "Life Is Just a Bowl of Cherries," but soon they too parted ways, and Ray Henderson was looking for a lyricist. Mercer would have been an excellent collaborator for the laid-back composer, but in this world of shifting collaborations, the job went to Ted Koehler. Koehler had originally teamed with Harold Arlen, and in the early 1930s they wrote such great songs for Cotton Club revues as "Stormy Weather." But when Arlen joined Ira Gershwin and Yip Harburg for a 1934 Broadway revue, *Life Begins at 8:40*, Koehler sought out other collaborators. These musical marriages and divorces were usually amicable, and despite the fact that their collaboration was over, Koehler and Arlen took the train to Hollywood together. For *Curly Top*, Koehler and Henderson, with colyricist Irving Caesar, wrote the classic Shirley Temple song "Animal Crackers in My Soup."

At the center of this game of musical chairs, Mercer recalled, was music publisher Jack Robbins. "He was a romantic about the music business and nothing pleased him more than to pub crawl late at night and find some undiscovered tune or singer. He would then appoint himself an instrument of fate to see that the tune got a lyric or the singer got a movie contract. . . ." Robbins knew that when Ted Koehler went to work with Ray Henderson, Koehler's previous partner, Rube Bloom, would be in need of a lyricist, and "in the best Sol Hurok manner, Jack teamed us up." Robbins then persuaded producer Lew Leslie to let Mercer and Bloom write the songs for his next *Blackbirds* revue.

Robbins clearly was type-casting Mercer in the role of blackface singer and songwriter when he united him with Leslie. Since the 1920s Lew Leslie had been producing *Blackbirds* revues, where he used white songwriters and black performers to attract audiences to Harlem spots such as the Cotton Club. Lyricist Dorothy Fields and composer Jimmy McHugh had written such hits as "I Can't Give You Anything but Love" and "On the Sunny Side of the Street" for Leslie's revues, so the prospect of writing songs for a new *Blackbirds*, which would open in London, was appealing to Mercer, who had never been abroad. Leslie, he recalled, was "a goodhearted man . . . a 'dese, dem and dose' guy, affected a beret and French phrases which he must have made up as I've never found anyone who could translate the words he used to lay on us!"

The trip started out wonderfully with a cruise across the Atlantic, and cruising would become Mercer's favorite form of travel. "We would stroll the decks preparatory to going in to the salon for caviar and grouse or woodcock under glass." But Mercer should have been suspicious when they were booked as second-class passengers. Leslie had only gotten a small amount of money to produce the show from two gamblers in New York, so he was still trying to raise the rest of the needed funds. Mercer and Bloom worked on the score during the crossing, then locked themselves into a room at the Savoy Hotel in London. While Ginger got to see the Tower of London, Westminster Abbey, and other sights, Mercer ate room-service food and stared at the four walls of the hotel room trying to come up with lyrics. He enjoyed collaborating with Bloom, however, a man who stuttered when he spoke but not when he sang. For Mercer it was a pleasure to take Bloom's melody, put words to it, then hand it back to the composer to sing. "Not only would his eyes light up but he would completely forget the impediment while he sang that song over and over like a caress." But Bloom was also a well-educated man who insisted that his lyricists be correct in spelling, grammar, and syntax. It could have been a nuisance, but Mercer made Bloom's punctiliousness into a game and tried to keep from getting caught in a grammatical error. (Johnny Burke, he later noted, "was even worse about this—a real pain in the ass. Poetry, okay. Pedantics, no.")

The fifty-member cast for *Blackbirds* included the Nicholas brothers, the spectacular dancing duo, and Tim Moore, who would later portray "Kingfish" on television's *Amos 'n' Andy* (on radio, Amos 'n' Andy were white men). They rehearsed their songs as soon as they came off the press from Mercer and Bloom. But Mercer soon realized that Leslie did not have the money to pay them. Not only had his dreams of Hollywood stardom come to nothing; he was now writing songs for an all-black revue in England and not getting paid. But the fact that he was interceding not only for himself but for the black cast might have bolstered Mercer's temerity. Putting aside all of his genteel upbringing, which would have deemed complaining, particularly about money, unseemly, he told the producer that until he and the cast received some money, there would be no lyrics. To prove his point, he stopped working and began taking in London sights and restaurants. He was surprised to find how popular his songs were in England and was invited to sing "I'm an Old Cowhand" on the BBC.

Leslie and his backers quickly came through with more funds, and Mercer and Bloom went back to work and finished the score. Although Mercer had seen that the cast got paid, most of them lost their money during the Manchester tryout when, on June 20, 1936, Joe Louis lost the heavyweight boxing title to Germany's Max Schmeling. Many cast members had bet heavily on Louis and were wiped out by their gambling losses. "They pitched in with a will, however," Mercer recalled. "And no company ever gave a more energetic, enthusiastic opening night." The show ran for six months in London, largely on the strength of the dancing of the Nicholas brothers, and had a New York run that included Lena Horne in her first Broadway stage production.

With his work on the show complete after the London opening, Mercer went to see a relative, his cousin Walter Mercer, in Scotland. "There for two or three weeks I sopped up my Scotch and Scottish forebears, dug the moors and the castles, the heather and the gorse." There he might have learned that his ancestry was even more closely entwined around his life. Before coming to America to fight in the Revolutionary War, Hugh Mercer had been a young surgeon attached to the Jacobite army that was trying to restore the Stuarts to the English throne. Rallying around "Bonnie Prince Charlie," the Scottish army was brutally crushed by the English at the Battle of Culloden in 1746, and Hugh Mercer had to flee to the colonies.

Before he died at the Battle of Princeton, Hugh Mercer had fathered five children, the oldest of whom, Ann Gordon Mercer, married Robert Patton, another refugee from the Scottish wars. One of their grandsons, George Smith Patton, was a colonel in the Confederate army who was killed in the Civil War. His widow fled Yankee troops with her two sons and made her way to Woodberry Forest, then a plantation in Virginia. The farmhouse was deserted except for the bodies of two Yankee soldiers, "one in the front hall, the other wedged in a second-floor window." Fearing that if the bodies were found, she and her sons would be accused of murdering Union soldiers, Sue Patton ordered the boys to drag the bodies outside and bury them. To make sure no one could identify them as Union soldiers, she had nine-year-old George strip them of their uniforms and burn the clothing while his brother Peter dug the graves. The family moved on to California after a year, and Woodberry Forest became the school that Johnny Mercer and his brothers later attended and where the legend grew that there were two Union soldiers buried on the grounds. George Patton, in turn, had a son, named, in honor of his slain grandfather, George S. Patton III, who would become the legendary tank commander of World War II.

While Mercer might not have known much of his family history, being in his relative's home in Scotland must have brought the weight of his prestigious heritage upon him, and perhaps he wondered how his forebears, who had been generals, doctors, and lawyers, would regard an offspring who was a songwriter, and a fledgling songwriter at that.

On the day they were to board the *Queen Mary*, a wire came saying that Warner Bros. wanted to put Mercer under contract to write songs. In a career of roller-coaster ups and downs, here was a rare second chance to make it in Hollywood. In accepting the Warner offer, Mercer offended the irascible Jack Robbins, who had felt that the songwriter was in his fold. Robbins issued the classic Hollywood threat, warning Mercer that he'd "never work in this town again." The film community was so close-knit that it could rely on oral promises rather than written contracts, so Robbins was not making an empty threat. He never made good on it, however, perhaps out of his recognition of Mercer's genius. When his daughter-in-law was distraught because her little boy had locked himself in his room and, given the tense times, she feared he'd been kidnapped like the Lindbergh baby, Jack Robbins offered these consoling words: "Listen, Rose, don't worry about it. Today I lost Mercer to Warner Brothers. More children you can have. Losing Mercer, you can't have."

While Robbins recognized Mercer's genius, Mercer himself was less sure of himself. His experiences in Hollywood had shaken his patrician self-confidence. "I remember," a friend said of these days, "Johnny was saying that he couldn't make a living writing songs." On the crossing, there was a dance aboard ship, and a man invited Ginger to dance. As they turned about the deck, he asked what her husband did. "Oh, he writes songs," Ginger said. "I mean," the man replied, "what does he do for a *living*?"

Six

Too Marvelous for Words: 1937–1938

I have always, since the time I can remember, and that may mean six months old or a year old, I have always been absolutely in love with songs. I knew them all, I sang them all. By the time I was ten or eleven, I knew every writer who was writing songs. . . . So that gives me an edge about fitting words to music because I have this musical sense anyway. I have a pretty good ear, and these words are always in the back of my mind as possibilities for titles. And when the tune comes along the subconscious does its work and finds the phrases.

Warner Bros., the most tightfisted of Hollywood studios, brought Johnny Mercer in only because its formula for making musicals was wearing thin. With its combination of gritty backstage realism, extravagant Busby Berkeley production numbers, and the jazzy songs of Al Dubin and Harry Warren, *42nd Street* had launched a series of successful musicals: *Footlight Parade* (1933), *Dames* (1934), and the *Gold Digger* series, from *Gold Diggers of 1933* through *Gold Diggers in Paris* (1938). Berkeley staged such Dubin and Warren songs as "I Only Have Eyes for You" and "Lullaby of Broadway" in increasingly opulent production numbers, but the same backstager formula about Broadway kids struggling to put on a show had become predictable. Dubin was escaping from the pressure to produce more and more lyrics by turning to drugs and alcohol, and Harry Warren told the penurious Warner brothers that they needed to hire more songwriters.

When Mercer arrived on the lot, producer Buddy Morris asked him which composer he wanted to work with. "I said, 'I'd rather work with Dick Whiting than anybody.'" Richard Whiting was, like Johnny Mercer, an outsider on

Tin Pan Alley. He was born in Peoria, Illinois, the son of a real-estate broker and a trained pianist. He began composing popular songs shortly before World War I and produced such hits as "Till We Meet Again" in 1918, "Ain't We Got Fun?" in 1921, and "Breezin' Along with the Breeze" in 1925. With the advent of talking pictures he joined the exodus of songwriters to the West Coast. At Paramount, he teamed with lyricist Leo Robin and wrote such standards as "Beyond the Blue Horizon" and "My Ideal." When his contract with Paramount was up, Whiting moved to Twentieth Century-Fox, where he wrote "On the Good Ship Lollipop" for Shirley Temple. Whiting returned to Paramount in 1935, but by then Leo Robin had settled into a new partnership with composer Ralph Rainger. When Warner Bros., in response to Harry Warren's plea for songwriting help, invited Whiting to join their music department, he accepted. Whiting was "another of my idols," said Mercer, who had admired the composer's work since boyhood. "A dear fellow, too. Modest and sweet,"—then, with just a whiff of anti-Semitism—"not at all pushy like a lot of New York writers are."

Whiting's experience at Fox and Paramount made him a father figure who guided Johnny Mercer through the labyrinth of Hollywood. Once they got their first assignment, to write songs for a movie called *Ready, Willing and Able*, Whiting explained that they had four to six weeks before they had to turn in songs, so they relaxed and worked beside Whiting's swimming pool. "He generally tried to initiate me into the studio mystique," Mercer said. Margaret Whiting recalls the way Mercer worked with her father: "He had to like the melody, and Dick would play it, and he would say, 'Why don't you try a higher note?' Very seldom, because they were really compatible." She remembers that they would sit by the pool or go to the golf course to work and Mercer would take out a typed lyric and ask her father, " 'What do you think about this?' And Daddy said, 'I think that's great.' . . . And then he would go and say, 'Do you think this fits? Do you think this is too hip? Is it sharp enough?' You know, 'How far should we go with it?' It was a complete collaboration."

Ready, Willing and Able was cast in the mold of Warner backstagers that went all the way back to *42nd Street*. It portrayed the struggle of a Broadway troupe to mount a musical despite financial woes and bickering in the wings. To freshen the stale formula, the studio replaced Dick Powell, who was on loan to Twentieth Century-Fox, with a Broadway actor, Ross Alexander, whose singing had to be dubbed but who could "talk" his way through parts of a lyric with flamboyant charm. Choreographer Bobby Connolly, accordingly, planned the big finale as flowing in and out of conversation (which would rhyme) as Alexander dictated a love letter to his secretary, which would be delivered to Ruby Keeler, the star of many of the Warner backstagers, who would then read it to her friends.

As conceived, the number posed a daunting challenge for a lyricist. In ear-

lier musicals, Al Dubin's lyrics would be repeated over and over for such production numbers, but Warners wanted Mercer to write different lyrics for
each repeated chorus, as well as rhymed conversation. After Mercer had written three or four sets of lyrics, Margaret Whiting recalls, "He was working
on the fifth lyric, and he said, 'I can't do it.' The studio calls them; they go
out. They did the four or five lyrics they had. They said, 'Wonderful. Do five
more. We'll cut it down to ten.' He came home, and he was struggling, and he
said, 'Dick, I can't do it. I have had it. I'm through' and he went home. And
my father raced to a book shop, got him a Webster's dictionary and put it in
the mailbox, and he said, 'Onward!' "

Mercer shrewdly turned his problem, "I'll never find the words," into its
own solution by building his lyric around a catchphrase of the day—"Too
marvelous for words." His fascination with the word "marvelous" went back
to his love letters to Ginger, when he was amused that it could be spelled with
one *l* or two. Even the dictionary found its way into the song:

> You're much too much,
> And oh, so very very
> To ever be in Webster's dictionary.

Connolly staged the number in a library, where skimpily clad chorines
climbed up and down ladders to shelve books (and display their legs). Ross
Alexander, alternately talking and singing (when his voice was dubbed by
James Newell) to his stenographer, dictates a love letter to Ruby Keeler:

> You're just too marvelous,
> Too marvelous for words,
> Like "glorious," "glamorous,"
> And that old stand-by "amorous."

As he and the stenographer come up with such phrases such as "So—I'm
borrowing—a love song—from the birds," Alexander breaks up Mercer's lyric
so that it sounds like spontaneous dictation. Along with the elegant polysyl-
labic vocabulary of "glamorous" and "amorous," Mercer throws in a pithy
slang expression:

> I'll never find the words
> That say enough, tell enough,
> I mean they just aren't swell enough.

Then Mercer moves into his next chorus, where he goes beyond the dictionary to coin "tintinnabulous" (based on the "tintinnabulation of the bells"
in Edgar Allan Poe's classic poem). Playing off another word, "apothegm," he

complains that words like "magical" and "mystical" "seem just too apothisti-cal." Turning poetic again, he concludes the next chorus with:

The sweetest words,
In Keats or Shelley's lyric
Aren't sweet enough
To be your panegyric.

The letter is typed, then dispatched to Keeler, who reads it to her girlfriends as they puzzle over such words as "tintinnabulous." They urge her to call Ross for a translation, and, as chorines hold dictionaries in front of him, he launches into litany of extravagant adjectives, from "euphemistical" to "eulo-gistical." Keeler then dances onto a Berkeleyesque set designed to look like a gigantic typewriter. As she and dance partner Lee Dixon (Ross Alexander couldn't dance either) tap-dance on the keys of the typewriter, chorus girls kick their legs to imitate keystrokes, and Mercer's lyric, with such absurd rhymes as "possible" and "collosable," appears on a massive sheet of paper at the top of the screen. The entire effect was to highlight words, and Mercer found that, for all of his struggles, he had found a superb showcase for his lyrics.

Although the rest of *Ready, Willing and Able* was nowhere as good as the finale, the staging of "Too Marvelous for Words" helped make the song a hit that lasted for six weeks on *Your Hit Parade*. Before the movie was released, however, Ross Alexander committed suicide, and the picture was reedited to reduce the importance of his part. The result placed too much pressure on Ruby Keeler, who had always relied on costars such as Dick Powell or her husband, Al Jolson. *Ready, Willing and Able* would be her last movie at Warner Bros.

The success of "Too Marvelous for Words," Mercer said, made him and Whiting "secure enough to sit around his poolside and throw rocks at the blackbirds." The Whitings invited Johnny and Ginger to dinner parties where he met such figures as the poet Edgar Guest, composer Alec Temple-ton, and other members of Hollywood's "intellectual" circle. One evening, the Whitings' daughter Margaret came downstairs in her bathrobe to sing for Johnny. "Margaret Whiting," Mercer recalled, was "then as now, a lyrical pure songer of the finest kind." After she sang, Mercer said, "I've just got two words of advice for you—grow up!"

Mercer felt so comfortable with Richard Whiting that he could work in the same room with him, a practice he seldom followed with other collabora-tors. "The two people that he would work with in the room," Margaret Whit-ing and her husband, Jack Wrangler, recalled, "were Richard Whiting and Harold Arlen. Only two. Other people, he couldn't stand having them around." With his gentlemanly reticence, Johnny Mercer rarely asked his collaborators to accommodate him. "He very seldom would change. If some-body put something in a specific structure, he would very seldom call them back and say, 'May I make that a half note or an eighth,' or, 'I really need this in order to make the thing flow,' or something. He would go right to what the composer gave him, and very seldom would go away from that."

Even when he worked in the same room with a composer, he would isolate himself in spirit. "They would play the tune for him, he would then lie down on his couch and he would, by all intents and purposes, fall asleep." Always the cavalier southerner, Mercer, even when he was working, appeared not to be toiling. Irving Berlin, by contrast, would recount his all-night struggles with a song, saying, "I sweat blood between 3 and 6 many mornings and when the drops that fall off my forehead hit the paper, they're notes." But John Herndon Mercer, without the faintest glow of perspiration, "would wake up, maybe an hour later, and he'd say, 'How's this work?' and hand him a lyric by just jotting it down right then and there. . . .

"The way Johnny put it, which later even Johnny said he thought was a lit-tle pretentious, he said he 'got in touch with the infinite.' Whatever he got in touch with, he'd go off into 'Mercer-land' and then all of a sudden it would form and he'd wake up and there it was." But the effort that churned beneath that sleepy southern mask was enormous. "The concentration, it was like steel," said Whiting. "It was absolutely extreme concentration. It was like a beam that would go through a table."

Mercer and Richard Whiting worked on three more musicals at Warner Bros.; none was a success, but each produced a hit song. *Varsity Show*, which starred Dick Powell with newcomer Rosemary Lane, featured the black dance team of Buck and Bubbles, and ended with a spectacular Busby Berke-ley production number. The hit that emerged from this film was "Have You Got Any Castles, Baby?" which stayed for eleven weeks on *Your Hit Parade*—more than twice as long as "Too Marvelous for Words," though it has not endured the way the earlier song has.

Their next picture, *Hollywood Hotel*, opened with Benny Goodman in a drum major helmet, leading his band in a car caravan to the airport to see Dick Powell off to Hollywood. Whiting's sprightly march melody threw Mercer for a while, but he mulled over the rhythm of its catchy title phrase with a "dummy" lyric. Dummy lyrics were nonsensical phrases that temporarily helped lyricists—most of whom, like Mercer, could not read music—remem-ber a melody while they worked out the real lyric. Occasionally a dummy lyric, such as Irving Caesar's "Tea for Two" or Ira Gershwin's "It Ain't Necessarily So," which Gershwin said could just as easily have been "An *or*der of *ba*con and *eggs*" or "To*mor*row's the *Fourth* of Ju*ly*," became the real lyric.

Mercer's dummy lyric for this Whiting melody was "*Piece* of ma-*ter*-i-*al* . . . *Piece* of ma-*ter*-i-*al*." Knowing it had to be a song about Hollywood, Mercer drew upon his own bitter experiences in Hollywood. "Hollywood seemed to me like a big put-on and I just tried to make a little fun of it," he said, but the satire had a biting edge. For a man with an aristocratic respect for talent and integrity, the hype of Hollywood, "where you're terrific if you're even good," was risible:

> Hooray for Hollywood!
> That screwy bally hooey Hollywood,
> Where any office boy or young mechanic
> Can be a panic
> With just a good-looking pan . . .
> That phony super Coney Hollywood.
> They come from Chilicothes and Paducahs
> With their bazookas
> To get their names up in lights . . .
> Go out and try your luck,
> You might be Donald Duck!

Mercer wrote several choruses, whose phrases bounce among members of Goodman's band—Frances Langford, Johnny "Scat" Davis, Gene Krupa, and others—in rapid-fire, swinging delivery. Then the song is reprised at the end of the picture with still more lyrics. Like other great catalog songs, such as Cole Porter's "You're the Top," the lyrics were updated over time, with Mercer adding such topical lines as "When anyone at all from TV's *Lassie* to Monroe's chassis is equally understood." With little attention to Mercer's sardonic lyrics, "Hooray for Hollywood" has become the anthem of filmdom, regularly performed at the annual Academy Award ceremonies

While Mercer could poke fun at the shallowness of Hollywood, he reveled in its pleasures. "Oh, it really was lovely," he later recalled. "Pre-world-war-two, pre-smog California was then many villages and orange groves with open spaces between, not too much traffic and hundreds of talented people all making the most money possible in an industry that was colorful, interesting, new and fascinating to be in." Still starstruck, he loved to see the movie stars who then walked around town. "The thing I remember about them was that the men were huge—twice as big as you expected them to be, and the women, while beautiful all right, were very theatrical, with orange or platinum hair and lots of eye make-up, wearing great fluffy furs and smoked glasses, so, as my sister-in-law explained, they would be *less* 'conspicuous'!"

As Hollywood grew, the kind of jazz Mercer loved in New York continued to move westward. "Joe Venuti or Benny Goodman would be at the Palomar, or Wingy Manone or Stuff Smith would be at the Famous Door on Vine. . . . Ginger and I were out at night more often than we were home." Reverting to his days with Paul Whiteman's orchestra, Mercer began to get up and sing at these clubs, and he developed a routine that later blossomed into what he called the "Newsie Bluesies." Using the traditional twelve-bar AAB blues format, he would improvise lyrics about people in the band or audience. The blues format is structured to make such improvisation possible, for it consists of a four-bar A line,

There's old Willis Conover sittin' over there,

which is then repeated, with some variation, as another four-bar A line:

I said there's old Willis Conover sittin' in his chair,

During that repetition, the singer has a few seconds to come up with a rhyme and improvise the new four-bar B line:

He's sittin' over there but to most people he is nowhere.

Even though Mercer, if he knew who would be in the band or audience, would prepare a few rhymes in advance, most of these songs were pure improvisations.

Among the jazz musicians who came to Hollywood was his former collaborator Bernie Hanighen, who played Mercer a swinging melody he'd written. To Johnny, it sounded like the call of the bobwhites he'd listened to as a boy in Savannah, and he created a hipster lyric about other birds criticizing the bobwhite for being square:

I was talkin' to the whippoorwill,
He says you got a corny trill,
Bob white!
Whatcha gonna swing tonight?
. . . Even the owl
Tells me you're foul,
Singin' those lullaby notes . . .
There's a lot of talk about you, Bob,
And they're sayin' you're "off the cob."
Fake it, Mister B.
Take it, follow me,
Bob white! We're gonna break it up tonight!

With its puns ("you're foul") and hip expressions ("off the cob"), "Bob White" was a compendium of big band era musician jive talk. Mercer later reflected that he and Hanighen "were way ahead of our time, rhythmically."

Bing Crosby liked "Bob White" and recorded it as a duet with Connie Boswell (who later changed the spelling of her first name to Connee so she didn't have to pause to dot the *i* in the thousands of autographs she signed for soldiers during World War II). The swinging recording was a landmark for Boswell as well as for Crosby, who, after the success of his saccharine "Sweet Leilani" and "Blue Hawaii," was undergoing a transformation from the bad boy of jazz to the bard of middle-class America (Decca even had him record Stephen Foster songs). Mercer and Hanighen's "Bob White" provided Crosby with a song he could deliver "in one of his most playful performances, indulging the staccato and vibrato called for in the lyric." For the sultry-voiced Boswell, who had been part of the Boswell Sisters until Martha and Vet Boswell found husbands and quit the act in 1935, "Bob White" was an opportunity to bolster her individual career and escape Decca's vigilant efforts to "tone down her jazziness." Boswell had suffered polio as a child and performed in a wheelchair that was concealed by costuming and lighting, but her skill as a pianist, cellist, and saxophonist bolstered her interpretive range as a singer and made her the idol of such younger singers as Ella Fitzgerald. "The compound of her molasses drawl and Bing's brisk virility" made "Bob White" a jazzy success at a time when popular music was increasingly receding into "middlebrow blandness." As Mercer's singing career developed, he would take Crosby's place as the hip jazz singer of the airwaves. He might not have achieved Crosby's stardom, but he kept faith with the early Crosby singing style he had loved as a boy. Many listeners, as they had when he was with Paul Whiteman, assumed Mercer was black. When he introduced himself to the maid at a party, she was astonished. "I am really surprised you are white, Mr. Mercer," she said. "We have always claimed you as one of our own."

Mercer himself was torn between the poles of hipster and square that he delineated in "Bob White." As much as he loved to go nightclubbing, Johnny was a homebody, and he loved their modest Cape Cod house at 8425 De Longpre Avenue in Hollywood, which he thought Ginger decorated beautifully. "Ginger painted it, and I gave her a mink coat as payment for the job!" Years later, Mercer sketched a picture of those days that mingled domestic pleasures with professional ones. "Life in these years, if it could be shown like the quick montages they show in the movies, would have shown me driving to the studios, recording on the sound stages, watching the stars sing the movie scores, making records with Crosby, golfing, playing tennis . . . singing in some small saloon, putting up a picket fence . . . going to private parties with entertainers 'on their way up,' and generally being a jack of all trades."

Much of Mercer's security was based on Richard Whiting's paternal guidance. On the one hand, Whiting was like "Peck's Bad Boy," a real "Gotcha!" guy, as another songwriter described him, playing practical jokes, setting off firecrackers just as a friend was teeing off at the golf course, and getting his friends drunk while he himself stayed sober. As a collaborator, however, he was a master of tact, going out of his way to protect his partner's feelings if he thought a lyric needed to be changed.

But working at Warner Bros. began to take its toll on Whiting. Hollywood studios in general treated songwriters, as composer Harry Warren put it, as "the lowest form of animal life." But at Paramount and MGM, the most regal of studios, songwriters were accorded at least some of the courtesy enjoyed by other artists. Warner Bros., however, was known as the working-class studio, where everyone was under constant pressure. Mercer recalled that at parties Harry Warren used to perform a song in which, as he played a frenetic melody, he described working at Warners:

> Warner Brothers . . . you're late . . . you're late
> Check in with the cop at the gate . . .
> Hurry up, Mr. Warren, you're late . . .
> Have you got the song finished yet?
> Mr. Warner says you're using too many Dixie Cups . . .
> Efficiency—efficiency . . . hurry up . . . hurry up . . .

Then he would shift to a soft, languorous melody:

> But at Metro . . . birds are singing . . .
> The sun is shining at Metro . . .
> Everybody smokes a pipe at Metro . . .
> See the beautiful stars . . .
> Everybody has the Book-of-the-Month Club under his arms at
>   Metro . . .

Warren would conclude the song by returning to the agitated melody for Warner Bros.:

> Busby Berkeley needs you . . . the song . . . the lyric
> Where is it? . . . We're shooting at noon . . .
> We're shooting . . . we're shooting . . . it's shot and it's shot . . .
> And it's shit!

Warner Bros. was hardly the place for Richard Whiting, a sickly man, Mercer recalled, who was "always feeling the veins behind his ears, got terribly nervous over little things, and made regular trips downtown to pick up what must have been his nitro pills." He was anxious about presenting their songs to the stone-faced producers at Warners. After they demonstrated one of their songs, a producer hurled the sheet music to the floor. Another producer told Mercer, "You really stink as a singer!"

As Mercer and Whiting were working on songs for their fourth film, *Cowboy from Brooklyn*, for which they had written "Ride, Tenderfoot, Ride," whose clip-clop melody made it a classic cowboy ballad, Whiting had a heart attack. He died on February 10, 1938, at only forty-six years old. Popular music lost one of its most artful composers, and the collaborative team of Mercer and Whiting, which might have gone on to write brilliant scores for movie musicals, was dissolved after little more than a year. Just as Mercer's collaborations with Hoagy Carmichael, Bernie Hanighen, and other song-writing partners had been disrupted by one circumstance or another, now all the promise of the Mercer-Whiting team was snuffed out. Whiting's death was like the loss of a father for Mercer, who now had no protective figure to help him through the maze of Hollywood; nevertheless, always brought up to be the kindest, most generous of men, he gallantly took responsibility for being a father figure to Whiting's daughters.

To complete the songs for *Cowboy from Brooklyn*, Harry Warren was brought in. Compared to the delicate Richard Whiting, Harry Warren was a workhorse, whose thirty-two-bar melodies had to be catchy enough to withstand the dozen or so reprises they endured through Busby Berkeley's extravagant production numbers. He also barked back at studio heads. When he demonstrated "Lullaby of Broadway" to Jack Warner, a lyric Dubin had written because he heard Warren's longing for New York in the driving melody, Warner dismissed the lyric and told Warren to tell Dubin to write a different one. Warren, who had changed his name from Salvatore Guaragna, showed a flash of his New York Italian toughness. "I'll write you a new song," he told Warner, "but I won't divorce this lyric from this melody." His faith in the marriage between words and music was vindicated when "Lullaby of Broadway" won the Academy Award for Best Song in 1936.

But the Warner work ethic was taking its toll on Dubin and Warren as well. In 1935, they wrote twenty-seven songs for eight movies; in 1936 they wrote fifteen songs for six movies. As their songs sounded more and more like variations on earlier hits, reviews turned sour, and other songwriters were brought in, such as Yip Harburg and Harold Arlen, to add numbers to Dubin and Warren's scores. Dubin, who was having marital problems and had already been relying on alcohol and drugs, became addicted to morphine when he was given a prescription after an operation. He would disappear for days but manage to turn up with lyrics scrawled on scraps of paper. It was Harry Warren who had beseeched Warner Bros. to hire Richard Whiting and Johnny Mercer to take the pressure off Dubin and himself. While he had always stood firmly behind his collaborator, when Dubin failed to show up with a lyric for the big production number for *The Singing Marine*, Warren's own work ethic was offended, and he asked director Busby Berkeley to send for Johnny Mercer. Mercer quickly turned out the serviceable "Night over Shanghai."

When Dubin finally showed up, he agreed to undergo treatment at the Mayo Clinic for his uncontrolled eating, drinking, and drug use. He returned to write songs with Warren for three more musicals, one of which, "September in the Rain," became a hit and has remained a jazz standard. But the studio was still concerned about Dubin's reliability and assigned Johnny Mercer to join him as a colyricist for the 1938 musical *Gold Diggers in Paris*. Even though he liked Mercer, Al Dubin exploded, and they had to work out "an uneasy division of the lyric writing between them." Dubin and Warren wrote four songs together, and Mercer and Warren wrote four together, so Dubin never had to collaborate with Mercer on lyrics.

In making *Gold Diggers in Paris*, Warner Bros. was simultaneously trying to revive its flagging tradition of backstager musicals and to impose a new economy on production costs. They cast radio crooner Rudy Vallee in the lead, following the trend to feature radio personalities in movies so that the public would come to see what their favorite radio stars looked like. They also imposed severe restraints on the budget for Busby Berkeley's production numbers. Berkeley managed to be innovative on a shoestring, but the rest of the picture was a failure, and Vallee never starred in a movie again. Dubin, Mercer, and Warren were next assigned to *Garden of the Moon*, where, as Dubin's antipathy to the younger lyricist abated, they worked as a threesome and produced such clever songs as "The Girlfriend of the Whirling Dervish":

While he's doing her a real good turn,
She gives him the runaround.
She's got a nervish, throwin' him a curvish,
Which of course he doesn't deservish,
Poor old whirling dervish!

But *Garden of the Moon* was beset with problems from the outset. Bette Davis found the script so awful she refused the part and was placed on suspension by the studio. Busby Berkeley could not pull off another choreographic miracle under the newly imposed budget constraints, and he never made another picture for Warner Bros.

The uneasy three-way partnership of Mercer, Dubin, and Warren persisted for two more movies in 1938, *Hard to Get* and *Going Places*, both starring Dick Powell, who, along with Dubin and Warren, was the last remaining figure from the team that created *42nd Street*. But the only successful songs from the films were ones that Warren wrote with only Mercer as his lyricist. "Al Dubin, unable to cope with his reduced status at the studio, asked for his release from his contract, and it was granted." Dubin worked off and on in Hollywood and on Broadway for the next few years until he collapsed on a New York street in 1945 and died a few days later from a drug overdose.

Johnny Mercer inherited Dubin's partnership with Harry Warren. There was a raffish, rhythmic drive to Warren's melodies that inspired Mercer's keen ear for vernacular phrases. When he heard Warren play one driving melody, his mind fastened on the initial ten-note musical phrase and leaped back to a visit to Savannah. When Ginger and his mother were going through an old family photo album, Ginger saw a picture of Johnny as a baby on a bearskin rug and said, "You must have been a beautiful baby," whereupon his mother produced a blue ribbon Johnny had actually won in a baby contest. In the lyric, Mercer turned the memory into a romantic compliment:

> And when it came to winning blue ribbons,
> You must have shown the other kids how.
> I can see the judges' eyes
> As they handed you the prize,
> I bet you made the cutest bow.

Then, as Warren's melody does a turnaround, Mercer follows with the perfectly complementary (and complimentary) lyrical phrase:

> Oh! You must have been a beautiful baby,
> 'Cause, baby, look at you now.

Whereas he crafted a title out of all the notes in Warren's opening melodic phrase for "You Must Have Been a Beautiful Baby," Mercer took only the first four notes of another melody for his title. He had heard midwesterner Henry Fonda use the expression "jeepers creepers" in a movie, and it struck him as a bowdlerized substitute for "Jesus Christ!" In the long tradition of poets celebrating their beloved's eyes, Mercer's lyric combines such regional slang as "Gosh all git up!" with city-slicker jive talk: "How'd they get so lit up?" With everything from an archaic "Woe is me" to the latest vernacular term for sunglasses, his lyric follows Warren's powerful musical accents with a collage of clashing colloquial idioms:

> Golly gee!
> When you turn those heaters on,
> Woe is me!
> Got to put my cheaters on.

"Jeepers Creepers" garnered Mercer his first Oscar nomination for the Best Song, but for 1938 that award went to one of the greatest songs ever written for a film, Leo Robin and Ralph Rainger's "Thanks for the Memory."

The last film at Warners on which Mercer collaborated with Harry Warren was *Naughty but Nice*, which was also Dick Powell's last musical with the studio. Powell, like Ruby Keeler, Busby Berkeley, Al Dubin, and Harry Warren, had been a mainstay of *42nd Street* and the backstager musicals that followed in its wake, his sweet demeanor playing off Keeler's spunky cuteness and his surprisingly strong tenor voice booming out such Dubin and Warren songs as "I Only Have Eyes for You" and "Young and Healthy." But by 1939

Powell's fortunes had fallen so low he was given second billing under "Oomph Girl" Ann Sheridan. Mercer and Warren wrote good songs for the picture, including "Hooray for Spinach," which, like a similar song written by Irving Berlin, was based on a popular *New Yorker* cartoon depicting a little boy glowering at a plate of broccoli and saying, "I say it's spinach and to hell with it." Mercer gives a clever twist to the idea, as the boy, now grown up, recalls:

> As a kid, I hated spinach and all its ilk,
> I abominated cod liver oil and milk

But now that he has found love, he exults:

> Hooray for spinach!
> Hooray for milk!
> They put the roses in your cheek soft as silk,
> They helped complete you till I could meet you, baby!

But even such lively topical songs could not save yet another musical based on the same old formula. The public, in effect, said of the Warner backstager, "I say it's spinach and to hell with it."

Harry Warren, the last major member of the company that had originated *42nd Street*, withdrew from Warner Bros. because of a personal tragedy—the death of his nineteen-year-old son from pneumonia. The Warrens were devastated by the loss and, long homesick for New York, sold their home in Beverly Hills. But when Twentieth Century-Fox head Darryl F. Zanuck learned that Harry Warren had negotiated an end to his contract with Warner Bros., he induced him to stay in Hollywood. At Fox, Warren was paired with lyricist Mack Gordon, who no longer wanted to collaborate with Harry Revel, with whom he had written such hits as "With My Eyes Wide Open I'm Dreaming" and "Did You Ever See a Dream Walking?" Together, Gordon and Warren would write "Chattanooga Choo-Choo," "I've Got a Gal in Kalamazoo," and other songs for Fox musicals featuring Glenn Miller and his orchestra. Once again, this star-crossed game of musical chairs left Mercer without a long-term collaborator.

With Warren's departure, following that of Dick Powell, his wife Joan Blondell, Busby Berkeley, and Ruby Keeler, a great era of musicals came to an end at Warner Bros. Soon, the studio would turn to a very different, and cheaper, kind of backstager—the "biopic" musical which traced the lives of great American songwriters such as George M. Cohan (*Yankee Doodle Dandy*) and George Gershwin (*Rhapsody in Blue*). Such biopics relied on their subject's most famous hits for their score and thus required no songwriters to produce new, untried songs. As Warner Bros. made fewer and fewer original musicals, it had less need for songwriters such as Johnny Mercer, who found himself, yet again, uprooted and alone as a songwriter in Hollywood.

Seven

Day In—Day Out: 1938–1940

You have to write, write, and WRITE. . . . Don't try to do too much too quickly. You write a number, and even if you think it's great, put it away and let it cook, let it simmer. Then you come back to it and you may have a different slant. You play with it, let it grow.

While Mercer had hit another dead end as a songwriter in Hollywood, his singing career revived in the late 1930s, and by combining singing and writing, he produced a stunning array of hits. It was the height of the big band era of Benny Goodman and Count Basie, Artie Shaw and the Dorseys, and Mercer's ability to perform with such bands set him apart from other lyricists of the day. "His was not a 'pure' trained baritone," said Dave Dexter. "He had difficulty sustaining whole notes on dreamy ballads. Yet on rhythm songs," Dexter said, Mercer was "great at improvising variations."

Singing also gave Mercer a rapport with musicians that enabled him to give voice, both as a singer and a lyricist, to the music they loved. Some of the songs he wrote during this period had started out as jazz instrumentals by band members, but every song lent itself to the swinging style of the era.

This turn in his career came, thanks again, to Bing Crosby. Johnny and Ginger participated in a series of informal minstrel shows put on by the "Westwood Marching and Chowder Club" that were initially staged at Crosby's house. The first show was held on April 16, 1938, and Mercer put on blackface to be one of the end men as Pat O'Brien, Jerry Colonna, and Crosby himself performed comic routines and sang old songs such as "Waiting for the Robert E. Lee." The show was an informal production for themselves and their friends, but, since most of the performers were professionals, they were slickly staged affairs, with elaborate costumes, such as Bessie Burke's cowboy chaps with "cutouts to display her buttocks." For white show business people raised on minstrel show traditions and accustomed to black-face performances throughout the 1930s, the racist caricatures in these shows would not have seemed offensive.

The first performance aroused so much interest around Hollywood that a second show was scheduled for June 25, and along with most of the original performers, the cast included Andy Devine, Fred MacMurray, and Bill Frawley (who would go on to play Fred Mertz on television's *I Love Lucy*). A small band was also brought in that included Tommy Dorsey and Spike Jones. Mercer later fondly recalled these early Westwood Marching and Chowder Club shows, where Pat O'Brien would sing,

Shame, shame on old Notre Dame
The Czechs and the Polacks have stolen your fame.

"It was all very spontaneous," Ginger recalled, "and as usual those are much more fun than when they get too well rehearsed." But one wonders if she was expressing Johnny's feelings more than her own. She seems to have loved sitting quietly to the side and taking in all the glitz and glamour. Her need to be there but apart from it was remarked by a nephew who attended several of their parties. "Ginger's idol movie star was Gary Cooper, and she very much didn't want to meet Gary Cooper. And at these parties in Hollywood where everybody would be there, including Gary Cooper, Johnny would get a couple of drinks, and his project would be to try to introduce Ginger to Gary Cooper." But Ginger would run and hide. "She said that she couldn't idolize somebody she knew."

The Westwood minstrels printed up programs and had large glossy photographs taken of themselves performing and watching one another perform, drinks in hand. These shows brought Bob Hope and Crosby together, and there was even talk at one point of filming one of them for Paramount. For Savannah-bred Johnny Mercer, that was going too far in mixing one's private and public lives.

The highlight of this second show, however, was a duet between Crosby and Mercer that Mercer had written as a blackface parody of the old ethnic vaudeville act "Mr. Gallagher and Mr. Shean." As " 'Lasses Mercer" and "Chitlins Crosby," he and Bing provided an "erudite analyseration of swing." Crosby had recently been given an honorary degree by Gonzaga University in his hometown of Spokane, Washington, and Mercer addresses him with mock deference as Crosby hums and scats:

Oh, Mr. Crosby, Dear Dr. Crosby,
Is it true that swing's another name for jazz?

And the first place it was played
Was a New Orleans parade
And the Southern Negro gave it all it has?

To which Crosby replies:

Oh, Mr. Mercer, Mr. Mercer, Mr. Mercer, Mr. Mercer,
I believe that its foundation came from them.

When Mercer asks, "Are you positive?" Crosby continues:

Yeesss. They just slowed the tempo down
And then they really went to town.

The verse ends with this folksy exchange:

Allegretto, Mr. Crosby?
Alligators, Mr. M.

While other numbers in the show were merely in-circle fun, this duet "dazzled the audience" with its "smooth-running wit." Within a week, Crosby and Mercer made a recording, and it became one of the big hits of 1938, with *Time* magazine calling "Mr. Crosby and Mr. Mercer" the "summer's most amusing ditty."

The recording rekindled Mercer's singing career, which had languished since he'd left Paul Whiteman. With a hit song, however, he was invited by CBS to come to New York, beginning on January 3, 1939, for the Tuesday edition of *Camel Caravan*, which featured Benny Goodman's orchestra. Mercer's association with Goodman went back to 1935, when Mercer's "The Dixieland Band," written with Bernie Hanighen, became one of Goodman's first big recordings. Their friendship revived when Goodman's band was featured performing "Hooray for Hollywood" in *Hollywood Hotel*. On the first *Camel Caravan* Mercer sang his three most recent hits—"Goody Goody," "I'm an Old Cowhand," and "You Must Have Been a Beautiful Baby." New York friends recalled how "California" Mercer looked with his casual sport clothes, big soft straw hat, and "crepe sole white wooden sneakers. . . . He was coming from California, and this is Christmas in New York with snow."

By the third week, Johnny Mercer had replaced Dan Seymour as emcee, and in addition to singing and announcing the show, he wrote special comic material. Mercer's fertile creativity in this period, as lyrics seemed to gush out of his imagination, is astounding. *Camel Caravan* originated not only from New York but from other major cities, where network affiliate stations would set up broadcasts in local theaters. When the program aired from Pittsburgh, for example, he tossed off a parody of "You Ought to Be in Pictures" called "You Ought to Be in Pittsburgh":

> George Washington surveyed it,
> And made a mental note,
> He WPA-ed it . . .

He also did a regular feature called the "Newsie Bluesies," based on the improvisational blues that he had performed in Los Angeles jazz clubs. "Newsie Bluesies" took current events and people in the news and satirized them; to keep the satire current, Mercer would wait until the night of the radio show, then go out on the fire escape at the studio and compose the lyrics. One friend compared him to "a typewriter," concentrating intensely, jotting down and crossing out ideas. "He'd go outside the studio and sit on the fire escape, and then he'd come back and have the lyric ready to do that evening." At Mercer's suggestion, all of these weekly programs were recorded, so that they now provide a priceless record of radio in the big band era. At the time, it was rare for a radio program to be recorded beyond making acetate "air checks" as protection against lawsuits over something allegedly said on the air or to prove to sponsors that their commercials had been aired.

The return to New York fueled a new burst of creativity in Mercer. During the course of the year he turned out a series of hit songs working with a variety of composers, each of whom presented him with a melody in a distinctly different musical style. For each, Mercer responded with a lyric that perfectly married words to music. However, the first of these hits, "I Thought About You," was written in one of the rare instances when Mercer did lyrics first. The idea came to him as he was taking the train back to New York. As he rolled past "all these little towns with the lights and cars parked and the glow worms in the dark," he wrote a wistful set of words around a title phrase so simple it is nearly banal but, as the lyric repeats it, resonates with understated longing:

> I took a trip on the train
> And I thought about you.
> I passed a shadowy lane,
> And I thought about you.
> Two or three cars parked under the stars,
> A winding stream,
> Moon shining down on some little town,
> And with each beam,
> Same old dream.

Mercer's imagery evokes small-town America right down to its lovers' lane, yet another lyric that stems from his boyhood in Savannah.

The refrain closes with another wry image that alleviates sentimentality. Mercer portrays himself trying to avoid thinking of his lover by pulling down the shade of the train window, but then he adds a comic touch:

I peeked through the crack
And looked at the track,
The one going back to you,
And what did I do?
I thought about you!

Beneath the comic image, however, the lyric registers the singer's helpless, obsessive preoccupation with his absent lover. Mercer always faulted himself, however, for using "you" twice for a rhyme.

He gave the lyric to Jimmy Van Heusen, who was just establishing a partnership with lyricist Johnny Burke—maybe Mercer hoped to have Van Heusen work with him instead. Mercer certainly found Van Heusen "easy to write with. . . . He seems to have a series of chords waiting at his command to which he can fashion a melody the moment his lyricist springs any idea on him." "I Thought About You," recorded by Benny Goodman's orchestra with Mildred Bailey doing the vocal, and then by Hal Kemp's and Bob Crosby's bands, became the first of a remarkable string of hits for Johnny Mercer.

Back in New York, he had the opportunity to work again with Rube Bloom, who was disappointed that no hit songs had emerged from *Blackbirds*. He played several of his other melodies for Mercer, who promised to write lyrics to them when he had time, threatening, "If you play these for anyone else, I'll never talk to you again." While Bloom would have to wait even longer than usual with his collaborator, Mercer first came up with one of his most passionately driven lyrics, "Day In—Day Out." Its soaring melodic line, which ranges beyond the standard thirty-two-bar chorus to fifty-six measures, is composed of short, jabbing phrases that were perfect for bringing out the big band sound. The opening phrase suggested the turnaround title to Mercer, and he also found a parallel pair of phrases in "Come rain, come shine," which he would later use as a title for another song. Mercer cleverly gave the "Day In—Day Out" title phrase, which suggests boring routine, a twist by using it to describe unrelenting excitement:

Day in, day out,
The same old hoodoo follows me about.
The same old pounding in my heart
Whenever I think of you.
And, darling, I think of you,
Day in and day out.

By using such tiresome expressions as "same old" and "I needn't tell you," Mercer keeps this theme of exciting routine going until it culminates in a kiss, and he compares it to the beating of the heart—at once monotonous and ecstatic:

> Then I kiss your lips
> And the pounding becomes
> The ocean's roar,
> A thousand drums

The song's climax comes when Bloom's melody shoots up to high F, and Mercer hits the note with the simple but impassioned "Can't," then follows with exasperated phrases that seem to grope for words:

> Can't you see it's love?
> Can there be any doubt?
> When there it is
> Day in and day out

Mercer juxtaposed the simplest words—"it" and "is" and "in" and "out"—and the deftly shifting meanings of "there," from "Can there be any doubt" to "there it is." While he was still the lyricist of hip slang and exotic imagery, Mercer could find poetry in the most ordinary of American words.

Singing with Benny Goodman's orchestra on radio brought still more opportunities to collaborate. Ziggy Elman, Goodman's lead trumpeter, played a fast klezmer melody he called "Fralich in Swing." As Mercer listened to it, he told Goodman that, if slowed down, it could be "kind of a Gershwinesque tune." George Gershwin had recently died, tragically young, at thirty-eight. The producer of *Camel Caravan* decided to make Mercer's writing of the lyric an on-the-air event by having Elman threaten to get Irving Berlin to set a lyric to his melody. Benny Goodman steps between the feuding pair and "orders" Mercer to write a lyric to it by next week's show. In the program, Mercer demurs and asks if he can change the title from "Fralich in Swing." The whole thing sounds like a prearranged plug for a completed song, but on the following week's program "lazybones" Mercer, as singer Martha Tilton labels him, still doesn't have a lyric and is given a one-week "extension" by Goodman.

Mercer was following his usual, methodical pattern of composition, crafting two different lyrics, "And It All Came True" and "And the Angels Sing," to the melody, then accepting the verdict of friends that the latter was better. It was another unusual and challenging melody, with sudden twists and turns of musical phrase, which brought out the virtuosity of big band musicians. Mercer matched those sinuous musical phrases with extended images such as

"Silver waves that break on some undiscovered shore" and "long winter nights with the candles gleaming." Tilton, backed by Ziggy Elman, turned it into another hit with a recording made the very next day.

Bing Crosby wrote Mercer to say that he thought "And the Angels Sing" was his best song to date: "You're Getting Practically Poetic." Cognizant of the ups and downs of Mercer's career to this point, in contrast to the unbroken, soaring rise of his own stardom, Crosby added that while they missed him in Hollywood, Mercer needed to "strike while the iron is hot" in New York.

The iron got even hotter in 1940, as Mercer had another hit with Rube Bloom, "Fools Rush In," which had been an instrumental entitled "Shangri-La," inspired by the classic 1937 Ronald Colman movie *Lost Horizon*. Mercer later said, "I think it's one of my better lyrics—a simple way to a very big, almost operatic kind of tune." The simplicity of the lyric—almost every word in the chorus is a monosyllable—creates a powerfully understated emotional plea framed by simple but subtly placed rhymes:

When we *met*,
I felt my life *begin*,
So open up your heart and *let*
This fool rush *in*.

Once again, Mercer played with the various meanings of the common word "there":

Though I see
The danger *there*,
If *there's* a chance for me,
Then I don't care.

There were many hit recordings of the song by the major bands—Glenn Miller's orchestra with Ray Eberle on vocal, Harry James with Dick Haymes, and Kay Kyser with Ginny Simms—but it was Tommy Dorsey's recording with Frank Sinatra's vocal that caught the plangent undertone of the lyric and made it one of the biggest hits of the year.

With all of these successful songs pouring out of him, Mercer found his work featured on another radio program, *Your Hit Parade*, which was sponsored by Lucky Strike cigarettes. The program showcased the ten most popular songs of each week, dramatically building up to the climactic number one song. Mercer was astounded that on one program his songs held the number one, two, and three positions, and on another, five of the ten songs on the program had lyrics written by him. "Imagine that," he later remarked, "one half of the Hit Parade!" Occasionally, he was invited to perform on the program himself, and he had the doubly pleasant task of singing his own hits.

But while it was a heady experience for Mercer to sing on the radio, radio was increasingly posing a threat to the quality of American popular song. It was the playing of popular songs that really established radio as an important medium after its initial development in 1921. Broadcasts of news, sporting events, even the presidential conventions of 1924 brought only a fraction of the public to their radio sets. But when radio stations began playing popular song recordings, the "free music" brought a boom in radio sales; from $60 million in 1922 to $430 million in 1925 to more than $800 million in 1929—an increase of 1,400 percent over 1922 sales—with a radio in one out of every three homes in America. Seasoned songwriters such as Irving Berlin immediately saw radio as a threat that would play a current hit so frequently that the public would soon tire of it and demand a new hit to replace it. Eventually, Berlin feared, radio's voracious appetite for hits would erode the quality of songs.

Radio station owners, like restaurant and nightclub owners before them, argued that their playing of songs should be seen as "free" publicity for songwriters, but the American Society of Composers, Authors and Publishers, an organization founded in 1914 to protect songwriters, demanded that stations pay a fee to play its members' songs, just as it had earlier forced restaurants, nightclubs, and other places to purchase a license for that privilege. The fees from those licenses were then distributed to the publishers, composers, and lyricists ("Authors") who were ASCAP members. In time, these ASCAP royalties would pay songwriters more than they had originally earned from sheet-music and record sales of their hits. Just as it had fought restaurant owners all the way to the Supreme Court, ASCAP went to court to force radio stations to a pay a similar fee. By the 1930s, ASCAP licensed nearly thirty thousand outlets for its music, which brought in fees of $10 million a year. Nearly half of these fees came from 657 radio stations; yet, while radio lined the pockets of songwriters, many of them felt that stations were still getting ASCAP songs for a small fraction of the money the songs were earning for radio stations. The battle between ASCAP and radio deepened as the time loomed for stations to renew their five-year ASCAP licenses, and Mercer was in the thick of the fighting. In May of 1940 he was elected to the directorate of ASCAP, the youngest of the twenty-four board members who administered an organization that had grown to more than a thousand composers and lyricists and nearly two hundred music publishers.

During the year Mercer served on its board, ASCAP demanded double its $4.5 million in fees from radio stations, and, in a battle waged in the trade papers, radio stations threatened to refuse to pay. If they didn't, ASCAP warned, they would not be permitted to play songs written by any of its members—virtually all of the major songwriters in America. When the deadline for renewal arrived, radio stations made good on their threat. ASCAP music was taken off the air, and programs were forced to change their theme songs.

Stations at first resorted to playing older songs that predated the formation of ASCAP in 1914. The songs of Stephen Foster, for instance, were aired so often that songwriters joked that Jeannie's light brown hair was turning gray. The public clamored to hear their favorite ASCAP songs again, but radio stations held firm and set up their own organization, Broadcast Music Incorporated (BMI), which signed up its own songwriters. Based in Chicago, BMI looked for songwriters in the Midwest and the South, promising to pay them "on the basis of the performance of music on thousands of independent stations as well as countrywide networks." Although few of these new songwriters had the talent of ASCAP writers, BMI precipitated a shift in American musical taste.

ASCAP music was, in effect, "city music," written largely by songwriters raised in New York—the Gershwins, Rodgers and Hart, Irving Berlin; their work was slick, sophisticated, and brassy. Nurtured by vaudeville and the Broadway musical, their Tin Pan Alley style was transplanted to the West Coast with the birth of the talkies, where it became even more pervasive. Even songwriters who did not come from New York, such as Cole Porter, wrote songs that radiated urbanity, and Mercer himself had learned to write in this style with such literately witty lyrics as "Too Marvelous for Words." But New York's dominance over most aspects of American popular culture began to weaken with the onset of World War II, and there were signs that musical tastes were opening up to a larger variety of songs. Tin Pan Alley had long marketed race records to urban and southern black communities, but already in the 1920s performers such as Louis Armstrong were moving blues and jazz directly into the mainstream. By the early 1950s, songwriters, many of them members of BMI, would draw on the tradition of rhythm and blues and make it the basis for rock and roll.

Tin Pan Alley also marketed "hillbilly" music to the South and the West, and slowly but steadily came signs that this music, too, was entering the major song market. The popularity of western movies, often with such "singing cowboys" as Tex Ritter and Gene Autry, called for folklike songs, and even Cole Porter wrote "Don't Fence Me In." Soon more authentic country songs began to cross over to mainstream popular music. One of the first of these was "You Are My Sunshine," sung by Tex Ritter in the 1940 movie *Take Me Back to Oklahoma*, which was the first big hit for BMI in its first year of existence. By the end of its first year, BMI had eleven hundred songwriters and drew in $1.5 million in licensing fees. In 1941, it had other countrified hits, such as "Deep in the Heart of Texas," which held the number one position on *Your Hit Parade* for five weeks.

ASCAP quickly threw in the towel, accepting, in 1941, the year Mercer's term on its board came to an end, an even lower annual fee from radio stations than it had been receiving—$3 million rather than $4.5 million. But it was too late. BMI had gathered a large group of young songwriters who were more responsive to a youthful audience than were the more polished and sophisticated songwriters of ASCAP with their Broadway musical traditions. First hillbilly music, then rock and roll would appeal to the young audience BMI reached. By 1952, BMI would license 80 percent of the music played over the radio. Perhaps the style of American music would have changed without the ASCAP-BMI war, but ASCAP's belief that it had a monopoly on American song hastened its undoing and precipitated a shift in musical style that would eventually leave songwriters such as Johnny Mercer behind.

During his year in New York, Mercer also ventured into music publishing. He had long known that the real money to be made in songwriting was not in composing music or writing lyrics but in publishing songs. Publishers owned the copyrights of songs and, while paying a few cents in royalty to composers and lyricists, kept the large share of the profits from sheet-music sales to themselves. Mercer formed a publishing company with business associate Edwin "Buddy" Morris, Mercer and Morris Music, and bought out catalogs from older companies that included songs, such as "I'm Always Chasing Rainbows," that Mercer had loved as a boy. While Mercer and Morris Music was short-lived, he continued to create music-publishing enterprises for the rest of his life.

Mercer also undertook another Broadway musical. Teaming with Hoagy Carmichael, he wrote lyrics for a show originally called *Three After Three* in its tryout run. As the show went from Philadelphia to Detroit, it was feverishly doctored by adding and dropping songs. It featured talented performers such as Kitty Carlisle, Mitzi Green, and Stepin Fetchit but did not fare well in New York, where it opened at the Ethel Barrymore Theatre on June 4, 1940, as *Walk with Music*. "We all liked the score," Carmichael recalled, which included a song called "I Walk with Music" that became one of his personal favorites, "but the show was too weak to give the songs much exposure."

Carmichael vividly remembered the pressure from the Shubert brothers, who produced the show. Like Mercer, he was a country boy who was not used to pushy New York tactics, particularly from two of the most notoriously ruthless men in the theater. The Shuberts had once reduced the young and brash Irving Berlin to nervous silence when he tried to demonstrate a new song to them. "Jake Shubert got under my skin on a few occasions," recalled Carmichael, "and most of us were disturbed anyway because we didn't think enough thought and money was being put into the production. Soon after the opening it appeared that one of our songs was not going to work out and in an impertinent manner Jake yelled at me, 'Write another song.' I'd had it. I followed him up the aisle, took him by the coat lapels and shook him. 'Don't ever talk to me that way again,' I said. This bit perhaps explains why I was never invited to write another Broadway show. He was a wheel—or did I misspell it?"

Brooks Atkinson's review in the *New York Times* pinpointed the problem with the show: Guy Bolton's book, which "hangs around the neck of *Walk with Music* like a stricken albatross. If it were not for the original book, with its mechanical complications, Hoagy Carmichael's music would seem gay and tingling, and an excellent cast of talented performers could dance on tip-toe straight through it." Atkinson bemoans the fact that "nearly everything but plot is present in excellent order," citing the songs in particular, to which "Johnny Mercer has fitted lyrics that are equally simple and light-hearted." The same problem with the book for a musical would dog most of Mercer's attempts to have an enduring success on Broadway. Yet he would never attempt what Charlie Miller had told Mercer's father Johnny had to learn to do: write the book, as well as the lyrics, for a Broadway musical.

In the summer of 1939, *Camel Caravan* replaced Benny Goodman with Bob Crosby's orchestra, but Mercer stayed on with the show. Crosby's arranger, Bob Haggart, had concocted a beautiful ballad as he was playing around with chord changes. The melody seemed perfect for trumpeter Billy Butterfield, and as "I'm Free" it became a hit jazz instrumental. Thinking to repeat the success of "And the Angels Sing," Crosby asked Mercer to write a lyric for "I'm Free." "He worked on it for two months," Haggart recalled. "But he said, 'I keep coming up with the same thing—I'm free, free as the birds in the trees, dad da da da.'"

The tune was then given to Johnny Burke, who took the advice of Larry Crosby, that he write in a less "poetic," more conversational style—"like 'what's new?' 'how's things' something like that, one-on-one." Burke transformed the melody into the classic "What's New?" which Bing Crosby, then Louis Armstrong, Frank Sinatra, Peggy Lee, and Linda Ronstadt, made into an enduring standard. Mercer and Burke had been vying to be the lyricist of the moment for Bing Crosby, and with "What's New?" Burke got the long-term assignment of writing songs, with Jimmy Van Heusen, for the Bing Crosby–Bob Hope "Road" pictures. For Mercer, the loss must have added to his envy of Crosby; now, having abandoned his dreams of emulating Crosby's stardom, he could not even serve as his in-house lyricist. Mercer would ever after carry a chip on his shoulder about Johnny Burke. In the 1960s, his son-in-law, a jazz pianist, was trying to write songs. When Bob Corwin showed Mercer one of his lyrics, Johnny scoffed at it: "Sounds like Johnny Burke."

Jean Bach, a journalist friend who met Mercer in 1939, recalls a remarkable evening she covered when the Bob Crosby band came to Chicago. Because James Petrillo, head of the American Federation of Musicians, had decreed that union musicians could no longer perform in informal—and unpaid—jam sessions in Chicago, Crosby's band chartered a boat so they could go out on Lake Michigan to jam. Joining the band was a group who called themselves the Harlem Hamfats, led by a large black guitarist named Kokomo Arnold. As young Chicago socialites looked on, Arnold, dressed in black tie and white wing tips, broke a beer bottle off at the neck, put the neck on his finger, and used it to play "frets" sliding up and down the guitar. Mercer sat beside him and, as Kokomo played "real, old timey blues," sang spontaneous lyrics about the people in the room. He might have done "a little woodshedding" ahead of time to find out who was going to be on board, Bach noted, but "it sounded as if it came off the top of his head." The scene captured Mercer's image of himself as the genteel Savannah boy, conversant in the vernacular and musical idioms of blacks, creating brilliant lyrics without any apparent effort.

The friend always marveled at Mercer's ability to pick up a phrase from a newspaper or magazine and turn it into a song lyric. In *Time* magazine he found one that he turned into "The Air-Minded Executive Dearly Loves to Fly." "That just knocked him out," Bach said. "He would just pick up everything and turn it into something entertaining."

When Mercer looked back upon this incredibly productive year in New York, he again expressed his typical disappointment with his achievements. "Outside of a few quotes in *Time* or *Life*, a record or two with Goodman, they ended as they had begun, pleasantly enough but without their major ambitions fulfilled." Whatever will-o'-the-wisp of success he hungered for had eluded him once more, and he returned to California with that characteristically melancholy sense of failure. "The programs over, the publishing company dissolved, the directorship of ASCAP vacant, I was to head back again to Los Angeles." One of his nieces saw in Mercer "that kind of melancholia" that his mother and others in the family had: "And he said to me on more than one occasion, he never felt he really got where he wanted to get."

In a more cheerful reminiscence of his big band days, Mercer reflected on all the great musicians he got to know—Woody Herman, Charlie Barnet, Louis Armstrong, Fats Waller, and many others—and how much he loved their artistic integrity, their independent lifestyle, and their humor. "I also felt, in a way, that *they* felt I was talking for them. I was the lyric writer who dug them and said the things (not completely, of course) they were too inarticulate to say." Perhaps this sort of achievement, giving voice to the great jazz musicians of the big band era, provided more of the satisfaction he craved than seeing his songs go to number one on *Your Hit Parade*.

During Mercer's year in New York, the world moved closer to war. Hitler invaded Czechoslovakia, Italy invaded Albania, and the Spanish Republic collapsed. When Germany invaded Poland on September 1, 1939, Great Britain and France declared war. One of Mercer's most powerful memories was of the frightened but determined faces of young American boys as Hitler moved the world to war. "I had seen examples of the fear he aroused in the young men in England, and now any thinking young man in America could feel the German juggernaut rolling, and judging from our past political leadership, knew that we'd be drawn into it despite many protestations and promises, including the President's, to the contrary."

As war clouds gathered and Mercer passed his thirtieth birthday, he might have felt the need to establish more stability and continuity in his life. In the summer of 1940, Ginger and Johnny Mercer took the train to Savannah and on that visit adopted an eleven-month-old girl, Norma Claire Barnes, who had been born on May 12, 1939. They named her Amanda. "Amanda was just beautiful when she was a baby," niece Joyce Pelphrey recalled. "She just had that, you know, white hair and big blue eyes and she just looked like a little angel. But she wasn't; she was a little devil."

The niece also said that afterward there was a scandal surrounding this and other adoptions, which had been arranged by Paul Whiteman's wife, who had adopted a child from a woman in Georgia and arranged for other Hollywood couples to adopt children through the same woman. But the woman, it was found, "would get babies by illegal means and then charge these people in Hollywood a lot of money." The niece described Amanda's efforts in later life to locate her birth parents. "We found out who the mother was, and we found out that she had been arrested for some minor thing—but then the trail stops—and what we think is maybe she was pregnant with Amanda—I mean, there's nothing about her being convicted or being let out or anything else, and this woman that was running this illegal adoption thing had connections with the sheriff and everything. So what we're thinking is maybe—she was in jail, she was pregnant, and the woman said, 'Give me your baby, and I'll get you out of jail.'"

Whatever circumstances later came to light, Mercer clearly adored his adopted daughter, and having her seems to have fulfilled one of the longings of his heart. He relished fatherhood so much that within a year he would write a paean to his daughter, "Mandy Is Two":

You ought to see her eyes of cornflower blue;
They really look as if they actually knew
That she's a big girl now. . . .
You ought to see how many things she can do,
She knows her alphabet and ties her own shoe,
And no one showed her how.

At the end of "Mandy Is Two," he inserted a line that suggests that Ginger shared the same love for their daughter—"Mommy is blue because her little girl is going on three"—evoking the image of a happy family of three, settling back down in southern California despite the threat of worldwide war.

But Pelphrey also noted that just before they adopted Amanda, Johnny had wrecked their car. In the accident, Ginger's jaw was broken on each side. When it healed, her face was distorted in a way that made it strangely resemble that of her adopted daughter. The incident was a grim foreshadowing of family ravages to come.

Eight

Blues in the Night: 1940–1941

You notice I haven't mentioned Malaise du Coeur, a wounded psyche nor any sadness of the spirit, but I've had them. You may find traces of them in my songs, however, and I hope it's the only place you do. I'm a private person.

When Johnny Mercer returned to California, he was thirty years old and could look back on a series of accomplishments that would have gratified a man twice his age. Although his dream of becoming an actor had not come true and he could only envy the stardom of Bing Crosby, he had found substantial success as a songwriter and singer in an era when it was rare for someone to excel in both arts. While he had not yet written a full score for an enduring film or stage musical, he had produced individual hit songs for nearly ten years. Yet among those hits, there was not a single song that really plumbed emotional depths. "Day In—Day Out" had passionate sensuality; "Too Marvelous for Words" was witty and sophisticated; "I Thought About You" was winsomely plangent. But most of his other songs—"Jeepers Creepers," "Goody, Goody," "You Must Have Been a Beautiful Baby"—had a jovial pixiness that characterized Mercer himself when he was not drinking. In thirty years, he had encountered frustration and disappointment but no pain that forced him to dig deeply into his emotional life. He had lost the first girl he loved in Savannah, had pursued and won Ginger with intense ardor, and had seen his father suffer a business failure. While these were not scars to be jested at, they were not the kind of wounds that tear a man's life apart. The next two years would bring him an ample, indeed a lifetime, supply of pain to pour into his lyrics.

Back in Hollywood, his string of recent hits made him a sought-after collaborator, and rather than look for another studio contract, which would make him write songs for whatever picture the studio assigned him to, he now enjoyed the luxury of accepting or turning down offers to write lyrics for individual motion pictures. In the Hollywood caste system, this was far preferable to being tied to a single studio, and it enabled Mercer to collaborate with some of the great composers he had admired since childhood. His first such collaborator in 1940 was Jimmy McHugh, who had written such Jazz Age hits as "I Can't Give You Anything but Love" and "On the Sunny Side of the Street" with the young lyricist Dorothy Fields. Early in the depression, Fields and McHugh had made the trek to Hollywood, where they had further success with such songs as "Don't Blame Me" and "I'm in the Mood for Love," but Fields was tapped to write with Jerome Kern for Astaire-Rogers films, and McHugh moved on from assignment to assignment with a variety of lyricists.

Mercer found Jimmy McHugh a difficult collaborator. In contrast to Mercer's quiet, intense, but still laid-back style, McHugh was a New York dynamo. He'd take anything a lyricist said and begin improvising melodies. "I'd come into the office at the studio and maybe I'd say, 'Mornin' Jim, how's it goin'?' and he'd start tinkling away on the treble, echoing 'Mornin' Jim, how's it going' to a dozen strains until I thought I'd go daffy. There was no way to break the spell either, or if you said, 'I guess I'll go to the men's room,' he'd switch to *that* theme and we'd be going to the men's room for half an hour in waltz time, rhumba, and fox trot." They wrote songs for RKO's *You'll Find Out* and Paramount's *You're the One*, and, while neither film was successful, the former produced a hit in "I'd Know You Anywhere," which garnered Mercer his second Oscar nomination for Best Song in 1941.

A much more agreeable collaborator was Walter Donaldson, who with lyricist Gus Kahn had written some of the greatest hits Johnny Mercer had grown up listening to as a teenager in the 1920s—"Carolina in the Morning," "My Buddy," "Makin' Whoopee," "Love Me or Leave Me," and "Yes, Sir, That's My Baby." After coming to Hollywood soon after the birth of talkies, however, Donaldson and Kahn seldom worked together, and neither had the extraordinary success they had enjoyed together in the Jazz Age. Before Gus Kahn died in 1941, he told Mercer he would trade all of the hits in his own catalog for the ones Mercer was destined to produce.

Mercer was thrilled to work with Donaldson, and his clever vernacular lyrics to two of Donaldson's melodies helped lift the older composer near the end of his career. "On Behalf of the Visiting Firemen," one of Mercer's novelty songs, conjured up a big-city bar as a group of conventioneers stroll in for a "smile," as a drink was slangily called then:

On behalf of the visiting firemen from Kansas City,
Let's have a "smile" on me,

On behalf of the gentlemen slicked up and lookin' pretty,
Let's make it two or three.

"Mister Meadowlark" was another "hep-cat" bird song, in which a city slicker asks the meadowlark to teach him to whistle so that he can compete for a country gal who's "got a country guy who whistles":

Mister Meadowlark,
If you should cop a gander
When I'm kissin' my chick,
Needless to remark,
I hope you'll have the decency to exit, but quick!

The two songs were in the same hipster vein as "Mr. Crosby and Mr. Mercer" and "Bob White," so Mercer and Bing Crosby recorded them in the spring of 1940. "Bing and Johnny," as a friend noted, "relished such tough-guy racetrack lingo mixed with jazz."

These songs with such old masters as Jimmy McHugh and Walter Donaldson were successful but still did not move Johnny Mercer into deeper emotional waters. That movement began with the death of his father on November 14, 1940. Mercer's mother called Johnny several days before to tell him his father was very sick and that he needed to come back to Savannah. Mercer wanted to board the train, but Ginger told him that would take too long; he'd have to fly. The very thought of flying terrified Mercer. A transcontinental flight in 1940 was a particularly harrowing experience—a hop, skip, and jump series of landings and refuelings—but for his father's sake Johnny boarded the plane, flew from Los Angeles to Yuma, Arizona, then to Nashville, and on to Jacksonville, Florida. He had always suffered from sinus problems, and the uneven air pressure in the cabin brought on a sinus attack that lasted for weeks. He landed at Jacksonville and boarded the train to Savannah, where his brother-in-law met him to tell him his father had died in the night.

The late arrival deepened Mercer's grief for a father whose diminutive stature made him seem like a child who needed to be protected by his sons; Mercer recalled him as "small but wonderful, with beautiful manners, a deep regard for all people, and a lovely sense of humor." George Mercer's death was all the more poignant because it was in large part brought on by his noble decision to liquidate his failed company rather than declare bankruptcy. "That had broken him," Mercer reflected, "and left him a nervous, harassed man, distraught at the thought of the money lost by widows and friends who had put their faith in his company. No good to tell him that his failure was due to the failure of other companies *he* had trusted in. He was never the same after that, and the ready laugh, the self-confidence, the erect bearing just seemed to disappear. He had gotten progressively older and weaker, and nothing my darling mother did could stop the inexorable process of time."

At the funeral, Johnny Mercer was overwhelmed with grief. In an age when men seldom cried at all and almost never in public, he gave vent to his loss with an abandon that would overtake him, privately, many more times during the rest of his life. "I never cried like that in public before or since. I wasn't ashamed of it, it was the most natural, spontaneous thing imaginable. I simply let go and all the feelings I had held in and not been able to reveal all those years were released that afternoon." His last meeting with his father had been the year before, when George Mercer traveled north to visit Johnny when he was working in New York. The senior Mercer was so impressed with his son that he dictated a memo when he got back to his office in Savannah. He noted that during the visit "in September, 1939 I had some long confidential and wonderful talks with him. I said to him, 'John, tell me how it is that a boy of your age can write over 500 songs and does not know music and cannot play an instrument. How do you account for it?' After pondering and thinking for a few minutes, John turned to me and said, 'Pop, to tell you the truth I simply get to thinking over the song, pondering over it in my mind and all of a sudden, I get in tune with the Infinite.'" What Johnny said might have been meant as flippant modesty, but George Mercer took his son's comment seriously and solemnly: "I believe that he then stated the real truth about his inspiration for his song writing. It comes from the Infinite and very high sources. That is why I believe that John's talent is from above and that he is a musical genius." He signed the letter, "Respectfully, his father, G. A. Mercer, Age 72." A son could scarcely ask for a fuller blessing.

When Johnny Mercer returned to California, he was emotionally vulnerable and about to undergo an even more convulsive experience. Judy Garland, after years of nothing to do at Metro-Goldwyn-Mayer but play bit roles or the jazzy counterpart to the elegant and operatic Deanna Durbin, had at last found stardom in *The Wizard of Oz* in 1939. But what MGM wanted for Garland was *child* stardom, putting her into movies with Mickey Rooney, while Garland wanted to play the womanly parts her close friend Lana Turner was being given. She rebelled against both the studio and her oppressive mother, and, while she dated other child stars such as Jackie Cooper, she was really interested in older men.

At eighteen, she developed a crush on bandleader Artie Shaw, who at twenty-eight had already had two failed marriages. Shaw refused to take advantage of Garland, then broke her heart when he whisked Lana Turner off to a whirlwind marriage. Garland saw it as a betrayal by both her friend and the man she loved, and felt even more keenly what Hollywood had always made her feel—short, stubby, and plain—or as Louis B. Mayer cruelly referred to her, "the fat hunchback." On the rebound, her friend Phil Silvers recalled, Judy "went off to Palm Springs with a writer. They had adjoining bungalows. On the way to the dining room, she stopped off for him, and found him kissing a man. I tried to persuade Judy it was not *her* fault. Not some fatal defect in her appearance or womanhood. She could never win that writer away from his male love. No woman could. Yet she clung to this rejection as if it were a senior prom corsage."

After that disastrous fling and still on the rebound from her crush on Shaw, Garland started seeing one of his friends, a twenty-nine-year-old composer named David Rose. It was clear to friends that her interest in Rose was not romantic or even sexual but a way for her to get out from her mother's dominance and gain some independence through marriage. Rose was cultured and affable, and despite opposition from Garland's mother, they became engaged.

At that point, Johnny Mercer entered Garland's life. They had met at a party two years before at Bob and Dolores Hope's. Hope, who had sung in Broadway shows before coming to Hollywood, had planned to sing a duet with Garland called "Friendship," from Cole Porter's 1939 hit show *DuBarry Was a Lady*. It was one of Porter's witty catalog songs, in which two friends exchange vows of friendship, one offering, "If you ever catch on fire, send a wire" and the other countering, "If you ever lose your teeth when you're out to dine, borrow mine." But at the last moment, Hope suggested Garland do the song with Mercer, and they took to each other instantly. Garland, wearing a red dress, was at her dynamic best, having just come off her extraordinary performance in *The Wizard of Oz*, for which she'd won a special Oscar for a juvenile performer (though the fact that she wasn't allowed to compete for the Oscar for Best Actress fueled Garland's bitterness that Hollywood would not let her grow up). Mercer told her that he had seen her in vaudeville, as one of the Gumm Sisters, when she was only seven years old but performed, in his words, "like a little electrical unit." She, in turn, had long been a fan of his lyrics; two of her favorite songs were his "Jamboree Jones" and "Bob White." They sang so well together on "Friendship" that David Rose suggested they record it, which they did, on Decca, in 1940.

Things turned more passionate at another party, one that Garland threw at her home on June 2, 1941, to celebrate, of all things, her official engagement to David Rose. Johnny and Ginger Mercer were among the more than six hundred guests, and one, the wife of one of Johnny's boyhood friends from Savannah, recalled that Mercer cut in on David Rose as he was dancing with Judy. Pouring on the southern charm, he again told her about his enthusiastic response to seeing her perform as a child in vaudeville.

" 'I spotted you then. I just thought you were so wonderful.'

" 'You're telling me this and you're Johnny Mercer,' " Judy flirted back. " 'I think you're so wonderful.' "

Mercer then turned the heat up: " 'You know, I've developed a crush on you, little girl, and I thought you were so adorable.' "

At which Garland stoked the flames by adding, " 'But I've been falling in love with you for years.'

"And they're dancing closer and closer and it's like what are we going to do," the friend recalled. She said that Garland, always trying to escape her mother Ethel's watchful eye, told Mercer to "come to lunch" the next day in her dressing room at the studio. "They would send out for lunch." There they first made love.

These lunchtime trysts had Mercer head over heels: "He was wandering around like a zombie." At dinner at his house, he was so entranced that another friend had to break through his romantic mist by saying, "Johnny, I'm speaking to you." "He was really ga-ga. . . . Oh, she was too—it was just like young love."

A recent biography of Judy Garland quotes Mickey Rooney as saying that in the spring of 1941, "She was at last in love with someone who loved her." But the question has always been who was this person. "Who this person was remains a mystery. . . . But it was not Rose." At thirty-one, Johnny Mercer was the older, talented, accomplished man who adored Judy Garland as Artie Shaw had not. Mercer, while a performer, was also a *writer*. Garland wrote poems herself and must have seen in Johnny Mercer an accomplished writer and intellectual who could give her the self-confidence she so desperately craved.

What Mercer would have loved in her was what he loved more than anything. As a friend recalled, listing the things his friendship with Johnny Mercer had taught him, the culminating lesson was "a deep, deep respect for the honesty and integrity of talent." In that respect, Mercer would have loved what was most truly at the center of Judy Garland—not the svelte sex goddess she wanted to be but the gifted artist that friends such as Phil Silvers, Mickey Rooney, and Gene Kelly, who could not bring themselves to love her romantically, adored in her.

Yet the sexual element was critical to the relationship. Garland was already known in Hollywood for "hot sex," a 1940s euphemism for fellatio. It might have been another way for her to prove that she was not a child but an experienced woman of the world, but it inflamed men to whom she made love, and Mercer would have been no exception. While his era of songwriting forbade any explicit sexual themes, his intoxication with sex is reflected in poems he wrote but never published, discovered among his papers after his death. Some of these may reflect his affair with Garland but could also be merely the reminiscence of a fling with a nameless chorine from one of his shows:

Watching you before the mirrors
How sinuous you are
How thrilling

Your lips and body reaching for mine
As mine strains toward yours.

How subtly they interweave
I intertwine
Until—all resistance gone—
They interlock
And melt into each other.

Oh, beautiful flowing hair
And aching flesh
Moving together
Until—all motion stopped
All passion spent
We lie—and smile at the mirror

To the side of the manuscript he inserted an additional line that underscores the physical intensity of their passion: "You didn't notice the bruise on your knee until the next day . . ."

Another poem recalls lovemaking in a swimming pool:

My ear still rings
From your anguished cry
As I held you in the water

The waves lapped against the poolside
From our movements . . .
The long beautiful afternoon was over
We were tired from our lovemaking
Full of lassitude and peace . . .

The closing suggests the kind of impulsive oral sex that Garland, later lovers confirmed, would perform upon them:

As if we didn't want the night to end
All of a sudden in the car
You held me

We are really insane you said
And made love to me

Until the full moon
Crossed halfway across the sky.

There is no date on these poems, but they are written on stationery with the address of the house in Los Angeles where Mercer lived the last fifteen years of his life. Whether or not they record his affair with Garland, they certainly testify to Mercer's love of sex, the only thing he enjoyed more than music.

But Garland was about to be married, and Mercer and Ginger had recently adopted a little girl. Ginger was as distraught over the affair as Johnny was enthralled by it. "What's going on?" she would wail helplessly to friends. "What's going on?" Suddenly, a man she had been able to control since their courting days was moving beyond her subtle force field. Now that her marriage had finally served as her entrée to the world of show-business high society, it would have been devastating to her to no longer be Mrs. Johnny Mercer.

Finally, a friend from Savannah took a cab out to the MGM studio, knocked on Judy Garland's dressing-room door, and told Judy the affair had to stop. "This poor guy is punch-drunk," she said, and Judy replied, "You're right. This has got to stop." Garland, who had fought so long and so hard to gain recognition in Hollywood, could have lost everything if rumors had spread that the dewy star of *The Wizard of Oz* was having an affair with an older, married man. Garland agreed to put an end to it.

But she did it in a cowardly way, never telling Johnny. Meanwhile, Mercer, a man who had been brought up to believe "You marry once and that's what the Bible says and you're stuck with it," a man clearly enthralled by his baby daughter, summoned up the courage to tell Ginger he wanted a divorce. On a Sunday evening, as he was breaking the news to her, Walter Winchell's voice crackled over the airwaves to announce that Judy Garland had just eloped and married David Rose in Las Vegas. If the announcement took the life's breath out of Johnny Mercer, it merely infuriated Louis B. Mayer, who had planned a mammoth publicity-grabbing wedding for his child star.

The aborted affair left all three—Judy, Johnny, and Ginger—rawly empty. Garland would divorce Rose four years later in 1945, then go on to marriages and affairs with numerous Hollywood figures, from Tyrone Power and Yul Brynner to Vincente Minnelli and Joseph Mankiewicz. The affair between Garland and Mercer would flare up again from time to time, but Mercer would grimly stay married, even adopt another child, John Jefferson, born on April 5, 1947. Yet he would grow increasingly bitter toward Ginger, the virulence he displayed when he was drinking turning more and more on her. At parties, he would make up insulting lyrics about her, lash out at her drunkenly, curse at her, and cruelly ask, "Why do you have to be always hanging around?" "He would be intoxicated and be terrible to her," a friend recalled. "He was so much more deft with language and so much more everything. He was entertaining and interesting and she would kind of laugh. And the drunker he'd get, the rougher he'd get, and she would in desperation start drinking. 'Yeah,' she figured, 'he's drinking, I might as well drink.'"

At this critical juncture in Johnny Mercer's life, tied to Ginger yet still reeling from his love affair with Garland, he was teamed with composer Harold Arlen, the most perfectly matched collaborator of his career. Despite the success Arlen had had with lyricist Yip Harburg on the score for *The Wizard of Oz*, the two men worked together on only one other film, the Marx Brothers' *At the Races*. "Harold went off with Johnny Mercer on some other films," Harburg recalled. "He felt he needed a change and so did I." But there was probably more to the breakup; studios fretted about Harburg's strong socialist views, first expressed in "Brother, Can You Spare a Dime?" and Arlen found him a trying collaborator. Mercer was a more easygoing partner, and there was a resonance between the two men that came from their deep devotion to blues and jazz. Arlen's father, a cantor, had immigrated to the United States through New Orleans and had lived for a while in the South. He was intrigued by black music, which he found closely related to Jewish cantorial traditions: when his son played him a recording by Louis Armstrong, the senior Arlen listened to an Armstrong riff and asked, "Where did *he* get it?" Moreover, Harold Arlen was a jazz vocalist, and his working with a fellow singer in Johnny Mercer gave a unique seamlessness to their collaborations. Finally, Arlen also felt trapped in an unhappy marriage, and the blend of his plaintive melodies and Mercer's melancholy words registered their mutual misery.

Although it is highly speculative to connect the writing of popular songs to the personal lives of their creators, there is a sudden and poignant sadness that appears in Mercer's songs with Arlen at this time. In previous lyrics, written with other composers, there had been passion, but with the songs he wrote with Arlen a completely new depth of sorrow suddenly registers itself that can only reflect his affair with Judy Garland. One of the first songs they wrote together was a song for the movie *Hot Nocturne*, in which a black man in prison hears a distant train whistle and sings a blues lament.

"I went home and thought about it for two days," Arlen said. "After all, anybody can write a blues song. The hard thing to do is to write one that doesn't sound like every other blues song." As the song developed, it stretched to fifty-two bars—much longer and more complex than the standard Tin Pan Alley structure of thirty-two bars divided into four eight-bar sections. Mercer found the meandering melody difficult to set, and the lyric he came up with began with the sentimental phrase "I'm heavy in my heart, I'm heavy in my heart." One measure of the compatibility between Arlen and Mercer is that Mercer accepted Arlen's suggestions for revisions in the lyric— something he seldom did with other collaborators. When Arlen saw that maudlin opening line, he felt it did nothing to bring out the emotional power of his music, but when he read through the rest of Mercer's lyric, he fastened on the hard-nosed expression of heartache in the section that began "My mama done tol' me," and tactfully suggested that Mercer move that to the beginning. When he did, "Blues in the Night" took off in a soaring, vernacular wail:

> My mama done tol' me
> When I was in knee pants,
> My mama done tol' me—"Son!
> A woman'll sweet talk
> And give ya the big eye,
> But when that sweet talkin's done,
> A woman's a two-face,
> A worrisome thing who'll leave ya t'sing
> The blues in the night."

Despite their harmony, Arlen and Mercer, like all collaborators, had disagreements. Arlen so liked the phrase "My mama done tol' me" that he thought it should be the title of the song, but Mercer insisted on retaining "Blues in the Night." So they took the matter to Irving Berlin. Berlin listened to them play the song and, with his practiced ear at placing a title phrase so that it figured prominently in a lyric, sided with Mercer. Once the studio heard the song, however, it retitled the movie *Blues in the Night*. The song was an enormous hit and was recorded by numerous artists, including Garland herself, who sang the "female" lyric Mercer wrote, which began "My Momma done tol' me when I was in pigtails . . ." But to Mercer, with his cavalier deprecation, "Blues in the Night" was "just another southern song," by which he probably meant a song in a black vernacular.

Another song from the same movie suggests that Mercer could regard the breakup of his affair with Garland with a more stoical eye. "This Time the Dream's on Me" accepts the end of an affair with a rueful shrug but takes solace in the admittedly imaginary prospect of a future reunion:

> Somewhere, some day, we'll be close together,
> Wait and see,
> Oh, by the way, this time the dream's on me.

Taking a drinker's phrase—"This time the drink's on me"—Mercer imbues it with emotional depth by substituting "dream" for "drink" and hints at the pain beneath the comforting but impossible dream of a future reunion:

> You'll take my hand
> And you'll look at me adoringly.

I'll understand.
This time the dream's on me.

The rest of the lyric suggests the pleasure Mercer, bred for kindness and generosity, must have felt at being able to comfort the distraught Garland as she struggled to realize her ambitions for stardom against the frustrations imposed by Hollywood studios:

It would be fun,
To be certain that I'm the one,
To know that I at least
Supply the shoulder you cry on
To see you through
Till you're everything you want to be—
It can't be true—
But this time the dream's on me.

The lyric that cuts closest to the bone of Mercer's loss of Garland, however, is "One for My Baby," which he and Arlen wrote in 1943. It is one of the most remarkable of popular song lyrics, conjuring up a time, a place, and a one-act dramatic monologue:

It's quarter to three,
There's no one in the place except you and me,
So set 'em up, Joe,
I've got a little story you oughta know.
We're drinking, my friend,
To the end of a brief episode.
Make it one for my baby and one more for the road.

If Mercer's pain over the affair with Garland was the inspiration for these lines, that pain is made all the more poignant by the way the singer never reveals the story of his lost love:

Could tell you a lot,
But you've got to be true to your code,
Make it one for my baby and one more for the road.

Mercer had intuitively learned Hemingway's secret of the "iceberg" effect, leaving the bulk of the emotion "below the surface" so that the small portion that did appear suggested enormous depths of feeling. Arlen called "One for My Baby" another of his "tapeworms"—songwriter slang for any song that exceeded the standard length of thirty-two bars. "Johnny took it and wrote it exactly the way it fell. Not only is it long—forty-eight bars—but it also changes key. Johnny made it work."

"Our working habits were strange," Arlen recalled. "After we got a script and the spots for the songs were blocked out, we'd get together for an hour or so every day. While Johnny made himself comfortable on the couch, I'd play the tunes for him. He has a wonderfully retentive memory. After I would finish playing the songs, he'd just go away without a comment. I wouldn't hear from him for a couple of weeks, then he'd come around with the completed lyrics." Arlen was amazed that Mercer listened to an unusually long and complexly structured melody only *once* before he left to work on the lyric.

What Mercer came back with was "That Old Black Magic," which friends of both Garland and Mercer said was written about their affair:

> That old black magic has me in its spell,
> That old black magic that you weave so well.
> Those icy fingers up and down my spine.
> That same old witchcraft when your eyes meet mine.

Mercer took the idea for a lyric about black magic from a line in Cole Porter's "You Do Something to Me," in which the singer elegantly and archly pleads, "Do do that voodoo that you do so well." It struck him that a whole song could be crafted around the idea of voodoo and love, and with that theme he opened all his emotional stops:

> I hear your name and I'm aflame,
> Aflame with such a burning desire
> That only your kiss can put out the fire.
> For you're the lover I have waited for,
> The mate that fate had me created for,
> And ev'ry time your lips meet mine,
> Darling, down and down I go,
> 'Round and 'round I go in a spin,
> Loving the spin I'm in
> Under that old black magic called love.

With the sensuous imagery of burning lips and icy fingers, the metaphors of spinning leaves and plunging depths ("And then that elevator starts its ride"), Mercer came as close as a lyricist of his era could to writing about the raptures of sexual intercourse.

Judy Garland, in effect, had become Johnny Mercer's muse, as Maud Gonne had been for William Butler Yeats, and he loved the "pilgrim soul" in her with a passion that lifted—and plunged—him to new levels of lyrical rapture and anguish. Without her, his lyrics might be remembered today as clever, vernacular, jazzy evocations of the swing era. Because of his love affair with Judy Garland, and his timely collaboration with Harold Arlen, the lyrics of Johnny Mercer endure as timeless standards that register romantic agony as poignantly as any songs in the history of American popular music.

It is one of those wonderful accidents of history that Harold Arlen collaborated with Mercer at the most critical point in the lyricist's emotional life. While they would work together, off and on, for many years, nothing would equal the songs they created in the early 1940s, when Johnny Mercer was devastated by the loss of the love of Judy Garland. Mercer admired Arlen as a sweet man—he compared him to a violin—and wondered how such a gentle soul could survive in the brutal music business. According to Mercer, he and Arlen never had disagreements, "only an occasional difference of opinion," and he wished they had worked more together. But Mercer appalled his gentle collaborator with his drunken behavior. One night the two men were eating dinner at a restaurant in Greenwich Village when Mercer suddenly began tearing the restaurant apart, furniture and all, and hurling racial slurs at the black waiters in a fit of drunken violence. On another occasion, at a party, Mercer vehemently turned on Arlen, saying, "I don't understand your music," and threw a punch at the composer, a punch that fortunately didn't land.

Even songs Mercer wrote with other composers during these years seem to carry inflections of his love for Judy Garland. Hoagy Carmichael had come out to Hollywood and adapted to the California lifestyle with alacrity. Reunited with Mercer, Carmichael found that Mercer's snail's pace at songwriting had not changed. He gave Mercer a melody that was to be used in a musical about Bix Beiderbecke. Although the production never materialized, Mercer hung on to the music. As usual, he was stumped for a title. "I couldn't write it and I couldn't write it, and finally I saw the word 'skylark' somewhere on a billboard or in a book. . . . It wasn't from the poem. It just associated itself with that tune. And I wrote that very fast. I don't think it took me half an hour."

By the time he took the song to Carmichael, the composer had completely forgotten the music. "I had shown Johnny a couple of tunes I was quite proud of," Carmichael said. "He took them home and I didn't hear from him for six months; he is the original 'Don't call me, I'll call you' guy, in reverse. But this time *he* called and sang to me over the phone. . . . Quite some kick to sit back comfy like that at the telephone and listen."

"Skylark," which Mercer insisted did not have its origin in Shelley's great ode, nonetheless expresses Shelley's same feverish longing for love:

Won't you tell me where my love can be?
Is there a meadow in the mist,

Where someone's waiting to be kissed . . .
And in your lonely flight,
Haven't you heard the music in the night,
Wonderful music,
Faint as a "will-o'-the-wisp."
Crazy as a loon,
Sad as a gypsy serenading the moon.

The lyric expresses a yearning that ran even deeper than love, for someplace where he could find peace, fulfillment, happiness—Johnny Mercer's emotional equivalent of Garland's "Over the Rainbow." "His heart," as a niece said, "didn't have a home."

Mercer gave voice to his longing for Judy Garland in "Skylark," celebrated her sensuality in "That Old Black Magic," and stoically bemoaned her loss in "One for My Baby," but it was to a simpler melody by Victor Schertzinger, "I Remember You," that he wrote most openly about his love for her. "I wrote it for Judy Garland," he told a Savannah friend. "I always had such a crush on Judy Garland I couldn't think straight, so I wrote this song."

I remember you,
You're the one who made my dreams come true,
A few kisses ago.

The lyric is a naked expression of emotion such as Irving Berlin was able to capture in his greatest songs. The words are almost all monosyllables, the rhymes utterly simple, and the sentiment unadorned with wit or sophistication:

When my life is through
And the angels ask me to recall
The thrill of them all,
I will tell them I remember you.

Only the quiet inner rhymes—"thrill" and "will," few," "you," "to," and "through"—underscore the understated pledge of absolute adoration. Mercer, it seems, had finally found—and lost—what he had been seeking in his lonely flight.

"I Remember You" was so clearly about his affair with Judy Garland that it was omitted from *Our Huckleberry Friend*, a collection of his lyrics edited by Ginger Mercer with Bob Bach, a family friend, in 1982. Although the collection contained all of his hits and many of his lesser-known lyrics, "I Remember You," which was made popular in recordings by Harry James's and Jimmy Dorsey's orchestras, doesn't appear. When Mercer's life was indeed through, and friends and family were planning his funeral in the summer of 1976, someone not in the know innocently suggested that the words "I Remember You" be inscribed on Mercer's tombstone. Ginger flew into a rage. In her later years, when she made a gift of Mercer's papers and established the Johnny and Ginger Mercer Archive at Georgia State University in Atlanta, the library staff was warned never to mention the name of Judy Garland in her presence. The song had the last word, however; when Ginger Mercer died in 1994, the program for her memorial service had her picture on its cover with the inscription, chosen by someone, again, not in the know, "I Remember You."

Nine

Ac-cent-tchu-ate the Positive:
1941–1944

*Needless to say, it was a gratifying feeling to know you were doing your duty,
especially out of the shooting zone, and I was proud I could bring a little cheer,
on a small scale, such as Bob Hope was doing on a large scale, to the men
wounded in the war and recuperating in California hospitals. Also the ones
doing their training in the desert and oceanside camps. I'll never forget the
faces of the colored troops the first time they heard us do "Accentuate the Positive." They must have been from the deepest part of Alabama or Mississippi,
for I don't think they had heard any white man sing just like that. They really
beamed.*

In 1941, on a Sunday morning shortly before Christmas, Johnny Mercer was
listening to the gospel choir from the I Will Arise Church in Los Angeles
when he heard that the Japanese had attacked Pearl Harbor. "It had finally
happened as we had all feared. Later, we listened to President Roosevelt, with
his marvelous, paternal delivery, declaring it 'a date that will live in infamy.'"
Within the week, he felt the onset of war even more intensely as he and Ginger had to drive home from a friend's house after the announcement of the
first blackout. "I can remember really 'feeling' our way home in the dark
(only about five blocks, all down hill) in our car with all the lights turned off.
The first bomb scare!"

Although his great-grandfather had been a general who led the First Georgia Volunteers, and his grandfather had been a colonel with Savannah's

Republican Blues in the Civil War, Johnny Mercer, with a newly adopted daughter, wanted to avoid the draft, for which, at the age of thirty-two, he was still eligible. Nevertheless, he wanted to do some service for his country. On a trip east in the frantic weeks after Pearl Harbor, he went to Washington to see Major Anatole Litvak, who in civilian life had directed the movie *Blues in the Night*. Litvak sent Mercer to a colonel in charge of strategic services, but the colonel turned out to be more interested in getting information from Mercer about Litvak as a security risk. Back in California, he got in touch with another army colonel, Tom Lewis, the husband of movie star Loretta Young, who told Mercer that the army wanted him to stay put in Los Angeles and entertain at army camps and naval bases. Boys from around the country were being rushed to California to train for warfare in the Pacific, so Mercer and other performers would do shows at Camp Roberts, Point Hueneme, Fort MacArthur, Camp Pendleton, and other military bases. They were also sent out to virtually every military hospital in California, including Palm Springs, where they entertained amputees and mentally ill patients at the El Mirador Hotel, which had been converted into a hospital. Mercer was so taken with the desert area that after the war he bought a luxurious home in Palm Springs, replete with swimming pool, tennis courts, and a mountain at the edge of his backyard.

In addition to entertaining troops in California, Mercer, along with Mel Tormé, Martha Raye, and other Hollywood stars, did broadcasts for such Armed Forces Radio Services shows as *G.I. Journal* and *Command Performance*. Mercer felt his contribution wasn't as noteworthy as Bob Hope's battlefield tours or Irving Berlin's all-soldier revue, *This Is the Army*, but it was a way for John Herndon Mercer, descendant of General Hugh Mercer, to contribute to his country's cause.

As the war drew on, Mercer's contribution would expand to writing songs that, directly or indirectly, expressed the feelings of American servicemen and their families back home. In response to a request from one soldier, he wrote a theme song for *G.I. Journal*, which became enormously popular on jukeboxes at military bases. He got the idea while waiting at the traffic light at the corner of Sunset and Vine as he noticed all the servicemen in uniform at that busy intersection. Then "he sat down at his typewriter," a friend recalled, "and dashed the whole thing off in a couple of minutes."

With his ability to steep himself in any regional argot, Mercer laced the lyric with clever twists of army terminology:

If you're a PVT your duty
Is to salute the L.I.E.U.T.;
But if you brush the L.I.E.U.T.,
The M.P. makes you K.P. on the Q.T.

Just as Irving Berlin had captured the ordinary soldier's griping perspective
on army life in World War I with "Oh! How I Hate to Get Up in the Morning," Mercer's "G.I. Jive" registered the grumbling acquiescence of American
boys to military routine:

> This is the G.I. Jive,
> Man alive,
> It starts with the bugler
> Blowin' reveille over your head
> When you arrive.

In addition to "G.I. Jive," he wrote songs about the wartime rigors of the
home front for such films as *Riding High* and *Star Spangled Rhythm*. When he
was a child during World War I, he recalled, "I didn't like the serious songs,"
but he loved the comic numbers about the war, such as "How Ya Gonna Keep
'Em Down on the Farm? (After They've Seen Paree)." It was in that satirical
spirit that he wrote songs from the tough-minded, female perspective of
Rosie the Riveter: "He Loved Me Till the All-Clear Came," "I'm Doing It
for Defense" ("If you think you're Cary Grant, brother, relax / —You're just
a rebate on my income tax"), and "On the Swing Shift":

> There among the nuts and bolts
> Plus a hundred thousand volts
> Shining from her eyes.
> She's a beautiful bomber!

Just as George M. Cohan and Irving Berlin had been America's troubadours
in World War I, Johnny Mercer, along with Berlin again, assumed the same
role in World War II. His songs and his voice on the radio captured the
nation's ear as well as that of servicemen abroad. As grim as the war was, Mercer took it and made it sing. One soldier stationed in England said that "the
only thing that made getting up at 8:00 in the morning on Tuesday" bearable
was hearing Johnny Mercer on *Swing Time*.

It might have been another soldier's letter, saying of a broadcast "I wish I
had a recording of that," that channeled Mercer's creative energy into an
unusual outlet. "I used to ask myself," Mercer recalled, "what talented people
did between picture and radio jobs. I thought maybe I could organize them
into some sort of co-operative and start a radio program." *The Angelinos*, he
thought, could be a program that featured Martha Tilton, who had left
Benny Goodman's band; Jo Stafford, who had left Tommy Dorsey's orchestra; and other performers who had found their way to the West Coast but
now, because of the war, were out of work. Mercer's benevolent impulse to

help such performers took a different form when he paid a visit to Music City, a large record store at Sunset and Vine owned by Glenn Wallichs. Mercer called Wallichs, who had started out as a radio repairman, an "electrical genius." Ginger had hired him to install a radio in Mercer's car as a birthday present. So impressed were the Mercers with his technical skill, they had him repair every radio in their home. In that era of radios and record players, people who could repair electronic equipment were prized as "Mr. Wizards."

By the time they met again, Wallichs had established Music City. "Because he had a liking for electronic things," said Michael Goldsen, who ran one of Mercer's publishing firms, "he decided it would be a good idea to have a little booth where he could record people." When Mercer dropped by to make some demo recordings in Wallichs's studio, the two men talked, and their conversation turned to putting out records. "This was during the war," Goldsen said. "There were no major record companies out here. All the companies were back East. There was Decca; there was RCA; and there was Columbia . . . and there was kind of a little jealousy because there was no record company out in California of note." Wallichs, the businessman, thought that the distribution tactics of the major record companies were outdated; Mercer, the artist, complained that "there were too many poor arrangements . . . technically irregular recordings, and general mishandling of talent in the business." It was a perfect union of business and art, but what Wallichs and Mercer lacked was money.

Johnny sought out Buddy DeSylva, who had produced several Shirley Temple musicals as well as such successful Broadway shows as Cole Porter's *DuBarry Was a Lady* and *Panama Hattie*. By 1941, DeSylva was head of production at Paramount, so Mercer asked if he thought Paramount would be willing to back a West Coast recording company. DeSylva said he didn't know whether Paramount would be interested, but he himself was and told Johnny to bring Glenn Wallichs to lunch. After listening to the two men pitch their project, DeSylva offered to back it and asked them how much money they needed. They asked for twenty thousand dollars, but DeSylva told them they'd need more than that and put up twenty-five thousand. "So Buddy came in," Goldsen said. "He put up the munificent fund of $25,000 to start the darn company."

Although it was initially known as "Liberty Records," Ginger, after hearing Johnny describe his aspiration to create a recording company that would be the very top in terms of its songs, its artists, and the quality of its records, told him they ought to change the name to "Capitol Records." Capitol Records was officially formed on April 8, 1942. It was registered with the American Federation of Musicians, which, led by James Petrillo, was planning a strike. The union was concerned that radio stations were increasingly relying on recorded music rather than live musicians, and Petrillo wanted record companies to guarantee that their recordings would not be used on radio or in jukeboxes. The antiquated copyright law of 1909, which was still in effect, required that recordings be labeled "For Home Use Only," but radio had long ignored that stipulation. Capitol rushed to make several recordings before the musicians struck, and then followed the practice of other companies in making recordings on which a singer was accompanied by a vocal group. (By a strange snobbishness, singers were not considered "musicians" and thus were not members of the AFM.)

As if the impending musicians' strike were not enough of a roadblock for the new company, on April 14 the War Board put a prohibition on shellac, the primary ingredient in the manufacture of records—but also of bombshells. Shellac was a substance secreted by insects in India, and with the onset of war imports were curtailed, so the government seized 70 percent of the shellac reserves. Margaret Whiting recalls Mercer and Wallichs hearing a report that a ship had been sunk in the South Pacific. "'How awful!' I said when I heard the news. 'Yeah,' Johnny said mournfully, 'and it was carrying shellac.'"

Glenn Wallichs heard about a shellac distributor in San Diego whose son wanted to be a recording star. Wallichs signed the boy to a contract and then persuaded the father to sell Capitol his shellac reserves. After the boy cut two records his contract was not renewed, but Capitol had a temporary supply of shellac. Wallichs's long-term solution was to buy up five hundred thousand pounds of old records, at six cents a pound, and grind them up to make twenty thousand new records a week. "Because of Glenn Wallichs' ability as a business manager and a businessman," Goldsen explained, "they succeeded."

However Goldsen added that "Glenn was what they called, in a friendly way, a 'square.' You know, his taste in music was old-fashioned and whatnot. So Johnny, it was Johnny's taste that was reflected; and, luckily, they hired people who were able to continue in a creative way to augment Johnny's taste." Mercer took advantage of the fact that much of the entertainment industry was moving to the West Coast, while the recording companies were still lodged in New York. He brought in such big band figures as Jo Stafford, Peggy Lee, and Stan Kenton and persuaded his old boss Paul Whiteman to record with the new label. Initially, Mercer had asked Whiteman to help fund the company, but the bandleader feared that Capitol would go the way of other record companies that had tried to rival Decca, Columbia, and RCA Victor.

"Those two guys had guts," Margaret Whiting said of Wallichs and Mercer.

Recording sessions, which were supervised by Mercer himself, were held primarily at the Radio Records studio on Santa Monica Boulevard. The first release was recorded on June 12, 1942; Capitol #101 was Paul Whiteman's "I Found a New Baby." Although it was not a hit, the next two Capitol records were jukebox blockbusters. Capitol #102 was "Cow-Cow Boogie" by Freddie Slack's orchestra with a vocal by Ella Mae Morse; the third release was Johnny Mercer's recording of his own "Strip Polka," a funny, folksy song about

Queenie, a burlesque dancer who strips to polka music as the audience chants, "Take it off, take it off":

> Oh! She hates corny waltzes and she hates the gavotte,
> And there's one big advantage if the music's hot,
> It's a fast moving exit just in case something r-r-rips,
> So the band plays the Polka while she strips!

"Strip Polka" became a huge hit among servicemen who listened to it on some of the four hundred thousand jukeboxes that spanned the country. "The number was just sexy enough for the guys without being dirty."

The recording of "Strip Polka" typified life at Capitol as Johnny envisioned it. Several friend dropped by the studio, including Phil Silvers, who improvised some introductory patter and joined the chorus in "Take it off, take it off." But while Mercer and others were trying out other new songs, Glenn Wallichs was on the phone and asked them to keep it down. When Mercer asked whom he was talking to, Wallichs explained he was trying to set up a distributorship in Pittsburgh. "Oh, the hell with that," Mercer said, and urged him to join in the fun of hearing the new songs. But though Mercer was laid-back, his ear for good songs and good singing was impeccable. When Ella Mae Morse was, she thought, rehearsing "Cow-Cow Boogie," Mercer called out, "That's it. That's a wrap." When she tearfully protested that she could do it better, Mercer said, "No, you can't." His judgment was proved right when the record sold a million copies.

Petrillo sent his musicians out on strike on August 1, 1942, but Capitol had managed to put out enough records to survive. "Capitol had enough things in the can that they could ride it out," a former employee explained. "The initial Capitol hits were already done and that leveled the playing field some and gave Capitol an edge they might not otherwise have had 'cause nobody else had anything done. Victor didn't—nobody could record union musicians." By the end of the year, Capitol had grossed $195,000.

On paper, Mercer was the president of the company, but in fact he was the top A and R man, overseeing "artists and repertory"—*who* sang *what* songs. His musical taste favored swinging big band stylists, but later he also sought out such sophisticated jazz performers as George Shearing and Miles Davis, even though their recordings held little commercial promise. But Mercer was also alert to the shifting taste in American music, and he brought in Tennessee Ernie Ford and Tex Ritter to do country and western songs.

Mercer's greatest discovery, however, came when he went to hear the King Cole Trio performing at the 331 Club in Los Angeles. Joining the growing number of people who urged Nat King Cole to sing as well as play piano, Johnny Mercer persuaded Nat King Cole to do a recording where he sang the lyrics of a song. Cole's first vocal recording was a novelty song, "Straighten

Up and Fly Right," which he had written back in 1937. He'd taken the title phrase from one of his father's sermons, but he'd sold the song to publisher Irving Mills for fifty dollars to pay his room rent. The loopy, slangy lyric about an errant buzzard was the kind that appealed to Mercer's hipster side. "Straighten Up and Fly Right" was the first big hit at Capitol for Nat King Cole, who would quickly become the major recording star of the label until Frank Sinatra was signed in 1953.

A friend recalled Johnny Mercer as the driving force, the "chemistry" of Capitol Records: "And that's why he did it—because of the love that people had for Johnny, the singers. And they knew they would be protected by him." Singers also knew Mercer could write songs especially for them. In 1943, Billie Holiday, while still under contract with Columbia's Okeh label, did a recording at Capitol with Paul Whiteman's orchestra under the pseudonym "Lady Day." For Holiday, Mercer fitted out a bluesy melody by Jimmy Mundy and Trummy Young with a stoical, understated lament:

> I'm trav'lin' light
> Because my man has gone
> And from now on
> I'm trav'lin' light.

Mercer fretted about the match between words and music. "The words don't go the same way as the melody," he said. "I never got them straight in my mind time-wise . . . because, you know, I don't read music." Billie Holiday's sultry singing, however, made the song another huge success for the new label. With Johnny Mercer writing songs and bringing in artists such as Billie Holiday and Nat King Cole, Capitol gave the established recording companies a run for their money. In 1943, their net sales totaled $1,950,217; in 1944, $3,674,723; in 1945, $6,391,685.

While Glenn Wallichs managed the business side of Capitol, Johnny Mercer served as chief talent scout. Another singer he recruited was Margaret Whiting, the daughter of his former collaborator. When she had first sung for Mercer, coming downstairs in her pajamas and bunny slippers, her song had been "My Ideal." Harking back to that childhood audition, Mercer decided she should record "My Ideal" as her first Capitol release. Whiting protested that it had been written by her father more than a dozen years earlier for Maurice Chevalier and had been recorded by several artists since then. "I don't care," Mercer insisted. "I love this song more than any other song, and I loved your father, so damn it, you're going to sing this song. I've gone through all this material—this is the one." Even though Mercer had cavalierly ignored the record's commercial prospects, Whiting had a major hit with "My Ideal" in 1943 that launched her career.

Whiting also provides illuminating insight into how Johnny Mercer would work with singers and songs, citing her recording session for "Moonlight in Vermont." "This is where he was great," she reflected. "This is where he was brilliant." Mercer told her to talk the lyric out as if it were a poem. For the opening line, "Pennies in a stream," he told her to imagine a New England snow-covered landscape as winter turns into spring. "Now describe spring," he told her. " 'It's coming from the cold into the first day of thaw. I can see little green things.' I was beginning to see it. Johnny led me through the four seasons." Then he told her to visualize falling leaves in a New England autumn for "falling leaves of sycamore." "What I want from you is four qualities," he said, "four seasons. You've got 'pennies in a stream'—that's not literal—that's the wonderful glittering look of metal when sun hits water. . . . I want you to give me the four seasons. Crunchy cold. Then warm. The first smell of spring . . . And just think of the images."

As intensely as he concentrated on imagery, Mercer was just as aware of sound. In a lyric notorious for its paucity of rhyme, the assonance running through "Penn*ies*," "str*ea*m," and l*ea*ves" ties the two opening lines together, and Mercer urged Whiting to linger on that long *ee* sound. The assonance continues into the next section with "I*cy* finger waves," and Mercer told her to get "colder" as she sang and think of a church in the snow, the smell of burning leaves, and maple syrup. Since neither he nor Whiting had ever been to Vermont, these were stock images of New England, but Mercer, always rooted in images from the natural world, insisted she visualize them as she sang. When she got to the line "Ski tows down a mountainside," Whiting panicked, saying she had no idea what a ski tow looked like. Mercer got on the phone and called the two songwriters, composer John Blackburn and lyricist Karl Suessdorf, and asked them if he could change the line to "ski trails down a mountainside." Both men were happy to make the change. Mercer had Whiting record the song with trumpeter Billy Butterfield's orchestra because he thought Whiting's voice had the crisp clarity of a trumpet. When the record came out, it sold more than a million copies and established Whiting as one of the major singers of the era.

In October 1943, after thirteen months of the strike by the American Federation of Musicians, Capitol, along with Decca, came to terms with Petrillo, and he lifted the ban on musicians performing in their recording studios. Columbia and Victor held out for another year, giving the young company more time to grow.

At Capitol, Mercer was creating his own version of the genteel, patrician world he had known as a child in Savannah, surrounding himself with a small aristocracy of talented people. Everything under his direction was done on a personal scale, with an absolute emphasis upon quality. Arranger and conductor Billy May, who came to work at Capitol in 1943, recalled the high caliber of Capitol recordings. "They really cared to put out a quality product. And the difference between their products—I'd worked for Decca, and I'd worked for RCA Victor, and I hadn't done too much work for Columbia. But Decca's records were just awful, poor quality. You listen to some of those old Andrews Sisters records, and, jeez, they were terrible. You could hear scratching all through them. Even when they would play them on the air, which should have been a good copy, they would be scratchy and bumpy. I did a lot of work for . . . Bing Crosby back in those days. And we used to always gripe about what a poor quality it was. And Capitol took great pains to put out a quality audio product."

Before it got its own studio, Margaret Whiting explained, Capitol artists used to record at McGregor Studios "because of the phenomenal sound." But one day "everyone broke for lunch," and the owner, "feeling flush with Capitol's success and the money it had given him," had the walls repainted during the lunch break. "When the engineers came back, they put on the earphones. The afternoon session began. Suddenly, everyone stopped. The sound wasn't the same." The new coat of paint had distorted the perfect acoustics Capitol people loved, and the company moved to another studio to try to recapture the sound quality. "It reminded me," Whiting said, "of alchemists frantically trying to rediscover their formula for gold. Johnny finally found a studio in Santa Monica that suited him, but he always talked wistfully about those halcyon days at McGregor's before the walls were painted. I guess it was like the South before the Civil War."

Such attentiveness to quality may seem extreme, but Fred Grimes, a former Capitol employee, recalled how bad the sound quality was on other labels: "During the war, if you pulled one of those old shellacs out, you could hardly *hear* a Decca record from the surface noise. . . . they were designed to break—designed to wear out and break. 'Cause when they broke, you had to buy another one." Capitol, by contrast, "had a very good product. In fact, they pretty much, I think, dragged the industry up to where they had to equal the quality of the pressings. They had a quality-control thing that was so rigorous."

Capitol "had a family feel to it" in those early years, Grimes said.

Billy May recalled a time when Mercer came to his house in Hollywood to hear a recording of Peggy Lee singing "I Remember You," for which May had done the arrangement. "So I was really kind of proud of the arrangement, and Peggy Lee sang good, and it was a wonderful rendition of the song." At the time, May probably did not realize that "I Remember You" was the song Mercer most closely associated with Judy Garland. He attributed part of Mercer's reaction to the recording to the fact that, because May's grandfather had worked for the fire department in Pittsburgh, Billy kept his grandfather's fireman's hat on his piano, as well as a radio that was tuned to the local fire department. "We were talking there, and the thing would go off every once in a while, the dispatcher, you know, telling where a fire was coming. And John was intrigued with this, you know? So when he heard—when I played the record 'I Remember You' for him, we were listening to it and everything, and he liked it so much he started to cry." Mercer, always liable to burst into tears, particularly when he heard a song he loved, must have been doubly moved at hearing his paean to Judy Garland arranged by a man whose fireman's hat and dispatcher radio testified to his reverence for his family.

Dave Dexter, a knowledgeable jazz journalist who edited *The Capitol Record*, the company's promotional publication, recalled Mercer as a wonderfully creative force at Capitol. "No man could have had a more pleasant executive to work with. Nor one with a better sense of humor." He painted a picture of Mercer, the company president, as elegantly casual about his business. "I recall Johnny would come into our tiny offices on Vine Street around 11 o'clock each morning, poke around with his mail, inquire as to which records were selling best—then he would unfailingly amble out the front door and head for the Key Club a block north to meet with musicians and songwriting pals over a noontime nip at the bar. He told a limitless number of funny stories, his broad Georgia accent making them all the more appealing."

Yet at times Mercer's genteel, laid-back style ran up against Glenn Wallichs's hard-nosed business sense. A young songwriter named Ervin Drake, who would go on to write such hits as "I Believe" and "It Was a Very Good Year," wrote a song in 1945 called "There Are No Restricted Signs in Heaven," a satire on racism in which Saint Peter greets black people at the pearly gates despite the fact that some white people in heaven look askance: "Welcome, welcome, there are no restricted signs in heaven." "I thought I could change the world," Drake said.

Johnny Mercer loved "There Are No Restricted Signs in Heaven," "but then he showed it to Glenn Wallichs." Wallichs, Drake said, "is a businessman. And Glenn said to him, 'John, the way things are in this country, if you record that song—we're a brand-new company. We will lose our total southern distributorship. And that will be the end of Capitol Records.' . . . And he couldn't do it." Apart from such conflicts, Mercer and Wallichs were in agreement, in Capitol's early years, that sound business practices and artistic integrity could go hand in hand. "In a business known for dishonest practices," a friend observed, "Capitol Records gained a reputation for scrupulous integrity. Mercer and Wallichs insisted on it." They refused to follow the practice of other record companies, which covered hits by their rivals with recordings by their own singers. Capitol only recorded songs it had developed itself.

During these early years at Capitol, Mercer continued to write his own songs. "He was writing like crazy then," Ervin Drake recalled. On one of his regular trips back to Savannah, he went to hear Daddy Grace preach, just as he had when he was a boy. In this particular sermon, Daddy Grace turned a phrase, "Accentuate the positive," which caught Mercer's ear. Back in California, riding with Harold Arlen on the way to Paramount, Mercer listened to the composer sing an "offbeat little rhythm tune" and the phrase "just popped into my mind." "With a beginning like that," Mercer said, "the rest of it practically wrote itself." As they drove, Mercer fitted it out with some of his slangiest lyrics:

> You've got to
> Ac-cent-tchu-ate the positive,
> E-lim-my-nate the negative,
> Latch on to the affirmative,
> Don't mess with Mister In-between.

"It was like getting an elusive crossword clue," he said. "By the time we finished our drive, the song was more or less complete." "It must have pleased John," Arlen recalled, in an indication of how heartbroken Mercer was during this period. "It was the first time I ever saw him smile."

From a revival rouser like "Ac-cent-tchu-ate the Positive," Arlen could provide Mercer with a quiet hymn, "My Shining Hour," which Fred Astaire sang in *The Sky's the Limit*, a 1943 war movie in which he played a fighter pilot and, for the first time in a film, was not once required to wear top hat and tails—a reflection of the solemn war years. Mercer captured that solemnity by setting Arlen's hushed melody with a bone-simple expression of anticipated ecstasy:

> This will be my shining hour,
> Calm and happy and bright.
> In my dreams your face will flower,
> Through the darkness of the night.

Nearly every word is a monosyllable, their edges notched with crisply alliterating consonants ("face" and "flower," "dreams" and "darkness"), subtly echoing vowels ("shining," "my," and "bright," "calm" and "happy"), and even subtler internal rhymes that stitch the lyric together ("This *will* be my shining hour *till* I'm with you again"). Mercer said that in writing "My Shining Hour" he was thinking of old World War I songs, such as "Look for the Silver Lining" and "Keep the Homes Fires Burning." Along with comic songs, such as "G.I. Jive," which dealt directly with the war, "Ac-cent-tchu-ate the Positive" and "My Shining Hour" voiced wartime emotions of affirmation and longing and underscored Mercer's role as America's troubadour during World War II.

Mercer regarded Harold Arlen's music as a fusion of classical Jewish music with early black jazz. "Harold's melodies are way out," Mercer said, "because

Jewish melodies are way out—they take unexpected twists and turns," and a lyricist had to be alert for anything. He saw a strong affinity between Arlen and George Gershwin in their grasp of black musical idioms. "When George and Harold were little boys growing up within about five years of each other, they were hearing records of men like King Oliver. They couldn't help being influenced, just as Irving Berlin, for instance, was influenced in 'Alexander's Ragtime Band' by the still earlier minstrel shows and street parades." Yet Mercer considered Arlen's music more soulful than Gershwin's. "The rhythm of both men is wonderful, but George's often strikes me as mathematical— listen to the precision of 'Sweet and Lowdown' or 'Fascinating Rhythm'— while Harold's comes from the bottom of his feet." Ginger Mercer bemoaned the fact that Johnny did not maintain a long-term collaboration with Arlen. The two men, she felt, had such rapport that had they maintained an exclusive partnership, they would have been given more opportunities to write Broadway musicals.

As much as Mercer loved working with Arlen during these years, nothing could compare with the opportunity to collaborate with the composer he most adored. In 1942 Mercer was given the chance to work with Jerome Kern on songs for the movie *You Were Never Lovelier*. Mercer had met Kern at Charlie Miller's music publishing offices on Tin Pan Alley back in the early 1930s and then had thought Kern "quick, probably irascible, and rather conceited." Now, in Hollywood, he would find what he had thought was conceit was a brusqueness that covered an extreme shyness. It was Kern, in fact, who had indirectly sought out Mercer as a collaborator, instigating a meeting through friends.

In awe as he was of Kern, Johnny Mercer could still hold his own as they worked together. Kern's sumptuous, soaring melodies sometimes drove lyricists, even seasoned lyricists such as Ira Gershwin, into overblown poetic language, but Mercer managed to stay his casually colloquial self in "I'm Old Fashioned." He set Kern's soaring music with an understated affirmation of his love for traditional romantic things—moonlight, rain drops on a window pane, and spring. When Mercer brought the lyric to Kern's home, the normally taciturn composer was so taken with it that he jumped up from the piano stool and kissed his lyricist on the cheek. Then he called to his wife to come hear the song. Mercer had told Kern that Margaret Whiting had a great ear for songs, so Kern invited her to his house and played the entire score of *You Were Never Lovelier*. After playing "I'm Old Fashioned," Whiting recalls, Kern paused, then told her that he thought Johnny Mercer was a genius.

"He was a great stickler for detail," Mercer recalled. "He'd written with lots of guys before me, and he was enormously experienced in collaboration with Wodehouse, Hammerstein, Fields, Harbach, but I think he liked me, in a way, because I made him laugh. He was just as interested in the dancing, and the book, and the lyrics of a show as he was in the music." One wonders why

Mercer didn't follow Kern's example in trying to fully integrate a song into a production.

There were also new collaborators to work with in Hollywood. Victor Schertzinger was a movie director, but he also composed songs for the 1942 musical *The Fleet's In*. "He gave you a tune on a lead sheet," Mercer said, "and whatever you brought in pleased him. . . . As they say, a doll to work with." One lyric that pleased Schertzinger was "Tangerine." "I don't know why I called it 'Tangerine,'" Mercer said later, "except that it had a kind of a Latin flavor, the melody." Latin America, the one part of the world not engulfed in World War II, became a favorite topic for songs and films for Americans who wanted momentarily to forget about the conflagration. Once he had concocted the rhyme with "Argentine," his course was set:

> And I've seen
> Toasts to Tangerine
> Raised in ev'ry bar across the Argentine.
> Yes, she has them all on the run,
> But her heart belongs to just one,
> Her heart belongs to Tangerine.

Amazingly, Mercer wrote the lyric to "Tangerine" in the same weekend he wrote several other songs for *The Fleet's In*, which featured the dynamic Betty Hutton. Two of the other songs, "When You Hear the Time Signal" and "Tomorrow You Belong to Uncle Sam," addressed wartime conditions more directly; but "Arthur Murray Taught Me Dancing in a Hurry" took a satirical look at the famed husband-and-wife dancing teachers who gave pupils a few cursory lessons, then assured them they would blossom on the dance floor:

> Arthur Murray then advised me not to worry,
> It'd come out all right.
> To my way of thinkin',
> It came out stinkin',
> I don't know my left foot from my right.

Arthur Murray, in a public relations gesture, offered Mercer and Ginger sixty free dance lessons. Ginger, after dancing professionally on Broadway, was underwhelmed by Arthur Murray's dancing, and Johnny found that Katherine Murray took the lead when they danced.

So successful were Mercer's songs that in 1942 he received a letter from Deems Taylor, head of ASCAP, telling him that his ASCAP ranking had gone from A to AA. ASCAP distributed performance royalties to songwriters on a classification basis; Johnny Mercer had now moved up to same top level that Cole Porter and Irving Berlin enjoyed. "And you didn't have to ask," Taylor added in a handwritten postscript, which must have pleased the patrician Mercer, who never deigned to be assertive or pushy.

Just as his songs wove themselves into America's sensibility during the war, Johnny Mercer's voice filled the air from jukeboxes, recordings, and radio programs, its folksy warmth soothing an anxious nation. In the summer of 1943, he substituted for Bob Hope on the Pepsodent radio show as emcee and performer. Pepsodent had added a new chemical, "irium," to its toothpaste to help whiten teeth, so to celebrate the new product Mercer wrote a commercial jingle about "Poor Miriam" who "forgot to use her irium." In 1944, he wrote a theme song for *The Chesterfield Supper Club*. "We were doing the Chesterfield show on radio," he said, "and I was just fooling around at the piano, and I got a series of chords that attracted me." He simply picked out chords at random, "fingered them out and everything, which is most unusual for me." Once again a new song grew out of an old one Mercer had loved as a child, in this case the 1920 hit "Whispering." Mercer insisted, however, that the melody was different enough from "Whispering" that he didn't "cop it."

With the melody completed, he wrote a lyric:

Dream, when you're feeling blue.
Dream, it's the thing to do.
Just watch the smoke rings rise in the air.
You'll find your share
Of memories there.

Mercer conceived of "Dream" as the theme song for the Chesterfield show, and that was the only reason he inserted the line about smoke rings rising in the air. Although Mercer said that "the words didn't really mean too much; it just seemed to go with the melody," the lyric, while virtually another commercial jingle, gave yet another expression of his longing for a world elsewhere, that home for his heart that he, like the skylark of his song, could never find.

As Mercer played the melody for Paul Weston, whose orchestra performed on the show, he was flattered that the trained musician "liked the chords." Weston recalled Mercer's hesitancy about his composition. "Johnny seemed dissatisfied with the sixth note, the one that falls on the word 'blue,' but I think that almost 'makes' the song and I convinced him to let it stay."

"Why don't we use it for the theme song?" Weston suggested, freeing Johnny from the unrefined position of making such a commercial suggestion himself. With its imagery of smoke rings, "Dream" seemed the perfect song to close out *The Chesterfield Supper Club*. Michael Goldsen, who then ran Capitol's music-publishing branch, Capitol Songs, was enthusiastic about "Dream." He went to his partner, David Shelley, the stepson of Buddy DeSylva.

"I said, 'Gee, Dave, we've got to get that song put right in the company—you know—we'll work on it.'

"So he says, 'Well, it's only a theme song.'

"I said, 'I know, Davey, but it's a great song. Regardless of whether it's a theme song—it's a great song.'

"And he says, 'Well, I didn't know whether you wanted it because it was only a theme.'

"I said, 'Oh, God, Davey, whatever you do'—I said, 'Get that damn song on a contract. Put Johnny's name on a contract right away.'

"Well, the Pied Pipers recorded it and everybody in the world recorded the song. It became a tremendous hit, sold over a million copies of sheet music. . . . And so Johnny felt very good about it, because our little company was able to make a national—worldwide—hit."

Although Mercer was replaced on the Chesterfield show by Perry Como, in June 1943 he was given his own show, *Johnny Mercer's Music Shop*. The program emanated from Los Angeles, where Mercer would do four fifteen-minute programs each week, Monday through Thursday; then on Fridays, when he and the musicians entertained troops at local camps, the program would be an acetate compilation of the previous week's shows, with commercials edited out, for broadcast over the Armed Forces Radio Service. In 1944, *Johnny Mercer's Music Shop* became a daily show, but at the end of the year it was taken off the air. According to singer Jo Stafford, the show was yanked because Mercer's singing sounded "too black." It certainly might have—in August of that year Mercer received a postcard, which he treasured, from Harris Owens, secretary of the Abraham Lincoln Junior Club of Chicago, a club for black teenagers, telling Mercer the club had voted him "the most popular colored singer on the radio." The club's sentiments were echoed by Eubie Blake, who sent Mercer a letter saying he was "the greatest Rhythm singer of all Ophays I've ever heard," and Louis Armstrong, who inscribed a photograph of himself and his wife with Johnny, saying, " 'Man' more *Spades* love you that you have *no idea*."

Doing radio shows from California in those days meant doing one broadcast for the East Coast and then, three hours later, another for the West Coast. Two young songwriters, Ray Evans and Jay Livingston, heard that Johnny Mercer could be found "five nights a week" at the Tropics, a bar near Capitol where musicians hung out between East and West Coast broadcasts of the Chesterfield show, and there they sought him out. To their delight, he took several of their songs, such as "Highway Polka" and "The Cat and the Canary," and sang them on the show. Evans and Livingston never forgot Mercer's generosity, nor did they forget how drunk everyone got at the Tropics before going back to do the West Coast broadcast. "They got pretty mowed on the second show," Evans recalled, noting one broadcast where the drummer fell off the back of the bandstand.

Evans and Livingston got their big break when Paramount asked them to write a title song to publicize a 1946 movie called *To Each His Own*. As when they wrote any song, Evans and Livingston asked themselves, "What would Johnny do?" Once they completed the song, they rushed to play it for Mercer, who, with his rigorous artistic standards, did not find it good enough for Capitol. "Johnny hated that song and wouldn't record it," Evans said. "Capitol was the only company that didn't like the song and didn't record it." Majestic put out a recording by Eddy Howard; Decca with the Ink Spots; RCA Victor with Freddy Martin; Columbia with Paula Kelly; and Mercury with Tony Martin. The first three of these were million-sellers; all made the top ten on *Your Hit Parade*. In 1960, the Platters had huge success with a rock and roll version of "To Each His Own." "Five of the Top Ten records—the other companies'—were versions of 'To Each His Own,'" Livingston recalled, "but not from Capitol. He didn't like it." Fifty years later, Evans and Livingston were still amazed. "It is so ironic. We wouldn't have had a chance to write if it wasn't for Johnny. Then, that was the one company that didn't record it." "He had the chutzpah," Evans said, invoking an odd term to describe the genteelly Gentile Johnny Mercer, "to turn it down."

But Mercer remained personally loyal to the two young songwriters. "We had Johnny and Ginger up here a lot," Jay Livingston said. At their parties, Mercer would sing while one of his collaborators played the piano. "He would sing songs that nobody had ever heard, you know, that he'd written, such as 'Poor Little Robin in the Rain.' He also sang 'Cottage for Sale' because he liked the guy who wrote it. Also he would throw his head back and talk Gullah." Frequently, the parties lasted all night. "In the morning about eight o'clock, Johnny would make us scrambled eggs." Livingston thought Mercer's love of cooking was a deep part of him and recalled that at a "secret desire" party Mercer came dressed as a chef.

But Livingston also recalled Johnny's drunken assaults. He would walk over to the young composer and, preying on his insecurity, sneeringly ask, "Why don't you write a song?" Finally, Livingston got up the courage to bark back, "Why don't *you* write a song?" Mercer threw back his head and laughed. Livingston also recalled going with Mercer to a nightclub where a particularly bad singer performed. Mercer put his head down on the table and seemed to be asleep until the singer finished the song, whereupon Mercer rose up and shouted, "I hate your brother's ass!" Another collaborator recalled being at a bar where the pianist had recently written his first big hit song, which he kept interspersing among the other songs he played. After hearing it over and over, Mercer shouted, "Hey, why don't you play us a medley of your *hit*!"

"Johnny was never a problem when we were recording together," Paul Weston affirmed. Weston, despite Mercer's frequent drunken assaults, followed by the customary roses in the morning, looked back fondly on these years: "All of us were earning big money, probably more than any group of musicians in the world. On Friday nights we performed in army camps throughout southern California. It was a memorable, happy period."

Songwriters formed a close community in Hollywood during those years. Jule Styne recalled how chummy they all were, partly in reaction to how little involvement studios gave them in motion pictures. Most of them had worked on Broadway, where lyricists and composers were central to a stage musical from the moment of its inception to final changes in lyrics before opening night. In Hollywood, however, they were told to write songs for certain moments in the narrative and sometimes not even given a script. They clung to one another out of a need to feel that their enormous talents were appreciated, at least by fellow songwriters. Every Monday night, said Styne, Ira Gershwin, Harry Warren, Mercer, and others would gather at Jerome Kern's home to talk about what was happening in New York and Hollywood and to play their new songs for one another. A major reason their songs are so good is that they were, in a sense, writing for one another, not just the American public, and at such a gathering one wouldn't dare use a false rhyme or a corny image with Ira Gershwin or Jerome Kern in the room. In these gatherings, Johnny Mercer must have found another simulacrum of the world he sought—an aristocracy of talent, of refinement, of *class*.

Yet even among these people that Mercer worshiped, his demons could not be controlled when he drank. According to one account, he once staggered over to Irving Berlin and snarled, "Well, Irving, you couldn't write a lyric out of a brown paper bag!" Berlin, knowing Mercer would be mortified in the morning, gently laughed. "Well, I think you're right, Johnny," he said. "Good night."

Ten

Come Rain or Come Shine: 1944–1948

I seem to catch the mood of a tune. If I have any gift at all I think it's that I can get the mood of the tune and try to write the words for it. I like it better than writing words first . . . A melody-less lyric is generally doggerel. I need the melody first to suggest ideas to me. The composer's emotion is his own private business; what I try to do above all is to match the mood.

Whenever Johnny Mercer was asked how he knew his words had brought out the latent emotional meaning of a melody, he always cited "Laura" as the supreme example of his ability to "hear" what music was "saying." David Raksin's haunting score for *Laura*, the 1944 film noir classic, had a recurring theme so loved by filmgoers that many wrote to Twentieth Century-Fox, pleading that it be turned into a song. The studio conveyed this enormous public interest to Abe Olman of Robbins Music, who sent a telegram to Johnny Mercer:

DEAR JOHNNY HAVE PHONED DAVE RAKSIN TO CONTACT
YOU IN REGARD TO THE LYRIC FOR THE MELODY FROM
LAURA TREMENDOUS CALLS FOR THIS TUNE FROM ALL
OVER THE COUNTRY AND POSITIVE IT CAN BE A NUMBER
ONE HIT STUDIO ADVISES THEY HAVE RECEIVED SEVERAL
THOUSAND LETTERS CONCERNING SONG HOPE YOU CAN
HOP ON IT RIGHT AWAY

What Olman did not tell Mercer was that he was the third lyricist to be considered for the job. Oscar Hammerstein, with his recent hit musicals *Oklahoma!* and *Carousel*, was the premier Broadway lyricist of the day, and he expressed interesting in setting Raksin's melody but stipulated that the song be published by his own music company, Williamson Music. Olman and others figured that if Oscar Hammerstein wanted to write the lyric, Raksin's melody must have the potential to be an enormous hit, and they were not going to lose out on the royalties.

They next approached Irving Caesar, an odd choice, for while Caesar had written lyrics to some of the biggest hits of the Jazz Age, such as "Swanee" and "Tea for Two," his success had declined with the increasing sophistication of lyrics by Porter, Hart, and Ira Gershwin. Even though Raksin had written a melody so the first two notes could be set with the word "Lau-ra," Caesar wrote a lyric called "Two Dreams." Although Raksin diplomatically did not name Caesar as the second lyricist, he said, "It was an abominable lyric." Abe Olman thought Caesar's lyric was serviceable and turned to Raksin asking, "Who are *you* to turn this down?"

"The composer, that's who."

A songwriter himself, Olman could sympathize with the young composer. "Well, who would you like?"

"Well, there's a guy I don't know, but he's such a wonderful lyricist I would adore to have him."

"Who's that?"

"Johnny Mercer."

"Oh, I know him."

Olman thereupon dispatched his telegram to Mercer.

When Raksin met Mercer, his impression was "a little guy with a funny hat—full of quiet reserve and charm." Mercer took the melody and, as usual, went off to work by himself. Although he wished it had been called "Footsteps in the Dark," Mercer immersed himself in Raksin's melody. The lines of the lyric he created evoke the mood and imagery of the movie, in which Dana Andrews plays a homicide detective pursuing the elusive, mysterious, and ethereally gorgeous Gene Tierney:

Laura is the face in the misty light,
Footsteps that you hear down the hall,
The laugh that floats on a summer night
That you can never quite recall.

The eerie resonance between film and lyric is all the more amazing given the fact that Mercer wrote the lyric without ever seeing the movie. "I hadn't seen the film it came from when I did the lyric," he told an interviewer. "I simply absorbed the tune and let it create an atmosphere for me."

Any other lyricist would have watched the movie to get a sense of its story and characters. But Mercer reasoned that if Raksin's melody had captured the mood of the film, his lyric could articulate that mood. Even before the words, however, came images, so that Mercer's lyric makes you see, hear, feel the emotional power in the music—the footsteps down the hall, the floating laughter, and Mercer's beloved train imagery:

And you see Laura on the train that is passing through

Then, thinking in cinematic terms, he cuts to a sudden close-up as the melody takes an abrupt turn:

Those eyes—how familiar they seem

Only at the end does Mercer's lyric lose touch with the film's narrative:

She gave your very first kiss to you

But by this point the theme of lost love has been so powerfully established that Mercer can reach into his own emotional past, perhaps for that haunting memory he always carried of the beautiful, dark-eyed Miss Elizabeth Cummins of Savannah.

In just sixty-two words, Johnny Mercer had brought out the emotional meaning in the seventy-two notes of David Raksin's melody. When Raksin heard the lyric, he was as stunned by its quality as he was by Mercer's characteristic nonchalance. "I thought Johnny's achievement was amazing, that he should get that feeling into the lyric. And I know that Johnny worked hard, sweated blood sometimes, but you would never have known it. He would show up without a hair out of place—with this thing he had written on the tip of his little finger." Clearly, Mercer felt he was an established enough lyricist that he did not have to pretend to have slaved over a song but could manifest his more characteristic genteel guise of having barely lifted a finger to produce such extraordinary artistry. Little wonder that the equally patrician Cole Porter sent Mercer a telegram saying "Laura" was his "favorite song—among those he didn't write."

Yet the purity of Mercer's talent, that refined concentration on the emotional mood of a melody, limited him as changes in the American musical theater demanded that lyricists think not only about the music they were setting but about plot, character, and theatricality. "Laura" would be inconceivable as a number in a musical comedy. Purely lyrical, it evokes no character or dramatic situation for the singer that can be staged, performed, acted out. While

"Laura" may be an extreme case of a purely lyrical lyric, most of the songs Mercer had written up until 1945 also lack a sense of theatricality.

Had Mercer written in the 1920s and '30s, he might still have had a successful career on Broadway. In that era, there was little of what later came to be called "integration" between the songs and the story of a musical comedy; a good show was simply a show with a lot of good songs. Most of the books for musicals were written by playwrights, such as George S. Kaufman and Guy Bolton, while lyricists such as Larry Hart and Ira Gershwin thought primarily in terms of the song rather than the story. Yet even in 1931, Charlie Miller, Johnny Mercer's boss at Miller Music, had written to George Mercer that his son needed to move beyond writing lyrics and learn to write the book for a musical show. The movement toward integration of book and songs had already begun back in 1927 with Oscar Hammerstein and Jerome Kern's *Show Boat*. Songs such as "Make Believe," "Can't Help Lovin' Dat Man," and "Ol' Man River" were closely tied to character and dramatic situation. Unlike most lyricists of his era, Hammerstein wrote the books for his musicals, usually adapting an existing play or novel, and the marquee for his shows typically read "Book and Lyrics by Oscar Hammerstein." By writing both book and lyrics, Hammerstein could tailor a lyric to character and dramatic situation, building a scene to the moment when dialogue flowers into song. In the case of Edna Ferber's *Show Boat*, Hammerstein wrote a book and lyrics that traced a somber tale of romantic failure and racial oppression, a far cry from the usual "gags and girls" fluff that characterized musical comedy in the Jazz Age.

Hammerstein had wanted to continue writing musical drama in this vein, but, as the depression took its toll on Broadway, he and Kern wound their way to Hollywood along with most other theatrical songwriters. While Kern flourished in Hollywood, however, Hammerstein languished. Writing for movie musicals simply did not present him with the depth of character and drama he needed to create his supremely theatrical lyrics. After years of frustration, Hammerstein retreated to his Pennsylvania farm to work on a labor of love: *Carmen Jones*, a black version of Bizet's opera. There he was sought out by Richard Rodgers, who had had enough of his brilliant but alcoholic and unreliable collaborator, Lorenz Hart. The last straw for Rodgers came when Hart refused to work on a musical based on Lynn Riggs's play *Green Grow the Lilacs*. Hart thought Broadway audiences would be bored by the story of cowboys and farmers in the Oklahoma Territory, so Rodgers announced that he was going to take the project to Oscar Hammerstein. A stunned Hart nevertheless had the class to reply that Rodgers could not have chosen a better collaborator.

In working with Rodgers, Hammerstein also wrote lyrics in a very unusual fashion. While Hart, Gershwin, Mercer, and other lyricists wrote *to* music, Hammerstein worked in reverse order. When he wrote lyrics, he had melodies in his head—either existing songs or "dummy" melodies that he would make up himself—but he would never tell Rodgers what these were when he handed him the finished lyric. Rodgers, as he sat down to compose *to* words, thus took inspiration from Hammerstein's lyrics, which were even more firmly rooted in his own musical book.

Originally entitled *Away We Go*, Rodgers and Hammerstein's show had a rocky time in out-of-town tryouts and was expected by nearly everybody to be a flop. After producer Mike Todd saw a Boston performance, he quipped, "No gags, no girls, no chance." But when it opened in New York, under a last-minute title change, *Oklahoma!* was a resounding success. From the opening curtain, which revealed, not the usual chorus line of gorgeous girls but an old woman churning butter to the strains of "Oh, What a Beautiful Morning," to its rousing finale, *Oklahoma!* changed the course of musical theater history. Integration between song and story became the watchword on Broadway. Earlier musicals had been moving toward the principle of integration—in 1941 Ira Gershwin and Kurt Weill's *Lady in the Dark* and even Rodgers and Hart's *Pal Joey* had closely tied songs to story and character—but it was *Oklahoma!* with its seamless union of Hammerstein's book with Hammerstein's lyrics that established a new age of musical drama on Broadway.

Many songs from *Oklahoma!* went on to become independently popular—not only the big romantic ballads such as "People Will Say We're in Love" but songs such as "The Surrey with the Fringe on Top" and "I Cain't Say No," which were closely tied to the plot and characters of the show. Their popularity stemmed from the fact that *Oklahoma!* was one of the first Broadway musicals to issue an original cast album. In a boxed set of 78-rpm records, listeners could hear the entire score of the show, from the overture to the rousing finale of "Oklahoma!" Such original cast recordings, particularly after the emergence of LP (long-playing) discs in the 1950s, would make hits of such thoroughly integrated songs as "The Rain in Spain" from *My Fair Lady* and "Trouble" from *The Music Man*.

Rodgers and Hammerstein went even further toward musical drama in 1945 with *Carousel*, and other songwriters who had worked in the loose form of musical comedy adapted to the new integrated form: Yip Harburg and Burton Lane with *Finian's Rainbow*, Irving Berlin with *Annie Get Your Gun*—even Cole Porter, who once evinced little interest in the books for his shows, created one of the most perfectly integrated scores for *Kiss Me, Kate*. In Hollywood, younger songwriters of Mercer's generation looked to Broadway as the place where they could exercise their full artistry. Jule Styne left a flourishing collaboration with Sammy Cahn to try his hand with another Hollywood transplant, lyricist Leo Robin, and had a smash with *Gentlemen Prefer Blondes*. Styne then went on to do such major musicals as *Gypsy* and *Bells Are Ringing*, never looking back at Hollywood. Mercer's friends lyricists Frank Loesser and Alan Jay Lerner also left for the Great White Way and enjoyed initial successes with, respectively, *Where's Charley?* and *Brigadoon*, then went on to write such monuments of the musical theater as *Guys and Dolls* and *My Fair Lady*.

Even Hollywood was producing its own great integrated musicals. The chief figure behind this movement was Arthur Freed, who had started out as a lyricist in the late 1920s, writing songs such as "Singin' in the Rain" with composer Herb Nacio Brown for the early talkies. In the late 1930s, Freed went to MGM head Louis B. Mayer and said he wanted to try his hand at producing, so Mayer assigned him, unofficially, to work on *The Wizard of Oz*. Freed fought to have Judy Garland, rather than Shirley Temple, play the lead in the picture and fought even harder to keep the song "Over the Rainbow" in the final cut. The success of that film gave him great stature at MGM, and Freed gathered around himself a talented group of artists that became known as the "Freed Unit"—stars such as Judy Garland and Gene Kelly, choreographers Robert Alton and Charles Walters, and directors Stanley Donen and Vincente Minnelli. Together they would go on to create such great films as *Meet Me in St. Louis, Easter Parade, An American in Paris, The Band Wagon*, and, as a tribute to Freed's own songs with Herb Nacio Brown, *Singin' in the Rain*.

A key member of the Freed Unit was Roger Edens, a young associate producer who had seen *Oklahoma!* on Broadway and told Freed he wanted to make a film musical set in the West. MGM had a story called *The Harvey Girls*, about the young women who went west to work in the chain of restaurants Fred Harvey had established, beginning in 1876, along the major stops of the transcontinental railroads. These "young women of good character, attractive and intelligent," were an important force in the taming of the frontier. Freed thought the story would make a good musical, and teamed Johnny Mercer with Harry Warren to do the songs.

It was from Edens that Mercer got his first lessons in writing for the new integrated musical. Still thrilled by *Oklahoma!*, Edens wanted Mercer to establish the principle of integration at the outset. "In a musical," he explained, "because of economy of footage, the music must tell a lot of the plot. . . . A love song must also advance the story. Even without a finished screenplay I would confer with Warren and Mercer, indicating situations which I wanted described in song."

Guided by Edens, Mercer began to think in these new integrated terms. In addition to his natural focus upon the mood of a melody, he paid more attention to plot and character. Still, it was Mercer's purebred talent to write *to* music that came out. Harry Warren gained a new appreciation of Mercer's intensity as he listened to a melody to hear what it "meant." He called Johnny "Cloud Boy" because when they worked on the score, Mercer would lie down on the couch and drift off into a reverie that could last for hours. With aristocratic aplomb, he would never appear to be really *working*, but when he came out of his reverie he would have lyrics that fit the music Warren had played for him. So intense was Mercer's concentration that Warren would greet him at the beginning of a work session with an innocuous question such as "Hi, Johnny, how's Ginger?" and after hours of silence as Mercer concentrated on a lyric, he would nonchalantly answer, as if no time had gone by, "Oh, Ginger's fine."

Mercer and Warren produced a score that, while not as integrated to character and dramatic situation as *Oklahoma!*, approximates the same effect of having songs grow out of the story. But one drawback to working on such integrated songs was that almost none of them went on to become independent hits—not "In the Valley," not "Wait and See," not "It's a Great Big World." The only song that did achieve popularity had its integrated character supplied primarily by Roger Edens and vocal arranger Kay Thompson. Edens had explained to Mercer and Warren that "we needed an elaborate number celebrating the arrival of the train with the Harvey girls." As Mercer and Warren started to work on the production number, Mercer mentioned that he had once noticed a railroad boxcar with the phrase "The Atchison, Topeka & Santa Fe." "I thought it had a nice, lyrical quality to it," he said; "like Stephen Vincent Benét says, 'I've fallen in love with American place names.'" When he suggested the phrase as a title to Warren, the composer said, "Fine, I've just the right tune for it." "It was an easy one to write," Mercer said. "As I recall, it took me about an hour."

While Mercer and Warren had created an excellent, rhythmic song, however, it made little reference to the scene of the arrival of the Harvey Girls. Roger Edens said he "wanted to clarify the identity of each of the Harvey Girls. So, Katie and I wrote and interpolated a section doing just that." Not only did Edens and Thompson not ask Mercer and Warren to write such an integrated series of verses; they did not tell the songwriters they had added to their song. Such highhandedness may indicate that Edens was aware of how slowly Mercer worked and that they could not hold up a huge production number until he polished enough artful verses to introduce each of the Harvey girls.

Shooting on *The Harvey Girls* began on January 12, 1945. They rehearsed the "Atchison, Topeka & Santa Fe" number for twenty days. When it came time to shoot, Judy Garland did the chorus, as Mercer and Arlen had written it, in a single take as Ray Bolger and a crowd of extras chugged alongside a huge locomotive. The rest of the number, including the added lyrics by Edens and Thompson that introduced the various Harvey Girls, took eight hours to film. When Mercer heard the added lyrics, he was incensed. "And when they were doing the thing about the arrival of the train," a friend recalled, "they realized they were going to do an interior of the train and identify the waitresses, where they were from, and all the stuff. They never contacted Johnny on that, that stuff. 'I'm from Paris,' and 'Paris, Texas,' and all those different lines that are all rhymes on the thing, they're not Johnny's. And he was livid about that, 'cause he thought they stunk, and he said 'they're going to make me look like an idiot. . . . everybody's going to think I wrote that junk.'"

He protested furiously to Arthur Freed, who as a lyricist himself could sympathize with Johnny's anger, but who as a producer must have realized that the public would never notice the makeshift qualities of the verses amid the opulence of the production number. He simply said, "It's done, it's too late. What are you talking about? It's wonderful." But Mercer remained outraged; not only were his artistic standards trammeled, but "On the Atchison, Topeka and the Santa Fe" was Judy Garland's big number in the picture. His manifestation of anger, uncharacteristic when he was sober, may have reflected the fact that he was still in love with her. But Garland had by then divorced David Rose and was about to marry Vincente Minnelli, which she did on June 15, 1945, denying to herself that he, as her own father had been, was homosexual.

If Mercer burned over the added lyrics to "On the Atchison, Topeka and the Santa Fe," Harry Warren exploded when he walked into a Beverly Hills music store and saw an advertisement proclaiming "Johnny Mercer's 'On the Atchison, Topeka and the Santa Fe." The ad referred only to the recording Mercer had made of the song, the most successful recording he would ever have as a singer, but Warren refused to speak to him for five years. Harry Warren always felt slighted as a Hollywood composer whose songs, no matter how popular, were not associated with his name as were the songs by such Broadway composers as Cole Porter and Richard Rodgers. Mercer later said that Warren was "Italian and everything that goes with it. He is Papa, he is quick-tempered, he is suspicious, and he is clannish." When "On the Atchison, Topeka and the Santa Fe" won the Oscar for Best Song in 1946, neither Mercer nor Warren would attend the ceremony, so Van Johnson had to accept Oscars for both men.

The Harvey Girls whetted Mercer's desire to write an integrated musical for the Broadway stage. Arthur Freed was backing a production of an all-black musical called *St. Louis Woman*. The success of *Porgy and Bess* in 1935 and, more recently, Twentieth Century-Fox's *Stormy Weather* in 1943, with an all-black cast headed by newcomer Lena Horne and veteran Bill "Bojangles" Robinson, indicated that a stage production using a black cast would find equal success. Freed and producer Edward Gross wanted Johnny Mercer and Harold Arlen to write the score for *St. Louis Woman*, certain that with such hits as "Blues in the Night" and "Ac-cent-tchu-ate the Positive," they could write songs in a black idiom. But Mercer was reluctant to take time away from Capitol Records. The young company was at a critical juncture, and Mercer was in the midst of negotiations with several major musical figures—Benny Goodman, Harry James, Julie London—as well as Judy Garland and Frank Sinatra—to have them sign with Capitol. Mercer was the key to such negotiations, since singers knew they could trust his personal and artistic integrity. The affiliation with Judy Garland was most critical because, for all of her success on the screen, Judy Garland did not produce hit recordings. Under Mercer's tutelage, she might have been given the appropriate songs and the careful coaching that had turned Margaret Whiting into a major recording star.

Mercer had also seen the script for *St. Louis Woman*, by Arna Bontemps and Countee Cullen, two black writers from the Harlem Renaissance of the 1920s, and he did not find it a "smash story." The diminutive hero, a jockey named Little Augie, was nowhere near the commanding presence of the crippled Porgy, and the tarty Della Green, the loose woman who makes him lose—then helps him regain—his luck, lacked the sensuality of Bess. But all of Mercer's reservations melted when Freed and Gross assured him that Lena Horne, currently under contract at MGM, would play the lead. Along with her would be the Nicholas Brothers, whose spectacular dance, in which the pair descended a huge staircase with bounding splits, had crowned the finale of *Stormy Weather*. To round out the cast would be a dazzling newcomer, Pearl Bailey. With the promise of that cast, Mercer took time off from Capitol Records to collaborate with Arlen on their first full musical score together.

But even as the collaborators worked, *St. Louis Woman* was becoming a pawn in a much larger cultural controversy. Fredi Washington was a light-skinned African American actress who had been considered for the role of Della. When it was decided the part would go to Lena Horne, Washington sought out Walter White, the executive secretary of the National Association for the Advancement of Colored People. The NAACP had been flexing its muscle during World War II, urging blacks to boycott *Gone With the Wind* because of its presentation of racial stereotypes and getting Irving Berlin to eliminate the word "darkey" from "Abraham," a song Bing Crosby performed, in blackface, in *Holiday Inn*. Walter White, like Johnny Mercer, was a Georgian, a descendant of one of Atlanta's most prominent black families. He knew that America's impending victory in World War II would open a brief window of opportunity for racial change, and he was determined to take advantage of it.

First, he advised Fredi Washington to use her theater column in *The People's Voice*, a black newspaper, to condemn *St. Louis Woman* for its racial stereotypes. Countee Cullen and Arna Bontemps had suffered this kind of attack before. While the Harlem Renaissance writers of the 1920s were widely praised by white writers and critics, middle-class blacks were offended by their portraits of blacks as sexually promiscuous and given to drinking, gambling, and fighting. One of the main points in Washington's article was a denunciation of the portrayal of Della as a woman of easy virtue—the very role she had coveted for herself.

White's second prong of attack was to put pressure on Lena Horne. Horne had loved the Mercer and Arlen score for *St. Louis Woman*. "It was a fantastic one, including among others, the great song 'Come Rain or Come Shine,'" but she had misgivings about the book with its racial stereotypes, particularly her role of Della, the "flashy whore." "There were all sorts of the usual cliché characters in it and I thought it very melodramatic and old-fashioned. I knew the book had been written by Negroes, but I still resented its pidgin English and the stereotypes they had written. . . . I knew there were other sides of Negro life you could write a play about, and I said so to Freed and the other MGM people who were putting a lot of pressure on me to take the part."

But Horne also acknowledged that she was being pressured by "people representing the Negro organizations" who "were telling me that I must not do the part. They were concentrating very hard just then on trying to end cliché presentations of Negro life. So I was caught between two very important forces in my life—the opinion of the Negro community and the opinion of people who had been important in my career." So Horne went to see Arthur Freed. Freed had produced most of the movies she had played in at MGM, and she trusted him. He told her that if *St. Louis Woman* was successful, he could make another all-black movie, perhaps even a film version of *St. Louis Woman* itself. She would not only be getting work herself but helping provide work for other black performers on Broadway. "Freed insisted that I tell him my own feelings. He was not insensitive about the situation." Horne told him that Fredi Washington, "a Negro woman whom I respected very much," had "condemned the script to me." Freed told Horne that Washington, after failing to win the role of Della for herself, "had secretly sent her sister" to him "to try out for the part that she was, simultaneously, advising me not to take." Nevertheless, Horne refused to take the part in *St. Louis Woman*. MGM retaliated by denying her the role she coveted—the mulatto Julie in a Broadway revival of *Show Boat*—despite the fact that composer Jerome Kern himself had requested that she play the part.

On August 14, 1945, VJ Day, Japan surrendered after President Harry Truman, succeeding Franklin Roosevelt, who had died during his unprecedented fourth term, ordered the dropping of atomic bombs on Hiroshima and Nagasaki. After four long years of war, America enjoyed the biggest celebration in its history. As a small part of the rejoicing, playwright Arna Bontemps boarded the train from Nashville to New York. *St. Louis Woman*, despite all the controversy, was about to go into production. Before rehearsals began, however, Countee Cullen died, broken by accusations that he had defamed his race. He and Bontemps, both teachers who had never known monetary success, had hoped *St. Louis Woman* would be their big Broadway hit.

Johnny Mercer, also looking for his first Broadway hit, was bitterly disappointed that Lena Horne would not play the lead. His disappointment was assuaged somewhat when on the first day of rehearsals he and Arlen performed the score for the cast. Both men were deeply moved when every black performer stood and applauded. "We sat in the room," Pearl Bailey recalled. "And this man just sat there and sang the whole score. . . . This man could sing his songs. He was one of the few people who could sing his songs better than anyone else could sing them. And every one was a masterpiece. . . . He wrote his heart, and he sang his heart."

The score was magnificent, Mercer and Arlen at their elegantly earthy best, and even in later years Mercer would say, "I myself am immodest enough to think it is one of the best scores written for a colored musical." Not only are the full-blown songs superb, there are wonderful stretches of recitative and lyrical fragments that grow out of the dialogue. Before Della's entrance, for example, men in the bar extol the virtues of "sweetening water" ("You take rock candy an' you pour on gin") in a blues round:

> He bought her Scotch but she was unimpressed . . .
> So I ordered her sweeten-in water an' she a-cqui-esced.

As Della enters, she picks up their theme and weaves it into a torrid declaration of female independence, "Any Place I Hang My Hat Is Home," where Mercer revels in regional slang and place names:

> Sweetnin' water, cherry wine,
> Thank you kindly, suits me fine,
> Kansas City, Caroline
> That's my honey comb
> 'Cause any place I hang my hat is home.

In this song Mercer once again went back to his roots in Savannah. He told Margaret Whiting that he would encounter an elderly man on the square near his home, and when Mercer asked him how he was he would reply, "Just fine, Mr. Mercer, any place I hang my hat is home."

Some of the best songs in the score went to Pearl Bailey, who played Butterfly, the comic counterpart of Della, paired with Fayard Nicholas, who played another jockey named Barney. She sang such importunate songs as "Legalize My Name":

> All you want to do is bill and coo,
> But you're empty-handed when the bill is due,
> If you really love me and you love me true,
> LEGALIZE MY NAME . . .
> If you prize me,
> Notarize me . . .
> LEGALIZE MY NAME.

In "It's a Woman's Prerogative," a title suggested by a phrase Ginger Mercer often used, Pearl Bailey again manifested a comically aggressive femininity:

> Promise everything,
> Honey, don't swerve.

Throw him a curve.
String 'em along till they show you what they got in reserve.
Though his bank shows a big balance,
And he seems heaven-designed,
If the boy's short on his talents,
It's a woman's prerogative to change her mind.

These numbers gained in comic effect because Fayard Nicholas could not sing, so he remained dourly silent during Pearl Bailey's harangues.

While Fayard's singing limitations could be turned to comic ends, however, Harold Nicholas, as the lead, had to sing. His voice was not strong, however, and Della and Augie weren't given a duet until the second act. Compared to the number of duets between the leads in *Porgy and Bess*, duets that bring their love passionately alive to the audience, the paucity of duets in *St. Louis Woman* hindered the development of the central romantic relationship. Still, their one duet, "Come Rain or Come Shine," was the best song in the entire score.

On this great ballad, the teamwork between Arlen and Mercer clicked again. When Arlen played Mercer the opening strain of the melody, Johnny instantly came up with "I'm gonna love you like nobody's loved you. . . ." But then he was stumped. "Come hell or high water?" suggested Arlen. "Of course," Mercer said. "Why didn't I think of that?" But what he thought of was "come rain or come shine," once again that fertile subconscious memory drawing on his lyric for "Dearly Beloved" from 1942. In that elegant Kern song the line had been "Come shower or shine," but for the more earthy blues sound of Arlen's melody Mercer fastened upon the more colloquial "come rain or come shine."

Yet, "Come Rain or Come Shine," for all its greatness as a song, reflects Mercer's limitations as a theater lyricist. While not as purely lyrical as "Laura," it, too, is a song that lacks theatricality. "Exquisite as this lyric is," one musical historian observed, "it simply isn't the sort that contributes to a show. . . . it is so anonymous. It is a pop lyric . . . more thoughtful than exuberant and spontaneous." " 'Come Rain or Come Shine' is beautifully written," another noted. "But as with 'Star Dust' and many other classic pop songs, it's hard to know what you'd do during the number to give it some dramatic propulsion on stage." Compared to the big romantic ballad from *Oklahoma!*, "People Will Say We're in Love," "Come Rain or Come Shine" gives no verbal cues to the performers beyond pure lyrical expression. Hammerstein's lyric, in contrast, supplies stage business for the singers, such as "Don't sigh and gaze at me" and "Don't start collecting things—give me my rose and my glove."

Mercer and Arlen hoped "Come Rain or Come Shine" would be the big ballad that would draw audiences to *St. Louis Woman*, so Mercer arranged for a recording to be released just before the show opened. He sent Margaret Whiting a copy of "Come Rain or Come Shine" and told her to learn it so they could make a recording for Capitol after he and Arlen arrived in New York. "Both Johnny and Harold were in the control room," she recalled, "the two of them such terrific singers themselves that just their singing of a song was enough to throw me. . . . They made the most unlikely, wonderful team. Johnny was a true son of the South, and Harold a true son of a cantor from Buffalo. But these two disparate heritages meshed. Harold wrote songs with a marvelous blues chord structure that was sensuous and sophisticated and also primitive. Johnny's lyrics blazed with originality and an American earthiness. They had the same understanding of the same kind of music, so it worked."

Such reflections on Mercer and Arlen inspired Whiting to take an unusual liberty with "Come Rain or Come Shine." "I had learned it note by note, remembering my father's cautionary words: 'Sing the song the way the writers wrote it. They worked hard to get it just right.' The very last note of this song was one long note on the tonic. I learned it that way, but when we did a take, something happened in my mind. I started thinking about Harold, the cantor's son. On that last note, I just let it wail:

I'm gonna love you, come rain or shine.

Well, Johnny burst through the door, mad as hell: 'What in God's name are you doing?' He was followed by Harold, who shouted, 'No, leave it, leave it! That's the way I should have written it.' That was the first time I dared do such a thing."

Once rehearsals began, *St. Louis Woman* was torn over racial issues. Cast members rebelled at the stereotypical characters and dialect; what might have seemed deeply and richly "Negro" in the Harlem Renaissance of the 1920s was offensive to blacks in 1946. At one point Rouben Mamoulian, who had directed *Porgy and Bess* and *Oklahoma!*, confronted angry cast members and, backed by Pearl Bailey, told them it was dramatically appropriate to portray such characters. As the New York opening neared, Ruby Hill, who had replaced Lena Horne as Della, was in turn replaced by Muriel Rahn, who had a more operatic voice. The cast rebelled, and a delegation protested to the producer. Ruby Hill was reinstated, while Muriel Rahn was paid her contractual salary of $650 a week while the production ran. The book problems, the casting problems—these might have been overcome by the great score; but when the NAACP threw its weight against *St. Louis Woman*, attacking the show in newspapers and picketing it on opening night, its doom was sealed.

Critics were unanimous in their praise for the songs, for Pearl Bailey, even the sets and costumes, but there was widespread criticism of the book. "Everything would be lovely," one critic lamented, "if the Bontemps-Cullen story didn't keep getting in the way. It's a foolish story at best. . . . A musical play . . . should improve as scene after scene goes by. It ought to walk in the beginning, step lively in the middle, run when it gets to the end. This, *St. Louis Woman* just does not do." The show closed after a run of only 113 performances.

So ended Johnny Mercer's first attempt to write a Broadway musical in the new integrated fashion of Rodgers and Hammerstein. He had to be content with seeing one song, "Come Rain or Come Shine," survive the debacle. In later years, he would try to look back on the failure philosophically, but his bitterness still surfaced. "But we can't have everything, can we? Sometimes you get so discouraged you feel it should read, 'We can't have anything, can we?' "

When Mercer returned to California, he found that another casualty of *St. Louis Woman* was that Capitol Records had changed dramatically in his absence. Originally a small, elite company that maintained the highest artistic and technical standards, Capitol now expected to sell 3 million records a month. By the end of 1946, its net sales were $13,082,797, nearly double its sales for 1945 and more than all the money the company had earned since it was founded in 1942. Capitol sold 42 million records that year—one-sixth of all records sold in the United States. The company, which had until then been renting recording space, floated a $3 million stock issue in order to buy its own recording studio; instead of being controlled by three men, Mercer, Wallichs, and DeSylva, Capitol would become "Capital," with stockholders interested not in artistic quality but in the size of their dividends.

Johnny Mercer's blue blood boiled. "John got upset when the company got so successful," said Billy May. "He liked it when it was just a little company, and he could write a song in the morning and record it that afternoon and have it a hit a week later. . . . wanted just a little, kind of quiet place where he could go in and tell his funny lines and his little funny rhymes and make a record and put it out. . . . he wanted the small little company where they didn't make too many records. He got mad when they started competing with the majors and everything like that. I mean, that annoyed him. . . . Glenn Wallichs told me that John would get mad. And Glenn was, of course, the other way. Glenn was a business man: 'Let's get ahead here and make it.' "

One of the new people responsible for the changing nature of Capitol was Alan Livingston, who was hired just after Mercer left for New York to work on *St. Louis Woman*. Livingston was an Ivy League business school graduate who wanted to go into the recording industry. He was fascinated by the fact that Capitol was the only major recording company on the West Coast and even more fascinated by the songs the company put out. "Now, I tried to get a job at Capitol Records, and they said, 'The only thing we're interested in is somebody to do children's records. We're not in that business and think we should be.' This was the end of 1945. And they hired me. I started to work January 1, 1946, and Johnny Mercer was in New York writing the score for *St. Louis Woman*, so I never met Johnny."

Livingston threw himself into his new position. "I sat down and created a character called Bozo the Clown. And I wrote the first album and had a new idea at the time—to put a book with it. And . . . Bozo, on the record, said,

'Whenever I blow my whistle, you turn the page.' And it was in synch with the record." Livingston got Billy May to do the music, hired a man to play Bozo, and worked with an artist to design the clown's face, figure, and clothes. "Children's records didn't sell then. They sold, you know, ten thousand—that was a lot. This sold over a million. This was a smash hit. . . .

"And Johnny still was this total stranger to me." Livingston built up children's recordings at Capitol by co-writing such songs as "I Taut I Saw a Puddy Tat." "I made a deal with Warner Bros. and got their rights to Bugs Bunny and Daffy Duck and all those characters, made a deal with Disney to do their original cast albums—they didn't have a record company—and I was very successful. When Johnny finished *St. Louis Woman* and came back to Los Angeles—that's the first time I met him. And I'll never forget the remark he made to me. He said, 'Well you're doing okay but just don't get too big around here.' I thought, 'What does he mean by that?' It put me off a bit."

Livingston knew it was a joke, but he was young and nervous in his first big job and didn't know how to take Johnny Mercer. They worked together on a children's record based on Disney's *Song of the South*. Mercer narrated the record and sang songs, but Livingston was frustrated by his laid-back attitude during the recording session. Livingston wanted to do another take, with all the technical people and musicians assembled, when Johnny decided to stop and eat a sandwich. "He worked very, very informally. When I'd do a session with him, it was almost like a party. I mean, he just didn't take it too seriously, but out would come his great talent. . . . He just took it so casually, and I was anxious to get things done because the musician's union was very strong in those days. I had, like a twenty-eight piece orchestra there, and I wanted to get the maximum number of sides I was allowed to do, and Johnny was just so casual about it all. I had to keep pushing him and say, 'John, please!' And he's eating a sandwich." It was again Mercer as the classic southern patrician— nonchalant, unconcerned about financial pressures, pouring out his remarkable talent without ever seeming to be working.

Yet Livingston found that Mercer's cavalier nature could work to his advantage. These were the days before sessions were taped, so if even the smallest thing went wrong, the whole song would have to be redone for the disc recording. "That was no problem for him. I mean, he'd shrug his shoulders and do it again." Having donned the role of the unflappable southern Brahmin, Mercer would work longer and harder—without allowing himself to show even a trace of sweat—than more temperamental plebian performers.

"His records sold," said Livingston, who as the consummate businessman regarded Mercer as one of Capitol's greatest assets. "Nobody could try and steal him away from Capitol. He was a major stockholder, and nobody would ever think that it was possible, which it wasn't. So he wasn't, like other artists, out there where record companies were competing for his contract or whatever. I mean, he *was* Capitol Records, period."

At the time, according to Livingston, Mercer was president of Capitol Records in name only. "Mercer's great talent and his tremendous contribution to Capitol was in finding and judging artists. . . . He just had a marvelous commercial ear for talent, and his contribution—in spite of the fact that he did not function as an executive, his contribution was tremendous. . . . He'd walk in and say, 'I heard a singer and I think you ought to pitch him.' He'd never push it. But, believe me, we listened when he made such a remark. And that's how Nat King Cole came in and Margaret Whiting came in and Jo Stafford came in and Peggy Lee came in—just on a comment of his. He didn't say—he was president at that time, but he wouldn't say, 'I heard somebody, you got to sign them.' Johnny would never talk like that."

It was not Mercer's way to be pushy, yet he had a tenacity that impressed the business-minded Livingston. "Johnny brought in Nat Cole—recommended Nat King Cole, who was a member of the King Cole Trio. Nat was a jazz pianist. And Johnny kept saying to him, 'We've heard you sing—you should make records singing.' And Nat kind of resisted it. But Johnny convinced him he should sing on records, and Nat Cole became one of Capitol's major artists." "And Johnny said at the time, he said, 'This can be the biggest vocalist in the country.' And he was the one that pinpointed it."

Livingston also got to know Mercer socially, going out for drinks with him and comedian Jerry Colonna. "Johnny was an alcoholic, and he was—he was fascinating because he was the sweetest man in the world and would do anything for you, and very generous with his time and his help and his advice." But when he was drinking, Livingston observed, "he became insulting to everybody around him, and treated his wife badly under those conditions. I never got the brunt of it. I was fortunate. . . . He did it to total strangers. . . . My brother gave a party, and my wife Nancy's mother was still living, and we took her to my brother's house, to the party . . . and Nancy said to Johnny, 'Oh, Johnny, I'd like you to meet my mother.' And Nancy brought her over, and Johnny said, 'I don't want to meet your mother. I don't want any part of it. And I don't even want to *talk* to you.'"

Another friend wondered if Mercer "used the drinking as an excuse to be nasty," especially to Ginger. "Now, that's because of the closeness, the fact that they'd been married, and you always attack the person closest to you. And she would drink too and go into submission. She wouldn't say anything, and I know she hurt." Livingston recalled that Ginger was the most frequent target of Mercer's abuse. "Johnny could be very sweet to her when he was sober and very mean to her when he had too much to drink. And she just put up with it. She loved being who she was, and as long as Johnny wasn't drinking, they had a good life together because Johnny was a kind person and very nice and maintained the marriage. I don't know how he felt, but he always maintained the marriage in a comfortable way, except there were times when he was not very nice to her. . . . There was one occasion where—I won't use his language, but there was one occasion when he was sitting next to her at a cocktail party, and he took his drink and looked at it and reached over and poured it over her head . . . Just like that, for no reason . . . She reacted, but she didn't scream at him or get angry. She never did. She just quietly—she knew he was under the influence, and, therefore, every now and then, she would have to put up with this, which she did."

Livingston also recalled how one man came up to Mercer at the start of a cocktail party and said, "Johnny, before you give it to me, I'm going to give it to you—and go f—— yourself.' And Johnny laughed." "He was very generous and very—wanted to be helpful to people—but when he got drunk he was a monster. . . . And the funny thing is, John remembered the next day what he had done. He was very, very sorry about it and would try to make amends and apologize. It isn't like a drunk who doesn't remember. He remembered and felt very badly about it."

The expansion of Capitol made it necessary for Mercer to relinquish the presidency of the company. "After a while the routine got a little bit too much for Johnny," Michael Goldsen said. "He had to okay title pages and everything, and he would be out playing golf or out at a party the night before, and he couldn't get in the office in time to do the work. You know, it got piled up so that they realized eventually that Johnny was not going to be able to handle all the work that was piled up; and it was also interfering with his career as a writer and a performer."

Glenn Wallichs officially replaced Johnny Mercer as the president of Capitol Records in 1947. "When they started the company," Alan Livingston recalled, "he had the title of president and Buddy DeSylva was chairman of the board, and Glenn Wallichs, who really ran the company—was the businessman who ran the company—was the executive vice president. As the company began to grow, the operation was such that Glenn felt he needed to have the title of president, and he asked Johnny to let him have that, which he did, so Glenn Wallichs became president."

"He was never businesslike," Livingston said. "He was just the opposite of businesslike. In his personal life—Ginger told me a story once where she found a check in a drawer that was like three months old for thirty thousand dollars, which was from ASCAP or someplace, which he had just put away in a drawer and forgotten about. I mean he had no sense or interest in business at all. So he could not function as president, and there was no question about that." . . . "Nobody nudged him out. He had the feeling they did. But Johnny was not interested in running Capitol and coming to the office every day. He resented giving up the title of president and he wanted it . . . and nobody wanted to push him out. Glenn Wallichs had to run the company. Johnny wasn't running it. It was growing and getting bigger and Johnny wanted it as a plaything. He just wanted to keep it a little company and be involved in finding new artists and doing things like that. Glenn had ambitions to make this a major record company. And Johnny didn't want it that way—he just wanted to have fun. But Glenn—that was Glenn's *career*! Johnny had his career as a songwriter. He just wanted this plaything."

"John got upset," Billy May recalled, when the company violated his policy of not covering hit songs by other companies with versions by their own artists. "And this was one of the things that got John mad about Capitol because they started recording pop tunes. Decca would have a hit, and Capitol would cover it. . . . And it was a fast, you know, 'Get the tunes in.' . . . And we would do them, and sometimes we were more successful, but John didn't like that competitive business that the record industry became. And, of course, it's worse now than it's ever been, you know. But he could see that that was going the wrong way."

Although Capitol was no longer that small, elite world that Mercer wanted to live in, he still sat in on recording sessions and gave advice. Billy May recalls that Mercer would come in to a recording session and frequently lie down and look as if he were asleep. "A couple of times, I know, he woke up suddenly and made himself aware. Some of the people didn't even know he was there. . . . He had a wonderful vocabulary, and he would come up with some kind of a crack, and people would say, 'Who was that?' . . . He would just make a general comment about the proceedings. . . . 'Why are you doing *this* song in the first place?'"

When Wallichs took over the presidency, Capitol moved from its tiny offices on Vine Street to the second floor above Wallichs's Music City store at Sunset and Vine. "And when we moved up there, Glenn had offices made for us," Livingston recalled. "And Johnny was given an office, of course, and a secretary, and he did not come in too much. . . . Glen Wallichs furnished an office for him there so he'd have a place to come. And he put in, instead of a typical business desk, he thought he'd make it informal, and he put in a kidney-shaped desk." While Mercer was not one to complain directly, he made sarcastic remarks about "a kidney-shaped desk! . . . He was an easygoing man, and he accepted it, but he used to make cracks about it," Livingston recalled. "He never let anybody up on that. . . . I can't remember him ever sitting in that office."

"He abruptly walked away from Capitol," recalled Dave Dexter. "It wasn't fun anymore. I stuck around Capitol for another quarter of a century, all the time deploring Mercer's absence and watching a covey of lawyers and Ivy League business majors take over the company's direction."

Acquiescent and pliable, Mercer stepped down from the presidency of Capitol Records without uttering an angry word. "And everybody wanted to know, you know, just about how he felt about it," Michael Goldsen said, showing a letter Mercer had written to him at the time, on which he signed himself "John Mercer, Ex-President, Capitol Records." "That shows you that down deep, he felt a little, not slighted, but just was sorry that he could not stay as head of the company."

Eleven

Autumn Leaves: 1949–1952

If everything sounds like sour grapes, it isn't really. I consider myself the luckiest of men. I am in a business I love, that I am perhaps better than average at. I have had more than my share of successes. It's just that if you are a perfectionist at all, which most creative people are, you hate to blow anything.

Despite the failure of *St. Louis Woman*, Johnny Mercer still longed to write a great integrated Broadway musical. As more and more successful shows were mounted—Lerner and Loewe's *Brigadoon* in 1947, Cole Porter's *Kiss Me, Kate* in 1948, then another Rodgers and Hammerstein masterpiece, *South Pacific*, in 1949—it became clear that Broadway was the elite echelon for writers of song. The successful revival of *Show Boat* in 1946 proved that such musicals would endure, preserving their songs as classic works of the American theater. Johnny Mercer tried again to enter the pantheon of Broadway musicals in 1949 with *Texas, Li'l Darlin'*, a political satire with a book by John Whedon and Sam Moore and music by Robert Emmett Dolan, with whom Mercer had collaborated on songs for Paramount films. *Texas, Li'l Darlin'* opened on November 25, 1949, and had a good run of 221 performances, but it was not the classic musical Mercer had hoped for, and there has never been a major revival of the show.

"It should have been called *Ride 'Em Cowboy*," Mercer said, noting that it was one of his favorite musicals. "We never had that big brassy production that might have shoved it over, and that the book and score deserved. We really put down *Time* and *Life* and the political establishment severely. Perhaps that's another reason we weren't better known." The satire on Texas politics gave Johnny Mercer, always alert to nuances of language, the opportunity to play with the breezy journalism of Henry Luce's *Time* and *Life* magazines. His lyrics bristled with such epithets as "Able, Beetle-Browed Harvey Small" and "Canny, Slab-Sided Hominy Smith." In *Time* he came across the word "affable" and was so intrigued by it that he wrote "Affable, Balding Me" as a send-up of what one reviewer called "*Time*style . . . Luce's elaborate conspiracy against the English language."

Once again, however, Mercer had left the writing of the book for a musical to others and chosen a collaborator who had never written for the theater. Robert Emmett Dolan provided Mercer with a musical score that included a rousing, rhythmic number, "It's Great to Be Alive," but little else. "Most of the music is commonplace," noted Brooks Atkinson, "and most of the lyrics are in a similar vein. But the book is the basic weakness of this cheerful-looking show." During the run of *Texas, Li'l Darlin'*, Mercer saw his friend and rival Frank Loesser score the kind of success he longed for with *Guys and Dolls*, a hit show that produced a string of hit songs and that would be revived for generations.

Mercer's quest for a Broadway triumph continued in 1951 with *Top Banana*, another satire, this time on the new medium of television, that starred the great burlesque comic Phil Silvers. "I suggested that we bring in the first musical to satirize the madness of week-to-week television," Silvers recalled. "In 1950 the tyrant of the tube was Milton Berle; on Tuesday night at eight, he had the whole country in his hand. I would do Uncle Miltie."

Silvers and Berle were friends, and Silvers used his knowledge of Berle to create the role of Jerry Biffle. "I knew every flip gesture of Berle's, every ruthless smile. Milton was, shall I say, an impatient man. He had to have his laughs, and he didn't care where or how he found them." But their friendship also obliged Silvers to tell Berle about *Top Banana*. Silvers made a golf date with him, and as they walked to the first hole, Berle asked him about his new show. Silvers took a deep breath and explained, "Milton, it's about a guy who's been 'on' all his life. His only goal is the laugh. It's got to come, no matter if it's at the expense of his mother, the President or himself. . . . He never listens to anyone's conversation—he's just thinking of what he'll say next. The poor guy's never had a chance to develop in any other areas. He's been on the stage since he was five years old. His dedication—the laugh must come." "I'll be a sonovabitch," Berle said, "I know guys just like that," and he promptly invested in *Top Banana*.

But as the show evolved through rehearsals and out-of-town tryouts in Boston and Philadelphia, it became clear that the book, by Hy Kraft, a veteran writer of Broadway and Hollywood, and Johnny Mercer's score, for which he wrote both music and lyrics, were overshadowed by Silvers's comic antics. During one rehearsal, for example, a wealthy businessman dropped by to review the show as a possible investment. As Silvers sang, he recalled, "I heard a dog howling melodiously in the lobby. And when I stopped—the dog stopped." The businessman apologized and explained that he had left his Airedale in the lobby and that "Sport" always burst into a "high, unearthly *ooooooowwwww*" whenever he, the master, sang in a certain key. Silvers pounced on the possibility of getting Sport to sing onstage with him.

Hy Kraft then had to write a sketch in which Jerry Biffle plays to the animal lovers in his audience just as Milton Berle pandered to the children who watched his television program. Mercer dutifully followed suit by writing "A Dog Is a Man's Best Friend," which defines a moment when the self-absorbed Biffle becomes sympathetic as he laments, "When I'm blue and lonesome too, nobody understands me like my dog." But then he becomes progressively jealous as the dog upstages him by raising his head to the heavens and yowling. Finally, Biffle roars, "If you want a pal that's quiet and peaceful—buy a *cat*!" To further milk the audience, Silvers would always give Sport a treat after they walked offstage so that the dog would start licking the star's hand in anticipation, thus making the audience think "there had to be something good in him if a dog loved him." When *Top Banana* opened on Broadway on November 1, 1951, Milton Berle and his mother were in the audience, leading the peals of laughter. Berle, characteristically, had to insert himself into the show. As the cast was taking a curtain call, he rushed onstage screaming, "I'll sue! I'll sue!" Sport, seeing only that a strange man was shouting and rushing aggressively toward Phil Silvers, leaped for Milton Berle's throat. Fortunately, perhaps, Silvers had the dog on a short leash. "The whole bit got a good laugh," Silvers recalled. "But Milton never did it again."

Top Banana ran for 350 performances on Broadway, and a friend of Mercer's who saw it described the show as "pee-in-your-pants funny," but the focus was exclusively upon Silvers and his burlesque sidekicks. "Phil Silvers finds himself without a program," one reviewer wrote, "so he puts on a dream entertainment of his own. The scenery parts and even a little dog—Ted Sport Morgan—has his play. And *Top Banana* is not top banana anymore. It is not much of any one thing." When Mercer's score was even noticed by reviewers, it was criticized: "The brilliant Johnny Mercer, who has written some of the best lyrics and composed some of the most memorable songs in American popular music, has provided a curiously commonplace score that didn't sound worthy of him last evening." An even harsher note came from Brooks Atkinson in the *New York Times:* "There is nothing beyond the skullduggery in *Top Banana* that need detain you long. Johnny Mercer's score is hackneyed. He has composed as though he hoped it would not sound like music—successfully from this point of view."

Yet Sheldon Harnick, an aspiring lyricist at the time, thought Mercer wrote an excellent score for *Top Banana*, though, looking back on it, he said, "Something about the show . . . I guess it was not a very substantial show because, as far as I know, it's never done." Harnick remembered meeting

Mercer during the out-of-town tour of *Top Banana*, "which my first wife was in. He was around the theater. He was a ladies' man. I think he made a play for a number of the young women in the show, including my wife. She wasn't offended. She was kind of flattered by it. . . . She knew there was no threat in it and that he was a gentleman and that all she had to do was say 'No' and he'd say 'Okay.' "

Harnick also recalled a cast party after the show in Philadelphia with Mercer in attendance. "He was mixing with everybody very affably. When I worked with Richard Rodgers, Dick did not particularly mix with the company, but Johnny mixed. People liked him. People approached him. He was easy to approach." As the party went on people began to perform, and those who knew Harnick had written some lyrics asked his wife to perform, and she sang some of his songs. "They were very enthusiastically received," Harnick recalled, "and I looked over to see what Johnny Mercer's reaction was, and he was sound asleep—with his drink next to him."

Even Phil Silvers, despite all the accolades that came his way from *Top Banana*, recognized the limitations of the show. The night before *Top Banana* opened on Broadway he went to see Judy Garland perform at the Palace—her great comeback on the stage after her humiliating departure from Hollywood. "She had come back to America after four triumphant months in Europe and the London Palladium. Her Sunday night show was dazzling, emotion-charged. There was by now a cult of Judy-worshippers. They screamed at every throb in her voice. Somehow, I felt my show was competing with hers. And how could I possibly measure up to her kind of mass hysteria? I felt I didn't even belong in the same city with Judy."

The simultaneous presence in New York of Judy Garland for her show at the Palace and Johnny Mercer for *Top Banana* rekindled their love affair. Although she had triumphed at the London Palladium, Garland was very apprehensive about performing at the Palace. "The Palladium experience was grand," Dorothy Kilgallen wrote in her Broadway column, "but it was, after all, England. New York is the terrible, wonderful test." Songwriter Hugh Martin called two friends, Jean and Bob Bach. "Listen, Judy's opening up tomorrow night at the Palace and she's scared stiff," he said. "It might just ease things if she could groove a little bit. . . . Could you ask a few sympathetic people over and we'll just have a little drink and she will do some songs." The Bachs arranged an intimate party in their New York apartment and, unaware at that time of Mercer's affair with Garland, included Johnny among the close circle of guests.

Jean Bach recalls Judy Garland opening her heart and singing. "She sat on the coffee table. She was getting very intoxicated. She kept handing me her drink and saying, 'Just put a little more in the bottom.' It was bourbon—straight bourbon. And I'm thinking, 'This woman could never be my best friend' because she's singing 'Over the Rainbow' and she's crying and everybody's crying, and then suddenly she sobers up and says, 'Could I have another drink, please?' Then back to the song." One guest recalls that Mercer and Garland went upstairs to the bedroom and were gone for more than an hour and a half: "It was a happening."

"This was a funny apartment," Jean Bach said. "In the back were swinging French doors that went out onto a huge terrace, which was the roof of the restaurant next door, and so we were in and out all the time." When they thought all their guests had gone, Bach and her husband decided to leave the mess and go to bed. But as she was closing the blinds in their bedroom, she noticed a limousine waiting in the street below. "Well, somebody forgot their car," she said. "Are you sure everybody's gone?" Bob said, "Look in the living room. There's nobody there." "So I said, 'Fine.' We went to bed, and the next day the limo's gone. . . . Well, it turns out, Judy and Johnny had rediscovered themselves. On our terrace. And it was fall. And I'd taken all the mattresses off the chaises, and I just had this terrible cot—an army cot—with kind of rusty springs. And I thought, 'What kind of romance overrides these conditions?' "

If Johnny was attracted to Garland by her talent and her vulnerability, the night of lovemaking must have given him the chance to be the kind and generous older man who could offer reassurance to the frightened star on the eve of her New York concert debut. Fortunately for Garland's voice, the October night was balmy, with a low temperature of fifty-four degrees. The tryst bolstered Garland's spirits, and she overcame her insecurity to triumph at the Palace. She sang, danced, joked with the audience about her weight ("I need to lose ninety pounds"), thereby disarming their possible criticisms of her appearance. Attired in a classic black-and-white costume, she projected an image of utter simplicity, at one point kicking off her pumps and saying, "My feet hurt." After singing one of her great songs after another, she received an ovation that ran more than three minutes. Critics were ecstatic, and Judy Garland played to packed houses for a record-breaking nineteen weeks, finally closing, by her own choice, on February 24, 1952.

If Mercer and Garland kept up their renewed affair during this period, it probably did not continue for very long, for while she was in the process of divorcing Vincente Minnelli, Garland had already taken up with Sid Luft, and would have his daughter, Lorna, in November of 1952. A few months after that, Mercer's irascible temper finally turned on Garland herself. She had always felt tormented by her mother, and as she became increasingly independent, she cut off ties with her, not even permitting Ethel Gumm to visit her new granddaughter. Ethel retaliated by granting interviews to gossip columnists where she would provide such tidbits as "She just brushed me off. . . . Judy has been selfish all her life." To support herself, Ethel had to take a job at Douglas Aircraft for sixty-one dollars a week. "My mother's a fucking riveter at Douglas," Garland, now thirty years old, scoffed. "That's where she belongs. It's too good for her."

As she was getting out of her car to go to work one morning, Ethel Gumm collapsed and died of heart failure. Her body was not found until four hours later. Newspapers harped on the story of how Judy Garland had turned on the mother who had started her on her career. "How could she have stood by and watched her own mother, who had contributed so much to her success, conclude her life so pathetically—broke, angry, and alone?" To Johnny Mercer, with his inbred love of family, Garland's treatment of her mother was unforgivable. At a party he accosted her as she entered and drunkenly shouted, "Why did you let your mother die in a parking lot?" Garland burst into tears, ran to the bathroom, and began cutting her wrists, so an ambulance was called. "The incident was so macabre," the host said, "that everyone left."

Mercer's bitterness in these years was exacerbated by his realization that the world of popular song, which he had ruled for more than a decade, was moving away from him and his kind of music. In the booming economy of the 1950s, teenagers had money to purchase records, and the music industry gravitated toward them. "As the age for purchasing went down," a former Capitol employee observed, "the quality of music went down with it. Bubble rock—here's the beat . . . As your level of sophistication, for whatever reason, goes down, that's where your market is."

Steve Allen, himself a songwriter, recalled how the very importance of songwriting eroded in these years under the economic pressures of the music business: "Eventually it occurs to vocalists—and if not to them, to their agents—that it is not absolutely necessary that 50 percent of the income derived from sales of the songs they record be shared with composers and lyricists, who may in fact not even be known to them. By creating their own material they could have *all* the money. At this point the question of ability naturally arises. Clearly the average singer simply isn't able to create melodies or lyrics on the level of the masters. But a popular song, in its essential form, is a simple little thing—compared, that is, to a symphony, a concerto, a play, a novel, or a great painting. This is particularly true of material based on simple and usually traditional or cliché harmonies, such as some country or rock music. Another contributing factor to the collapse of quality in American pop music is that in the old days almost all of it was written at the piano. In the modern day a lot of it has been written not by pianists but by guitar players, and often just by people who have minimal knowledge of that instrument."

Johnny Mercer, a man who, even in the most pressing times, maintained a supreme self-confidence, began to doubt himself. "He had an insecurity about him—strange," Alan Livingston said. "He never thought of himself being the successful man he was. And in his forties, he kept saying—he said, 'I'm an old man. I'm through. It's over.' And we'd laugh at him because, you know, he was still tremendously successful and important. And he was a young man by any standards, in his forties. But he didn't feel that way."

Livingston saw Mercer's eclipse as part of the whole shift away from his kind of music. "Rock came along and just changed all that, and, of course, Johnny went with it. And so he was—the music business moved beyond him—not beyond him, but away from him. And I guess if he felt that he was unhappy that he couldn't record, that was the reason. It had nothing to do with his talent. . . . It had to do with where the young people's interests were. He was born at the right time for his talents. If he had been born later, his talents would never have come out. There was no market for them."

Mercer himself put it more succinctly: "We aren't greedy. We just have so much to say, it seems a shame that there is no room to say it anymore. Rock and roll has shoved so many of us onto the 'flip side.'"

Between Mercer's affability and his insecurity in these years, he was a prey for less talented collaborators who would seek him out to write a lyric to their melody. With his generous nature, Mercer would consent, but the results were unsuccessful songs. "Johnny was so easygoing," Alan Livingston recalled, "that he wrote with some composers who really he shouldn't have been working with, because they went after him, and he couldn't say no. . . . People got to Johnny. . . . Johnny was a patsy for composers."

The same sentiment was echoed by others. "Paul Weston used to say that he would write with the first guy who showed up in the morning," recalled Ray Evans. "He had a lot of people that hung around him trying to get some help," said Billy May, "and I know he wrote some lyrics for people where someone would come and say, 'I'm stuck with a lyric,' and John would take it and rewrite the whole thing and give it back to the guy. And I know that's not a good thing for a guy to give away his talent like that, but he was such a nice guy, and if someone was a friend, he would help. I know of at least two instances where he really rewrote the man's song for him." The southern gentleman in Mercer had the aristocrat's proud disdain for showing how much he prized his own talent; rather than refuse to share it, he was a prodigal who cavalierly gave it away.

To Livingston, Mercer's easygoing affability was part of his genteel refusal to fight for what he wanted. "He never inserted himself strongly," he said. "He wasn't strong about trying to take charge. That was not his nature. . . . He was not aggressive in his relationships, not aggressive in choosing composer-writing partners. Those who came after him, he went with, and sometimes the wrong people. And we were, at times, critical of him for that. But he was such an easygoing man that he would never think of saying no or turning somebody down or not being social or polite or whatever. . . . He was not aggressive in any manner at all. If somebody took advantage of him, he'd complain about it, but he wouldn't do anything about it."

Livingston found Mercer's refusal to fight for what he wanted, attend to business, or enjoy the fruits of his success puzzling. "Johnny never lived up to his income or stature, ever. He had a little house in a very middle-class part of town. And he had a business manager who got to him, who was not, certainly, an important business manager in this town, who did not necessarily handle his funds as well as they should have been handled. But Johnny didn't care. He just went along and whoever came to him, he said, 'Okay.' He just didn't—he didn't live up to who he was, ever."

Despite Mercer's genial manner with everyone, Livingston saw him as an essentially lonely man: "I don't think Johnny had any close friends. He went with people who called him and said, 'Let's go out to dinner,' or whatever it is, or invited him to a cocktail party or a dinner or whatever it was. And he would always come. But I don't think he ever developed a really close, intimate, warm relationship or had a best friend. I don't think Johnny had a best friend."

Mercer's willingness to collaborate with virtually any composer did bring him some rewards. For example, he would agree to write English lyrics to popular foreign songs—something many lesser lyricists disparaged because it meant royalties had to be split with the foreign songwriters. Such assignments gave Mercer better melodies to work with than he usually was given by sundry American composers. Michael Goldsen, who headed Capitol's sheet-music publishing wing in the early 1950s, loved French popular songs and asked Capitol's French representative to send him songs that were popular there. "So he got back to me, he sent me a pile of records this high. And I listened to them, and I heard one song, I think Edith Piaf had recorded, called 'Les Feuilles Mortes.' And I listened a minute, and I said, 'Oh, man, this is the greatest song I've ever heard.' And so I got ahold of him, and I found the name of the publisher, and I made a deal."

The deal, however, stipulated that the English lyric had to be written within four months. At the time, Goldsen was not aware of Mercer's protracted working habits. "So I gave him the lyric, and I was busy with other things, and, finally, it was three weeks before the deadline, and I hadn't the lyric." To Goldsen, it seemed that the English lyric should not have taken so long to write. "You know, it wasn't a big song. And, to me, it sounded like you could write that in twenty minutes, you know? But here it was almost three months, and he hadn't written it." When Goldsen called Mercer to ask for the lyric, the songwriter said he was going to New York in a few days, and if Goldsen would drive him to the train station, he would write the lyric on the train, then send it back in the mail. On the day of Mercer's departure, Goldsen was delayed and got to Mercer's house about ten minutes late. "So I drove up to his house, and I see him sitting on the steps of his house, and I walked up, and I said, 'Gee, John, I'm awfully sorry I'm late.'

"He said, 'Well, you know, I didn't know if something had happened, so while I was waiting, I wrote the lyric. Here it is.'"

Once again, Mercer was able to give the impression of the effortless aristocrat who, without ever *working*, created works of genius. "And he wrote it on the back of an envelope or something. And as I'm driving, he read it to me, and tears came to my eyes. It was such a great lyric. . . . Everything about that lyric was just so, so Mercerish."

"*Les Feuilles Mortes*," literally "The Dying Leaves," had music by Joseph Kosma, who set a poem by Jacques Prévert, which, in a literal translation, begins:

> The falling leaves (are so abundant) they can be collected by shovelfuls,
> Memories and regrets, as well
> But my silent and faithful love
> Still smiles and thanks life.

Although Mercer might not have tried to write his English version during the three months he had the French song, his mind must have ruminated on it during that time, for the English lyric he crafted was one of his most exquisitely spare and moving. Into it may have gone his own anguish at seeing the changing musical world pass him by, but he rendered that anguish with superb artistic control.

Instinctively he must have known that French, as a Romance language, was rich in rhyme; there are fifty-one rhymes for *amour* in French, including such evocative rhymes as *toujours*. By contrast, English, a Germanic language, has far fewer words that rhyme; there are only five rhymes for *love—above, dove, glove, shove,* and *of*—only the first two of which really lend themselves to romantic parlance. The real poetry in English, moreover, lies in its hard accents and harsh consonants. The earliest poetry in English employed not rhyme but alliteration ("Bitter breast cares have I abided"), and Shakespeare laced his unrhymed iambic verse with crabbed consonants ("I had rather hear a brazen candlestick turned or a dry wheel grate on the axletree"). Even modern advertising slogans employ the rough accents and alliteration at the poetic heart of the language: "When better cars are built, Buick will build them."

Johnny Mercer's English lyric used only three rhymes, relying instead on alliterating consonants in what could be described as a lyrical "Concerto in *T* and *D*":

> The falling leaves *d*rif*t* by the win*d*ow,
> The au*t*umn leaves of re*d* an*d* gol*d*.
> I see your lips, the summer's kisses,
> The sunburne*d* han*d*s I use*d t*o hol*d*.

With the paucity of rhymes, those harsh *t* and *d* sounds underscore a loss at once personal and universal.

He even wittily inverts the seasonal change, as a Japanese poet might do in an elegant haiku:

Since you went away the days grow long,
And soon I'll hear old winter's song.

Days, of course, do not lengthen but shorten through the autumnal season, but Mercer, creating a twist not in the original French lyric, underscores the overwhelming loss of love with a seasonal image that suggests a reversal of natural process. When asked about his lyric for "Autumn Leaves," Mercer offered only a series of brief understatements that reflect his characteristically patrician disparagement of his achievements: "It's all right. It fits the tune. I don't think it's very original." "His talent was number one," Alan Livingston said, but he recalled how often Mercer would shortchange himself: "He never thought he could sing. He'd say, 'You call that a voice, you know?' And his writing talents he took for granted and didn't think much of."

The success of "Autumn Leaves" in 1950 prompted Goldsen, a year later, to present Mercer with another French song, *Le Chevalier de Paris*," by lyricist Angela Vannier and composer M. Philippe-Gerard. "This was also an Edith Piaf record, and it was a thing with verses and a chorus. To me, it felt like a great song. . . . So I went to Johnny with the song, and I got him a translation of it. And he looked at it, he listened, and he says, 'Gee, I love this thing.' He said, 'I really feel it.'" Within three weeks, Mercer had written two sets of lyrics so that the song could be sung by either a male or a female vocalist. "In other words," Goldsen explained, "if the song was written for a man, it would limit it. And so there was always that option, and some would either change the lyric or add lyrics so a girl could do it; and Johnny was smart enough to realize that. . . . And of course the artists that we got on the thing were just tremendous—including Sinatra. . . . Peggy Lee recorded it. Well, she wouldn't have recorded it if it didn't have a girl's lyric."

Mercer's felt response to the French chanson probably reflected the fact that the lyric could describe his own life. In the male verses, the narrator, a sophisticated man about town, reflects on his urbane lifestyle:

It isn't by chance I happen to be a boulevardier, the toast of Paris,
For over the noise, the talk and the smoke,
I'm good for a laugh, a drink or a joke.
I walk in a room, a party or ball,
"Come sit over here" somebody will call.
"A drink for M'sieur! A drink for us all!"
But how many times I stop and recall:

The brief refrain then takes the narrator back to his rural boyhood:

Ah, the apple trees,
Blossoms in the breeze,

That we walked among,
Lying in the hay,
Games we used to play,
While the rounds were sung,
Only yesterday,
When the world was young.

Clearly, the lyric expresses Mercer's own longing, for all of his cosmopolitan shuttling between New York and Hollywood, for that pastoral world he knew as a child in those summers "on the water" in Savannah.

Mercer was flattered when, on a visit to Paris, people told him his English lyric to "When the World Was Young" was superior to the original French lyric, but he was again casually understated about his achievement. "It seemed to me just my way of remembering how it was in the old days, because the song in French, as well as in English, talks about a man who has been to war, comes back disillusioned, or girl who's been around the pool comes back disillusioned and remembers how it was when she was young. Before the world got to her and everything. . . . I just remembered all these things that I remembered as a boy."

Equally nostalgic, but much more flippant, were the English lyrics he set to an old German song, "Glühwürmchen," written in 1902 by Paul Lincke. The first English lyrics were written by Lilla Cayley Robinson when the song was featured in the 1907 musical *The Girl Behind the Counter*. Several recordings were made of the song as "Glow Worm," and Mercer, with his omnivorous love of songs, probably knew it as a child. His updated, hipster lyrics are some of the cleverest he ever wrote:

Glow, little glow-worm, fly of fire,
Glow like an incandescent wire,
Glow for the female of the specie,
Turn on the A-C and the D-C . . .
When you gotta glow, you gotta glow,
Glow, little glow worm, glow. . . .
Thou aer-o-nau-tic-al boll weevil,
Il-lu-mi-nate yon woods primeval;
See how the shadows deep and darken,
You and your chick should get to sparkin' . . .
You got a cute vest-pocket Mazda
Which you can make both slow or "Fazda" . . .

Mercer made his own hit recording of "Glow Worm" for Capitol, but it was the Mills Brothers who came to "own" the song.

The most unusual foreign composition for which Johnny Mercer provided lyrics was Nikolay Rimsky-Korsakov's "Song of India," which Tommy Dorsey recorded in a swing instrumental version in 1937. In 1953, Mercer took the melody and set it to soaring imagery:

> Then I hear the song that only India can sing,
> Softer than the plumage on a black raven's wing.
> High upon a minaret I stand
> And gaze across the desert sand
> Upon an old enchanted land.
> There's the maharajah's caravan,
> Unfolding like a painted fan.
> How small the little race of Man!

When Mel Tormé first heard the song on the radio, in an operatic recording by Mario Lanza, he called the station to inquire who had written the lyric. He was amazed to learn it was Johnny Mercer. Tormé later asked Mercer, "How do you do it?" Mercer said, "Mel, read everything. If you are in the breakfast room, read the cornflakes box; you can never tell when there's going to be a lyric in it."

These foreign songs were virtually the only successes Mercer had in the early 1950s, and it is ironic that their nostalgia reflects Mercer's own alienation from the world of popular music. In "Autumn Leaves," in particular, he had poured out, in its stringent syllables, his own despair and sense of loss. Over the years, the song has endured as one of the great standards, an expression of a universal sense of mutability and transience. Years later, as the classic quality of the song became increasingly apparent, Johnny Mercer sought Goldsen out and said, " 'You know something, Mickey? "Autumn Leaves" is the biggest income song I have ever had, and I only wrote the lyric to it, and I only collect in the United States and England.' That's how big the song was."

Twelve

I'm Old Fashioned: 1952–1954

When I lived at the beach, and the kids were growing up, I spent a lot of time with them—tried to. . . . I love the water. I love especially the ocean.

As the world of popular song moved away from Johnny Mercer, he clung to the things he had. "Johnny got very attached to things," a niece recalled. "He was old-fashioned, and he was loyal, and he was—he never put on airs, he was very unassuming." One of the things he was most attached to was his house in West Hollywood at 8425 De Longpre Avenue, which presented the same impression he liked to give of himself: from the outside, it was an unimposing Cape Cod bungalow, so very different from the palatial homes of other Hollywood notables. Over the years, however, the Mercers had added on to and improved the house so that it was quite comfortable, though still not ostentatious.

But by 1953 it became clear that they would have to move out of the neighborhood. "The neighbors started selling, and they started building apartments around there, and Johnny just refused to move." Even in California, the land of quick turnover, Johnny Mercer clung to his roots, refusing to sell a home that he knew would be torn down to make way for a high-rise apartment building. "Finally, I think he was probably one of the last people, he was just absolutely forced to sell the house. Well, then, he wanted the house. They said, 'Okay, you know, we are going to give you the money. You can buy the house back for a dollar and move it.'" But all the additions and improvements made the house immovable. "The house was a very old house and had been added on to, and the old parts didn't meet the building codes, and so they couldn't. They wound up—much to Johnny's dismay—just having to go and buy a whole new house. But he tried. I mean, he must have taken a year trying to find some way to get that house moved." Their interior decorator recalls that, rather than let the house be torn down, Mercer gave it, or rather part of it, to his secretary. "They sawed it in half and took it down in the dead of night when there was no traffic to Long Beach at ten miles an hour."

"He was the same way with cars," the niece added. "In the early fifties, he had this Cadillac convertible that at that time was about ten years old. And his agent kept telling him, 'This isn't good for your image, you know. You really need to get a new car.'

"'I like this car,'" was Mercer's only reply.

In 1954, the Mercers bought a vacation house at 108 Via Karon on Lido Isle at Newport Beach and decided to live there until they could build a house in the fashionable Bel Air district of Los Angeles. "What happened was, though," their daughter Amanda said, "they got my brother and me down there, and it was like—we threw a hissy fit. We had gone to school and savored the life of a small town and enjoyed it very much in Newport. It was a typical beach, small-town place, and nobody knew who anybody was or cared. You know, half of the kids had never even been up to Hollywood, and they didn't know what Hollywood was like. And it was really, you know, a great life, and we threw a hissy fit. We were supposed to move back. And my father gave in, which he shouldn't have done, I guess. But it was the greatest thing that ever happened to my brother and me . . . growing up in a small town and not in that, you know, Hollywood setting."

Giving in to his children's demands to live in Newport Beach further alienated Johnny from Ginger, who missed the social whirl of Hollywood. "My mother," Jeff Mercer recalled, "didn't really care for it down there."

But Mercer found living in a small town on the ocean brought back his boyhood in Savannah, and he would pile his children, along with kids in the neighborhood, into his pickup truck and take them to the beach to go sailing, swimming, and surfing. "He loved to bodysurf," his son recalled. "We used to bodysurf at Tybee in Georgia and at Huntington Beach." He also took up painting in these years, as other songwriters, such as Irving Berlin and George Gershwin, had done. But whereas Berlin and Gershwin painted in oils, Johnny Mercer chose the lighter, more informal medium of watercolors. "I used to paint watercolors, which is a lot of fun," he said. "I'd sit outside under the trees and paint."

A neighbor recalled how much Mercer loved living near the ocean. "He loved to go to the bay . . . and he had an inner tube . . . and he would go out to the dock with his tube, and he'd swim off the dock with the tube; he'd paddle around with the tube." The sight of a wealthy, world-famous songwriter behaving like a country boy with his inner tube always amused the neighbor.

"And he's sitting out there with a tire tube." While Via Koron was a fashionable neighborhood, the Mercers' house had no view of the bay. At a neighborhood party, a woman said, " 'You know, Johnny, you love the water and all—how come you're not living in one of the waterfront houses?'

" 'Oh, man, they're expensive, I can't afford it.'

"That's the kind of guy he was," the neighbor reflected. "He could've afforded, you know, to buy up a whole row of houses, but he never felt that he was rich." It might again have been Mercer's patrician disdain for a display of wealth that kept him in more modest quarters. "He didn't live according to his income. He just lived according to his taste. If he wanted something, he bought it. So he was that kind of guy."

Despite the time he devoted to his children while they lived in Newport, friends said, "He was not a good father. . . . People would always say what a sweet person he was. He was always kind to people. . . . But he could get to be quite mean. Ginger always bore the brunt of most of that . . . and of course it was extremely hard on his two children, who had to live with him all the time." Toward Mandy, "He was a protective and loving father." She grew up rather dazed by the glamorous world her father moved in. At parties, their house would be filled with movie stars she had seen on the screen, and even as an older woman she radiates a starstruck excitement as she recounts her memories. Some are fond, such as the shy Mel Ferrer slipping away from the other guests to sit in her room and talk to her:

"I'd say, 'What are you doing in here? Why aren't you out at the party?'

" 'Oh, it's too boring. I would rather talk to you.' "

Other memories were not so pleasant, such as wearing a beautiful new dress to a party only to have it ruined when Frank Sinatra threw his drink across the room at agent Swifty Lazare.

By the time she was in high school she had clearly had enough of the Hollywood lifestyle to throw the "hissy fit" that enabled her to grow up in the normal, small-torn atmosphere of Newport Beach.

As a child, however, she was awestruck by her father's world and by him. She remembers he would lie on the couch, but if she made noise, her mother would shush her.

" 'Daddy's asleep.'

" 'No, he isn't,' " her mother would say. " 'He's writing songs.' " Although her father "worked" by lying down on the couch with his eyes shut, she was amazed when songs came out of him. She would listen as he sang a lyric to her mother and asked, "What do you think?" When she was older, he would pay her the supreme compliment of asking *her* what she thought of a lyric. "Just pretend you're my public," he'd say.

Early on, she realized that her father was a performer: she heard him on the radio, and at her school the parents of other children crowded around him. "He pursued it. He loved to entertain. That was his dream. That was his life." At first she tried to dismiss his fame, saying, "You're famous to them—you're not famous to me." As she got to know more about the world in which her father moved, however, she became fascinated with it. "He baby-sat me a lot," she said. "I don't know what my mother was always doing, but he was always baby-sitting me. . . . He'd take me to the set; and he would dump me off on some set where there were a lot of kids, and then he'd go do his work." Wandering around the sets, she would see the same stars who came to her home, moving in the magical world of Hollywood studios in their vintage years. "I was, I guess, a movie fan like every other kid in Hollywood and spent most of my waking hours in the movies." She even got a taste of being on-screen herself. One day he took her to the television studio where a children's program was airing. "So he takes me and he sits me down on *The Bozo Show*. And I had to be on *The Bozo Show* while he went and worked. I mean, like, I *had* to be on it, right?"

While Amanda could be enraptured by Hollywood stardom, she was annoyed when fans hounded her father for autographs: "I'd say, 'Daddy, let's go! I want to go home now!' He'd say, 'Sit down! If it wasn't for them, you wouldn't have any food in your mouth, so you sit down.'" Moreover, when Mercer signed an autograph he graciously took extra time to draw a caricature of himself. Mandy's first husband recalled that Mercer tried to be a good father but that "one of the things he really didn't understand was probably paying attention to his children in public. Because when you would go out to dinner with him, everybody would come to the table and they would ignore everybody at the table except Johnny." A child who was already shy would feel even smaller at such moments. While Ginger seemed to relish being part of that world, even though she herself was not the center of attention, her daughter would have felt more like a member of the audience before her father and the other famous stars she knew.

Mandy soon grew showbiz savvy as she accompanied her father on his Hollywood rounds. On one television show, *Musical Chairs*, Johnny sat on a panel with stars such as Bobby Troup, Rose Marie, and Mel Blanc (the voice of Bugs Bunny). Viewers would send in musical questions to try to stump the stars, and at the end of each show the panelists had to collaborate on a lyric, each one improvising a line. On one episode, the host told them to write a song about Hollywood. Bobby Troup started off with a line about how wealthy everyone was in Hollywood, Rose Marie improvised a line about people walking around in "diamonds and furs," Mel Blanc added still other possessions, and Mercer, seemingly with utter spontaneity, concluded, "And matching swimming pools marked 'His' and 'Hers.'" It was Mercer at his casually genteel best, effortlessly producing witty lyrics at the drop of a hat. "Of course," Amanda explained, "it was a song Daddy had written, you know. He sat down before the show and wrote out these lines and said, 'Okay, this is what we're doing.'"

At times her father's glamorous world overwhelmed her, such as the day he brought home Nat King Cole, "my big crush of all time." As Mercer and Cole worked on songs, Amanda hid under the huge mirrored table in the living room. "I know they knew I was there, but I pretended like I was hiding." Nearly fifty years later, the ecstasy of that moment is undiminished: "Oh, oh," she recalled, sighing. "My heart still beats thinking about it. It was just the most thrilling thing in my life."

But Amanda also remembers the bitter fights between her parents, fights in which Ginger would throw at Johnny the far greater fame and money her old beau Bing Crosby was making in Hollywood. By pressing the Crosby button Ginger proved herself to be a formidable domestic warrior, for while Crosby's wealth would not have aroused Mercer's envy, the reminder that he had once hoped to emulate the crooner's stardom would have cut deeply.

"They would fight about anything," a friend of Ginger's recalled. "They fed off each other." They fought about money, the money Johnny lavished on friends and family—Ginger's family as well as his own. "Johnny was always sending the mother and sister on trips. "Her mother would call and say, 'We are leaving in two days for Europe' or 'Hawaii.' And she'd say, 'Where did you get the money?' And she'd say, 'Johnny sent it. Didn't you know?'" Such gestures sprang from Mercer's native generosity, but they seem also to have been his way of getting back at Ginger, who resented his munificence.

"He just adored his family," Amanda said. "That was the most important thing in the world to him, you know. That came before everything, and when my mom would get mad at him and say, 'You should save more money and do this and do that' and nah-nah-nah-nah . . . and he says, 'It's my money. I spend it the way I want.'" But as an adult Amanda could recognize the absurdity of Mercer's generosity. "He was ridiculous. He spoiled us all to death."

Neither Johnny nor Ginger, according to a niece, understood money. "Ginger *thought* she was a very down-to-earth, normal person who did not take advantage of having money and position. But, you know, you don't realize it when you're in it. She had people who paid her bills—she and Johnny didn't pay bills. They were very much taken advantage of. . . . But they did not pay attention to money. Johnny didn't give a damn about money." She recalled that the Mercers had three cars but were so dependent on a local filling station to maintain and repair them "that there were times when they had *no* car." Another niece said, "I remember all the people—people that you *go* to—the hairdresser, the massage therapy. I remember them coming out *there* to do her. Have her hair done, have her massage."

Amanda also recalled her own arguments with her parents. Her father always admired her "sweet and patient spirit," she said, "and he was patient to a point; then we'd both blow up, usually at each other. 'Cause we couldn't blow at Mom because she would hold it to us unless she blew. He and Mom blew all the time. But between us he would blow. It was easier for Daddy and me to

Moon River, Savannah, Georgia, formerly the Back River, renamed in honor of Johnny Mercer's best-known song.

The Mercer summer home "on the water" at Vernon View, outside Savannah. *Georgia Roux Collection, M2001-6/2, Popular Music Collection, Special Collections Department, Pullen Library, Georgia State University*

Susie Lokie, Johnny's nurse, holding his sister Nancy, January 17, 1913. The following year Nancy died of diphtheria at the age of three. PHOTOGRAPHY BY FOLTZ STUDIOS, SAVANNAH. *Johnny Mercer Papers, M81-1/62, Popular Music Collection, Special Collections Department, Georgia State University*

George Anderson Mercer, Johnny's father, ca. 1905. *Johnny Mercer Papers, M81-1/65*

Lillian Ciucevich Mercer, Johnny's mother, ca. 1905. *Johnny Mercer Papers, M81-1/89*

Johnny Mercer, approximately two years old, probably taken at the Mercer summer home at Vernon View, ca. 1911. *Johnny Mercer Papers, M81-1/50*

Johnny Mercer, age eight, May 1918, at Vernon View. *Johnny Mercer Papers, M81-1/52*

Johnny Mercer, far left, with classmates at Woodberry Forest School, Virginia, ca. 1926. *Johnny Mercer Papers, M81-1/618*

Ginger Meehan (Rose Elizabeth Meltzer), when she and Johnny were courting, ca. 1930. *Johnny and Ginger Mercer Papers, M1995-15, 1/73, Popular Music Collection, Pullen Library, Georgia State University*

Newspaper photograph of Elizabeth Cummins, Johnny Mercer's "girl back home" in Savannah, announcing her engagement to another man. *Savannah Morning News*, October 19, 1930.

Mr. and Mrs. Johnny Mercer on the boardwalk at Atlantic City, October 1, 1933. PHOTOGRAPHY BY G. DOBKIN STUDIO, NEW JERSEY. *Johnny Mercer Papers, M81-1/134*

Johnny Mercer and Paul Whiteman at the National Broadcasting Studios in Times Square, March 24, 1932, two days after Whiteman selected Mercer as one of the winners of the Pontiac Youth of America singing contest. *Johnny Mercer Papers, M81-1/342*

Johnny Mercer and Hoagy Carmichael, 1947, perhaps reminiscing over their string of hit songs that started in 1933 with "Lazybones." PHOTOGRAPHY BY *DOWN BEAT* MAGAZINE. *Johnny Mercer Papers, M81-1/287*

Johnny Mercer, upper berth, on the set of *Old Man Rhythm*, RKO, 1935. *Johnny and Ginger Mercer Papers, M1995-15, 1/6*

Johnny Mercer and Richard Whiting working on a song for Warner Bros., ca. 1937. *Johnny and Ginger Mercer Papers, M1995-15, 1/12*

Ruby Keeler and Lee Dixon tap dancing to "Too Marvelous for Words" in *Ready, Willing and Able*, Warner Bros., 1937. *Photofest*

Johnny Mercer, standing, and other minstrels in a Westwood Marching and Chowder Club performance, March 23, 1940. *Johnny Mercer Papers, M81-1/397.*

Johnny Mercer singing on the radio, 1944. PHOTOGRAPHY BY CHARLIE MIHN. *Johnny and Ginger Mercer Papers, M1995-15, 1/18*

Mercer and Harold Arlen, perhaps working on *St. Louis Woman,* ca. 1945. *Johnny Mercer Papers, M81-1/299.*

Pearl Bailey and Fayard Nicholas in
St. Louis Woman, 1946. *Photofest*

Mercer and Lena Horne, ca.
1950. Photography by Jules
Davis. *Johnny Mercer Papers,
M81-1/322*

Judy Garland in the production number for "On the Atchison, Topeka and the Santa Fe," *The Harvey Girls*, MGM, 1946. *Photofest*

Mercer and Nat King Cole at a recording session at Capitol, ca. 1950. *Johnny Mercer Papers, M81-1/623*

Johnny Mercer "working" on a lyric at home, Los Angeles, 1949. PHOTOGRAPHY BY ROBERT. S. HANAH. *Johnny Mercer Papers, M81-1/601*

Johnny Mercer, always the laid-back boy from Savannah, even in New York City. *Johnny Mercer Papers, M81-1/282*

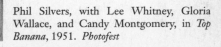

Phil Silvers, with Lee Whitney, Gloria Wallace, and Candy Montgomery, in *Top Banana*, 1951. *Photofest*

Seven Brides for Seven Brothers, MGM, 1954. *Photofest*

Fred Astaire and Leslie Caron dancing to "Something's Gotta Give," *Daddy Long Legs*, MGM, 1955. *Photofest*

Peter Palmer and Edie Adams singing "Namely You" in *Li'l Abner*, 1956. PHOTOGRAPHY BY FRIEDMAN-ABELES, NEW YORK. *Photofest*

Johnny Mercer during a Broadway rehearsal, perhaps of *Saratoga*, ca. 1959. PHOTOGRAPHY BY GJON MILI, NEW YORK. *Johnny Mercer Papers, M81-1/238*

Carol Lawrence and Howard Keel in *Saratoga*, 1959. PHOTOGRAPHY BY CECIL BEATON. *Photofest*

Bert Lahr in *Foxy*, 1964. *Photofest*

Johnny Mercer, John Jefferson, Ginger, and Amanda, probably at their Newport Beach home, 1957. PHOTOGRAPHY BY BUD SELZER, HOLLYWOOD FILM STUDIO. *Johnny Mercer Papers, M81-1/124*

Mercer and Henry Mancini, ca. 1962. *Johnny Mercer Papers, M81-1/328*

Mercer and Bing Crosby, trading banter during a recording session, August 1960. *Johnny Mercer Papers, M81-1/41*

Johnny and Ginger, 1962. PHOTOGRAPHY BY HERB CARLTON, HOLLYWOOD. *Johnny Mercer Papers, M81-1/128*

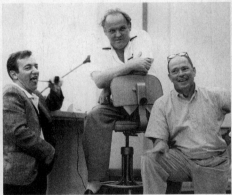

Bobby Darin (at left), bandleader Billy May, and Johnny Mercer recording *Two of a Kind*, 1963. PHOTOGRAPHY BY GARRETT-HOWARD, INC., LOS ANGELES. *Johnny Mercer Papers, M81-1/34*

Judy Garland performing on *The Judy Garland Show*, ca. 1963. *Photofest*

Mercer at a party at the Manhattan apartment of Jean Bach after his appearance in the "Lyrics and Lyricists" series at the 92nd Street Y, March 14, 1971. PHOTOGRAPHY BY HELEN MARCUS, NEW YORK. *Johnny Mercer Papers, M81-1/559*

Mercer near his boyhood home on Moon River, Savannah, 1970. PHOTOGRAPHY BY FREDERICK BALDWIN, SAVANNAH. *Johnny Mercer Papers, M81-1/219*

blow because then we forgot it the next day. My mother would *never* forget. I mean, you had a fight with her, ten years later she would drop it on you."

A friend remembers a bitter argument between Ginger and Johnny over Mandy. "It wasn't anything profoundly serious," he said. "And what struck me was how Johnny defended Mandy. It was like he didn't want to hear anything bad said about anybody. . . . I felt more than that. I felt like he was, you know, he was trying to put a good face on something that might have been problematic."

"Mandy did a complete turnaround," another friend said, recalling her rebellious teenage years. "She'd sit and stick her tongue at me and blow smoke in my face. But I'd say, 'You're not supposed to be smoking you little brat.' . . . And then, she ran away from home and spent one night out, and, my God, you would've thought she'd been captured by white slavery. Johnny went crazy. So did Ginger. She was at a neighbor's. You know, it was no big thing, she was just rebelling."

Amanda's daughter remembered her grandfather "Beebah" and grandmother "Granginger": "Even my mom would tell me they were awful to each other. I never saw that. See, they never did it in front of us." She said that Mercer did not believe in divorce and told his son-in-law, when he and Mandy were having marital difficulties, "You married for life." Ginger too was committed to marriage, though the commitment sometimes came out in bizarre fashion. The granddaughter recalled a ceremony where Ginger was to accept an award posthumously for Johnny. "She got so drunk she couldn't get on stage, so me and my mom went up." But as the wife of one of Johnny's collaborators also went up to accept an award, Ginger "was trying to dive over the table" and "beat her up . . . calling her a gold digger." What incensed Ginger was that at one point in the woman's marriage the couple was broke and the wife left her husband until he made more money. Ginger "hated her because of that. She had some type of dedication to marriage."

She recalled her grandmother as a terrifying figure in old age. "I remember peeking out every night in my room and she would just be drinking—sittin' in her little, you know, what do you call those long—chaise?—but it's like a fancy bed, you know, with an antique frame—satin. . . . She'd be drinking and smoking—it used to kind of scare me." Another memory, more poignant than terrifying: "She had a little bit to drink and she put her arm around me and said, 'I never—I always had a hatred toward your mother because he loved her so much and she wasn't mine.'" A child adopted to bring Johnny and Ginger together turned out to be yet another wedge driven between them.

Asked about her memory of her father, Amanda responded with a word: "Loving. He was the kind of person who loved unconditionally. And he was very caring about his family. I mean he would just grab you and hug you, you know. It seemed like no reason at all. It was just 'cause he felt like it and he loved you." Asked what her father gave to her as a daughter, her first word again was "Love. Love, mostly. You don't think about those things, and you don't realize how important it is. And when he died, I realized I still had that. That it was something I'll have all the rest of my life—his love."

Pressed for more memories of Ginger, Amanda simply said, "I don't like to talk about my mom."

About her brother John Jefferson's childhood, a family friend said, "It was a rough, rough—his father gave him anything he wanted. If he wanted an alligator in the bathtub or crocodile, he'd buy it for him. Whatever he wanted. Just spoiled him. There was no discipline. No anything. And of course Jeff's mother, she had always heard that if a child was hugged demonstratively by a mother, he might turn out gay. . . . So she was not demonstrative at all. He had a rough one."

"Neither of them had any clue as to how to raise a child," a niece recalled. "I was painting one year, wanting to do some painting. And I asked for some oils and some brushes. And they were here for Christmas, and I think Jeff was eight years old. And the Christmas presents in our house . . . took up almost the whole living room and most of them were for Jeff. And Jeff got a really professional artist's thing of oils and brushes—and he was only eight years old." A Savannah friend explained that Mercer was always solicitous toward Jeff because when he was adopted, "Johnny wasn't sure he'd been fed well." He also recalled Mercer's attempt to pull a string to get Jeff admitted to Woodberry Forest, whose headmaster, Joseph Mercer, was Johnny's cousin.

" 'Joe, take him on probation. And maybe in the past they didn't really give him the necessities.'

"And he said, 'Johnny, if I take him on probation, I have to take anybody on probation.'

"And so Johnny says, 'Okay, Joe, but tell your office not to send me any more requests.'

"Johnny was a good benefactor to the school," the friend explained. "He said, 'I didn't ask him to do anything but give the guy a chance.' . . . He said, 'Take him and see if you can help him and if you can't I'll understand.' But he didn't say, 'Take him.' He cut 'em off." On the one hand Mercer was his characteristically genteel self in asking, but not insisting, that Woodberry Forest admit his son; on the other, he was vindictive enough to cut off his contributions to his alma mater.

In his mid-fifties, a father himself, Jeff Mercer could look back upon his father with kindness, even though he admitted their relationship was distant. "He was a grandfather is what he was. He would have been better suited as a grandfather than a father. . . . He tried. He'd take me to the beach and we'd play, and stuff like this. He was pretty competitive. We'd play croquet or something on a lawn and if I was beatin' him, he'd get mad. He'd turn it up a notch. He'd have to beat me. He had a little—he had a hard time setting aside his aggression when it came to winning. And that's what made him a great songwriter. Because he wanted to be the best. He had that drive. So sometimes you can't turn it off."

Jeff thought that competitiveness drove his father to give up golf. "He played golf when he was younger. He loved the sport. He always told me it was the greatest sport ever invented and that I ought to get into it. I think he liked it more as a social event and also his Scottish ancestry. He enjoyed it, but I think he was one of those types of people that—he was so competitive—now he *claims* he had to quit because his knees got pretty beat up. . . . I think it was just his ego." Mercer himself would probably never admit to such plebian aggressiveness, but his son not only recognized it but, ultimately, forgave it.

Mercer also indulged Jeff's love of exotic animals. "My father was always pretty lenient about that kind of thing. He liked animals." On a visit to Savannah they traveled to a game reserve in South Carolina, where Jeff caught some baby alligators. "There was a female that had a bunch of babies, and they told me—I was about eleven or twelve—so I went over there, and we used a casting net and caught 'em, got chased out by the female, but I brought 'em back." From Savannah, they took the train to New York, and the alligators went along. "I had to take 'em with us to New York, and we stayed in the Plaza Hotel. And when I put the alligators in the bathtub and kept them there it kind of freaked out the maids and things."

When they got back to California, Mercer had a tank built for the alligators. A niece said that Johnny "caught Jeff feeding one of his frogs to one of the alligators."

"And he says, 'What are you doing?'

"And Jeff says, 'That's life, Dad. That's the way of the world—that's the way things are.'

"And Johnny says, 'Not in my backyard, it's not.' And that's when he gave the alligators away. . . . He was very softhearted, and he wouldn't kill a fly or anything like that."

Jeff had also brought a turtle back with him from Savannah. "When I got rid of the alligators," he recalled, "I said, 'Well, I can't let this turtle go here. It's a diamondback terrapin and it's from the marsh, you know, near Florida and Georgia.'" On their next trip to Savannah, the turtle went along. "I just carried it back in a carryall," Jeff said, "and took it back to Savannah and let it go where we found it—crossing the road at Tybee. We physically let it go right where we found it. . . . He was fine when we let him go. Waddled right back into the water and was gone."

The niece remembered how the incident became part of Mercer's comic repertoire: "'Can't you imagine when that turtle gets back to Savannah, and the other little turtles say, 'Well, where have you been, man? We haven't seen you for a long time.' And this little turtle says, 'Well, man, I've been to Hollywood!' And then Johnny went into this long story about what the turtle is going to tell them about Hollywood."

Mercer's indulgence continued into Jeff's early adulthood. "I found a lion for sale at this pet shop . . . an African lion cub." He bought it for $250, put it in his Jeep, and drove home along the freeway. "It was about six months old, so it was just starting to grow its mane, and it was already about a two-hundred-pound animal. And I went, 'Jeez, a little bigger than I thought.'" When he got home, he tried to sneak the lion into the empty dog run in the back of the house. "I figured I'd just put it back there and tell my folks over dinner. And my mom was washing dishes in the kitchen, and I was going around the back but where the kitchen window is, and I came underneath with the lion, and my mom kind of looked and her eyes popped out, and I just kept moving real fast and she just went back to doing her dishes. I don't think she realized what she saw. And I put him in the dog run. And my dad came home and I told my dad first. . . . And he went out there and he looked at him and he said, 'Oh, boy, your mom's going to not like this.' But he said, 'Ah, but he's beautiful.'"

During the night, however, the lion roared under Johnny Mercer's bedroom window. "Definitely that lion is going to have to go," Mercer said the next morning.

Some of Jeff Mercer's fondest memories of his father were of their train trips together. "Fred Harvey used to run the restaurant on the train, and he knew my father, so it was cool; we'd get wined and dined, we had the luxury thing." They also went to ball games: "He always liked baseball; it was a casual type of sport, he could go sit and have a hot dog and a beer." He also recalled his father working on songs. "He would work at night and he'd be in his bedroom, and I'd walk in and say, 'Hey, good night, Dad.' And he'd look up, 'Oh, good night.' And he'd think of something. 'Oh, thanks.' I went, 'What'd I do?' 'Well, you just made me think of something.' And he'd scribble it down."

Jeff remembered his father's cavalier attitude toward money. "He was a generous tipper, yeah, he tipped everybody way more than he should have. He was real generous with money. I mean, he never even made any profits on *anything*. He didn't believe in the stock market. He didn't believe in owning real estate other than to live in a house. He wasn't into turning over money. He wasn't a capitalist." Because he had money, Mercer could ignore it, a blithe spirit impervious to the dollar-driven world around him.

Jeff Mercer could recall only vaguely the fights between his father and mother. "I was in the house when they'd argue and yell at each other. I think most kids grow up with that." Except for an occasional threat from his mother such as "I'll just take you to the cleaners," he was certain, given his father's commitment to family, that they would never have let him hear any discussion of a possible divorce. "They got into fights, but, you know, I really tried to slough that off. It wasn't my business. I mean, they're the couple. I don't have any claims to them being the couple. And that's the way I felt. I would deal with both of them individually or whatever. It didn't bother me. Now, when I was a little kid it might have bothered me. But it didn't bother me when I was an adult."

Friends who knew them in this period recalled how the friction between Johnny and Ginger stemmed from their differences from each other. "She was totally opposite from Johnny," one Newport friend remarked. "She was sophisticated, and he was a 'huckleberry friend.' You know. He was a boy from the South in a Panama suit and a straw hat." The friend recalled how Johnny's drunken belligerence would alienate her more and more. At a Mexican restaurant where a mariachi band was playing, Mercer called out, "Who are these no-talent people?"

"I'm going to take out my compact," Ginger said, "and pretend I've never seen the son of a bitch before in my life."

Yet the same friend recalled driving them to the train station from Lido Isle: "They argued and argued and argued all the way. And, finally, he climbed on the train, and he said, 'You don't want to come on and have a drink with me?'

"Ginger said, 'No, we've got to get back.'

"And he said, 'Well, give me a kiss.' So she turned her cheek to him, and he kissed her on the cheek. And I gave him a hug and a kiss, and he climbed on the train, and we waved as he went. And I turned around and Ginger was standing in back of me, and she's crying.

"I said, 'I don't believe you! I mean, here you are arguing with him all the way into town. And I turn around, and you're crying!'

"And she said, 'You want to know something? Tomorrow, I'm going to miss him.' "

As Ginger received less and less love from her husband, she became increasingly enamored of expensive things—clothing, cars, jewelry. She bought an ermine coat and had it dyed red so she could wear it at Christmas. All there was to know about Ginger, according to a friend of Johnny's in Savannah, was "she was money-hungry." But she clearly needed love as well, after the abuse she received from Johnny. "In a marriage," one of her friends said, "when a man knocks, knocks, knocks, *knocks* at you—many, many years of that, the thing becomes cold." There were rare times, she recalled, "when I'd see them off alone and away from their problems and their children. . . . They were happy and sweet. Good companions. But I don't think there was any great romance left in it because when a woman has been done by a man— wronged in that way, I don't think there is anything." According to another of her friends, Ginger began an affair of her own as early as 1945 with a man who later became her constant companion after Johnny died.

Their alienation from each other was reflected in the chaotic life of their home. Friends recalled parties at the Mercer home where dinner would not be served until midnight or even later. On one occasion, Johnny invited eight people for dinner—but never told Ginger they were coming. "And so we're having drinks, and, you know, eight, nine, ten, eleven o'clock . . . and nothing. There was no food. What happened was that Johnny invited all these people and never told Ginger they were coming for dinner, so Ginger didn't have any dinner prepared, so after about eleven o'clock, we started to phone around and find out if a restaurant was open, and we finally found a restaurant, and we all went out there to have dinner. But that was the way Johnny lived."

Living in Newport Beach meant that Mercer had to drive to Hollywood to work, a commute that became even more inconvenient after he acquired so many tickets for drunk driving that his license was suspended. Fortunately, friends were happy to drive Mercer between Hollywood and Lido Isle. "Johnny was commuting," one recalled, "which is insane." During these years, however, there was not much work for Mercer in Hollywood. Television was rapidly replacing the movies as America's primary form of family entertainment, and the first movies to go were musicals, which required an elaborate company of songwriters, choreographers, dancers, and musicians. In 1938, Hollywood made fifty-nine musicals; in 1950, twenty-one.

From writing songs for three or four movies a year during the 1940s, Mercer wrote for only one or two movies a year in the 1950s. Some movie musicals that were slated for production were canceled, as happened with *Keystone Girl*, for which Mercer had written songs with Hoagy Carmichael. At a Hollywood party, Carmichael and Mercer performed "In the Cool, Cool, Cool of the Evening," one of their songs from the canceled film. At the party was Frank Capra. "My father heard the song," Frank Capra Jr. explained, "and loved it. He asked Mercer and Carmichael if he could use it in a film he was directing, *Here Comes the Groom*." The film was a typically charming "Capra-corn" film that starred Bing Crosby as a roving reporter who adopts two French children but must marry a suitable mother within five days or give them up. With Mercer's folksy dialect, Carmichael's regional rhythm, and Crosby's laid-back persona, "In the Cool, Cool, Cool of the Evening" fit in perfectly:

In the cool, cool, cool of the evenin',
Tell 'em I'll be there.
In the cool, cool, cool of the evenin',
Better save a chair.
When the party's gettin' a glow on,
'N' singin' fills the air,
In the shank o' the night,
When the doin's are right,
You can tell 'em I'll be there . . .

If I ain't in the clink,
And there's sumpin' to drink,
You can tell 'em I'll be there.

When *Here Comes the Groom* came out in 1951, the song brought Mercer his second Academy Award. The award created a mild controversy. Ironically, the problem stemmed from the fact that, back in 1942, Oscar Hammerstein and Jerome Kern had won the Oscar for "The Last Time I Saw Paris," beating out Mercer and Arlen's "Blues in the Night." "At the time," Robert Emmett Dolan said, "I was in New York and Oscar Hammerstein said to me, 'When you get back to Hollywood, tell Johnny Mercer he was robbed.'" Hammerstein's guilt stemmed from the fact that he and Kern had written "The Last Time I Saw Paris" as an independent song, dedicated to Noel Coward, lamenting the fall of Paris to the Nazis. The song, however, was interpolated into the 1941 movie *Lady Be Good* (which should have only featured songs by the Gershwins) and therefore was eligible for an Oscar. Both Kern and Hammerstein felt that "The Last Time I Saw Paris," as an interpolation, did not deserve the award and worked to get the Academy rules changed. But in 1951, because "In the Cool, Cool, Cool of the Evening" had not been recorded or published before it was used in *Here Comes the Groom*, it was deemed eligible for the award.

Although the movie musical was in decline, it went out with a bang at MGM, where the Freed Unit created *An American in Paris* (1951), *Singin' in the Rain* (1953), *The Band Wagon* (1953), and other opulent productions. One of MGM's musicals from this period, *Seven Brides for Seven Brothers*, gave Johnny Mercer the opportunity to write his greatest film score. A niece from Savannah was visiting the Mercers for the summer in 1954 and remembered driving with him to Hollywood. "I went one day with him to the studio. He took me in, and I was starting to be a little awed by it, but he was still mostly my uncle, and it was a lovely studio. It was like a living room with a grand piano and fireplace and cocktail tables and upholstered armchairs and wing chairs. And I curled up over on one of the wing chairs, and he said, 'We're going to be busy. We're going to do a little bit of work, and then I'll take you to lunch.'

"I said, 'Okay.'

"So I was listening to them write these lyrics. . . . Sometime around three o'clock, he turned to me, and he said, 'Oh,' he said, 'I guess you're getting hungry, aren't you? Is it time for lunch?'

"That was at three o'clock, which just speaks to the ability of those men's— able to focus, their focusing ability and to shut out the world. And he always had that ability. He did that all the time. He was a little absentminded at some things, too. There was a time he threw a huge royalty check into the fireplace."

Although writing songs that were tailored to character and dramatic situation did not come naturally to Johnny Mercer, by 1954 he had mastered the art of integration, and he provided the film with some of his most brilliant lyrics. Yet while *Seven Brides for Seven Brothers* was one of MGM's most glorious musicals, it was not produced by Arthur Freed and lacked the sumptuous high-budget effects that characterized Freed Unit productions. One can only speculate that the Freed Unit, which included many homosexuals, such as Minnelli and Edens, and was known, sneeringly, on the MGM lot as "the Fairy Unit," did not relish a production that has been called "one of the most virile of all musicals."

On the other hand, *Seven Brides for Seven Brothers* might have been a victim of the economic rule of thumb in making film musicals: Rather than bank an original, untried story, make a film version of a Broadway musical that has already proven successful onstage. While filming something that was originally conceived for the stage would seem to provide the worst of both worlds, audiences flocked to such wooden films as *Oklahoma!* and *Carousel*. "*Seven Brides for Seven Brothers* was supposed to be a much more expensive picture than it was," recalled costar Jane Powell. "But they really wanted to put the money into *Brigadoon*, which they did. So they cut the budget on *Seven Brides for Seven Brothers*." Jack Cummings insisted he could still produce on a relatively low budget, "but it was a sleeper. It was not supposed to be as successful as it was. If it had had a bigger budget, it might not have been what it turned out to be."

The movie was based on "The Sobbin' Women," a story by fellow Savannah native Stephen Vincent Benét about seven brothers in the mountains of Oregon who, inspired by the eldest's account of the Roman rape of the Sabine women, set out to find wives in a nearby town. Benét's folksy story was skillfully adapted into a musical screenplay by veteran Hollywood writers Albert Hackett, Frances Goodrich, and Dorothy Kingsley. To write the score, Mercer was paired with composer Gene de Paul, who had written film scores at Universal; Mercer liked de Paul's laid-back style, which he compared to that of Richard Whiting: "He's shy and prefers to keep in the wings when possible. . . . he doesn't work so very much, isn't too prolific." Except for "too prolific," the same description could have applied to Mercer himself.

Although Powell remembered Mercer as a smiling, gentle presence, she had some intuitive sense of his dark underside: "There was a depth to him and a sadness to him . . . a real, underlying hurt someplace. . . . I guess that's why he could write such poignant songs."

"*Seven Brides* was an enjoyable and unusual assignment to work on," Mercer said. "Choreographer Michael Kidd had this idea of casting seven professional dancers in the leading roles, and this led to some interesting song-and-dance routines like 'Lonesome Polecat' and 'Sobbin' Women.' There you have a classic example of how a songwriter has often to take his cue from his collaborators and, if he's a thorough-bred pro, he'll come up with something that fits the bill and keeps everyone happy. Michael Kidd explained to us his conception of the 'Lonesome Polecat' scene—the rhythmic lament of the brothers for their 'brides'—and Gene and I went away and thought out lyrics and music to match."

Johnny Mercer was in his element. He could throw himself into these regional characters and situations and revel in their dialect. When Howard Keel goes into town in search of a wife, he sees the winsome Jane Powell working in a restaurant and confronts her with the romantic forthrightness of "Bless Yore Beautiful Hide." As Keel's brothers bewail their bachelorhood, they howl "I'm a Lonesome Polecat." Mercer's tour de force, for a lyricist who once balked at having to write numerous refrains for "Too Marvelous for Words," was "Spring, Spring, Spring." For this piece sung near the end of the film as the brothers and their captive women celebrate that most poetic of moments, the coming of spring, Mercer joyfully, and with the fecundity of nature itself, came up with a refrain for each brother and each bride:

Oh, the barnyard is busy
In a regular tizzy,
And the obvious reason
Is because of the season.
Ma Nature's lyrical
With her yearly miracle,
Spring, Spring, Spring!
All the henfolk are hatchin'
While their menfolk are scratchin'
To insure the survival
Of each brand new arrival . . .
In his hole, though the gopher
Seems a bit of a loafer,
The industrious beaver
Puts it down to spring fever . . .
Slow but surely the turtle
Who's enormously fertile
Lays her eggs by the dozens,
Maybe some are her cousins . . .
Even though to each rabbit
Spring is more like a habit,
Notwithstanding, the fact is
They indulge in the practice . . .
To itself each amoeba
Softly croons, "Ach du lieber,"
While the proud little termite
Feels as large as a worm might . . .

Ev'ry bug's snuggled snuggy
In its own baby buggy,
And in spite of policing
Seems the tribe is increasing.
'Cause Missus Katydid
Once did what her matey did,
It's Spring, Spring, Spring!

The robust Howard Keel as Adam, and his six brothers, all of whom were spectacularly athletic dancers, "imbued the film with a balletic quality . . . without ever losing the essentially masculine 'feel' of the piece." *Seven Brides for Seven Brothers* remains one of the finest and best-loved film musicals.

Yet not one song from the film became independently popular. It is difficult to imagine a pop singer recording "I'm a Lonesome Polecat" or "Bless Yore Beautiful Hide," which were songs that were so thoroughly integrated into *Seven Brides for Seven Brothers* that they could not stand alone. It was as if, in writing integrated songs, Mercer could not also think in terms of writing a popular hit. Writing free-standing popular songs was his natural gift; when he had to think in terms of tailoring a song to character and dramatic situation, that gift deserted him. With *Seven Brides for Seven Brothers*, however, his lyrics would endure. On a visit to Spain, he would be amazed to find that the film had been playing for years at the same movie theater, always to packed houses. In fact, a local Spaniard who knew no other English had seen it so often that he could sing the entire score for Mercer. Finally, Mercer's longing to produce a musical classic, a film that would preserve his lyrics for generations, had been fulfilled. But he still wanted more.

Thirteen

Something's Gotta Give: 1954–1956

I never force things. If ideas don't flow freely I leave it all alone, go away, relax, move on to something else. You can't just switch yourself on and off when you feel like it; your subconscious is working all the time and it doesn't necessarily consult your convenience when deciding to turn out its pockets. I'm a great believer in the subconscious, letting it do the work. You generally get what you want in the long run, as long as you don't try and twist its arm.

For all the success of *Seven Brides for Seven Brothers*, what Johnny Mercer really wanted was an equivalent hit on Broadway, always the more illustrious venue than Hollywood. Finally, in 1956, he seemed to have achieved precisely such a triumph with *Li'l Abner*. Some of the same team from *Seven Brides for Seven Brothers*—notably composer Gene de Paul and choreographer Michael Kidd—collaborated on this musical based on the Al Kapp comic strip. The show ran for a smashingly successful 693 performances, yet it was subtly flawed in ways that have relegated it to the boneyard of Broadway. In nearly half a century, there has never a major revival of *Li'l Abner*. But during its long run, it gave Johnny Mercer the satisfaction of having brought in his big Broadway show.

It was a show, moreover, where his lyrics took center stage, rather than serve a star vehicle as they had in *Top Banana*. The lead actor of *Li'l Abner*, in fact, was a newcomer to Broadway. Peter Palmer was a six-foot-four 220-pounder who had been a football player (and music major) at the University of Illinois. Edie Adams, then married to television comic Ernie Kovacs, played a buxom and bouncy Daisy Mae; and Stubby Kaye, the closest thing to a star, who had stopped the show as Nicely-Nicely in *Guys and Dolls* with "Sit Down, You're Rockin' the Boat," had an equally dynamic number in *Li'l Abner*, "Jubilation T. Cornpone":

> When we fought the Yankees
> And annihilation was near,
> Who was there to lead the charge
> That took us safe to the rear?
> Why it wuz—
> Jubilation T. Cornpone,
> Old "Toot-Your-Own-Horn-Pone,"
> Jubilation T. Cornpone,
> A man who knew no fear . . .
> There at Appomattox
> Lee and Grant were present, of course
> As Lee swept a tear away,
> Who swept up—back of his horse . . .

It was another showstopper, and Mercer supplied numerous verses to satisfy audiences that clamored for encore after encore.

For Palmer, Mercer recast "Lazybones" in a yokel idiom as "If I Had My Druthers," which Abner and his cronies sing while fishing from a log:

> If I had my druthers,
> I'd druther have my druthers
> Than anything else I know.
> While you'd druther hustle,
> Accumulatin' muscle,
> I'd druther watch daisies grow . . .
> I'd druther have my druthers
> Than work anywheres at all.
> It ain't that I hates it,
> I often contemplates it
> While watchin' the raindrops fall . . .

Yet for all the wit and charm in such lyrics, not one song from the show became independently popular.

Mercer's dilemma, which limited him to writing either a popular song or an integrated song, seldom a song that could fulfill both ends, is most apparent in "Namely You," which should have been the "big ballad" of *Li'l Abner*, recorded by numerous popular singers. Mercer wove a tender romantic duet around the simple catchphrase "namely you," which captures Daisy Mae's aggressive pursuit of the bashful Abner:

> You deserve a gal who's willin',
> Namely me,
> One who'd love to have yo' chillen . . .

While Abner responds with wholesome innocence:

> You deserve someone good lookin',
> Namely me.
> Someone who, as yet, ain't tooken,
> Namely me.
> That is how I'll remain unless you get me, shall we say
> In the family way . . .

But the dialect and the characterizations make this so integrated a lyric that it could not possibly become an independent song in the way, for example, Lerner and Loewe's "I've Grown Accustomed to Her Face" and "On the Street Where You Live" transcended their roles in *My Fair Lady* to become enormous hits.

Most reviewers praised the score, and Mercer's lyrics in particular. Some compared *Li'l Abner* to *Guys and Dolls*, another musical that reveled in the argot of a particular region. Both Loesser and Mercer were skilled at capturing slang idioms—Loesser, the racetrack talk of Damon Runyon's tinhorn gamblers; Mercer, the hillbillyese of Al Kapp's cartoon characters. What reviewers most singled out, however, was the dances staged by Michael Kidd, which gave the show a "furiously fast and funny" pace. Walter Winchell celebrated the erotic elements of the show: "The best girlesk show in town," he wrote with lecherous relish. "Blonde, Brunette, Busty, Boy-Bait."

Given its stunning success on Broadway, it is surprising that *Li'l Abner* did not become the classic musical Mercer had hoped for. It may be a period piece, tied to the popularity of Al Kapp's cartoon in the 1950s. Begun in 1934, *Li'l Abner* was carried by more than seven hundred newspapers by the 1950s, but it has long since faded from syndication. For some reviewers, however, the very premise of the show was flawed. "Whether characters who are full-fashioned in pen and ink can ever do as well in flesh and blood may well be doubted," wrote Louis Kronenberger, "but it is less the characters than the characteristics of comic-strip life that make for trouble on Broadway." . . . *Li'l Abner* "sometimes gloriously explodes, sometimes damply sputters as a big Broadway show." The thin texture of the comic strip, Kronenberger speculated, simply does not stand up for an evening on Broadway. Brooks Atkinson made a similar analysis, noting that the libretto "does not have the lightness, simplicity, and speed of the Dogpatch folks. . . . Mr. Kidd has caught the spirit of Dogpatch civilization brilliantly enough to suggest that ballet is a more suitable medium than words for animating Al Kapp's cartoon drawings."

While other Broadway songwriters were intimately involved with every aspect of a musical through rehearsals and tryouts, Mercer, Edie Adams recounted, "hated being around the set . . . You always saw him at a jazz club somewhere. He didn't like to hang around the theater. He wasn't there a lot. . . . he'd come in and get the material, he was always there with a rewrite on a lyric and stuff, but he did not hang around." Adams contrasted Mercer's reluctance to be around the theater with cartoonist Al Kapp's lecherous presence. "He was there a lot because he liked to pinch the girls and be obscene . . . exposed himself and did all kinds of charming things."

But Mercer, in a more discreet way, also took advantage of his Broadway shows to make his own overtures to women in the cast. An actress was taken aback at a party in Manhattan when Mercer led her out on the balcony and propositioned her with the teasing question "Would you like to try some?" "Well," she thought, taking in the view, "at least he chooses his spots well." Although she declined his advances, pretending she didn't understand what he was talking about, she found something boyishly wholesome about his sexual appetite. On another occasion, when he invited her to dinner, she asked if she could bring a friend of hers who was visiting from England. Mercer picked the two women up in a cab and took them to Bookbinder's. The actress remembered that her friend had on a long cape, buttoned at the neck, and when they got to the restaurant, the woman removed her cape, revealing her very ample bosom. Other men would have quietly delighted in the sight, but Johnny Mercer could not contain himself. Ogling her breasts as they rested on the tabletop, he exclaimed, "Those are the biggest knockers I ever saw!" The woman was so humiliated that she returned to London and underwent breast-reduction surgery.

When he worked on shows in New York, Mercer frequently took the train down to Savannah, renewing contact with the world that had nurtured him. There he could again be the young "Mercer boy," beloved, respected, "down home." A niece remembered his visits with his mother: "She always, you know, had southern hospitality. She didn't cook. I think she knew how to cook one thing. . . . She cooked leg of lamb or something. But in those days help was cheap, and I guess she always had help. . . . Of course, Johnny was her baby and her pride and joy, and she always kind of babied him." Friends recalled how Johnny would devote himself to "Miss Lillian" on these visits, speaking with his mother in Geechee during what one friend described as their "lovefests."

"When he would come to town," Nick Mamalakis, who had worked for the Mercer family firm, recalled, "he didn't want any commotion. My wife met him one day in the grocery store. He was shopping for his mother. And he was there with his floppy shoes and socks and unshaven. And so, of course, Anna knew Johnny, and she slid up to him carefully and says, 'Hello, Mr. Mercer.'" Mercer shushed her so as not to draw attention to himself, but, knowing how much he liked Greek pastries, Anna Mamalakis promised to make him some when he returned at Christmas. "So Anna fixed him all kinds of fancy sweets, including some with a lot of powdered sugar on them," and when they brought them to Mercer at Christmas "he immediately wanted to go into it. And Ginger said, 'Johnny, we've got this four o'clock reception, and now you don't want to go into eating sweets right now. And, besides, you are going to get that sugar all over your clothes.' And he said, 'Well, I'm just going to take one.' And by the time he took one, all that sugar was on his dark suit. . . . But that was Johnny."

While in Savannah, Mercer also loved to party. One friend recalled "the party of the century" where she invited the mayor of Savannah: "Everybody got drunk. The French cook fell on the floor of the kitchen. The mayor's wife kept saying, 'Oh, Mr. Mercer will you sing. . . . ' He says, 'If you call me "Mr. Mercer" one more time I'm going to knock you on your fucking ass. It's *Johnny.*'" Such behavior on his part was accepted and forgiven in Savannah, where he was regarded as the scion of a prominent family—to the manor born but, when drunk as a lord, wild and unruly.

"He would visit his friends and they would have, sometimes pretty raucous visits," Mamalakis said. "But when it came down to fundamentals, Johnny was a high-type person. His entire family was with that reputation, just honorable people, and he wouldn't veer away from that. His life recorded the fact that he respected the honorable issues of life."

It's unusual for a man to visit his boyhood home as frequently as Mercer did, and it suggests that there was something about his early life there that Mercer was always, like the wandering skylark of his lyric, trying to recapture. How American such a longing was. Like Fitzgerald's Gatsby, Mercer seemed always to be reaching out for a future that was "already behind him" in his lost youth—"the orgiastic future that year by year recedes before us. . . . So we beat on, boats against the current, borne back ceaselessly into the past."

When he returned to Hollywood after *Li'l Abner*, Mercer was given one of his last opportunities to write a full score, lyrics and music both, for an original Hollywood musical. As the era of the Hollywood musical was passing, so too was the career of its greatest star. Since the mid-1940s, Fred Astaire had made musicals with younger costars—Lucille Bremer in *Yolanda and the Thief* (1945), Judy Garland in *Easter Parade* (1948), Jane Powell in *Royal Wedding* (1951), Vera-Ellen in *The Belle of New York*, and Cyd Charisse in *The Band Wagon* (1953). In all of these films the disparity between Astaire's age and that of his leading lady was a problem. In 1955, teamed with the even younger

Leslie Caron in *Daddy Long Legs*, the problem seemed insurmountable. A script conference dissolved without a solution, and Mercer was asked to try to resolve the age disparity with a song.

That night he went to bed but woke up in the middle of the night. "I don't know what woke me up . . . I don't know whether I had a problem about that, wanted to write that song, or whether this was a worry that I had about the score I was doing. . . . I woke up in the middle of the night and wrote the whole thing . . . Words and music. I went to the piano in the front room, out of bed, and quietly picked it out with one finger. And I wrote it down in my little hieroglyphics, which is my way of writing music. And then finished it the next day."

Whatever the inspiration, Mercer produced an extraordinary song, musically and lyrically. Shedding the regional idioms he had used in *Seven Brides for Seven Brothers* and *Li'l Abner*, he assumed Fred Astaire's debonair vocabulary:

> When an irresistible force such as you
> Meets an old immovable object like me . . .
> When an irrepressible smile such as yours
> Warms an old implacable heart such as mine

"Irresistible," "immovable," irrepressible," "implacable"—it's as if Mercer were leafing through the I section of one of his favorite dictionaries. After building a lyric around these erudite terms, he shifts to the vernacular title phrase:

> You can bet as sure as you live,
> Something's gotta give, something's gotta give,
> Something's gotta give.

Then in the release, he reverts to Astaire's urbane style at its most refined:

> So *en garde*, who knows what the fates have in store
> From their vast mysterious sky?

Then back to a punchy colloquial idiom for the conclusion:

> Fight, fight, fight, fight, fight it with all of our might.
> Chances are some heavenly star-spangled night,
> We'll find out as sure as we live,
> Something's gotta give, something's gotta give,
> Something's gotta give.

Such shifts of tone registered the internal struggle Astaire underwent as he succumbed to Caron's charms, so that his concerns over their age difference, along with those of the audience, were overcome in the resolution of the song. For once, Johnny Mercer had written an integral song that also became an enormous hit. On June 20, 1955, he received a brief note from Frank Loesser:

> Dear Johnny:
> Just a note to tell you how crazy I am about "Something's Gotta Give."
> It's a real pleasure to see carriage trade writers getting the hits.

The note must have been gratifying, but Mercer envied Loesser's ability to write smash Broadway shows that produced, to borrow one of Loesser's own titles, "A Bushel and a Peck" of hit songs. Mercer would ruefully say to friends, borrowing a racetrack catchphrase, "Loesser passed me at the turn."

While the song and the film were successful, during the course of shooting, Fred Astaire's beloved wife, Phyllis, died. Astaire was devastated by the loss; Leslie Caron recalled that after a take he would sit down, put his face in a towel, and weep helplessly. So devoted was Astaire to his marriage, he was one of the few major costars Judy Garland could not seduce.

Johnny Mercer was always more at home with a song rather than a score, working by himself rather than with a collaborator or a company. He proved this side of his genius yet again one day in 1955 as he was driving from Hollywood to Newport Beach. On the car radio he heard a jazz instrumental by Lionel Hampton and Sonny Burke called "Midnight Sun." Mercer was so moved by the melody that he pulled into a filling station, called the radio station, and said, "This is Johnny Mercer. Would you mind playing that again? I love it." On hearing it a second time, Mercer committed the melody to memory, and during the drive home he worked out the lyric.

What makes this feat all the more amazing is that the melody for "Midnight Sun" forced a lyricist to face one of the profession's greatest challenges: coming up with a series of "feminine rhymes," two-syllable rhymes where the accent falls on the first syllable. And yet Mercer said that when he first heard the melody, it was those rhymes that popped into his mind, first "aurora borealis," which he associated with the title, followed by "palace" and "chalice." Mercer used such lilting rhymes to underscore images that oscillate between sensuous reality and shimmering fantasy:

> Your lips were like a red and ruby *chalice*,
> Warmer than the summer *night*,
> The clouds were like an alabaster *palace*,
> Rising to a snowy height,

Each star its own aurora bore*alis*,
Suddenly you held me tight,
I could see the midnight sun.*

"I know of no lyric in the world of popular music," one critic wrote, "in which so many unwieldy and seemingly alien elements have been so cleverly fused to form a natural union."

But even Mercer's ear for "hearing" what a composer's melody was "saying" was not infallible. Once when he was working with Harold Arlen, the composer played what he called one of his tapeworms, a long, complicated melody that went well beyond the standard thirty-two-bar length—in this case, sixty measures long. "It was a jazz tune like 'I've Got the World on a String' or something like it," Mercer recalled, "rhythmical, you know." The lyric he set to it was elegantly literate:

I've seen Sequoia, it's really very pretty,
The art of Goya and Rockefeller City,
But since I saw you, I can't believe my eyes.
You're one of them there things
That comes equipped with wings:
It walks, it talks, it sings,
And it flies.
I've touched the table that held the Declaration,
And Betty Grable (in my imagination),
But you're a fable that's hard to realize.
Yes, I've seen a view or two,
But there ain't no view like you.
Believe me, baby, I simply can't believe my eyes . . .

But the song was never completed. "I don't even know what picture it was for," Mercer said, "or why it wasn't used."

In 1954, when Harold Arlen was collaborating with Ira Gershwin on songs for *A Star Is Born*, Judy Garland's big comeback picture after she had reestablished herself as a concert singer, he played a melody at Gershwin's home in Beverly Hills. When Leonore Gershwin called out from another part of the house, "Sounds like Gershwin to me," Arlen immediately stopped, always sensitive to criticism that his music derived from that of George Gershwin. Instead he began playing the melody he had worked on with Mercer, never telling Ira that Johnny had already written a lyric to it. Ira listened and leaned over the piano. For one of the few times in his career, a title, which he called

---

*"Midnight Sun" (Lionel Hampton, Sonny Burke, and Johnny Mercer) © 1954 Crystal Music Publishers, Inc.; © renewal 1982. Reprinted with the permission of the Copyright Proprietor.

the most difficult and "vital" part of a lyric, popped into his mind: "The Man That Got Away," he said. "I like," Arlen replied.

Arlen must have played the melody more slowly this time, for the lyric Ira Gershwin set to it, unlike Mercer's original, was filled with helpless and hopeless loss as he matched syllables to the same notes Mercer had:

> The night is bitter,
> The stars have lost their glitter,
> The wind grows colder,
> And suddenly you're older,
> And all because of
> The man that got away . . .

When Judy Garland sang "The Man That Got Away" in *A Star Is Born*, it marked one of her greatest screen performances, though she failed to win an Oscar, which went to Grace Kelly for her performance in *The Country Girl*, and the song lost out to Cahn and Styne's "Three Coins in the Fountain."

"The Man That Got Away" came on the radio one day as Johnny Mercer was driving Alan Bergman to the beach to help the aspiring songwriter with some of his lyrics. Just as Yip Harburg and other songwriters had helped Mercer when he started out, so Mercer freely gave his time to younger lyricists who sought his help. Bergman, not knowing about Mercer's own lyric for Arlen's melody, began raving about "The Man That Got Away," telling Mercer he thought Ira Gershwin's lyric was the kind of lyric he wanted to write. Johnny Mercer leaned over and turned the radio off. "I liked the first version better," he said.

It must have galled him that Ira Gershwin's lyric had not only turned Arlen's melody into a classic song but had given his beloved Judy Garland, who did not often have successful records, one of her biggest hits. In later years, Mercer looked upon the song more philosophically. "You know, this is sort of a silent agreement with most collaborators that if the song doesn't make it, they have their tune back, we have our lyrics back and we forget it. It was a nice try and that's all." But still he pointed out that Arlen's melody "went faster when he first wrote it. It wasn't so dramatic," he said defensively. "Not the same. I don't think you can compare them."

At the time Mercer was helping Alan Bergman, he was also tutoring another young lyricist, Marylin Keith, and he would eventually suggest that she and Alan not only work together but get married. They did, and went on to write some of the finest lyrics of the latter part of the twentieth century, such as "The Windmills of Your Mind" and "Nice 'n Easy," as well as scores for such films as *The Way We Were* and *Yentl*. "Johnny not only matched words with music," another lyricist quipped, "but people."

While Johnny Mercer worked on Broadway shows and Hollywood films in the mid-1950s, Capitol Records continued to grow. One of its finest additions was Frank Sinatra, whom Alan Livingston had signed when the singer was widely regarded as a has-been. Bobby-soxers no longer screamed for a singer who was balding and pushing forty, and who had divorced his first wife, Nancy, to marry the sultry Ava Gardner, who, in turn, had divorced him. Even his magnificent voice was showing signs of wear, and when Mitch Miller insisted he do novelty and country-flavored songs at Columbia, Sinatra said, "I'm not going to do any of that crap" and was summarily let go. (Sinatra's version was "Hey, I just fired Columbia.") Sinatra's agent called Livingston to ask if Capitol might be interested in signing the aging singer. When Alan Livingston said yes, the agent asked, in amazement, "You would?"

It was a propitious moment for a Sinatra comeback. Before their breakup, Ava Gardner had used her influence to get Sinatra the role of Maggio in *From Here to Eternity*, for which he won the Academy Award for Best Supporting Actor in 1954. At Capitol, Sinatra continued to record singles, such as "Young at Heart," on the 45-rpm discs that were replacing the old 78-rpm records, but he also began recording LPs. LPs had originally been used only for classical recordings and Broadway scores, but as 45s were increasingly marketed to teenagers to play on their little "changeable" phonographs, the LP was seen as a recording for adult listeners to play on their more expensive "hi-fi" (high-fidelity) players. Since an LP could hold from twelve to sixteen songs, the problem was where to get that many good songs to fill an album. The problem was solved, for Capitol and Sinatra, by recording older songs by such songwriters as Rodgers and Hart, Cole Porter, and, of course, Johnny Mercer, whom Sinatra revered, saying, "A Johnny Mercer lyric is all the wit you wish you had and all the love you ever lost."

Through the albums Sinatra made at Capitol, these songs became the "standards" we know today. Those songs, in turn, helped Sinatra redefine his singing persona. Most of them, such as "My Funny Valentine," "The Boy Next Door," "The Lady Is a Tramp," "Dancing on the Ceiling," and "It Never Entered My Mind," came from Broadway shows and Hollywood films, where they had originally been written for female performers. Traditionally in musicals, women were given songs of greater emotional range and depth. With some minor lyrical changes ("The Boy Next Door" became "The Girl Next Door") Sinatra could sing them, but their essentially feminine sensibility remained, rendering him more tender, pensive, and vulnerable as a singer.

The success of Capitol stirred interest in the company abroad. "EMI came along when we were very successful," Alan Livingston recalled, "and wanted to buy Capitol." EMI, Electric & Musical Industries, was a vast British holding company that owned the Angel label, described by Russell Sanjek in *American Popular Music and Its Business*, as "the oldest record trademark in Europe, dating back to 1898." It was the first attempt by an international conglomerate to acquire an American record company and reflects how popular

American music had become in England and Europe after World War II. "Recordings of American origin accounted for about one third of Europe's purchases, and the combined total of 75 million disks sold in Great Britain and West Germany in 1954 represented a third of the American market."

But Glenn Wallichs did not want to sell the company he had helped make into such an industry giant. "When EMI came along and wanted to buy Capitol Records," Livingston recalled, "Glenn had a problem. He didn't want to sell. But he had to do something about it because he had an obligation to the stockholders. He couldn't just make the decision, 'No, we won't sell' . . . and the money they were offering was a big profit for everybody." Buddy DeSylva had died five years earlier, and even at that point the success of the company was indicated by the fact that despite DeSylva's enormously successful career as a songwriter and Broadway and Hollywood producer, his greatest asset at the time of his death was his share of Capitol Records. Now EMI was offering to buy the 248,435 shares owned by Glenn Wallichs, Johnny Mercer, and DeSylva's widow at $17.50 a share—$4.50 above the market selling price of Capitol stock at the time. That meant that Johnny Mercer, who held one hundred thousand shares of Capitol stock, stood to gain $1.75 million from the sale. He could walk away from a company he had founded and seen grow too big and commercial for his taste, and watch it be devoured by an even bigger enterprise. Yet the southern patrician in him resisted doing something purely to make money. He described his decision as a gentlemanly gesture to accommodate the widow of a friend. "Mrs. DeSylva had lost Buddy; he had died, and she was not interested in staying in the record business," he said. "He was the guy who had put up the money. And I felt an obligation to her." But he also obliquely confessed to his own ungentlemanly avarice: "I was also tempted, because it was a nice, you know, price. . . . And I—I sold it with reluctance, because I knew that, you know, it was a great—great company."

Although Wallichs remained with Capitol, he no longer ran the company. "Glenn, I think, retained a little bit of stock," Livingston recalled. "I think Johnny sold all his stock. So that was his official separation. And EMI became our major stockholder. Which worked out in many respects. But there was certainly not a role to play for Johnny Mercer anymore. He didn't like it, didn't want it." "To complete the negotiation," according to Russell Sanjek, "EMI had to purchase two thirds of the remaining 476,230 outstanding Capitol shares by March 14, 1955, at the same figure, representing a total investment in one of the Big Four American disk companies of $8.5 million." It was, at the time, the biggest transaction in the history of the recording industry. When it was completed, Johnny Mercer was a millionaire. At a Capitol company picnic afterward, Fred Grimes, a former employee, recalled, people wondered if the company would be able to build its distinctive tower, in the shape of a stack of records, on the Los Angeles skyline. "This means," Grimes said, "we *will* be able to finish the tower."

A close friend of Ginger's remembers when Johnny received his check from the sale of Capitol. "He brought it to our first apartment, which was smaller than this, if you can believe it, with a baby. He was just tickled." He had finally equaled Crosby's success, at least financially. She recalled that Johnny proposed an extraordinary way to spend a good deal of the money. "The minute he said to Ginger. 'Do you want to do this?' she said, 'It's your money.'"

A few days later, George Hunt, who was still head of the Chatham Savings Bank in Savannah, received a letter from Johnny Mercer, inquiring about the current state of the liquidation of his father's company. "I was in conference with Walter Mercer after hours," said Nick Mamalakis. "Mr. Hunt knocked on the back door, and we let our friend in. 'Walter, Johnny wants to know the figure to pay off the certificate holders. He has no obligation whatever. He can't even take a tax loss as a write-off on income taxes. What shall I do?' Walter advised Hunt to answer the letter and give Johnny the figure."

Hunt wrote back to tell Johnny that his father's faith in liquidation rather than declaring bankruptcy had almost been fulfilled. When George Mercer died in 1940, only 34 percent of the original debt of $1,070,807 had been repaid, but by 1955, 72 percent had been paid back to the three thousand certificate holders. The problem, Hunt explained, was that no payments had been made for several years, and if the original assets, the remaining real-estate lots, were sold at current value, they would repay only another 10 percent. Hunt then wrote, very diplomatically:

> From the tone of your letter, I conclude that you are thinking that you
> might do something extra for the people who still have not been paid
> in full. Of course, I do not know to what extent you would like to go
> with such an idea (if that is your idea), but . . . if you would be willing
> to buy all of the present real estate of the old G. A. Mercer Company
> at a figure to be placed by appraisal of the Savannah Real Estate Board,
> it would be a grand gesture, and enable us to complete this liquidation
> to the great pleasure of many individuals.

"I figured he had in mind doing something," Hunt recalled, "but never for a minute did I dream that he would undertake to pay off the entire amount of $300,000!"

What Hunt suggested to Mercer was that if he would "buy up the remaining assets, which amounted to about a hundred thousand dollars, we could then make a substantial final payment to all certificate holders and close up the whole thing." Hunt was certain this would be more than anyone could have hoped for. "I knew the holders would be happy to go along with this as we haven't been able to pay them a cent in the past 10 years."

In April, Hunt opened a letter that had been addressed to the bank from

Chicago. "It was in a plain envelope without a return address," he recalled. "Inside was a personal check for $300,000 and a little note that wasn't even dated":

> It has been my ambition since my boyhood to pay off my father's debt in this venture, and I thought that this would be appreciated by the certificate holders and would in effect clear the name of the company.

"Shortly thereafter on another after hours conference with Walter Mercer, a knock on the back door brought Mr. Hunt back, this time to say that he received a check from Johnny," recalled Mamalakis. " 'But,' Hunt said, 'he forgot to sign it!' "

That's Johnny," George Hunt reflected. "The best-hearted boy in the world, but absent-minded."

"After Hunt's departure," Mamalakis said, "I opened a new approach." He wrote to Johnny and urged him to use the money to set up scholarships at Savannah's Armstrong State College in his parents' names. "In that way," he reasoned, "their names will always be remembered." Mamalakis received his letter back in the mail with a handwritten note on the bottom: "Nick, you are talking with your head, but I'm speaking from my heart." "And he initialed it 'J.' How often I have regretted not keeping that letter. . . . When I looked into that statement, I found that he had promised himself that if he ever made it, nobody who bet on his father would lose one cent. That was speaking with the heart."

A few days later George Hunt received another letter from Johnny, with a second check for three hundred thousand dollars:

> I made out that check and carried it a few days unsigned just in case I lost it. When I got around to mailing it, I suppose I forgot to sign it. But if by chance I did sign it, please tear up one or the other of them.

Even the second check had to be returned because Mercer had made it out to the wrong account. "He agreed," Hunt said, "and told me to tear up the check and he'd put another in the mail immediately. 'I can't tear up that check, Johnny,' I said. 'It would be a sacrilege. Besides that, I'm going to sue you. The sight of it has blinded me.' "

On Mercer's next trip to Savannah all of the complicated paperwork was completed. With the self-effacement that characterized the Mercers, he asked only that his name be kept out of it: "It's just a family affair. I didn't want any publicity. . . . It's been my ambition to pay those debts so that there be no slur on the family name. Everyone will be paid every dime they thought they might lose in the company. . . . It's strictly a family affair. It concerns only my mother, my brothers, and myself." Hunt tried to comply and downplay the publicity the story generated by telling reporters that it was "simply the act of a boy who had been raised to believe that a good man does good deeds in the dark of the night."

But with so many people involved, the story began to spread in newspapers, and soon tales followed about the impact of Mercer's gesture: the old woman in Baton Rouge who went to church to pray for money for an operation for her blind grandson and received a check from the Chatham bank the next morning; the impoverished Oregon couple with the brilliant son who had not been able to contemplate going to college until the Chatham check arrived.

Letters began to pour in directly to Johnny Mercer. From Henry J. Stokes, pastor of the First Baptist Church of Macon, Georgia, came this letter:

> No doubt your most generous and commendable act in memory of your father has brought numerous letters of praise and appreciation. As an heir of an estate that held some of the G. A. Mercer certificates and one who has received the check for final settlement, I wish to thank you and give to you an account of how your munificence will be used in one instance. My oldest daughter is studying piano at Sophie Newcomb, New Orleans, and this will insure her completion of college work. She is on a scholarship there, but it has been a squeeze for one who has three other children to educate. As a musician, I thought this might be interesting to you.

Then Pastor Stokes adds an eerie memory but refrains from drawing a spiritual moral:

> It would be inconceivable for you to recall, but years ago in the late '20s or early '30s when I was at Yale Divinity School and was in New York with a crowd of Savannah youngsters (Mills Lane, Sally Nash, and others) you were in the crowd. When we boarded a subway I recalled that you were short some change and I handed you a coin. Why such would still stand out in memory is one of those tricks of the mind. Ever since then it has bounced in my mind when I read of or heard one of your tunes.

Of the many other letters that came in, a friend said, the general message was "You've restored my faith in human beings . . . Yes, in human beings, in human dignity—beautiful gesture."

By paying off all the certificate holders, Johnny Mercer inherited what was left in the G. A. Mercer Company. George Hunt said, " 'Now, what do you want to do with the residue?'

" 'Mr. Hunt, what the hell is residue?'

" 'That's what's left over.'

"And Johnny took his pencil out and on the back of an envelope wrote 'residue.'

"And Mr. Hunt said, 'Well, I'll let you know later what the residue is.'

"Johnny said, 'I don't care about what is the residue. I want to remember that word because I might want to use it in some lyrics.' So whenever he would hear a word like that, sometimes it impressed him, and he would write it down."

And that is what he did. In a satirical song from *Li'l Abner*, "The Country's in the Very Best of Hands," Mercer gives an innocent Dogpatch perspective on the rhetoric of Congress:

The money that they taxes us—that's known as revenues,
They compounds the collateral, subtracts the residue,
Don't worry 'bout the principal and in'trest that accrue,
They're shipping all that stuff to foreign lands.

The "residue" from G. A. Mercer Company came to forty-five thousand dollars. "He asked us to let it sit for a while," Mamalakis recalled, "and he would decide what to do with it. And eventually he gave fifteen thousand to the Crippled Children's Hospital in Atlanta, the Elks; and fifteen thousand to his Episcopal bishop for the diocese work in Savannah; and then the last fifteen thousand he gave to the Jenkins Boys Club for the gym, which they named in honor of his father."

Johnny's half brother Walter was a major supporter of the Exchange Club of Savannah, which sponsored Jenkins. "We built a brand-new building," Mamalakis said, "a gym building, and we were struggling to pay off the last of the mortgage. So Johnny came to town to visit his mother and had a day extra on his schedule, so we asked him to look at the Boys Club, and we went there in the middle of summer. The swimming pool was jumping. The basketball courts were full of boys—and the game rooms, shooting pool and reading."

When George A. Mercer had walked along the streets of Savannah, he would take coins out of his pocket and give them to little black children. Now, his son could afford much more sweeping gestures of magnanimity.

" 'Well, how much you owe on this gym?' " Johnny asked Mamalakis.

"And I said, 'Approximately fifteen thousand dollars.'

"And he said, 'Mark it paid. Mark it paid.' "

Johnny Mercer had done his "good deed in the night" and removed even the faintest blotch on the Mercer escutcheon.

Fourteen

Midnight Sun: 1957–1962

Music is a life enhancer, like a growing thing. There is no death in it. It is full of life, and the more perfect it is—the more life-giving, the more warming, the more comforting it becomes. A song is born in excitement, has a robust life climbing the popularity charts and traveling to the ends of the earth and then, like rare old wine, brings back nothing but sweet memories. And even if the memories are bittersweet, a song takes you back to a time when you were younger, stronger, and the blood was coursing through your veins, the sun seemed to shine brighter, the nights were cooler and the girls softer and rounder and made to fit in your arms as the music played.

By the end of the 1950s, changes that had been accelerating in American culture for more than a decade finally took hold. Television supplanted the movies as America's primary form of entertainment; radio played songs aimed exclusively at teenagers; and Hollywood, by and large, stopped making original musicals. Except for children's films such as *Mary Poppins* or teenage movies featuring rock singers such as Elvis Presley, when Hollywood made a major musical it was usually an adaptation of a Broadway show, such as *My Fair Lady* or *The Music Man*, that had already proven successful onstage. While he occasionally had the opportunity to work on a score for an original film musical, such as *Merry Andrew* in 1958, Mercer had to content himself with the piecework of writing title songs and theme songs for dramatic motion pictures. None of these—the title songs from *Spring Reunion* (1957), *Love in the Afternoon* (1957), and *The Facts of Life* (1960)—was even mildly successful. Mercer's only film song to become a hit in these years was the title song he wrote for Pat Boone's film debut in *Bernardine* in 1957. It was Mercer's only attempt to write in the idiom of rock and roll, and despite the song's success, he never essayed that style again.

Still in his forties, at the height of his creative powers, and eager to write lyrics to *anything*, he accepted Capitol's invitation to set words to some jazz instrumentals that Duke Ellington had recorded for the label. One of these, "Satin Doll," was the closest Mercer came to a hit song in 1958. With its truncated, abrupt melody, "Satin Doll" posed as much of a problem for a lyricist as the feminine rhymes of "Midnight Sun," but Mercer matched those brief musical shards with slangy exclamations that were woven together by subtle rhymes:

Cigarette holder,
Which wigs me,
Over her shoulder
She digs me . . .
Telephone numbers,
Well, you know,
Doin' my rumbas
With uno . . .
Speaks *Lat-*
in
that
sat-
in
doll.

Such cool sophistication makes one wish that Mercer and Ellington had collaborated, truly collaborated, more often, or at least that Mercer had been given the task of setting lyrics to all of Ellington's instrumentals. Ellington's beautiful melodies, such as "Caravan," "Sophisticated Lady," and "Mood Indigo," had been saddled with florid, overblown lyrics that strained to be "poetic" by various staff lyricists at Mills Music in the 1930s. They have endured, not so much as songs, but as the jazz instrumentals they originally were.

From a time when Mercer dominated *Your Hit Parade*, he now was grateful for even one mildly successful song in a year, but in some years, such as 1959, he didn't have even that. Friends recall how Mercer went "through a rather—oh, period of depression actually, because of the fact that music was changing so drastically in the fifties. And, of course, with the advent of rock and roll, that's what young people wanted to hear. So, the poet that he was, the demand for his—for that kind of lyric, you know, just—wasn't there." Mired in this depression, he was reluctant to try another Broadway musical, but Broadway had become the one outlet for writers of his kind of song. Harold Arlen persuaded him to do a show based on Edna Ferber's novel *Saratoga Trunk*. Assuring Mercer it would not end as unhappily as had their 1946 collaboration on *St. Louis Woman*, Arlen told him the musical promised to be as big a hit as *Show Boat*, which had also been based on a Ferber novel.

The director, moreover, would be Morton Da Costa, who had just done *The Music Man* and *Auntie Mame*. Rock Hudson and Carol Lawrence, who had starred as Maria in *West Side Story*, would play the leads; Jane Darwell, most famous for playing Ma in the film *The Grapes of Wrath*, would have a supporting role; and the magnificent Cecil Beaton, who had won a Tony for *My Fair Lady*, would design both the sets and the costumes. So promising were all these components that money poured in to produce *Saratoga*—four hundred thousand dollars, primarily from NBC and RCA Victor Records. It would be, at the time, the most expensive musical ever mounted on Broadway.

Despite such omens, Mercer instinctively recoiled from *Saratoga*, yet he agreed to do it for Arlen's sake. "As I understand it," Sheldon Harnick said, "he really didn't want to do that show, but he did it as a favor to Harold Arlen. Arlen very much wanted to do a show, so he did it against his better judgment. He did it as a generous act of friendship." Always the patrician who could not bring himself to initiate a project or seek out a collaborator, Mercer was also an easy mark who could not bring himself to say no. Years later, he would say that "the decision that saves you the most heartache is the first NO. If you can make that one and not go along hoping that things will get better, you will save yourself a lot of trouble. When in doubt, DON'T. Learn how to say very politely, but very firmly, 'I'm sorry, but it's not for me.' Believe me, it'll be worth it in time and labor saved."

What Mercer did not know at the time was that Rodgers and Hammerstein and Lerner and Loewe had all said "No" to Edna Ferber when she offered them *Saratoga Trunk* as the basis for a musical. Once again, the heart of the problem was the book. Da Costa had a proven record as a director, but he also took on the task of adapting Ferber's sprawling novel for the stage— his first attempt at writing a book for a musical. Carol Lawrence speculated that "if Morton Da Costa had allowed Lillian Hellman to cowrite with him, it would have been a better show." At their one meeting to discuss his script for *Saratoga*, Hellman bluntly told Da Costa, "It's very obvious you can't write."

"John would be there," said a friend who was present during the planning of *Saratoga*, "and he did not want to get involved with that at all. He read the book—the Da Costa book—on the train and he didn't see how anybody could make anything of this thing. Harold, however, felt that it was because of Da Costa's track record up to that point." "The book was twenty years behind *Show Boat*," Mercer said later, "and no amount of style nor gloss could cover the humorless and out-of-date book."

Before rehearsals started in September, Rock Hudson "bowed out . . .

after only a few music lessons and pressure from his movie studio," but he was replaced by Howard Keel, who had performed magnificently in *Seven Brides for Seven Brothers*. Once rehearsals started, Jane Darwell, nearing eighty, could not remember her lines and had to be replaced. Then the problems with Da Costa's script began to emerge. According to an actress in the cast, Da Costa was required by the great Edna Ferber herself to adhere closely to her novel even though simplifying the narrative would have made it work better as a stage musical. "With a cast that included thirty-two speaking roles and a large singing and dancing chorus, and scenes that shifted from elaborate settings in Paris to New Orleans and Saratoga, the show was unwieldy."

"Edna Ferber was right there," the actress said, "and she wouldn't let us change a thing." Da Costa "had to work right with her, but she wouldn't let him cut out things which would have expedited the musical numbers. So I remember when we found out she was in the audience we all just fell on our faces. And when you have Miss Ferber in the audience, you know, you have to do what she says."

Mercer told a friend he disliked the "swishiness" Da Costa gave to the show. "It was all for the gays, which made Johnny crazy," said another friend who was there on opening night. "They made it gay." The most lavish aspect of *Saratoga* was Cecil Beaton's sets and costumes. The sets were on huge turntables and covered fifteen changes of setting with more than two hundred costumes. "I mean," the friend said, "you don't go out singing the scenery or the costumes." She felt that the gay emphasis downplayed the romantic relationship between Howard Keel and Carol Lawrence, which was the linchpin of the story: they "never looked at each other."

Carol Lawrence believed that Da Costa set out to prove himself in *Saratoga* by taking on both the writing and the directing. "In truth, Morton had never felt validated in what he contributed to shows. He thought, 'Now, I'm going to do all those things and they'll realize how much I did.' . . . Well, he put himself in the hospital." With Da Costa hospitalized, it was up to Harold Arlen and Johnny Mercer to take charge of the production; but then, Lawrence recalls, "Harold became ill, so we had both of them in the hospital. All the changes fell to Johnny to make." Suddenly, *Saratoga* was without its composer, its director, and its playwright. From the hands-off approach Mercer had taken with other Broadway musicals, he was suddenly put at the center of the arduous process of pulling a show together. No one could have been more temperamentally unsuited for such a role.

"I'm convinced most hit shows need a strong man (or team) to lead them into the hit column," Mercer later reflected. "When we get into those conferences out of town, and everybody starts telling each other what's wrong, a dog fight was never as loud, a cat fight never as fierce. Everybody is screaming at once. Here is where you need an Abbott, a David Merrick or a Harold

Prince and a Jerome Robbins to take charge. Not that they are the ultimate talent, but not every creator can be the boss, and all should leave it to one who commands the respect of the others, to decide."

Even though Johnny Mercer was clearly not the man for such a job, he threw himself into *Saratoga*, cutting dialogue and numbers and writing three replacement songs, words and music. Howard Keel, who described *Saratoga* as a "catastrophe," reflected, "We opened in Philadelphia, and they ripped us to shreds. And everyone left us. Johnny came back and worked with both words and music. He was the only one who really tried. Harold Arlen never showed up again. We didn't see Da Costa for three weeks. Everyone went into a trauma. It was not a happy event and it took me months to get over it. But that's what show business is. You just keep going."

An actress in *Saratoga* recalled that Mercer didn't like to come to rehearsals "because if something annoyed him, he didn't like to say so. So he'd go to Sardi's instead." Always the proud patrician who could not criticize others, Mercer would call her over for consolation. "He was sitting on the steps from the lobby to the balcony, and he motioned and I came over and sat down, and he said, 'This is the dull part, isn't it? But it's necessary.' And so he sighed and he said, 'This really isn't my kind of music. . . . This is really not the kind of thing I like to write.'"

When *Saratoga* moved on to Boston, Sheldon Harnick was working there on *Fiorello*, which would go on to win the Pulitzer Prize. "He was with *Saratoga*, and we were with *Fiorello*. We talked a little bit; unfortunately, when I saw him, he would come over to our theater. I don't know—maybe being around *Saratoga* distressed him—but he would come over to wherever it was that we were playing with *Fiorello*, and he would stand in the back next to me and just kind of shake his head enviously . . . but we couldn't talk because the show was going on, and he knew that I was trying to observe it to see what further changes needed to be made. I was working." Seeing Sheldon Harnick so intently at work must have made Mercer, a lyricist who labored best when he could recline on a couch and drift off to "Cloud Land," feel how little he was suited to the rigors of the musical theater.

Just as *Saratoga* was about to open in New York, Nick Mamalakis came up from Savannah on business. "'Do you want to go down to see the rehearsal for *Saratoga* with me?'" Mercer asked. "And I said, 'Sure, I'd be delighted to.' So we start walking down Fifth Avenue and suddenly we stopped at the corner where there was a little church, and they referred to it as 'the church around the corner,' a little Episcopal church. And he says, 'Nick, wait here a second. I want to go in and say a little prayer.' And I said, 'Well, Johnny, you blue-blooded Episcopalians don't let any other Christians go into your church?' He stopped and pivoted around, and he came over. 'Nick, I apologize. Honestly, please forgive me. I shouldn't have said it that way.' So we both went into church together. You know, he was an acolyte when he was

growing up. And he sang in the boys' choir at the church, so he was reli-
giously trained and oriented. So when we came out of church, we started
walking toward the rehearsal arena, and I said, 'Well, I guess you prayed for a
little help on *Saratoga*.' And he said, 'Nick, I have never asked the good Lord
for anything. I just thanked him for all of his blessings that he has bestowed
on me. I've never said, "Lord, please do this." I always said, "Thank you,
Lord." ' Well, that's from his background, his father's background, his own
background. But he was just adamant on the fact that his prayers were prayers
of thanksgiving."

In the case of *Saratoga*, he should have prayed for help. It made its New
York debut on December 7, 1959, at the Winter Garden Theatre. "The show
had a fabulous cast," Carol Lawrence recalled. "It was a diverse mixed company, buddies in the trenches trying to make the thing float. That much was
fabulous. . . . It was a shame—Cecil Beaton's costumes and sets drew gasps
from the audience—they were transported! Nothing we said on stage lived
up to that. . . . I learned so much about sustaining character and—singing forever in a whalebone corset because Beaton insisted on authenticity. I was
changing costumes constantly and wearing stockings that matched upholstery
material."

Another of Mercer's Savannah friends was in New York when *Saratoga*
opened. "He asked me to come to the opening with him, and I told him that
I didn't think I would want to come to the opening, that I would meet him for
lunch the next day and we could have a celebration or a wake. And I turned
on the television in my hotel room that morning, and a drama critic described
Saratoga as being the biggest bomb to hit Broadway in many years. I said, 'Oh
my. This is going to be some lunch.' And sure enough, I met Johnny and
Ginger at the 21 Club and that lunch lasted about two and a half hours as
Johnny drowned his sorrows."

The New York critics condemned *Saratoga* and pointed their finger at the
book, which was described, variously, as "dull," "jumbled," and a "fiasco."
Brooks Atkinson, as usual, was the most surgically ruthless: "Give Mr. Da
Costa a script or a scenario by someone else and he can invest it with excitement on the stage. But he has not been able to sail his own scenario out of the
doldrums. *Saratoga* is an uninteresting show."

Facing competition from *Gypsy* and *The Sound of Music*, *Saratoga* closed,
after only eighty performances, on February 13, 1960. Harold Arlen wrote to
a friend, "I don't think an audience nor the critics realize (alas why should
they?) how much is taken from a writer every time he goes to bat." Mercer's
dour comment was "I thought my work the poorest I have ever done—even
ruining one of Harold's tunes with a mediocre and unimaginative lyric."
Musical theater historian Martin Gottfried tried to put the failed collaborations of Arlen and Mercer into perspective: "Though a first-class composer,
Harold Arlen was not a man of the theater. He didn't have show judgment or

the plain knack for the stage. His wish to write for the theater may have out-stripped his propensity for it. He was not a composer to think in terms of book, production, and characters. He was interested mainly in his music, pol-ishing a song for its own sake rather than the sake of the production. His care may have resulted in many musically perfect songs, but at the expense of the-atrical spark." That lack of theatricality was reflected in the lyricists Arlen worked with, most notably Johnny Mercer, who "never achieved a theatrical reputation commensurate with his ability because he, too, thought in terms of the song rather than the show. Like Arlen, Mercer was a poor judge of book material, and the musicals they worked on never stood much chance of success."

The debacle of *Saratoga* left Mercer more depressed than ever. He was fifty years old, and everything seemed to be leaving him behind—the Broad-way theater, the Hollywood musical, the world of popular song. It was at this time that he lashed out most viciously at family and friends, snapping at a niece when she brought her school friends to *Saratoga*: "Why don't you invite the whole world?" he bellowed. This was also the time when he made a drunken pass at another niece, just as she was going through a divorce. Even the quiet and demure Jo Stafford had enough of his abuse and stopped him with an uncharacteristic riposte. Just as he was starting to tear into her at a party, she snapped, "Stop it, Johnny, I don't want any more of your fucking roses."

In hindsight, he would bewail to Margaret Whiting the loss of Capitol Records. "All of a sudden, Capitol was gone. He wanted it that way, but he was very sorry." Then, in an instant, he could turn on her, shouting, "Why the hell do you have to sing so goddamned *loud*?" She received her roses in the morning as an apology. "He would run people out of the room. . . . Now, he's got nothing to do," she said. "I mean, he was doing five pictures a year. . . . And he would come over to the house, so we'd walk, and he says, " 'Nobody wants me anymore.' "

One of the changes that put songwriters out of work in Hollywood was that the composers who wrote the scores for films demanded to write the songs as well. Dmitri Tiomkin had started this trend in 1951 when he wrote the musical score for *High Noon*, insisting that he also be allowed to write the theme song, "Do Not Forsake Me," for which the stalwart Hollywood lyricist Ned Washington supplied the words. Tiomkin knew that the lucrative side of film music was not the scores but the songs, since songs could go on to inde-pendent popularity and earn royalties. Tiomkin and other music scorers fought for the right to write film songs, and the success of "Do Not Forsake Me" supported their case.

But to veteran songwriters such as Ray Evans and Jay Livingston, these "background writers," most of whom had been classically trained in music, were not true songwriters. "They wrote with their heads. . . . They would sit down and write interesting melodies, but they weren't songs. There was no heart, no feeling. You write with your feelings, from your stomach . . . from the heart, it's instinct. They didn't have that. . . . Background composers decided they were going to write all the songs in their pictures [or] they wouldn't score it. . . . It started with Tiomkin, and he said, 'I'm going to write this.' . . . And they killed the music writers. . . . Harry Warren couldn't work after that."

Evans and Livingston responded to the changing scene by presenting themselves as colyricists and working with film scorers to set words to their songs. "That's how we kept going," Evans said, pointing out that Johnny Mercer was also able to adjust to these changing circumstances: "Johnny latched on to Henry Mancini." They characterized Mancini as one of the few film scorers who could also write true melodies. Mercer had heard "Joanna," Mancini's theme melody for the television show *Peter Gunn*, on the radio and called Mancini to ask if he could put words to it. It must have been difficult for Mercer, who typically waited for collaborators to seek him out, to drop his genteel guard and ask the younger Mancini to collaborate, but he was in desperate straits. "Joanna" met with little success as a song, but it established a rapport between Mancini and Mercer, so when Mancini was asked to write a score—and theme song—for a film based on Truman Capote's *Breakfast at Tiffany's*, he turned to Mercer for a lyric. "I do believe," said Virginia Mancini, "that was the motivation for Henry calling him to see if he was interested in collaborating with him."

She recalled that Mancini was "oh, elated, elated" to work with Mercer. "Of course, to collaborate with a master like Johnny Mercer was wonderful for Henry because Henry never considered himself a songwriter. He was a film composer, and because of his gift of melody, his mentors were Victor Young and the composers who had a great gift of melody, which he had as well. And so the fact that the melodies were so strong and lent themselves to a song, you know, a typical song, in the Tin Pan Alley fashion—it was a thrill for him to work with Johnny Mercer." The two men were perfectly matched for the assignment. "When *Breakfast at Tiffany's* came along, and there was a need for a certain, haunting song that would depict Holly Golightly as a little girl from a small town who is trying to be very sophisticated in big, bad New York City, there had to be a happy medium that would work for this—for this young woman. And the melody came after a while to Henry. And John certainly put a wonderful lyric to it."

Mercer was a great lover of Capote's book and might have seen in the story of small-town southern girl Holly Golightly trying to succeed in New York a reflection of himself after he left Savannah to try to make it as an actor on Broadway. But Mercer saw the theme song as a purely aesthetic exercise, for he doubted it would have any chance in the current popular song market. " 'Hank, who's going to record a waltz?' he asked. 'We'll do it for the movie, but after that it hasn't any future commercially.' I gave him a tape of the melody," Mancini said. "And he went home."

Several days later Mercer called and said he had three lyrics to the melody. Mancini had not known that Mercer frequently wrote several lyrics for a song, then let his collaborator choose his favorite. One of the lyrics was "Holly," in which Mercer took the first three notes of Mancini's melody and matched the upward sweep between the first and second notes with a simple declaration of the main character's name:

> I'm Holly,
> Like I want to be,
> Like holly on a tree back home.
> Just plain holly,
> With no dolly,
> No mama, no papa,
> Wherever I roam.

When Mercer sang this lyric to Mancini, the composer agreed that the producers might like a song that was so clearly tied to the movie's main character.

Then Mercer sang his second lyric, "Blue River," which he said could also be called "Red River" or "June River." "Red River" smacked too much of "Red River Valley" for Mercer and lacked that melancholy *oo* vowel in "Blue" and "June." Mancini thought "June" sounded too "summery," so it seemed it would be "Blue River," but when Mercer learned that his friend Joseph Meyer had already written a song called "Blue River," he insisted, even though he knew a title could not be copyrighted, upon changing "Blue" to something else. The river he was thinking of was the Back River, a branch of the Vernon River that ran past his family's summer home, but since "Vernon" and "Back" were not very singable, Mercer did what Stephen Foster had done a century before when he wrote "Old Folks at Home": he looked at a map and, as Foster had found the mellifluous Suwannee River in Florida, found a Moon River a little north of Savannah near Bluffton, South Carolina. With "Moon River" he could still keep that melancholy *oo* vowel of "Blue" and "June," and the lunar image gave the lyric a dark, brooding edge.

That was the only change in the lyric as he sang it for Mancini. Mercer had reached back in his memories of traveling back and forth across America by train to the image of crossing the wide Missouri, then even further back into his boyhood, when he and his cousin Walter Rivers used to pick huckleberries along the spreading fingers of the Vernon River as it poured into the Atlantic. Into those memories went his own boyhood longing to leave that idyllic scene for the city of New York, whose skyline he had beheld from the deck of a ship one chilly morning:

Moon River,
Wider than a mile:
I'm crossin' you in style some day.
Old dream maker,
You heart breaker,
Wherever you're goin',
I'm goin' your way.

Mercer managed to capture both youthful ambition and mature stoicism,
reflecting, perhaps, the part of him that always regretted leaving Savannah.
As the song swelled to a close, he conjured up the image of "Two drifters, off
to see the world":

We're after the same
Rainbow's end,
My huckleberry friend,
Moon River and me.

When the melody soars upward, Mercer, with his uncanny ability to hear the
music in words, placed "same" and "rainbow" together on the two climactic
notes, knowing that the long *a* in "same" was exactly the same as the long *a* in
"rainbow," so that the two words, like the two friends, stand side by side.
Drawing on the image of Tom Sawyer and Huckleberry Finn on the Mississippi, Mercer merged his lyric with America's folk tradition. When his cousin
Walter Rivers heard the song, he called Johnny to tell him how the "huckleberry friend" line made him recall their days of playing along the Back River,
and Mercer said, "Well, you ought to because you're the 'huckleberry
friend.'"

The phrase was problematic, however, and when he and Mancini demonstrated the song for Margaret Whiting, whose judgment Mercer trusted, she
said, "Gee, I don't know. . . . It tells a beautiful story, but I just don't like
'huckleberry friend.' What is a 'huckleberry friend'? . . . That particular
phrase throws the whole thing out of context for me. . . . It changes the
whole song. It simply won't work." Mancini slumped over the piano, but
Mercer held his ground. "Well, I'll tell you what. I'll think about it. But, boy,
I really liked that lyric." Three hours later he called Whiting to say, "Kid, I
gotta go along with my instincts. I gotta keep 'huckleberry friend' in."

When *Breakfast at Tiffany's* was previewed in Los Angeles, audience reaction was tepid, and a hasty conference was called to discuss problems with the
movie. "I don't know about the rest of you," the producer said, "but that
damned song can go." Yet "Moon River," sung charmingly by Audrey Hepburn, stayed in the picture and was recorded by Andy Williams. A friend who
had been at the preview said he knew by the third note of the song that it

would win an Oscar. Another friend recalled how the Mancinis came to Mercer's home on Oscar night, and, going to separate rooms, they donned their tuxedos. "Let me see your shoes," Mercer said when Mancini came out of the bedroom. "Oh, I like those shoes." A limousine pulled up to escort them all to the ceremony, and as they pulled up to Chandler Pavilion, crowds swarmed around them. "People were looking into the cars and asking 'Are you anybody?'" Virginia Mancini recalled. "It cracked Johnny up."

Mercer's son-in-law Bob Corwin said that up until "Moon River" Mercer had felt "over the hill. I remember one day we were sitting in the house, and he said, 'You know, I haven't had a hit song in years.' It was really interesting because that night the phone rang and Mancini was on the phone, and he said, 'This new song we recorded—it's really doing well.' It was 'Moon River.'" Until then, however, "There was like a big gap." During this dry period, Mercer's depression, drinking, and belligerence grew worse. "When he was drunk, I was his guardian," Corwin recalled. "I used to go into bars with him, and I just took the job upon myself to get him out of there before he got killed because he was so belligerent. I remember one time I was really afraid. He started insulting somebody big-time, so I went to the bartender. It was a club in Beverly Hills, and I asked the bartender how to get him out of there, and the bartender said, 'Give him this.' It was his next drink—he put something in his next drink. I guess that's what they call a 'Mickey Finn.' Five minutes later, he said, 'Let's go.' And so we left. He got sick as a dog." The son-in-law thinks that Mercer's viciousness was "competitive." "The more famous you were, I think the more belligerent he got."

Not even the stunning success of "Moon River" could calm Mercer's dark anger or satisfy the restless, questing skylark in his soul. "Moon River" became so associated with him that he grew to loathe it; as he entered a restaurant and the orchestra struck it up in his honor, he said to a friend, "I hate that fucking song."

With a new hit song on the charts, Johnny Mercer once again found himself in demand. He was invited to appear as a guest star on such television programs as Steve Allen's Sunday evening variety show, much to the delight of songwriter Allen, who considered Mercer the greatest of all American lyricists. The two sat on stools, and Allen would sing a few bars from a great standard by another songwriter, challenging Mercer to match them with his own lyrics about the same subject. If Allen, for example, sang "Witchcraft," Mercer would respond with "That Old Black Magic." It was, of course, all scripted, but it sounded wonderfully spontaneous and showcased the enormous emotional range of Mercer's lyrics, from sophisticated ("Satin Doll") to folksy ("In the Cool, Cool, Cool of the Evening"), from childish ("Jeepers Creepers") to nostalgic ("Autumn Leaves"), from gleeful ("Goody Goody") to wrenching ("One for My Baby").

One of his most emotionally complex lyrics emerged in 1961, when he and

Mancini were assigned to write the title song for *Days of Wine and Roses*, a brutal look at how alcoholism destroys a marriage. Mercer, however, did not know what the film was about, assuming from its title, that it was a romantic swashbuckler set in the medieval Wars of the Roses. The title was taken from a poem by Ernest Dowson, one of the Decadent poets of the 1890s, himself a victim of alcohol:

> They are not long, the days of wine and roses:
>> Out of a misty dream
> Our path emerges for a while, then closes
>> Within a dream.

As he drove home from the studio with Mancini's melody in his mind, Mercer agonized over writing a lyric with such a lengthy title. "Oh, my God," he thought. "What am I going to write?" Margaret Whiting later asked him how he had come up with the lyric, and Mercer walked her into the room that held his piano. As they turned the corner into the bar, she said, "There was a wall." Mercer explained that as he was leaning against that wall the lines suddenly came to him,

> The days of wine and roses
> Laugh and run away
> Like a child at play . . .

Within five minutes the rest of the sentence followed:

> Through the meadowland toward a closing door,
> A door marked "Nevermore,"
> That wasn't there before.

Andy Williams, who had a hit recording of "Days of Wine and Roses," professed he could not understand the significance of "Nevermore" in the lyric. "Allegorically," Mercer explained, "it's like a Dali painting, you know. You're walking through a meadow and suddenly there's a door and there's a word on it. You see past that and past that you can't go."

Ernest Dowson would have grasped the significance of Mercer's image. He shared with the French Symbolist poets the quest for "verbal sensation, the haunting cadence, the cultivated languor," and he believed in their theories of "verbal suggestiveness and of poetry as incantation." Poetry, he thought, could be created by "mere sound and music, with just a suggestion of sense." Certainly these elements figure in Mercer's evocative choice of the word "Nevermore," which goes back to Edgar Allan Poe's "The Raven." Poe, a poet beloved by the French Symbolists, chose to have the raven repeat the word "Nevermore" because he thought the sound of that word the most melancholy in the language.

Mercer's account of his composition of "Days of Wine and Roses" also reflects the Symbolists' belief in poetic inspiration as a sudden, intoxicated effusion of musical words. "I think I wrote it in five minutes. I couldn't write it down fast enough. . . . It just poured out of me. I have no idea. I labored over it later, but the song came to me first, the words came to me, leaning against that wall, looking in at the bar." . . . "I can't take credit for that one. God wrote that lyric. All I did was take it down." The creative rush is reflected in the syntax of the lyric, which consists of merely two sentences, whose phrases tumble inexorably into each other so that, even when the song is sung slowly, as it usually is, the underlying syntax registers the swift passage of time. In some strange, mystical fit of creativity, Mercer's childhood memories of the meadows around their summer home in Savannah, his futile longing to find satisfaction, and the memory of an old love, perhaps, coalesced:

> The lonely night discloses
> Just a passing breeze
> Filled with memories
> Of the golden smile that introduced me to
> The days of wine and roses and you.

If the "golden smile" in Johnny Mercer's mind was that of Judy Garland, it would add yet another figure of dissipation to the network of Edgar Allan Poe, Symbolist poets such as Verlaine and Rimbaud, Ernest Dowson, and, finally, Mercer himself.

Jack Lemmon recalled the day that Mercer and Mancini brought the song to the studio. All morning he and Lee Remick had been filming a long, grueling scene for *Days of Wine and Roses* that ended with Lemmon dissolving in tears. "We finally got it," he said. "We had it." Director Blake Edwards cut, said, "Print," and "we did it once more for protection—in case something happened to the film in the lab, and that was it. . . . I was an emotional mess by lunchtime. . . . I was exhausted. I didn't even want to eat lunch. I merely wanted to go back to my dressing room at Warner Brothers."

But Blake Edwards prevailed upon Lemmon to accompany him to another sound stage. Lemmon described what followed as a scene that could have come from "an old MGM musical." They walked into a dark and empty stage—"Nothing except this enormous empty stage—one work light way over in the corner—one tiny light and the rest is just total blackness. And beside it an old, beat-up, upright piano. And not a stool—just a little broken-backed chair." Lemmon vividly remembered Mancini sitting at the piano, and Mercer taking a folded piece of paper out of his pocket. "And he opens it up—I swear to God, I'm beginning to cry—he started to sing this song and I have never been through anything like it in my life. . . . When I heard this, I was wiped out, I was gone. And I'll never forget the circumstances. It was one of the most thrilling moments that I've ever had in thirty-five years of being in this business."

Mancini returned home to tell his wife of their reaction to "Days of Wine and Roses." " 'When they were finished,' he said, 'both Blake and Jack had tears streaming down their faces.' " . . . When Virginia Mancini first heard it, "I said, 'My goodness, that undoubtedly is going to win an Academy Award.' And it did."

After Mercer won the Oscar, his fourth, a Savannah friend sent him a telegram that incorporated all four of his Oscar-winning songs. "I said, 'Now hop 'The Atchison Topeka, and the Santa Fe,' come to 'Moon River,' and let's have some 'Days of Wine and Roses' 'In the Cool, Cool, Cool of the Evening.' And so he got a bang out of that, and he wired me back. He said, 'Take the whole gang to Johnny Harris,' which was a watering hole, 'and tell them the drinks are on me.' That was his thank-you for the message."

The success of "Moon River" and "Days of Wine and Roses" lifted Mercer out of the worst depression of his life, and he could thank, yet once more, his childhood in Savannah for inspiration.

Fifteen

When October Goes: 1962–1964

Music can still make me cry. More so than the really sad things. I'm inured to those, expecting death and taxes and taking them as a matter of course.

For all their success, "Moon River" and "Days of Wine and Roses" were still *songs*—individual hits that could pass the way of most popular songs. What Mercer still longed for was that great Broadway score that would preserve his lyrics in a classic musical. Having had a few hit songs again, however, must have helped him forget the failure of *Saratoga* and made him receptive to the prospect of another musical. As usual, it was not Mercer who took the initiative; with his genteel reserve, he waited for someone to approach him with a project.

The initial idea for that project came from preservationists in the Canadian government who thought that Dawson City, the scene of the Klondike gold rush of 1898, could be turned into a historical site that would attract tourists. The crown jewel of Dawson City was the Grand Opera House, which in the town's heyday had provided lavish entertainment, featuring such stars as Douglas Fairbanks. When the gold ran out, however, prospectors deserted Dawson City for Alaska. From a population of 40,000 in 1899, Dawson City dwindled until, by 1960, it boasted only 735 people, half of them Indians. By then, the Grand Opera House "had become a derelict shell, ravaged and distorted by the elements." Fearing that this landmark site of the Klondike gold rush would disappear, the Canadian Department of Northern Affairs and Natural Resources stepped in to try to save the opera house and turn Dawson City into a tourist attraction.

The old building, however, was beyond restoration, so in 1961, after it was carefully studied and measured, the existing structure was torn down and an exact replica was built on the site. To celebrate the re-creation, the Canadian government, in conjunction with theater people in Canada and the United States, planned an annual "Gold Rush" festival of musical shows to be staged at the opera house. Broadway producer Robert Whitehead agreed to mount the first production as part of a festival in Dawson City. Whitehead presented the project to two Hollywood screenwriters, Ian McLellan Hunter and Ring Lardner Jr., neither of whom had ever written a stage musical. Hunter, who had worked on films with Johnny Mercer, suggested he be approached to do the score, music and lyrics.

While Mercer agreed to write lyrics, he did not want to take on the music as well, so he suggested Robert Emmett Dolan, who had composed the score for *Texas, Li'l Darlin'*. "We decided to do a show about gold," Mercer said. "The minute we said that word *Volpone* came to mind." Ben Jonson's Renaissance satire on avarice could easily be adapted into a story about Klondike prospectors trying to bilk one another out of their gold. The choice would have especially appealed to Mercer because when he was struggling to make it as an actor in New York in 1928, one of the bit parts he got was that of a policeman in a Theatre Guild production of *Volpone*. The big catch was getting Bert Lahr to play the lead. Lahr, nearing seventy, had had glorious success in burlesque, vaudeville, and the loose Broadway shows of the 1920s and 1930s, as well, of course, as the Cowardly Lion in *The Wizard of Oz*. But, like Mercer, he had had difficulty adapting to the new "book shows" that had been ushered in by *Oklahoma!* *Foxy*, as the new musical was to be called (playing off *Volpone*, Latin for "fox"), would give Lahr, as well as Mercer, another chance, for a big Broadway hit. For a costar, the production signed the young actor Larry Blyden, who had been a sensation in the television production of *What Makes Sammy Run?*, to play Lahr's partner in larcenous intrigue.

The logistics of mounting the production were staggering. Getting the cast, crew, sets, and costumes from Broadway to Dawson City, 4,700 miles away, took a series of seven airplane flights, and for Lahr and director Robert Lewis, who refused to fly, an even more complicated series of train, ship, bus, and automobile changes. Mercer, along with Ginger and son Jeff, sailed up the intercoastal waterway to Vancouver, where the company rehearsed for three weeks. They then packed into cars and drove the 300 miles to Dawson City. "I was only fifteen," Jeff Mercer recalls, "but my Dad let me drive the whole way. It was just one dirt road."

In writing for the great Bert Lahr, Mercer instinctively wrote free-standing patter songs that let the comedian chew up the scenery. In "Bon Vivant," Mercer played with British place-names as inventively as he had with American ones:

> Manchester and Dorchester
> And Chichester and Perth,
> Sailing on the Firth of Forth
> Or is it Forth of Firth?

Although he had objected to the "swishiness" Morton Da Costa had injected into *Saratoga*, Mercer gave Lahr lines he could use to strike a limp-wristed pose:

> Birmingham and Nottingham,
> And Sandringham and Crewe,
> Shrewsbury and Tewkesbury
> And Shaftsbury and Lewe,
> Where I starred as Portia
> In "The Taming of the Shrew."
> As we would say in school,
> I've been around the pool.

For Blyden and the other performers, however, Mercer and Dolan wrote songs that were more integral to the story and characters:

> I think, by proxy,
> For my friend, Foxy,
> A man—whose innocent mind
> Is kind—
> But rather cloudy.

These two different kinds of lyrics underscored a tension that ran throughout the production.

Lahr, the last of the comics who had come up through star revues built around themselves, found that the libretto lacked laughs, so he began to ad-lib lines, mug, and generally turn *Foxy* into a one-man show. At one point, for example, he was to hop off a dog sled, toss a bag of gold to his two Eskimo drivers, and say, "Here, buy yourself a couple of fishhooks." But after a few performances, Lahr substituted the funnier—but less dramatically realistic—line "Buy yourself some chocolate-covered blubber." Director Robert Lewis, who had spearheaded such hit musicals as *Brigadoon* but had never worked with an old-time star, was caught helplessly between holding to the script or letting Lahr go for laughs. Blyden dug in his heels. "Every time he does that," he told Lewis, "I'm going to do it!"

Blyden saw the struggle as a conflict between the old theatrical tradition represented by Lahr, a dog-eat-dog world where each actor fought to keep the spotlight on himself, and a new theatrical world where everyone worked to bring out the organic power of the play. "He came up with a school of butchers. They were killers, those guys. You can't expect anyone who started at fifteen and is now seventy to change. People are props. He said to me, 'Well, in this sketch we should do so and so . . .' Well, it is not a sketch. It's a book musical. There are scenes connected to each other. In a sketch you go from one laugh to another, then blackout. In his mind, *Foxy* was a sketch."

Even without the internecine squabbles, *Foxy* faced insurmountable odds in Dawson City, trying to fill its five-hundred-seat opera house every night with the nearest town, White Horse, 350 miles away. The rest of the Gold Rush festival failed to materialize, and *Foxy* had to draw audiences by itself. Still, Ian Hunter recalled that the opening night audience was receptive, and *Foxy* received a standing ovation: "The rich people who arrived on opening night, by and large, came by seaplane of all things and landed on the Yukon River." But soon *Foxy* was playing to nearly empty houses on weeknights and half-full ones at best on weekends. After three weeks, its losses forced a closing notice, but the Canadian government stepped in at the last minute and funded *Foxy* for the rest of its eight-week run.

Whitehead had originally planned to produce *Foxy* on Broadway, but he had to step down after he agreed to oversee the new Lincoln Center Theater. As he sought out another producer for *Foxy*, it was announced that the show would reopen on Broadway "sometime in the future," a phrase that normally sounded the death knell for a production. Amazingly, however, *Foxy* revived. Wealthy oilmen from Calgary had seen the show in Dawson City and wanted to back it on Broadway. "The whole show was budgeted, I think, at three hundred and fifty thousand," Lardner recalled. "I think they put in two hundred and fifty, Johnny Mercer put up about thirty thousand, and I put up about fourteen thousand." For a while it looked as if Billy Rose would take over as producer, which would mean replacing Robert Lewis as director, since he and Rose were enemies. "We had considered some alternative directors to Lewis when he and Rose couldn't get along," Lardner said, "among them Jerome Robbins." But Robbins was about to commit to another project. "'Obviously, *Foxy* is going to be the hit of the season,' he said. 'But for ethnic reasons I have to do this Jewish thing.'" "The inference," Lardner said, "was that he was going to do this even though he knew that it would never amount to anything, and that our show was going to be the hit." The "Jewish thing" Robbins was committed to was *Fiddler on the Roof*, which turned out to be one of the most successful Broadway musicals ever. Finally, Whitehead asked David Merrick to produce *Foxy* on Broadway, and Merrick agreed—because, Lardner thought, "he didn't have to really put up any money for it, or raise any money from his normal backers . . . Except for about fifty thousand he got from RCA, who normally did the cast recordings for his shows. So they were the only backer he was any way responsible to."

As soon as rehearsals began, the same rift between doing *Foxy* as an integrated musical and presenting it as a star vehicle for Lahr broke out again. "We had a lot of trouble in rehearsal," Lardner said, "because Bobby Lewis couldn't take charge. He couldn't control Lahr and, to a certain extent, Blyden." Bert Lahr went to David Merrick, whom he trusted as an old-fashioned theater man, and Merrick backed Lahr. "Lahr knew where to find the laughter," Blyden recalled, "but it always had to relate to him. At one point, Foxy is chasing a girl who, on discovering he's rich, turns track and pursues him, crying, " 'Play me like a harp.' It topped him. He did everything in his power to kill her laugh. In fact, he said, 'Honey, I'm sorry I'm going to have to kill that laugh.' Then, he put in another line for himself: 'Yeah, but I got a sore pinky.' Finally, he figured if he waited, and let it hit, then said his line—he would top it. But had he not topped it, he would have killed it. . . . He has to have the biggest laugh in the scene; and he has to have the last laugh of the scene, and the biggest line that ends it. . . . Otherwise, he's going to be hungry; he's going to be fifteen and nobody's going to love him; and he's going to be looking for a job."

As the show increasingly became a vehicle for Lahr, Mercer and Dolan added new songs that were less integrated into story and character but promised to become independently popular. "Since the tryout in the Yukon," Mercer told a New York columnist during the out-of-town run, "Bobby and I have written five new songs for *Foxy*. Two of them could well be hits before the show opens in New York. . . . Frank Sinatra has already recorded 'Talk to Me.' " But the columnist was skeptical of a show "written by talent which is primarily tuned to writing popular songs rather than highly integrated scores where songs are so much a part of the plot that they fail to become hits. Mercer and Dolan, Merrick and Lahr, in *Foxy* are bringing in a musical which is frankly aimed at the notion that hit-songs-sell-tickets. And the musical integrationists will be watching the results closely."

"The worst thing that happened to us," Lardner recalled, "was the successful opening of *Hello, Dolly!* while we were out of town." *Hello, Dolly!* was another David Merrick production, and the producer quickly lost whatever interest he had in *Foxy*, which he even considered closing out of town. Johnny Mercer and other investors persuaded Merrick to bring the show to Broadway, but, according to Ian Hunter, "he brought it into town cold," spending very little money on advertising. It opened on February 15, 1964, and reviewers, while praising Lahr, noted the conflicted nature of the show. "The show, as a show, isn't ever firmly certain which side of the bed to get into," said Walter Kerr. "It begins, for instance, with a sly, quiet, confidentially tricky monologue sung by Larry Blyden that suggests at once an intimate, cozily styled, perhaps even literate entertainment (the suggestion of literacy stems not from Ben Jonson but from the articulate intricacy of Johnny Mercer's lyrics). But lo and behold, no one knows how to follow through on that. . . . We are listening to the ensemble roar out any number of those irrelevant snappy tunes that are so interchangeable these days from show to show."

While New York critics were usually hard on shows written by songwriters based in Hollywood, the palpably pop nature of a song such as "Talk to Me Baby (Tell Me Lies)" raised their integrationist hackles. Still, the songs were catchy, and there were enough positive comments about Lahr's performance that *Variety* predicted a solid run for *Foxy*.

But David Merrick, according to Lardner and Hunter, was dead set against *Foxy*, and after the show had run for a week, the newspaper ads virtually stopped. "It's a wonder," Bert Lahr said, "we played as long as we did with the treatment Merrick gave us." Merrick's next bit of treachery, according to Lardner, was "agreeing with the RCA backers that they didn't have to make a cast recording." Original cast recordings of Broadway shows were routine in the 1960s and not only sold well themselves but were an important means to promote a show, drawing in people who had bought the album or heard selections on the radio. Cast recordings were normally made on the Sunday after a show opened, which explains why even a short-lived show, such as Stephen Sondheim's *Anyone Can Whistle*, which ran for only nine performances, was preserved in an original cast recording. The only money Merrick had raised to produce *Foxy* came from RCA Victor, but after RCA lost money on two other original cast recordings, for *110 in the Shade* and *Jennie*, Merrick agreed to release the company from its contract, and no original cast recording was made of *Foxy*.

Without a cast album and with no advertising, *Foxy* steadily lost money. The Ziegfeld Theater had the capacity to gross $78,305 a week, but in its best week Foxy took in only $37,961. In its seventh week, *Foxy* was hit by a post-Easter slump that affected all Broadway shows, and drew in only $26,099. At that point David Merrick finally stepped in and closed the show. "We could have made it," Lahr said, "if the producer cared." When the Tony Awards were announced a few weeks later, *Foxy* received two nominations: Bert Lahr for Best Actor in a Musical and Julienne Marie for Best Featured Actress in a Musical. Bert Lahr went on to win the Tony, in a ceremony where *Hello, Dolly!* took most of the trophies. Had Merrick kept *Foxy* running, that award alone would have drawn crowds. "He should never have taken it on," Ring Lardner Jr. said. "He couldn't resist the fact that he didn't have to do the money raising"—an ironic explanation of the failure of a musical version of Ben Jonson's brilliant satire about avarice.

"*Foxy* I thought was salvageable," said Johnny Mercer, as free of avarice as anyone could be, "and I don't rap our work on that, but I'm sorry I didn't save myself a year or two's worry by just saying 'no.' Working with Bert Lahr was great fun, and I loved everybody in the show, but I just don't get any kick out of spending all that time and effort, getting into backstage politics, bitching and being bitched at, when one song can make me twice the money and never say an unkind word to me."

Mercer must have been thinking of the enormous time and energy he had spent on *Foxy* between 1962 and 1964, a two-year span when the continuing success of "Moon River" and "Days of Wine and Roses" earned him far more than *Foxy*, in terms of both financial profit and personal and artistic achievement. "You don't even have the satisfaction of having written a prestigious work that succeeds in failure by being talked about at all the bars in town. Who has time to talk about old shows that died on the vine when everybody and his brother are coming out with new shows, new movies, new albums? Make one effort count. Make someone happy, and make that someone yourself!"

Even while he was involved with *Foxy*, Mercer had made himself—and others—happy by writing individual songs. Back in 1957, he had received a letter from Sadie Vimmerstedt, a fifty-eight-year-old grandmother who worked at the cosmetics counter of a Youngstown, Ohio, department store. She had been outraged when Frank Sinatra divorced his first wife, Nancy, to marry Ava Gardner; when Ava Gardner left Sinatra, Sadie relished the fact that the cocky singer had gotten his comeuppance. Tearing several sheets from an old desk pad calendar, she wrote to Johnny Mercer, asking him to write a song about how "Frankie boy" got his just deserts for leaving Nancy. She suggested a title, "When Somebody Breaks Your Heart," and gave Mercer the idea of the lyric: "I want to be around to pick up the pieces when somebody breaks your heart." She put the sheets in an envelope and addressed it simply to:

Johnny Mercer
Songwriter
New York, NY

The post office forwarded the letter to New York's ASCAP office, and eventually it reached Mercer.

Although he was usually responsive to correspondents, Sadie's letter came at the low point of Mercer's career, when his confidence in his songwriting ability was at its ebb. With the success of "Moon River" and "Days of Wine and Roses," however, his creative spirits surged, and in 1962 he wrote back to Sadie Vimmerstedt, apologizing for not responding sooner but telling her he had written the song, lyrics and music, and had been waiting for a major recording artist to do it. "He said he didn't want to record the song until he got the best singer," Sadie Vimmerstedt said. "When he told me that Tony Bennett was going to record it I really got excited." Bennett, coming off the success of "I Left My Heart in San Francisco," was the biggest star at Columbia Records, and his recording of "I Wanna Be Around" sold fifteen thousand copies the day it was released. Mercer explained to Sadie that he wanted to publish the song and split the royalties with her. He suggested she receive one-third, since she had had the idea for the song, and he receive two-thirds for writing the lyric and the music.

The song, which recast the theme of romantic vengeance Mercer had established in 1936 with "Goody Goody," had a rhythmic, vernacular pulse to it that resonated with the era of rock:

> And that's when I discover that revenge is sweet;
> As I sit there applauding from a front row seat,
> When somebody breaks your heart
> Like you broke mine.

The song was a huge hit, and Sadie Vimmerstedt found herself a celebrity. She would write to Mercer about people coming into the department store to ask for her autograph and being interviewed on the radio in Cincinnati and Cleveland. "I'm getting to be very famous," she wrote to him. "You can't believe how, it's like a fairy story, a Cinderella story." Then she was invited to appear on network television, but after her experience in New York, she wrote to Mercer, "I'm *tired*. I think I'm getting out of show business."

Friends recalled the early 1960s as a time when, with his songs once again topping the charts, Mercer was as happy as they'd ever seen him. He could even enjoy some of the new music that had displaced Tin Pan Alley. "I think one of our happiest three or four days together," Jean Bach recalled, "was when he was East, and the family was out in the West." She and her husband rented a red convertible and, with Mercer and singer Blossom Dearie in the backseat, drove to the Newport Jazz Festival. "They got along so wonderfully well, Blossom and Johnny, it was sensational, and I never saw him happier in my life. We're driving along in this crazy red convertible. And it was the time of Chuck Berry's, what was it, 'School Days.' . . . I believe it was 'Hail, hail rock 'n' roll.' He was singing along and it would come on the radio and he'd sing along, leaning out of the car, banging the tempo on the side of the car. I just thought, 'It can't get any better than this.'"

Mercer and Blossom Dearie became friends, and Mercer, with his absolute admiration of pure talent, included her in his circle of the gifted. "Blossom was being a pixy. She's very odd, you know, and they were perfect together. And he was fascinated by her, because—she's her own person, shall we say, is the kindest way to put it. She's eccentric. But she too is absolutely pure when it comes to music. . . . They were great buddies that weekend."

Blossom Dearie introduced Mercer to a French song she wanted to record on an album, "Valse de Lilacs," which Michel Legrand had composed with Eddie Barclay. As he had done with "Autumn Leaves" and "When the World Was Young," Mercer agreed to write an English lyric to it. "She was recording songs for the album, and they had taken the cover photograph, and they were waiting for Johnny to get this darn lyric done. It was supposed to be done in the spring; he took all summer." Mercer, characteristically, took great pains with the lyric, which he entitled "Once Upon a Summertime":

> Once upon a summertime, if you recall,
> We stopped beside a little flower stall.
> A bunch of bright forget-me-nots was all
> I'd let you buy me.

The song is sung from a woman's point of view, and here, in a few lines, Mercer manages to establish a sense of character, present an arresting image, and create a dramatic scene. But he labored painstakingly over the release, with its many long *e* sounds:

> You were *sweeter* than the blossoms on the *tree*.
> I was as proud as any girl could *be*,
> As if the mayor had offered *me* the *key*
> To Pa*ris*.

"There was one word in there that he wasn't pleased with. He was such a perfectionist, and he was waiting for the *mot juste*. . . . I don't know what was wrong in his head, but something wasn't working, and I think they finally speeded him up and said, 'Let's take it as it is' or something." What the consummate cabaret singer Mabel Mercer found awkward about the line was that it seemed inappropriate for an innocent young girl to be thrilled by receiving the key to the city, but after many performances she delivered the line with a shy giggle that brought it back into character.

"Once Upon a Summertime," like "Autumn Leaves" and "When the World Was Young," registered for another great cabaret singer, Tony Bennett, Johnny Mercer's ability to capture a French sensibility: "He had an American understanding or view of his love of Paris, like no other composer I know of, even the French composers. I don't know of anybody that had more of a . . . kind of longed for the *soul* of Paris, the *feel* of Paris. When he wrote about Paris, something else happened to Mercer, something, something magnified in his own talent. . . . something about him and Paris makes me cry . . . it's just beautiful." A friend who stayed with the Mercers in Paris for an extended visit recalled how Mercer steeped himself in the everyday life of the city, going marketing every morning and communicating with all the vendors even though he spoke not a word of French.

Happy as he was in the early 1960s, the monstrous side of Mercer still came out when he drank.

Jean Bach recalled one party at her home when Mercer was so drunk he attacked the family cat. "That was really terrible. He was lashing out at everybody, and throwing insults around and embarrassing all of us, here in this house. And I had this marvelous housekeeper . . . a black lady who—she'd seen enough of him not to get her feathers too ruffled, although she was a sensitive person. But she had a pretty good sense of humor herself. But she said she drew the line when he turned on Seymour, and he looked at him and he said, 'And you, you're nothing but a cat and a terrible alley cat' or something, he was really insulting. She said, 'Just a minute.' She said, 'You can insult my madame, and you can insult me, but you can't do it to Seymour.'

"Oh, you'd go out with him, and of course everybody was so thrilled to have him in the room. You know, you'd go to a supper club or something. We were at the Copacabana, and they had a big dance floor where they had the revue and the chorus girls come out and dance, and we had a ringside table. And by the time the emcee came out and said, 'Ladies and gentlemen, we're honored tonight to have with us that distinguished songwriter, Johnny Mercer' and they'd put the spotlight on him and he's sound asleep. . . . He could sleep through anything. You know, having had a drink, he was out of it. He did a lot of sleeping."

On the other hand, Bach recalled, Mercer was filled with a vital responsiveness to life. "I was always knocked out by the way he picked up immediately on sounds and phrases, topical references," she said. "I think he was a magnet, everything stuck to him. . . . He entered into everything. He really savored every experience, and I guess that's the artist. Their pores are open, they pick up more than the rest of us. Either we think, 'Oh, it's too obvious, let's don't do it.' Or we're put off by things being, kind of, not too interesting, but he just found fascination in every realm, every phase of life, it was terrific."

That vibrant, spontaneous Johnny Mercer was captured in 1963 when he recorded an album with Bobby Darin, who was then at the center of the new musical world with such popular hits as "Splish Splash," "Mack the Knife," and "Beyond the Sea." Both had done a television show in New York called *The Big Party* when Steve Blauner, Darin's manager, thought of having them do an album together. "I just got this idea, and I said to Bobby, 'Would you like to do an album with Johnny Mercer?' He said, 'I'd love to.' So I went over to Johnny Mercer and introduced myself, and I said to him, 'Mr. Mercer, how about you and Bobby Darin doing an album together?' He said, 'I'd love to.' I said, 'Okay, I'll put it together.'" Years later, when Darin and Blauner were in California, Blauner arranged a three-day recording session with Billy May, who had done so many swinging albums with Sinatra. "I wanted to do an album of all Mercer tunes, but Johnny did not want to do that. So I think in the album there are maybe only two or three of Johnny's songs. That's all." Between Mercer's characteristic self-effacement and his love of older songs, a love shared by Darin, the album consisted largely of such classics as "Back Home Again in Indiana" and "Paddlin' Madeline Home."

But the album needed a title song, and Mercer came up with "Two of a

Kind." "I remember when they were writing the lead song," Blauner said. "We were on a set someplace, and Johnny would be in the dressing room, and Bobby would go off and do some scene, and he would come back, and Johnny had a pencil, and he would be writing something down, and Bobby would give him a line here and a word there. The next thing you know they wrote the song. I mean Johnny really wrote the song, but he wrote on it 'Written by Johnny Mercer and Bobby Darin.' When Bobby saw his name on the song, he said to Johnny, 'Why are you including my name?' Johnny said, 'You helped me write the song.' So out of this album, of course, Bobby has the honor of being credited with having a song written with Johnny Mercer."

With "Two of a Kind" written, they were ready to record. "In those days all albums were done in three sessions," Blauner explained. "You do four songs a session, three different days and you would have your album, twelve songs. So we do the twelve songs, we got the album. Then both of them come over to me after the last session and say to me, 'Listen, we have to do another session.' I said, 'Why?' Their response was 'Because we don't have the album yet!' I said, 'Of course we have the album.' They insisted, 'No, no.' Then I realized, why am I carrying on for? They were having such a good time together singing that they wanted to do another session together. So we did three more songs."

Blauner recalled the camaraderie between the two singers. "They had such a great time working together, and they would crack up, you know, and they would have to do another take or they would have to stop the band." Blauner decided to leave their clowning—even some of their flubbed lines—on the album to capture the spontaneity of the sessions. The singers trade scat solos; sing in accents and falsetto; do imitations of Groucho Marx, W. C. Fields, and Bing Crosby; improvise lyrics; and banter between and during the songs. In "Back Home Again in Indiana," while Darin sings the original line about "moonlight on the Wabash," Mercer follows up with an interjection about things being "peachy on the old Ogeechee." Darin snaps "Where's that?" but then, as Mercer says, "Savannah," Darin makes up his own line about the Hudson River, and Mercer rounds off with "We all know where that is." "As I remember the album," Blauner said, "there is one time that Bobby just bursts out laughing and they keep trying to top one another with the asides. When you listen to the album, it is more spontaneous than any album you're used to hearing." *Two of a Kind* is a magnificent time capsule of two singers, from different generations, joining in a celebration of classic American song.

Bobby Darin talked about how much he loved working with Mercer. "He is such a pleasure to watch," he said. "When a song starts to feel good to him, he puts his hands over his head, in a sit-up exercise position, and smiles. And all the tracks you hear, most of them you hear were done while his hands were over his head, and he sings that way. That's great! My hands are usually in my pockets." Yet Mercer, Blauner learned later, had misgivings about doing the album with Darin, not because of Darin's singing but because he was worried that the young performer would not be able to keep up with him on the repartee. "He was afraid Bobby couldn't cut it." But Mercer's misgivings were not about just Darin's quick-wittedness. "When they were all through and just about ready to leave, Mercer came up to me and said, 'Steve, I gotta tell you something. I thought you were putting me on. I didn't think anyone would have any interest in singing with me again.'" For all of his renewed success, Mercer still secretly feared he was over the hill.

It was at this precarious moment in Johnny Mercer's life, as he was poised between gnawing fears and renewed confidence, that one of the cataclysmic events in American life during the twentieth century befell. On November 22, 1963, President John F. Kennedy was assassinated. Johnny Mercer was as devastated as any American. "The Kennedy assassination stunned and horrified me, and I can remember all the hardened Broadwayites sitting in Dinty Moore's looking like pole-axed oxen as they watched TV." Although Mercer was not a political liberal like Ginger, who was active in women's political groups in California, he was a good southern Democrat. He might have felt, as so many people did at that time, that with the young president's death a vibrant future for America had been snuffed out. Now the coming years, for himself as well as his country, seemed dark, uncertain.

He was at a point in his life when some men reach out to recapture a lost moment from their past. He had just turned fifty-four, his daughter was married, and his son was nearing graduation from high school. Just as he was enjoying a resurgence of hit songs and singing appearances on television, Judy Garland had had a comeback career onstage, capped by a triumphant appearance at Carnegie Hall in 1961. At the time she also had a successful weekly television program, *The Judy Garland Show*, where she was joined by such guest stars as Ethel Merman and Lena Horne in presenting what still comes off as a dazzling showcase of songs. Garland was, for one of the few periods in her life, ravishingly beautiful and svelte in gorgeous evening gowns. Although Mercer does not appear in the recorded shows that survive, his songs are cast across the programs, as in a show when Frank Sinatra and Dean Martin competitively woo Judy in song, Sinatra singing "Too Marvelous for Words," and Martin, "You Must Have Been a Beautiful Baby." Garland is in absolute command of her audience and radiates sensuality. Now that she has reached her mid-forties, there is a new heft in her voice; if Gatsby thought Daisy Buchanan's voice was full of money, then Garland's was bursting with sexuality.

Then, in the show of February 9, 1964, there is another dimension—maternal and caring. Even without Mercer's physical presence, an intimate moment binds him to Garland and her children in a kind of surreal family portrait. The show is one of several "concert" shows Garland did for the program, in response to viewers' requests that, instead of inviting guest stars to join her, she devote the entire program to singing songs as she did in her famous concerts. In this program, she dedicates a segment to her children. She sings "Liza" for her daughter Liza Minnelli, then brings her son Joey Luft to the edge of the stage and sings "Happiness Is Just a Thing Called Joe" to him. She then explains that her daughter Lorna Luft has always felt envious of her siblings because no song has ever been written about a "Lorna." But, Garland explains, tonight she will sing "Lorna's Song," whose music was based on the theme song for the television show. To put lyrics to that song, Garland tells the audience, she called upon "one of America's greatest lyricists, Johnny Mercer." At the mention of Mercer's name, the audience bursts into applause, and Garland summons the child up to the edge of the stage and serenades her with Mercer's words. Attired in a stunning evening gown, Garland is ravishing but also very clearly the tender mother, hugging her child as she sings Mercer's words.

It seems certain that at this time the affair between Mercer and Garland had rekindled. Both had made astonishing comebacks and were at the top of their form artistically and personally. Garland had just finalized her divorce from Sid Luft, so it was a propitious moment for two old lovers to start over.

Johnny told Ginger he now, again, wanted a divorce and would give her anything she wanted in the way of settlement. Ginger was as thrown as she had been at the time of the original affair in 1941, but she had become more savvy about putting off her husband. Neither Amanda nor Jeff recalls being told about a divorce, but Jeff said their parents would not have discussed such a taboo subject in front of their children and recalls tumultuous arguments when their mother could be heard threatening to "take you for everything you're worth." A niece confirmed that "they were having some marriage problems at that time. . . . Ginger I think was drinking too much, and Johnny didn't like it—which was okay when he drank, but they were talking about a possible divorce at the time."

It must have been as difficult for Mercer to broach the subject of divorce in 1964 as it had been in 1941. "He had this great regard for conformity," a friend said, "and he got absolutely defensive about family. . . . He would say, 'But children, that's what it's all about.' I don't know if he believed it or not, but it was the kind of point of argument in his case. And it was like he wanted it to be that way even if it didn't materialize. I mean, he'd be taking gas at the way the world is going now, with families collapsing all over the place. He's lucky to be out. I mean, we're the poorer, but he wouldn't care for this world at all."

On the one hand, Johnny Mercer could coolly ask a male friend, "You know, I've had the opportunity to go with all sorts of diverse women when I've been doing movies. Do you think I'm making a mistake by just sticking with Ginger?" "You have to live with yourself," the friend said, "and he said, 'Yeah, you're right.'" On the other hand, he was "old-fashioned and prudish," said a niece. At one point he let Ring Lardner Jr. stay in his house in Palm Springs, "and he found out later that he had taken his girlfriend, and Johnny was so angry at Lardner for doing that. He was furious, and he would not let him stay in the house again."

A friend was amazed that Ginger withstood Johnny's abuse for so many years instead of simply divorcing him and living comfortably. "She must have adored him to the bitter end," she said. "That truly supports the idea that money does not buy happiness." But another friend shrugged. "He was abusive to other people when he was drunk, so why wouldn't he go after her? And she was such a meek little thing. She even got to the point—and maybe this was as a result—but she got to the point where she would talk quieter and quieter and quieter . . . so you couldn't understand a word she said. You had to lean way over to even hear what she was saying."

If Ginger had developed some desperate social strategies after years of verbal bludgeoning, she also managed to fend off Mercer's request for a divorce. "He asked Ginger for a divorce," a friend said. "He told her, 'You can have anything you want.' He said he was going to marry Judy Garland. . . . He really loved her. He truly did. That much I know." Ginger shrewdly stalled for time by asking Johnny to let her take a trip with her sister Debbie, whose husband had just died, promising that if he still wanted a divorce when she returned, she would grant it. She had always wanted to visit the Far East, so Mercer arranged a cruise for her and Debbie to the South Seas, Australia, China, and Japan, where they attended the 1964 Olympics with former decathlon champion Bob Mathias as their escort.

On the cruise back, however, Ginger contracted a severe case of hepatitis and had to be quarantined. She and her sister shared one of two luxury cabins on the ship, the other of which was vacant, so Ginger was moved in there. Debbie nonetheless visited Ginger to comfort her for the remainder of the voyage. Once the ship docked, Ginger was rushed to Cedars Sinai Hospital.

A friend who went to see her said, "You had to go in with a mask on. Very infectious." When Johnny went to see her, her doctor told him she did not have long to live. As he went to her bedside, Ginger said, "Will you stay with me? I'm really frightened."

"I'll stay with you," he vowed, "as long as you live."

She recovered—and lived for another thirty years.

Sixteen

Summer Wind: 1963–1969

The lyric gets to so many people. . . . I started out just wanting to be a success, but you reach a point where you begin to feel responsible, to yourself and to those like you. You have to go ahead and just write your best. There will be those who understand, and think that what you do is important poetry, and there will be those who will simply be pleased, and enjoy it.

After the Kennedy assassination, America spun increasingly out of control, and Johnny Mercer, along with other songwriters of his generation, found himself left behind. "They didn't want anything to change," the grand-daughter of one of his collaborators said. "They were all very, very stubborn." As much as they abominated rock and roll, "It's like they were the rock stars of their day. Whole movies were dependent on their talents. . . . They all went and drank their lunches. . . . All the girls wanted to be around them. . . . There were a million parties. . . . Girls who were dancers would get up and dance, pick up their skirts." At one party, at the home of Harold and Gloria Hecht, she recalled, "Johnny went into the closet and went to the bathroom on Gloria's shoes." "He liked sex," a friend confirmed, recalling that the daughter of one of Mercer's collaborators told her, " 'God damn it, when he got a drink, he was after everybody, even me.' I didn't want to hear that," the friend said. The more Johnny Mercer felt left behind by the musical world, the more caustic became his drunken behavior.

Even as his kind of song was being displaced by rock, folk, and country music, Johnny Mercer continued to collaborate with Henry Mancini, but their songs gradually lost their magic. In 1963, Mancini extracted a sinuous melody from his score for *Charade*, at once a romantic comedy and a sinister murder mystery that starred Cary Grant and Audrey Hepburn. " 'Charade,' I think, is one of the finest melodies ever written," Mercer said. "The only thing I don't like about it is the title, but that belonged to the film." Mercer wove his lyric out of imagery drawn, first, from the game of charades:

> When we played our charade,
> We were like children posing.
> Playing at games,
> Acting out names,
> Guessing the parts we played.

Then, knowing that the movie, set in Paris, had a theatrical motif that included Punch-and-Judy shows and a climactic scene in the Paris Opera House, he connected the childhood game to the world of theater, particularly vaudeville, which had its origins in medieval entertainments in the French town of Vau-de-Vire:

> Oh, what a hit we made.
> We came on next to closing,
> Best on the bill,
> Lovers until
> Love left the masquerade.

Mercer's allusion to the "best of the bill" coming on "next to closing" indicates his familiarity with vaudeville, where the act that got top billing was always scheduled next to last in order to hold the audience.

In the next section, he returns to the world of childhood with images from marionette theater:

> Fate seemed to pull the string.
> I turned and you were gone.
> While from the darkened wings
> The music box played on.

"It was a lovely metaphor that he had written," said Virginia Mancini, "depicting life and losses and loves in terms of the stage and the theater and the love affair that was so great and fell apart." "Charade" was nominated for an Oscar but, although it was one of Mercer's most brilliant lyrics, lost to Sammy Cahn and Jimmy Van Heusen's "Call Me Irresponsible."

Considerably less sophisticated was "The Sweetheart Tree," which Mercer wrote with Mancini in 1965 for the campy *The Great Race*, which starred Jack Lemmon, Tony Curtis, and Natalie Wood. The movie was at times hilarious, in the vein Lemmon and Curtis had established in Billy Wilder's *Some Like It Hot*; at other times, it was labored, as when Curtis and Wood sang "The Sweetheart Tree" and the lyrics appeared on the screen with a bouncing ball. "As was his habit," Virginia Mancini recalled, Mercer "would come in with several sets of lyrics, depending upon, you know, the assignment. And when he came in with some lyrics to 'The Sweetheart Tree,' the first thing he sang, and it might have been his way of joking, but the first lyric was, 'There are ninety-nine cars on a freight train.' And so Hank said, 'What else have you got?'" Mancini, by this point, was no longer the neophyte songwriter who felt privileged to work with the great Johnny Mercer; the year before, he had written the score for *The Pink Panther*, which included one of the best-known of movie theme songs.

Mercer and Mancini at last got an opportunity to write a full-blown movie score in 1969 for one of the few original Hollywood musicals made during the decade. *Darling Lili* starred Julie Andrews as a German spy during World War I who poses as a London entertainer and falls in love with an American squadron commander played by Rock Hudson. The multimillion-dollar production was not successful with critics or the public, but it has since gotten more recognition, as have the songs, particularly "Whistling Away the Dark." Mercer told an interviewer that he was "especially fond" of his score for *Darling Lili*, but the movie's tepid reception might have ended the Mercer-Mancini collaboration. Mancini, however, had also caught the brunt of Mercer's temper. "Henry Mancini told me," a friend recalled, "'the one thing that you never did with Johnny—' . . . Henry said, 'I learned that you do not call Johnny Mercer and ask him if the lyric's ready yet.' He said he made that mistake only once. He phoned and he said, 'Johnny, how about that lyric?' And Johnny bit his head off, and screamed at him over the phone, and he said, 'I never!' He said when Johnny was ready with a lyric, he phoned you, you *never* phoned Johnny." Years later, when Mancini was asked by a radio interviewer why he and Mercer had not written more film scores or even a Broadway show, the composer politely answered, "'Well, there was a difficulty in getting things on time.' That's all he would say." Off the air, however, Mancini remarked that working with Mercer had aged him twenty years and almost given him an ulcer.

Another collaborator in these years was Johnny Mandel, with whom Mercer in 1964 wrote "Emily," the theme song for the cynical World War II comedy *The Americanization of Emily*. Mandel's brief, lilting melody gave Mercer very few notes to work with, and the title, "Emily," had no true rhyme. Mercer did not try to hide from the problem but instead brought it to the forefront and wrote *about* its sound in images that create a visual rhyme:

Emily, Emily, Emily,
Has the murmuring sound of May.

All silver bells, coral shells, carousels,
And the laughter of children at play.

He manipulates his images as if he were a cinematographer, zooming in on his lovers as they, in turn, watch images:

We fade to a marvelous view.
Two lovers alone and out of sight
Seeing images in the firelight.

Mercer concludes the lyric with two off-rhymes for "Emily"—"family" and "dreamily"—which, between their sounds, approximate a rhyme for his title. "Emily" was not a hit, but both Frank Sinatra and Tony Bennett made sensitive recordings of it.

In 1965, Mandel wrote the theme melody for *The Sandpiper*, and Mercer was asked to craft a lyric for it. Trying to use images that related to the movie, he wrote:

Today I'm in a mood I can't explain.
It might be just a sudden summer rain.
Today I saw a bird that broke its wing,
Which isn't in itself a tragic thing.

The producer did not like it, however, and Mercer later learned that several other lyricists had also been invited to set a lyric to the melody. The one chosen was by Paul Francis Webster, "The Shadow of Your Smile," which bore little relation to the movie but better suited Mandel's melancholy music. To add to Mercer's irritation, "The Shadow of Your Smile" won the Academy Award, beating out his and Mancini's "The Sweetheart Tree."
Songwriter Ervin Drake recalled that Mercer's resentment found expression in his "mischievous and sly sense of humor. Now, despite being a giving man, he was human. And he had written a lyric to a tune for a film. And they didn't tell him that they were making a sweepstakes out of this. They were submitting it to other lyric writers . . . and it was a song that came out and came to be known as 'The Shadow of Your Smile.' I don't think he loved the fact that somebody else beat him—he probably felt he had a much better lyric, though I don't know what his lyric was. And he said to me, 'By the way, "The Shadow of Your Smile"—doesn't that kind of suggest the faint mustache on a lady's lip?' That's how he got even." Mercer might joke about his failure, but it still pained him. Michael Goldsen, his music publisher, recalled that on the wall near the piano in Mercer's home "he had a lyric stuck up with a pin in it. And it said, 'You can't win them all.' And I looked at the lyric, and

I said, 'What is this?' He says, 'That's the lyric that they turned down on "Shadow of Your Smile." ' "

Mercer did have his own big hit in 1965 with "Summer Wind," another of his foreign "translations," this time of a German song with a melody by Henry Mayer. When he heard the music, Mercer's imagination carried him back, yet once more, to the summers of his boyhood on Savannah's seacoast, and his theme was, again, the loss of love and youth:

> The summer wind came blowing in across the sea,
> It lingered there to touch your hair and walk with me.
> All summer long we sang a song and strolled the golden sand,

Mercer's ear was as acute as ever, subtly rhyming "*strolled*" and "*gold*en," but, as always, it was imagery that came from the deepest wellsprings of his creativity:

> Like painted kites the days and nights went flying by.
> The world was new beneath a blue umbrella sky.
> Then, softer than a piper man one day it called to you,
> I lost you to the summer wind.

The images of kites and beach umbrellas invoke the world of childhood, as does the pied piper man who leads children out of innocence.

No other songwriter, in an age of sophistication and urbanity, was as obsessed with this theme of the lost world of childhood. "Summer Wind" held the same nostalgic appeal for an America mired in Vietnam and convulsed by the civil rights struggle. In 1965, amid the Beatles, Bob Dylan, and the battles between rock and folk music, it became an enormous hit through recordings by such singers as Frank Sinatra. As much as any song Johnny Mercer wrote, "Summer Wind" drew deeply on his Savannah summers "on the water" and touched the American public's longing for a pastoral past.

For years, Mercer composed light verse for his family's annual Christmas card, and these poems grew quite lengthy as Mercer tried to incorporate many of their friends' names into the verse. The cards were prized by their recipients. Jack Lemmon wrote, "You should be the first man to receive an Academy award for a Christmas card," and Irving Berlin countered with a bit of light verse of his own:

> Only God can make the tree,
> Where presents lie for you and me,
> But only Mercer makes the rhyme
> That cheers us all at Christmas time.

But Mercer's verse for his 1965 Christmas card reflected the darkening times:

> For though love makes the world go round,
> It's getting harder to be found
> And in our riot, war torn land,
> The Scrooges have the upper hand.

He even incorporated a surreal allusion to the war in Vietnam:

> The old and new—a lovely sight
> They made almost as bright a light
> As that far tree in Viet Nam
> Whose one bright bauble is a bomb.

At times, he could laugh at the bizarre changes that were transforming the America he knew. "We were in New York City," producer Bill Harbach recalled, "and we were talking about the mores of living in the sixties, and it was, everybody was doing with people's wives, and, everything was an open—seemed like an open field. And he said, 'I've got a great title, but I would never write it as a straight song. It would have to come out of a show, of a situation in a show.' And he said, 'Bill, if I tell you, don't tell anybody, because someday—I think it's a cute title, and I'd like to use it. But it's got to be in a situation about somebody having an affair with some man's wife.' And I said, 'I'm sealed.' And I said, 'What's the title?' And he said, 'Your Wife Is the Love of My Life.' Isn't that a marvelous title? And he said, 'But don't tell anybody.' Now, after he died, I told Steve Allen. And Steve wrote a very nice lyric, not like Johnny could write it; and, in it, he says, 'with apologies to John Mercer, whose idea this was.'"

But Mercer's overriding mood was of sadness as he watched the world he knew pass away. The pristine California he had known in the 1930s and '40s had been overrun as many of the soldiers stationed there in World War II returned with their families after the war, their cars congesting the freeways, polluting the air. Although he had seen California go from a lush paradise to an overcrowded hell, he could still cherish signs of nature's endurance. "I still hear many owls around the place," he said, "whooing in the trees at night, but the squirrels have all but disappeared. I hope they have learned to go further back into the hills, but I don't think that's the case. You just don't see as many on the road—living or dead. . . . I'm afraid the traffic has taken them. . . . Driving home very late, I almost ran a doe down that was standing in the middle of the canyon road. . . . As I slowed down, she turned but I had to follow slowly, honking my horn very slightly, as it was about two in the morning, so that I would not wake the neighborhood, before I could get her to finally leave the road and take off into the underbrush."

He was also concerned about the civil rights movement, with blacks assuming what for him was a strange new belligerence, threatening to destroy the way of life he had loved growing up in Savannah. Mercer had always been fiercely protective of the South. When Michael Goldsen asked him to write lyrics for the theme song for *Ruby Gentry*, Mercer refused because he disliked the way the film portrayed the South. Mitchell Parish, who was also born in the South, took the assignment and had an enormous hit with "Ruby."

Similarly, composer Jule Styne wanted to write a musical show based on Tennessee Williams's *The Rose Tattoo*, which had been a hit on Broadway and made into a successful film. "Jule had always wanted to work with Johnny," a friend recalled, "and Jule optioned *The Rose Tattoo*, and he wanted to do a musical of it, so he thought, 'Well, the South and everything. Well, that's got to be just perfect for Johnny Mercer.'

"He called Johnny Mercer and he said, 'I've got the thing of *Rose Tattoo*, I'd love to do a musical of it, would you consider doing it?'

"He said, 'Well, I think that would be wonderful. Fly on out here. I'll read it.'

"He apparently had never read it. And so Jule flew out to California, he went to the house . . . rang the doorbell, got inside, and there is Johnny with a drink, standing at the top of the stairs with the script of *Rose Tattoo* in his hand. He threw the script at Jule Styne and said, 'That goddamned Tennessee Williams doesn't know anything about the South!'"

The friend thought Mercer's ire was understandable: "Tennessee Williams's version of the South, which is about decay, and Johnny Mercer's version of the South, which was about romantic yearning, a place that still exists, that's frozen in time, and 'Ain't that grand?' He thought it was so wonderful that Savannah never changed; to Tennessee Williams it was the decadence that he was seeing. He could not understand that, threw the script at Jule. Jule got back up the driveway, got on a plane, and went back to New York."

Mercer's attitude toward blacks was complex and very much involved with the way he regarded himself. Friends recalled how warmly Mercer was treated by blacks on his many cross-country train trips. "There were always those black porters," one said, "and there was that lovely feeling. It wasn't just that he was going to give them a good tip or something, but they understood each other, and his accent would become heavier in that world. And there was something, an understanding and a rapport, a certain thing certain whites of a certain age had toward the blacks. But I don't think he was a person who could have been a racist."

On one trip, Bill Harbach recalled, "He asked for some apple pie, and they were out of it. And Johnny looked very, you know, sincere. He wanted one. So he said, 'Well, all right, just a cup of coffee.' And the waiter saw he was disappointed. Now, the waiter—all the waiters—that's another thing—all the waiters, after years and years of traveling, all knew him. 'Mr. Mercer's aboard my train today!' Oh, absolutely. He'd know 90 percent of all the Pullman porters and everything. So all the porters, through the years, got to know the Mercers because they were always on the train, either going east or west. And this waiter went back to the kitchen for about eight or nine minutes, and he came out with a big smile on his face and had an apple pie. And Johnny's telling this story, and he had that marvelous southern accent, and he said, 'This marvelous waiter said, "Mr. Mercer, this is the onliest apple pie on the train." ' "

Mercer's son, Jeff, remembered his last train trip east with his father. "He would tip, and we went on the train, and he'd tip all the porters and everything. Well, the last trip I remember, the porters refused the tip. The whole trip was on them. Then we got to the Plaza Hotel, and we get out of the cab (course he tipped the cabbie—he didn't know). The doorman came and said, 'Mr. Mercer, how are you?' and he pulls out a wad of money, and the guy says, 'No, this stay is on the house—all the way around.' " All of the train porters and the blacks who worked at the Plaza had gotten together and paid for all of Mercer's expenses on the trip. "The room, everything, they wouldn't let him pay a dime. They got together and paid the *whole* thing. He was so generous for so long they just wanted to do that." The extraordinary gesture of all of these black workers must have crystallized Mercer's vision of himself as a southern gentleman who in his own way loved, and was in turn beloved by, blacks.

Yet there was another side to Mercer that marked him as a child of Savannah. "Every black I ever liked," he wrote, "has conquered his 'blackness'—is a civilized man of dignity and independence. Few are pure black. Though Nat King Cole, Bill Cosby, Quincy Jones, Willie Mays, and my friends in the South are very black—most others like Lionel Hampton, Shelton Brooks, Teddy Wilson, Flip Wilson, Sammy Davis, Harold Nicholas . . . are light-skinned, showing the influence of other races." Building on this tortured distinction, he asserted, "But they are not angry. Inside perhaps—but they have overcome their anger and have been too busy overcoming life to stay mad." What the southern gentleman in him hated, it seemed, was the anger the heretofore gentle blacks were displaying. At a party after the Oscar ceremonies, a young woman from Savannah was introduced to Mercer. "When he heard I was from Savannah, he said, 'Do you know what NAACP stands for?' . . . He was drunk. . . . He said, 'Niggers Ain't Acting like Colored People.' "

A Savannah friend recalled that "Johnny definitely adhered to the belief that music had no color" and was friends with Count Basie, Duke Ellington, and other black musicians. As tensions over civil rights mounted, some black musicians "snubbed Johnny and hurt him deeply." Yet another friend recalled Mercer would freely refer to "spades," even as Ginger would say, "Johnny, I told you not to use that word." His mother would refer to blacks with what she must have considered the polite term "darkies." When Mercer took her to see Nat King Cole perform at the Copacabana, he said, "Mama, do you want to go backstage and meet him?" She said, "No, if he wants to see me, bring him up front to the audience." Miss Lillian was furious when she saw a newspaper photograph of Johnny with his arm around Nat King Cole. "I don't like it in the paper," she told him. "We don't do things like that down here."

Jean Bach visited Mercer in Savannah and remembers the tension over race after the federal government declared segregation unconstitutional. She recalled that Mercer "would hang out with his old buddies . . . and they're all so anti-Negro . . . these funny songs making fun of 'coons' and everything. . . . Desegregation had just been passed, but you'd be in the train station, and the walls were this kind of old curry color with age. And there'd been a sign hanging up that said 'Colored Only' that they'd taken down, because you could see the white space. And all the black people stayed on one side even though there weren't signs, and all the white people on the other. So they were still practicing racial discrimination."

Bach recalls Johnny singing at a party at her New York apartment to the accompaniment of Bobby Short, and when Bobby Short asked him which key he wanted for his next song, Mercer replied, "Oh, just play some colored key." For all of his genuine affection for blacks, he wanted them to remain in a different social place from his own. A California friend recalls another encounter with Bobby Short, walking out of Sardi's in New York with Johnny and Ginger. "And up pulls a taxi and out jumps Bobby Short. And Bobby Short had on a porkpie hat, a buttoned down collar shirt, a knit black tie, a suit from Brooks Brothers, and penny loafers on with white socks. And he hugged all of us and kissed Ginger on the cheek and Johnny, myself, gave us a hug." After a brief chat, Short left, and Johnny turned to his friend and said, "Man, how white can you get?"

Perhaps the most revealing insight into Mercer's racial attitudes comes out in his relationship with Ronnell Bright, a young black composer with whom Mercer collaborated on several songs in the 1960s. Bright was then the accompanist for Nancy Wilson, and in 1964 Wilson wanted to do an album called *Tender Loving Care* and asked Bright to write a title song. When Bright created a melody built around a repeated five-note title phrase, Wilson took him to Johnny Mercer and asked Mercer to do the lyric. Bright played the title song and some of his other melodies for Mercer, and Johnny said, "I'd like to write lyrics to these." Mercer invited Bright to his house, fixed him a huge "Dagwood" sandwich with many layers of meats and cheeses, then sat down at his piano and picked out the notes to Bright's melody. "Could you add some more notes," he asked. "I need more room." Once they had worked out the melody, Bright left Mercer to work on the lyric, as usual, alone.

Bright was surprised when Mercer called him a few days later to say he'd finished a lyric. "I wanted to sing my lyric for you before I gave it to Nancy to make sure you thought it fitted your beautiful melody." Bright felt as if Mercer were treating him with the same respect he would give such eminent collaborators as Harold Arlen and Hoagy Carmichael. Bright was also touched by Mercer's generosity of spirit at a formal dinner for members of AGAC, the American Guild of Authors and Composers. Bright, attired in a tuxedo, was accompanied by his sister. When they were introduced to the assembly, before the announcer could say that they were "sitting at lowly table number thirty-nine, Johnny Mercer, sitting at table number one, stood up and called out, 'Table number one.' So we sat at table number one, while Paul Francis Webster sat at table number two."

Yet Bright was hurt when he told Mercer about his ambition to go beyond writing individual popular songs to compose film scores. They were at a restaurant on Wilshire Boulevard—Bright recalls that Jack Lemmon was sitting at the bar—and Mercer asked him, "Ronnell, what do you want to do?"

Bright said, "I want to write for the movies."

He was stung by Mercer's reply: "Don't you think the time might not be right for that?"—meaning, Bright was sure, that Mercer felt it was all right for a black man to write popular songs but not to break into his own echelon of Hollywood songwriters.

"I'll not let anything stand in the way of my dream," Bright shot back.

"You ought to write with Billy Strayhorn," Mercer said, which infuriated Bright even more, since it sounded like Mercer was pairing blacks with blacks.

In retrospect, Bright thinks the Strayhorn suggestion might not have been racist, for he learned later that Mercer had tremendous admiration for Strayhorn, who had written "Take the A Train" and had collaborated with Duke Ellington. But to the young composer, Mercer's statement that the time was not "right" for a black man to write for the movies was unmistakably racist, even though it came from a man who had shown Bright enormous kindness. "I knew what he meant."

As the saying goes among blacks, "In the North, the white man doesn't mind your getting ahead of him; he just doesn't want you to live next to him. In the South, the white man doesn't mind you living next door to him; he just doesn't want you to get ahead of him." Johnny Mercer, who was raised by a black nurse and played with black children, was completely comfortable in the presence of blacks and could show genuine warmth toward them. It was when they forgot their "place" that disturbed and bewildered him, having only treated them with loving kindness.

One benefit for Bright was that Mercer, even when he was drinking, would never launch into his vicious attacks as he would with white friends. As he slid into depression, Mercer would mutter something like "All my friends are gone," but before his monstrous side could show itself, Bright recalled, Mercer would withdraw. "You could never tell when a drink would kick in, but suddenly his face would freeze, and he would abruptly leave the table without even a word and sit glumly by himself or leave the place completely." The first time these dark clouds passed over Mercer, Bright thought he had offended him, but Ginger smiled and reassured him, "That's just Johnny."

As Mercer's career gradually declined during the 1960s, Judy Garland's plunged into ruin. Drug use was taking its toll on her magnificent voice and made her increasingly unreliable, so producers would be delighted to have her for brief appearances in movies or on television shows but would not give her major roles. She was rejected for the role of Mama Rose in Hollywood's movie version of *Gypsy* and, despite composer Jerry Herman's pleading, was not allowed to follow Angela Lansbury in *Mame*. "If it falls apart because she doesn't show up on opening night," Herman's producers told him, "we will have destroyed everything we all worked so hard to create."

Those who did give her a break got burned. Garland did a wonderful job hosting ABC's Saturday night variety show *The Hollywood Palace* in 1965, but the next year, when she returned, she got laryngitis while the show was being taped and locked herself in her dressing room, crying, "That beautiful voice! It's gone!" Someone had to crawl through a ceiling hatch, enter the room, and open the door so taping could continue after a four-hour delay. In retribution, Garland trashed the dressing room. "She smeared all its painting with lipstick, she dumped ashes and cigarette butts between the keys of its piano and she set its sink and toilet to overflowing." She would cut herself and set fires, screaming in interviews, "I'm an angry lady! I've been insulted! Slandered! Humiliated! I wanted to believe, and I tried my damnedest to believe in that rainbow that I tried to get over—and I couldn't." Along with all her personal and professional woes, Garland was deeply in debt, and, according to a lover at the time, "Everybody was dropping her flat because she was broke. Nobody would help. She couldn't get anybody on the phone. Everybody was, like, never home."

Johnny Mercer was one of the people Garland called. His grandchildren remembered Ginger talking, with a kind of pride, about Johnny's affair with a "big" movie star. Finally, one asked, "'Who was it?' She said, 'Judy Garland.' She said she would call, Judy would call, at all hours of the night.... She'd ask Johnny to come over, crying, and was very distraught. And most of the time he didn't go. But occasionally he went, and then he didn't hide it from her."

"Judy would call—she'd call every day," another grandchild recalled. "My grandmother wasn't very nice to her."

A woman who had always felt unattractive, Garland prostrated herself before men. In some of her affairs, such as her romance with Frank Sinatra that had begun in the 1940s and been rekindled in the 1950s, sex consisted solely of Judy performing fellatio. "I'm worried about Frank," she told a friend. "All he wants is blow jobs. . . . you've gotta fuck once in a while, you know." By the late 1960s, Garland's abasement had reached new depths. She would crawl "under the tablecloth at a Santa Monica restaurant to perform oral sex." At another lover's request, she sang "Over the Rainbow" after giving him a blow job "so he could hear those famous words sung through a mouthful of his semen."

Her lowest point came in 1967, when she was forced to sell her house, and in a tape-recorded memoir, she asked, "How do you act when they take something from you that you thought belonged to you? . . . Are you supposed to laugh—or sing?" At that point she sang a snatch from an aria from *Porgy and Bess:* "Ole Man Sorrow's come to keep me company, / Whispering beside me . . . Telling me I'm old now since I lost my man."

Judy Garland, after other affairs, other marriages, died of a drug overdose on Sunday, June 22, 1969, in the bathroom of a London hotel.

Mercer's niece knew about his love for Judy Garland—"He told his mother, and she told me"—and tried to comfort him, but she wanted to be discreet about the extent of her knowledge of their relationship. "I said, 'I'm sorry to hear about your—friend.' He just cried."

Later that fall, Johnny Mercer turned sixty. One day as he was driving along a California freeway, a medley of songs from *Show Boat* came over his car radio. When he heard the plangent strains of "Make Believe," he said, "I pulled over to the side of the road, parked, and cried like a young boy."

Seventeen

Dream: 1969–1976

I want to tell the young ones that we older writers are honest too. On a tougher basis—a harder pattern. Our songs may not smell of sweat and the earth, but our rhymes are pure, not just "time" and "mine"—not just "wrong" and "alone" or "home." Sure, when a line is great you can skip the rhyme. But how many are that great?

By the time he turned sixty, Johnny Mercer felt utterly alienated from the world of popular music, but he tried to accept that estrangement with equanimity. "The old order changeth," he told an interviewer. "Frankly, I can't comprehend the new stuff and Lord knows I'm not just talking about the noise. . . . I like the younger generation but I don't want to write music for them. I don't dig their music, and they don't dig Mercer's." At other times he expressed the same sentiments less stoically: one friend recalled how he would moan, "They don't want what I do anymore." Another described how Mercer would go to a bar for a drink and put his head on the table and say, "Oh God, I should be dead." Still another remembered Mercer's summing up his career by saying, "I tried to be a singer and failed. I tried to be an actor and failed. So I just naturally fell into songwriting."

Out of his reverence for the songs of an era that had passed, Mercer helped establish the Songwriters Hall of Fame in 1970. His vision was to have an organization, ultimately with its own museum, that would annually induct a few great songwriters, just as baseball players were inducted into the Baseball Hall of Fame in Cooperstown, New York. With his characteristic benevolence, however, he also saw the Songwriters Hall of Fame as a charitable organization that would help impoverished songwriters who had seen their hit songs, along with their royalties, fade into oblivion. Together with music publishers Abe Olman and Howie Richmond, Mercer approached Irving Berlin and asked him to serve as the organization's first president. But Berlin, at that point sliding into an irascible old age, said, "A songwriter writes words and music. That's what a songwriter does. And I'm a songwriter. The rest of them are lyric writers and music writers." So Johnny Mercer, despite his genteel aversion to running things, agreed to serve as the organization's first president.

At the first induction ceremony, five songwriters were included: Irving Berlin, Duke Ellington, Richard Rodgers, Dorothy Fields, and Hoagy Carmichael. Mercer spoke at the ceremony and stressed the fact that newer songwriters, such as Jimmy Webb, were carrying on the tradition of artistic songwriting. Although the Songwriters Hall of Fame still lacks a permanent home, it continues to recognize artistry in songwriting with an annual award, the "Mercer." It is apt that etymologically, a "mercer" is someone who deals in expensive fabrics, and to "mercerize" a cloth is to give it luster and strength by treating it with caustic chemicals.

Mercer himself was honored on March 14, 1971, when he was invited by New York's Ninety-second Street YMHA to perform his own songs as part of its "Lyrics and Lyricists" series. Before an audience that included Yip Harburg, Harold Arlen, and many prominent people in show business, Mercer sang such comic numbers as "The Girlfriend of the Whirling Dervish" and "Strip Polka," then finished with what he called his "Big Medley" of hits, culminating in "Days of Wine and Roses." Between songs he told anecdotes, fielded questions, and even gave a sample of his "Newsie Bluesies":

> There's Mr. Harburg, sitting in the very first row
> And with him's Harold Arlen, with whom I wrote a very unsuccessful
>   show
> And what an old Episcopal choirboy's doin' up here I don't know.

On that night, the most successful night he ever had on Broadway, Johnny Mercer could even laugh at the debacle of *Saratoga*. He also, however, could not resist pointing out the anomaly of his career in a profession dominated by New York Jews. "Johnny was *in*," Margaret Whiting said.

In his last years, he drew closer to Savannah. In addition to his homes in California and his apartment in New York, he bought a house in Savannah, to anchor himself in the three-city triangle that had shaped his life. When Mercer's mother came to visit them in Palm Springs, Amanda Mercer recalled, "she was getting so bad, and she was saying, 'You have to have a home there.'" The house they initially planned to buy was the scene of a terrible accident, when a boy fell from the roof and was impaled on the wrought-iron railing, so the Mercers purchased a different house but still "on the water," where he had spent his boyhood summers. He christened it the "Moon River House" and visited there often.

Family had always been important to him, and now he doted on his three grandchildren. "He was, like, a professional grandfather," Jim Corwin recalled. "I never even knew he was famous. . . . I'd go, 'I've heard of Bob Hope. I've never heard of you, though. I've heard of Fred Astaire. I've never heard of you.'" Jim recalled Mercer taking them to a store to buy some toy submarines. "You put pellets in, and it would sink to the bottom. And then the pellets would fill up and the boat, the submarine, would rise back up." But Mercer's Bel Air house didn't have a pool, so Mercer cavalierly made use of his neighbor's swimming pool. One submarine refused to rise from the bottom of the pool, "so he was looking around for a net to fish my submarine up," Jim recalled, "and here comes Jim Ray," the neighbor, "and Jim wasn't a very pleasant man."

On another occasion he took his grandchildren and their friends to the circus, but first they stopped off at the toy store to buy "these little teeny plastic pellet guns." At the circus Mercer encouraged the children to shoot at the circus animals and performers. "We were hiding in this little box, and we were going 'Pew—pew!'—shooting these little pellets at the entertainers as they were parading around Ringling Brothers. And then I hit an elephant; and this elephant responded. And my grandfather was all, 'Oh, we'd better stop that, guys. We can get in trouble.'"

Jim and his mother described a family ritual, perhaps one that went back to Mercer's own boyhood: "When we'd go swimming—see, he had this theory: he loved to lock himself in a hot car until he got all sweaty. We'd lock ourselves in the car for an hour, forty-five minutes, or an hour until we were dripping sweat. Then we'd be—we'd turn on a baseball game and we'd be listening to it. We'd be dying."

"My brother did this, too," noted Amanda.

"Oh, we'd be dying. We'd jump out of the car and would go running into the pool. We'd jump in the pool. Then, we'd dry off, and we'd get back in the car. . . .

"He had a 1971 beige Pinto with a red interior," Jim recalled, "because he'd buy Grandma the elegant Jaguar. She always had a Jaguar every other year or something. She'd get the Jaguar. But he wasn't into a fancy car. So he bought this beige Pinto, one of the old hatchbacks . . . and then in that Pinto, he would—what he'd do is he would take his hands off the wheel—because in Bel Air, you know, driving around Bel Air, he'd take his hands off the wheel and go, 'Oh, no! we're out of control!' 'Grandpa—wait, wait!'

"And he was steering it with his knees. I'd be screaming. . . . It was like a roller coaster."

"He did that to me when I was a little girl, too," Amanda said. "We'd be on our way to Palm Springs, and I'd go, 'No! No! No!' I'd grab hold of the wheel."

"The way he bought cars," she explained, was purely whimsical. "He bought a Skylark because he had written the song."

Jim recalled how lavishly Mercer treated him and his friends. "My Little League team won the championship one year, and he rented out an ice-cream parlor for both teams to come for the day and spent about a thousand bucks in 1973 for twenty-two kids and their parents." But he also recalled how terribly Mercer could behave in restaurants. "I remember once at Thanksgiving in '73, and we went out to this restaurant, and he and my grandmother would get pretty buzzed, and they'd just argue. . . . I mean just vehemently about, you know, how they raised the kids. . . . And he brutalized the waiters and waitresses, just be brutal to them, then he'd give them a hundred-dollar tip as he left."

His impression of his grandparents was that they were total opposites. Ginger was "very polished, very cultured, very learned." By contrast, his grandfather "was very family-oriented. I mean, she used to be very frustrated at how generous he was not only to *his* family but to *her* family. He was very generous financially with her mother and her sisters which agitated her no end. She was very into, you know, their financial status . . . almost like a Joan Crawford–type person in the movies. . . . He loved helping the family. When he was alive, I used to get a thousand-dollar check at Christmas.

"I think the challenge was that she was just becoming very mean-spirited, and it was a challenge for him to really function in the circles he liked to go in because she was not very cooperative going to events, holding events, as his stature declined a little bit, she'd get more aggressive on how he handled the money, wanted to be more in his affairs. They did not get along towards the end, and I remember times when they would argue then, and then they would have a couple of drinks, both of them."

Despite the tensions between Johnny and Ginger, Mercer seemed a loving grandfather to his grandchildren. "I think he liked being a grandfather more than he did being a father. And he put a lot of time into it too. He did with me. . . . You know, he'd have little hats and glasses of his own wardrobe duplicated and he'd put me in them. . . . I'd put his hat and his glasses on, and dress just like him. . . . I miss him. I wish I knew him now, man. That's the tough part . . . to think he'd still be writing great songs. Think how many songs he wrote right before he died. I mean, he probably had another two or three hundred songs in him."

One of the songs Mercer still had in him was for Jim's Cub Scout troop. "He brought all the boys, all the little boys, over to the house," Amanda said, "and he taught them all the song. And he typed it all up so that the den mothers could have it. And they sang it in the big pack meeting:

We're men of the Werewolf Den!
We're fearless, brave, and true!
We're men of the Werewolf Den!
And we know what to do!
Our hair is neat,
And our nails are clean.
We help old ladies across the street.
We're men of the Werewolf Den!
Ahooo! Ahoooo! Ahooooo!

"I called him 'Beebah,'" Jim said. "That's the name I called him, growing up . . . 'Beebah and Granginger.' I didn't even know they had names for ten, twelve years."

"And in the South," Amanda added, "he was 'Bubba.'"

Another grandson, John Corwin, had been born during his father's first marriage and only came into the Mercer family when his father married Amanda. He felt no prejudice because he was not a blood relative and had fond memories of his grandfather at the Palm Springs house, playing croquet, swimming, barbecuing. "Here is where he really just let his hair down," he said. "That's where I saw him in his straw hat." The straw hat marked Mercer as a southerner—laid-back, down-home, but still genteel. "On the outside, I just saw him in his straw hat, and he seemed like a very simple guy, but he wasn't."

John recalled his grandfather through objects that help him "go back to where I was with him. . . . He always did everything, like, the high-class way. He got this phone book that's like solid cast iron made in Spain. That was like, his phone book." Then one Christmas "he gave me a boomerang from Australia. My parents would always get me typical little toys, but no one ever gave me a boomerang. . . . He would just buy the things that were a little bit classier. He just always had an eye out for everything." Yet Mercer's indulgence of his grandchildren produced a backlash. "He would take us to the store and buy us toys or whatever to just make us happy. I mean, I feel bad now 'cause I remember thinking he would buy me stuff and I was never satisfied with what he bought me. . . . 'How come he didn't buy me this?' That's so frustrating that he died so young because I have so much to say to him now."

Among John Corwin's possessions were photograph albums that Mercer compiled of each of his homes. With his southern sense of roots, he had a professional photographer take pictures of each room in each of his homes, as well as exterior shots, including an overhead photograph of his Palm Springs house taken from an airplane. In each house, the albums show, Johnny and Ginger had separate bedrooms; hers would be elegantly and delicately decorated in French styles, while his were "kind of the rustic, down-to-earth" style, usually in Scottish plaids. The impression John Corwin carried of his grandparents was of how "separate" they were—separate bedrooms, separate cars: "For me it was kind of like he was here and she was there . . . not 'big happy family.' . . . By the end, Ginger was driving a Jaguar and he drove a Pinto. He didn't care. He did what he wanted to do."

Even when they took up hobbies, Ginger and Johnny went their separate ways. She went into yoga; he started jogging, and with his accident-prone history soon broke his ankle.

But the joys of playing with his grandchildren, of watercolor painting, of traveling with Ginger to Europe and Hawaii, where, away from their children, they could sometimes enjoy some peaceful moments—these were not enough to fulfill that restless, questing skylark in Mercer's soul. Not even writing an occasional song, such as "My New Celebrity Is You," bristling with witty images for Blossom Dearie to titillate cabaret audiences, satisfied his hunger for the one big Broadway hit he had never had.

When Bill Harbach asked him in these years if he had any disappointments, Mercer said, "Yes, I had one. I never had a Broadway hit." Harbach rattled off a list of some of Mercer's greatest songs and asked Mercer if he was slighting them. "No, they are marvelous songs," he replied. "But I never had a hit on Broadway."

Songwriter Ervin Drake, who had had his own frustrations on Broadway, recalled that when he was visiting Mercer in the 1970s, Mercer brought up the recent failure of Drake's *Her First Roman*, which had folded after only three weeks: "He twitted me when I was in his home.

" 'Hey, wait a minute,' " Drake shot back. " 'Let's review your record on Broadway.'

" 'You know,' he said, 'sometimes I have the feeling that I'm just not cut out for Broadway.'

" 'What do you mean?'

" 'Well, it's a very special kind of writing for Broadway, something that Alan Jay Lerner has and something that Steve Sondheim has. . . . You know, these guys like Harold Rome and Stephen Sondheim know how to write the book. . . . I don't know that I have it. I'm okay for songs by themselves for movies, but what has developed in the theater is quite different from when I first came around to the theater. And I don't know that I should really be trying so hard.' "

Having a big Broadway musical must have seemed to him, all the more as the years drew on, the only sure way to achieve the kind of immortality every artist wants. A show like *Guys and Dolls* or *My Fair Lady* would be revived for generations, while individual hit songs, even a "Laura," could be swallowed up by time, as had so many of the songs he had loved in his youth. Who, in 1970, would even remember "Coquette," which had made him weep at his first dance at Tybrisa pavilion by the sea?

Dropping his customary reticence, Mercer sought out a collaborator in

André Previn, the composer of many film scores and a successful Broadway musical, *Coco*, which he had written with Alan Jay Lerner in 1969. Previn, who was then serving as the conductor of the London Symphony, had once casually suggested they write a show together, and one day, out of the blue, came a call from Johnny Mercer. "We've never worked together," Previn said, "and I'm not a songwriter," but he had always wanted to collaborate with Johnny Mercer. As they tried to choose a property, Mercer sent Previn a letter proposing that they do a musical based on *Little Women*. "You may think this is a crazy idea," Mercer wrote, but he said he wanted to do it before somebody else "fucks it up." He even included lyrics for three possible songs.

Previn did think it a crazy idea, so they considered other properties. "There's this book I've loved all my life," Mercer finally said. J. B. Priestley's novel *The Good Companions* had been turned into a successful play on Broadway in 1930, and Mercer, because of his love for the book (one friend recalled that he read it to Ginger on their honeymoon), must have seen it. It tells the story of a struggling acting troupe as it wends its way across the English countryside, and it would have resonated with Mercer during his own struggles to make it as an actor with the Theatre Guild touring company. "It was his favorite book," Previn said, "bar none."

Previn agreed to the project, but Mercer did not even consider adapting the book into a libretto himself, as Alan Jay Lerner, Oscar Hammerstein, and other lyricists had done to create their successful shows. He never would follow the advice Charlie Miller had given to George A. Mercer back in 1932—that Johnny needed to learn how to write the book, as well as the lyrics, for a musical. Once again, Mercer turned that task over to a young playwright, Ronald Harwood, who collaborated by mail until Mercer could come to England. Harwood realized that, in turning to an English setting, Mercer was emulating Lerner's success with *My Fair Lady*, but he doubted that Mercer could have adapted his own book. "He did not have a good sense of dialogue," he said. "He never interfered with my work. He never said, 'That line could be different.' He didn't have any confidence in that—in himself."

Something should have warned Mercer that for an American to try to write lyrics for a musical based on a very British novel—for London audiences—was a very difficult undertaking. He would not be writing lyrics in anything like his native idiom, as he had in the black dialect of *St. Louis Woman*, the yokelese of *Li'l Abner*, and the showbiz argot of *Top Banana*. Even if he did manage to please British audiences, would a show about a theatrical troupe in provincial English towns in the 1920s be likely to interest Broadway audiences in the 1970s? A warning sign should have gone up, for example, when Harwood wrote Mercer to ask him to cut one song and replace it with a different one:

I don't think the present song does what we want it to. Let me give my reasons: what I think we need is a song that says: EVERYTHING IN

BRUDDERSFORD IS DREARY / THE ONE HIGH SPOT OF
THE WEEK IS THE FOOTBALL MATCH / AND TODAY IT
HAS BEEN A GOALLESS DRAW. It would create the feeling of
those Northern towns, of gloom, and smog.

Hardly a promising premise for a song in a show destined for Broadway, but,
Harwood said, Mercer's lyric about a "Goalless Draw" was brilliant: "He had
a real gift for entering the spirit of another person, another world, another
country." Mercer, always agreeable, had known and loved Priestley's novel
for so many years that he had completely absorbed its spirit: "The lyrics kept
bursting out of me."

As Mercer was about to leave for Europe to work on *The Good Companions*
with Harwood and Previn, he agreed to give an interview to Hugh Fordin,
who was writing a book about Arthur Freed and the great musicals Freed had
produced at MGM. "The first time I saw him, the first day I saw him, Ginger
hadn't come in yet," Fordin said. "He was there alone . . . lonely! You'd think
he didn't have a wife. You'd think he didn't have many friends. That's the kind
of, it was a failure sense I sensed about him. God, failure! I mean I can tell
you about failure from some of the other writers that I've talked to. And
understandably failure. But Johnny was certainly not a failure in anything."

As they talked, Fordin realized that the sense of failure he had detected in
Mercer stemmed from the fact that he had never written a classic Broadway
musical. "Okay, so the shows were not hits, and they're not the first song that
comes into your mind if you wanted to do a Broadway medley of songs. But
when you hear some of the songs he's written, you'd say, 'Oh no, Johnny
Mercer didn't write that.'" Fordin compared his meeting with Mercer to
encounters with other songwriters who, because they had written enduring
Broadway musicals, felt confident that their work would live on, even in the
age of rock. Such changes in the musical world, Fordin said, "didn't matter to
a lot of other people. I mean I sat and played poker with Ira Gershwin at that
time too. Ira had a kind of a, even though Ira was even more introverted than
Johnny, it was a kind of security that you had about yourself. . . . Attention's
not drawn to lyric writers in the East, unless they're Broadway, and that's
unfortunate. It shows you how narrow-minded they are, you know? I mean,
why does it always have to be Larry Hart, why does it always have to be Cole
Porter?" Not having had that big Broadway show, Fordin sensed, "was a big
hole, one of the many holes in his heart."

In London, the Mercers took an apartment near the American embassy on
Grosvenor Square. André Previn lived in Sussex with Mia Farrow and had a
heavy touring schedule with the London Symphony, so it was difficult to find
time to collaborate. Mercer was frustrated at Previn's absences. André Previn
was, one friend of Mercer's recalled, "a little tougher. You know, you have to
be a son of a bitch to be a symphony conductor, that's a given, you can't be

Mr. Nice Guy, and I think he was a little demanding. Johnny was kind of more relaxed, and he worked better with people that just kind of leaned back. So that was not a happy association."

André Previn, however, had only warm memories of working with Mercer, whom he, unlike most of Mercer's other collaborators, found as nimble a writer as himself. "I write quickly," Previn said, noting that he wrote the melody for "Dance of Life," a very complex and brooding song, in about ten minutes. But he also noted that Mercer wrote with equal ease, crafting the witty and vernacular "Ta, Luv" in ten minutes. Previn's pleasure with Mercer's alacrity was based on his experience with Alan Jay Lerner on *Coco* and pointed up the difference between Lerner as a "theater" writer and Mercer as a "song" writer. "Lerner worked like a playwright," Previn said. "Took forever to write a lyric and frequently would leave a few lines unfinished, so he could always say, 'The lyric wasn't finished.'" Previn found Lerner a maddeningly slow collaborator because he always thought in terms of character and dramatic situation; Mercer, by contrast, usually thought purely in terms of the music.

The major problem that Previn and Mercer encountered was that Previn liked to have the lyric first and Mercer preferred having the music first. Previn did not normally compose at the piano; he would look at his collaborator's lyric, determine its meter, then compose a melody in his head. Mercer found that practice strange, unlike any collaboration he'd done. "I just can't get used to this," he said. But the men met each other halfway, sometimes working from music, sometimes from lyrics. Still, there were glitches. At one point, Mercer gave Previn a lyric and Previn composed a melody for it. "Oh, that's very pretty," Mercer said when Previn played it. "Let me take it down so I can set words to it." He hadn't realized that the melody was set to a lyric he had already given Previn.

Previn found it a genial collaboration and had to endure only a few flashes of Mercer's legendary temper. "I'd like to see a couple of English musicals," Mercer said, " 'cause I don't know what that's about." After the first act of one show, Previn found it so dreadful, he said to Mercer, "Let's not even stay for the next act." Mercer knew that the absence of the conductor of the London Symphony would be embarrassingly noticeable, and, with his patrician sense of propriety, exploded at Previn. "I know this isn't very good, but this is the first musical these writers have ever written, and we owe it to them to stay for their next act." After they sat back down, however, Mercer opened his program and said, "Wait a minute. This isn't their first show—this is their third show. Let's get out of here."

Previn recalled a time when Johnny and Ginger came to his home in Sussex. Mercer loved walking in the surrounding woods and drinking while looking out at the countryside. The composer recalled that he could even be gentle with Ginger. After years of battering by Mercer, Ginger had found that one way to garner attention was to tell interminable stories, and as she was telling one such story to Previn, Johnny said, "in a pleasant way but obviously with some irritation, 'Tempo, Ginger, tempo,'" to hurry her along. "But he didn't say it meanly or angrily," Previn said. "Just gently moved her along."

By contrast, Previn said, Mercer was a consummate raconteur. "He loved to tell the story of a woman who asked him how he wrote lyrics.

"'I like to write songs myself, and I just wanted to know how you go about it technically.'

"'Well,' he said, 'I try to think of the title first, and then find out where the title goes in a song. And then I take out my rhyming dictionary . . . '

"And she stopped him: 'Rhyming dictionary—no wonder!'

"Johnny loved that story."

Previn also remembered a moment as Johnny and Ginger were leaving his home. "He stumbled and held on to Ginger, then he had to sit down. He said to her, 'I don't know what's wrong with me.'"

Whatever the problem was, it did not affect Mercer's work on *The Good Companions*. Ronald Harwood recalled how brilliantly Mercer wrote lyrics for the show. When they decided they needed to add a number about "Camaraderie," Mercer "went off into the gentlemen's lavatory at Her Majesty's Theatre, scribbled something, and came back with a pretty well complete lyric. He must have been gone about twenty minutes. But I think he must have been thinking about it because it was too terrific to do it just like that. But that was the impression he gave—that he just thought of it." Mercer was still projecting the image of the southern aristocrat, producing brilliant work with barely perceptible effort.

But Harwood also recognized Mercer's limitations. "I think he was one of the great songwriters of the twentieth century—lyric writers. He had very little theatrical instinct at all. He'd come to rehearsal and say, 'I saw a great little act on television last night—some guys playing a brass band. Could we get them into the second act?'" Or he would say, "'I've got a terrific song—I don't know where it can go.' He'd do that. And then we'd try to accommodate it. But on the whole he was subservient to Previn and to me." For Harwood, "His instincts for the theater were not as good as his gift, not nearly as good as his gift for writing the lyric."

Harwood recalled one evening when he saw Johnny Mercer as the pure lyricist. They were working in Mercer's flat when the phone rang. "I couldn't get who was on the other end of the phone, but Johnny sang a song, one of his songs, very lightly, to the person at the other end. Then he put down the phone, and I said, 'What was that about, Johnny?' And he said, 'Oh, that was Frank Sinatra. He wanted to know how to phrase something.'"

Harwood said that Mercer was very involved in rehearsals, going from room to room to see how dances were going, songs were being sung, dialogue was being rehearsed, but he noted that Mercer never worked with performers directly. He always made his suggestions, as he did with his other shows, through the composer or the director. "He was very modest, Johnny, in that way. He never threw his weight around. He just liked his lyrics to be clearly sung." Harwood believed that Mercer's many years on Hollywood sets had "made him cautious about interfering," but Mercer's genteel southern upbringing would also have made it seem unseemly to assert himself. Harwood also speculated that while Mercer never said it, he thought "that Previn wrote too difficult a melody . . . to match the simplicity of his lyrics, and in one or two instances he was right." Once again, however, Mercer would not be the man to complain.

Previn noted several problems that emerged during rehearsals. The director, while excellent with straight drama, was not good with musicals. The choreographer, moreover, was young and inexperienced. "What do you want this number to be about?" he would ask Previn and Mercer. Both men had worked with Jerome Robbins on Broadway: "That's why you're here," they would say.

"I remember him sitting at rehearsals," said Harwood, "and he would nod or smile or laugh. I think he was disappointed in our musical. I don't think he loved it." Harwood knew that *The Good Companions* had been Mercer's idea and that he'd had a vision of it based on the novel he loved. "I don't think we fulfilled that vision." Harwood explained that the charm of the book is that it has many characters who pass in and out of the story as the theatrical troupe wends its way across the countryside. "We couldn't do that theatrically. It's impossible. And he was disappointed. I think that's the conflict between his theatrical instincts and the reality of the theatrical world.

"I just think we didn't get the thing right," Harwood added. "I was very much the junior partner. I was very inexperienced. It's the only musical libretto I have ever done, and I've never done one since. It was not a happy experience." Between Johnny's reticent demeanor in the theater and Previn's frequent absences to be with the London Symphony, the burden of the production fell on Harwood's inexperienced shoulders. He recalled a dreadful opening night in Birmingham, after which he and Previn agreed to rework the show the next morning, but when he went down to breakfast, he learned that Previn had suddenly had to fly to Helsinki to conduct. A friend of Mercer's recalled that Johnny too was frustrated with Previn's absences, but she attributed them to his preoccupation with Mia Farrow, who was pregnant at the time. "John said he could never get hold of Previn when he needed him."

After playing for several weeks in Birmingham and Manchester, in the region of England where the story is set, *The Good Companions*, featuring the veteran John Mills and the vibrant newcomer Judi Dench, opened in London on July 11, 1974. British reviewers were positive but pointed out the difficulty of turning Priestley's sprawling novel into a musical and noted the absence of a big romantic ballad "the audience comes out tra-laaing for dear life." Mercer's lyrics came in for praise: "Johnny Mercer's lyrics have, as you would expect, zip and dexterity. He manages English English at all levels well, and the rhymes chime away like bells."

Yet Johnny Mercer's bad luck in the musical theater still dogged him: bad books; stars such as Lena Horne, who dropped out of productions, and Bert Lahr, who dominated them; and organizations such as the NAACP, which picketed them, now found their British counterparts. The Irish Republican Army set off bombs in Birmingham and Manchester on July 14, their first terrorist assaults in England. Then, on July 17, a bomb blast killed tourists at the Tower of London. "We had a great misfortune," Harwood recalled. "We were doing rather well." He said business dropped alarmingly as people stopped coming to London. "We were not a big enough hit to survive." The show ran for only five months. Previn thought the run could have been longer, but the theater had already scheduled a new musical by Andrew Lloyd Webber. "It closed after three performances," Previn noted. Initially, he explained, they had planned to take *The Good Companions* to Broadway, and one producer was interested in the show, provided it could be made more "American," but it had gotten "more and more English." Still, Previn remembered Mercer taking the closing in good spirits: "Let's give it a rest and then let's try another one."

It must have been a tremendous disappointment for him, at this point in his life, to have failed once more to get his big Broadway hit. One of Harwood's last memories of Johnny Mercer was going out to a "rather grand" restaurant with him, Previn, and other members of the company. There was a woman playing the piano and playing very poorly, but nonetheless Mercer left her a huge tip. "That was very nice of you, Johnny," Harwood remarked. "Yeah, I have a soft spot for musicians who never made it."

His daughter and grandson, however, recall Mercer's experience with *The Good Companions* as a fulfilling one. "Well, he loved that era because, see, England appreciates—they still knew him. See, the problem with America is he was kind of a forgotten guy, even when he'd win an Academy Award or something—they just didn't know who he was. He wasn't an entertainer anymore. He was primarily a movie score writer. He was in the background. He was still earning money, but he wasn't in the limelight at all. But he'd go to England, and they'd go, 'The world-famous Johnny Mercer!' and they'd have him on every TV show, every radio show down there. And young people knew who he was. *The Good Companions* actually did very, very well there. . . . it was a very popular play. So, he never had a Broadway hit, but that was the closest he ever came."

On this last trip to England, he revisited the Scottish relative he had called upon back in the late 1930s. Dr. Walter Mercer was now Sir Walter Mercer, knighted by Queen Elizabeth. He had been Sir Winston Churchill's personal physician during World War II and had written the authoritative book on bone surgery. "When I went to visit him," Mercer said, "the thing he wanted me to see was not the Mercer genealogical chart, but his study. For there were the bits of paper, the diploma, the awards of a lifetime. This is understandable, for after all the bills are paid, the shouting and the tumult dies, the band stops playing and all the dancers have gone home, what do we have to show for our lives?"

As Mercer wrote those words, he went on to cite his own four Oscars, two Grammys, and other awards, but he knew he would live or die by his songs, and he cherished, not just awards, but moments such as hearing "a newsboy on a little railway station in faraway Scotland whistling 'Goody Goody'" and "three husky truck drivers pulling up to a diner marked 'EATS' singing in unison, 'Take it off . . . take it off. . . .'" Then there was the time he was sitting in a bar and one of the only two other occupants put a coin in the jukebox and said to his companion, "Get a load of these words, pal." "It was Tony Bennett singing 'I Wanna Be Around to Pick Up the Pieces When Somebody Breaks Your Heart.' . . . There was no way—no way—he could have known that the guy sitting a couple of bar stools away was the writer of the words to that song. That was a kick." Equally thrilling was walking into Toots Shor's as several guys were talking about baseball and had come to an agreement that Joe DiMaggio was the greatest ballplayer of all time. When one of the group, songwriter Jerry Bock, looked up and saw Mercer enter, he said, "I don't know about you guys, but that's my Joe DiMaggio."

While he was in England, the dizziness that had bothered Mercer at Previn's home worsened. Accounts differ as to whether he fell getting off a London bus or whether he was actually struck by the bus, but he was not seriously injured. A British physician, however, recommended that he have exploratory brain surgery when he returned to California.

"When he got sick," his daughter Amanda recalled, "he said, 'Take me home, Ginger, I want to go home.'"

By home, of course, he meant Savannah, and when they returned to New York, while Ginger wanted him to return with her to California and undergo surgery, Mercer, with his lifelong fear of doctors, refused and took the train to Savannah. A grandson remembers Johnny and Ginger at the train station before he boarded. "He had his arm around Ginger, she was like kind of holding him." He thinks the memory stuck in his mind because he had never seen them be affectionate before. "The two standing there. It just so impregnated in my mind. . . . But he was there with just his arm around her, standing at the station."

"That was the last time he visited Savannah," said friend Nick Mamalakis. "When he was in England, collaborating with André Previn, he was asked by the physicians over there to return early because they detected that he was having some kind of problem in his head. He was misstepping and sort of weaving, and they thought he might have some blockage in his brain. So Johnny came on back." Mamalakis asked him what songs he was working on.

" 'Well, Nick, I can't write any more lyrics for this generation.' He says, 'I am so disgusted with what they are calling lyrics and how nasty they are.'

"And I said, 'Aw, Johnny, you have been writing for two and a half generations. Don't give up.'

" 'I rode from my mother's old house to the office, and there was only one tune on the radio. And it was ugly, nasty. And it was just going up and down the scale, up and down. And all it was saying, that "I want it, I gotta have it, I need it." . . . What kind of lyric is that? Why are they letting that go on the air?' "

The primary reason Mercer made the trip to Savannah was to see his mother, who had been put in a nursing home. When he visited her, he also entertained the residents of the home and, noticing that many of their television sets were not working, later called a friend and told her to see that they were all repaired and send him the bill. But seeing his mother in that condition devastated him.

"I can't do it, I can't do it!" he moaned as he was riding in a car with the friend, adding, "I do some of my best crying in a car."

"Well, hell," she said, "go ahead," and Mercer let loose with a flood of tears while she grimly drove on.

Still, touching his hometown roots was important in making him feel that, amid all the changes that were engulfing him, the early center of his world still held. "Savannah's still like it used to be," he said, idealizing the world he had known in his youth; "everybody goes around and sings songs, and drinks, and loves one another."

When he returned to New York, he called a niece on the phone, and she knew immediately that something was wrong by the sound of his voice. "He didn't have that squeaky, personality, Savannah, Southern quality in it." When they went out to dinner at the Palm, "where they had these five-pound lobsters and these big steaks," she noticed that Mercer chewed, but could not swallow, his food. "He very discreetly put it on his napkin."

Bill Harbach also went out to dinner with Mercer in New York. "He had his cousin with him or his nephew, his nephew with him to hold—he was bouncing off the walls," Harbach said. "He was being held by his nephew, but he would bump into the wall, then he would pull him away from the wall, and his whole equilibrium was lost. But he was talking fine and everything like that."

After dinner, they went back to Harbach's apartment and played records. "I started talking to him like a Dutch uncle. I said, 'Johnny, you've got to go for the operation.'

" 'Bill, I don't want to be a vegetable.'

" 'Johnny, you've got to take a shot at it because you're going down the toilet now, and, you know, you're bouncing off of buildings and it's getting worse.'

" 'I know,' " Mercer said. " 'Ginger wants me to, she's begging for the last two years.'

" 'Johnny, play the big game because this is a dead end where you are.'

" 'I guess you're right. Call up Ginger and tell her I'll go for the surgery.'

"I went to the phone in the library, and I said, 'Ginger, I'm here with Johnny. He's on his train tomorrow night. He said he'll go for the surgery.'

"She said, 'Oh, thank—thank God.'

"And I said, 'Johnny, I applaud you.' "

Harbach recalled the records they listened to that night. "I was playing this new thing called bossa nova. And I think it was the Sinatra with, I think, it was Jobim, you know. And it's beautiful, you know, with the new beat and the whole thing. And I remember him sitting on the edge of the couch with his eyes shut, looking straight down and his eyes are shut, listening to the music.

"And at the end of this song, this beautiful bossa nova song, he said, 'God, why didn't the kids go this way?' "

When Mercer got back to California, an extraordinary invitation was presented to him. The Beatles, who had dominated popular music throughout much of the 1960s, had split up in 1970, each going his separate way. With the breakup of the group came the dissolution of the successful songwriting team of John Lennon and Paul McCartney. McCartney had written many songs on his own, but as a British writer observed, "McCartney has always needed a good lyric writer."

According to some, Mercer admired the songs of Lennon and McCartney, predicting they would endure as standards. Others recall that Mercer had a different estimate of their artistry. In 1967, he told an interviewer, "The Beatles don't really sing, and they don't really write too well, but they're an attraction." A British friend recalls that Mercer, appalled by McCartney's title song of the James Bond film *Live and Let Die*, said, "You call that a lyric?"

McCartney, however, was an unqualified admirer of Johnny Mercer's and wanted to collaborate with him. Margaret Whiting was the go-between. "One day his music firm came to me and said, 'You can work miracles with him. Will you go and talk to him about the fact that Paul McCartney wants to write with him?' " Whiting went to Mercer's home. "He had no idea. Sitting in front of a fire, 'having a cup of tea. I don't know what he was thinking really, and said, 'Johnny, I am thrilled with this and I know that you like this man's writing. I don't know how you'd feel about this, but Paul McCartney wants to write with you. He loves the idea of the two generations, and he thinks you two publicly would be marvelous and that you could write so well together. He wants to write with you.' And, without a moment's hesitation, he said, 'I would give anything to write with him. I adore him. I think he's great, but I don't think Ginger is well, so I can't do anything now.'" Whether Mercer was using Ginger's own imminent surgery to avoid collaborating with what he considered a less than stellar songwriting talent or whether he genuinely wanted to work with McCartney but was afraid his own debilitating condition would affect the quality of the collaboration, a great opportunity was lost. Instead of trying for success in the world of musical theater, which was not the arena where his gifts lay, working with McCartney would have returned him to his native sphere of pure songwriting. Had Johnny Mercer and Paul McCartney collaborated, it might have spanned the gap between the eras of Tin Pan Alley and rock, a gap that remains impassable to this day.

After Mercer consulted six different doctors in California, the consensus was that a benign tumor was putting pressure on his brain, but that it was inoperable. Then, a close friend of Ginger's said, they "finally found one doctor that would operate." She remembered that by then Johnny's skull was misshapen. Johnny Mercer went in for surgery on October 15, 1975, at Huntington Memorial Hospital in Pasadena. Before he checked into the hospital, however, he had his son Jeff drive him all around Los Angeles to a series of banks. "He had safe-deposit boxes in every one, and he grabbed—he opened them and took all the stuff out."

The doctor who agreed to perform the operation was Theodore Kurze, known among colleagues as a "very aggressive" and "theatrical" neurosurgeon who "played to the audience" of his patients' friends and family. "If six other doctors had refused to operate on Mercer's tumor," said Dr. Michael Kadin, who treated Mercer after the surgery, "Ted Kurze would have gone in there aggressively." Kadin explained that the other doctors must have seen that Mercer's tumor was very large and located in a critical part of his brain. "I would have recommended a biopsy, which would have been safe, and then radiation treatments." Such treatments would have possibly improved or at least kept stable Mercer's "remaining quality of life" and helped him stay "hopefully functional" for the rest of his "albeit short" life. "I only know that once you go into the brain and see the extent of tumor, the adage 'do no harm' applies." At that point, Kadin thought, a neurosurgeon should have performed only a "minimum operation . . . i.e., biopsy, and then get out. . . . But Kurze went in there aggressively. . . . He didn't know when to stop."

"Ted Kurze had a very prominent reputation as a neurosurgeon from Boston, had been profiled on television . . . a celebrity doctor. *Nobody* told him what to do and he was more aggressive than most neurosurgeons at the time." Kadin recalled a similar case a few years later, when Kurze let one of his residents operate on a man with a condition similar to Mercer's. When the man came out of the operation a comatose "vegetable"—as Mercer feared *he* would—Kadin confronted Kurze about operating on a man's tumor when he knew the surgery could leave him in such a state.

"I shook my head in disbelief," Kadin said, "and muttered, 'You're nuts!'"

"Kurze told me that 'since the residents get little practice in operating on patients, this was a good opportunity for him to learn how to.'"

Dr. Kadin shook his head, said again, "You're sick," and walked away.

Like many neurosurgeons at the time, Kadin explained, Theodore Kurze did not think beyond the surgery to the quality of life the patient would enjoy afterward. "He was doing Mercer no favor by operating on him." When Mercer went under the knife, it turned out that the other doctors had been right: "It was inoperable," a friend of Ginger's said: "the doctor came down crying." Theodore Kurze, in later years, was a man with "no humility," said Kadin, who was surprised to learn that Kurze had wept when he told Ginger that the tumor was malignant. Had Kurze not operated, Kadin speculated, Mercer would not have lived long, but he would have remained conscious. Eventually, as the tumor grew even larger, he would have suffered seizures but still had some "quality of life" before he died. Kadin, a radiation oncologist, was brought in to confront the hopeless task of trying to bring Mercer out of his coma with radiation treatments. "I hope I'm not too harsh on Ted Kurze, but the Mercer case and the following resident case remained in my memory for the last twenty-seven plus years."

"Dr. Theodore Kurze," he said, again, did Johnny Mercer "no favor by operating on him."

"The thing that got me was he did become a vegetable," lamented Bill Harbach, who had urged Mercer to undergo the surgery. "Whether he should have just gone out with nothing going on—I've always felt a little guilt about that. But I still thought you should play the big game and get it checked. Now, I talked with the surgeon after the operation, and they found it was cancer. Now, the surgeon said eight out of ten are not cancer if it's in the brain, and it has been in the brain a year and a half or two years, as it was, because the brain is so full of blood the cancer grows much faster. And he'd had this for two years."

Harbach said the surgeon, Dr. Theodore Kurze, said, "'I swore to you, it would be benign.' And he said, 'I opened him up, and I said, "Oh, God."'"

"At the risk of being a bore," Harbach asked Kurze, "how do you tell?"

"'Well, you know the difference between a chicken and a duck?'"

"He said it was a big cancer. But I would have, he would have, put money that it wasn't because it had been there so long and brain tumors, he said, don't, if they last long, are not cancerous." In an effort to clarify some confusion about the exact nature of the illness, Dr. Kurze later wrote a letter explaining that Mercer had "a midline malignant glioma which had invaded his brainstem prior to his surgery." The tumor grew along the center of his brain and then spread to each side; had Johnny overcome his fear of doctors and gone in earlier for surgery, the tumor might have been removed before it damaged more and more of his brain.

On Johnny Mercer's sixty-sixth birthday, November 18, 1975, his family came to see him in the hospital and watch *Old Man Rhythm*, the movie that had brought him to Hollywood forty years earlier. For his daughter, that last birthday brought back her father's young dream of becoming a Hollywood movie star. "See, he always wanted to perform," she said. "He always wanted to be on, so if he could get a TV show or a television—or a radio show or whatever was there at the time. He wanted to be an actor. He came out to Hollywood to act. Yeah. He came out to Hollywood, and he said, 'Okay, I'm going to write, and I have to be in the movie.' And they said, 'No. Okay, we did *a* movie. We don't need to do any other.'"

His granddaughter Nickie remembered that he "held my hand and he smiled, and the nurses and everyone said that was the only gesture, emotion that he showed the whole time, and the tears rolling down his eye, and he squeezed my hand. And that otherwise they say he pretty much acted like a vegetable." That magnificent fount of wit and song lost the power of speech, apparently as a result of a tracheotomy that frequently must be performed on postoperative patients who remain in a coma, simply to keep them breathing. "That would have devastated him," a friend recalled. "It would have just closed up."

Amanda's son Jamie had a grimmer recollection of that last birthday. "Now, that was a tough time," he said. "You'd go in and he'd lost—I mean, he was a hearty man, and he was probably down to 150 pounds. He was real skinny. And it was weird because he was—"

"They kept saying he was depressed," Amanda said. "He *was* depressed."

"He would look right at you," Jamie said. "He couldn't talk. But his eyes were open. He would look like he was alert, but he couldn't respond. He couldn't respond at all."

"Except he'd cry," Amanda said.

"He'd blink his eyes," Jamie said. "Yeah, he'd cry occasionally. And the tough part was a lot of friends really wouldn't come and see him."

"They couldn't," Amanda countered. "They weren't allowed to."

"They weren't?"

"Mom wouldn't let them," she said. "They weren't allowed to come. Mom wouldn't let them. She didn't want them to see him the way he was. No, she wouldn't let them. And she wouldn't tell them he was dying either. It was hard for the people. It was hard for me to talk to people. Because I wasn't allowed to talk to them, to tell them anything, or to talk to them or anything."

"It was not known how deep his problem was. They kept it very quiet," said Bill Harbach. "One night—I was taking Ginger out once every two weeks or something—once a week when I was out in Beverly Hills doing other shows—and one time Ginger came in to him in this hospital room and said, 'Johnny, Bill's here. He's going to take me out to dinner.' And he smiled, which made me feel so marvelous. He just smiled. But his eyes were shut. . . . the smile is the last thing I saw."

When Mercer's medical insurance expired in March, Ginger brought him home and turned his study into a hospital room. She hired a husband-and-wife team to nurse him around the clock. "They made a little hospital room and had nurses around the clock. I think it was over $350,000 a year of nurses," John Corwin said, "and he was on a machine at the end and basically a vegetable."

Friends, unaware of how much Mercer had deteriorated, wrote and called. Henry Mancini sent love from himself and his wife, adding, "Being the 'music' half of the team, I'm not very good with words." Bing Crosby wrote to Ginger in February 1976, saying, "I've been thinking of Johnny a lot, since his hospitalization and surgery, and just wanted you to know that I'm praying for his complete recovery. I know this must be a very difficult time for you. I suppose you see him every day or so, and I would be grateful to you if you would give him a message from me that I'm pulling for him and hope before long that he'll be up and around and that I'll be able to talk to him person-ally." A friend who stayed with Ginger every night in the hospital and then at the house said that "she closed herself off from everybody, to the extent that she wouldn't even talk to Irving Berlin when he called once a week. I talked to him. I took the call."

Mercer had instructed his doctors before the operation that if they found he was inoperable, he wanted to be allowed to die; he did not want his life preserved by machines. After months of lying semicomatose, he had to be put on a respirator, and he finally died on June 25, 1976. It was Ginger's birthday. "My brother," said Amanda, "said it was his way of getting even with her."

His body was cremated, then flown to Savannah. "I'm not sure Johnny was so thrilled about being cremated," a friend said. "That wasn't his way. That was more Ginger's way." Then, after a pause, "They were an interesting couple."

Flying haunted Johnny Mercer even after his death; for several hours in Las Vegas, his ashes could not be found to be transferred to a flight to Savan-nah. Once they arrived at the Savannah airport on July 2, they were received by Nick Mamalakis. After some discussion of scattering his ashes along Moon River, where he had played as a boy, the family decided to bury them in Bonaventure Cemetery. Eventually, he would be flanked by his mother on his right and Ginger on his left. During the graveside ceremony, a bobwhite sang out from the trees overhead.

And the Angels Sing

On my last trip to Savannah, I drove along the streets that James Oglethorpe laid out in squares when he founded the colony of Georgia in 1733. Because of the layout, few streets run in long straight lines; instead, every few blocks, they open onto a square, so you have to slow down and go around half its perimeter before you pick up your street again. The grid forces you to proceed slowly, deliberately, politely. The squares are filled with trees, giving Savannah its nickname of "the Forest City," and stately houses face one another on all four sides. The streets, the squares, the houses, impose a public demeanor that would, if you grew up here, nurture a genteel forbearance, enforced by the scrutiny of neighbors who literally surround you.

At the corner of one of these grids, on Broughton Street, around from the Episcopal church where Johnny Mercer sang in the choir, was the Tea Room, one of the city's oldest restaurants. There I met another of his nieces, the only child of his sister Juliana. When I called to arrange the meeting, I asked how we would recognize each other; she said, "You'll know me. I look like him."

Struck by the opulent Victorian decor when I walked into the tiny restaurant, it took me a moment to see the resemblance. She had his blue eyes and light brown hair but not his most characteristic feature—the large gap between his two front teeth that showed when he smiled. The same kind of gap, Chaucer's Wife of Bath claimed, marked her as an amorous child of Venus. Johnny Mercer, who would also fit under that description, used to brag that he could spit through the gap for ten feet.

Raised by Johnny Mercer's mother, Nancy Gerard felt she had a particularly deep understanding of the man who was the closest thing she had to a father. "I think I know him, knew him, better than any of us other than his mother. And the reason I think is because his mother, my grandmother, was very, very attached to me and I to her. And he told her everything, and she told me everything. And I think I have more understanding about him than many of the other people in the family. And this understanding about him has only come recently. Because I have some sobering experiences with him too."

Our tea came, served with an unassuming elegance that must have been centuries old. "You know, he was always expected to be so wonderful," she said with southern languor, slowly describing the rigorous standards of kindness, generosity, and chivalry set by his mother and father. "I think he expected himself to be as well." She thought those demanding expectations prompted many of Mercer's noble acts, large and small. But she also thought they could become an unbearable burden that he flung off when he drank, violating all of his inbred great expectations with violence and viciousness. "If he was being irritable or he was in one of those dark places, I think that was a survival mechanism. . . . We get to places where we can't handle life, where we just want to get away, get out, give me mental space. And you think of that creative genius that was going on all the time and also having to produce on deadlines and create on deadlines and subject to other people's opinions as to whether this was good or not good or gonna fly or not fly or gonna make money or not make money or—I think it started with the little sister who died."

The little sister who died. For a second, I didn't know whom she was talking about, but then I remembered there was a sister who died of diphtheria when Mercer was a child. I had seen her gravestone, near his, at Saint Bonaventure Cemetery: "Nancy Mercer, 8 February 1911–11 May 1914." But I had not attached much importance to her, dying when he was so young. Later, when I checked the typescript of his unpublished autobiography, I couldn't find any mention of her in the chapters on his childhood. I went over the entire manuscript and, near the end, in a chapter entitled "Into Each Life Some Rain Must Fall," where he recounts the physical injuries he received as a child, there she was—buried in an aside. He writes that all of his accidents "must have been distressing to my poor mother, who had lost a little girl slightly my junior at the tender age of three." Then, in a twisted turn of syntax, he adds, "Fortunately, for her, none of my injuries were fatal and she had another little sister to look after."

It was not the death of his sister itself, a sister he could probably barely remember, that so affected him, but the devastating effect the death had had on his already sad-hearted mother. "There was not a day in that house that that little girl's death was not brought up," his niece said. "I have things written by my grandmother after the death of her little girl Nancy, for whom I'm named. And that little girl was named for our grandmother's mother, Nancy. . . . She was never able to speak about her little Nancy without tearing up. I could remember as a child and I'd ask her about that. Because she had the picture of little Nancy and I'd ask her about it, and she would just say, 'Oh, I just can't talk about—' and she would tear up." If Lillian Mercer was still so shaken by the death thirty years later, how wrenchingly evident her grief must have been to Johnny Mercer at five years old.

Nancy Gerard thought her grandmother's sorrow over the loss of that baby drove Johnny to do everything he could to try to comfort his grieving mother. "I remember one time, I guess it was after the death of that little baby, I think she said something about, you know, he was so loving and so kind and so sweet, and I'm thinking he was probably six, seven years. . . . And I have this scene that she put in my head . . . and he was hugging and kissing her, 'Don't cry, Mutha. Don't cry.' "

As a child, Johnny Mercer must have done everything he could to stop that crying, to stanch those unstanchable tears. His mother loved to tell the story of how, when he was six, seven, or eight, "Bubba came up to me one day and said, 'Mother, are there some jobs I can do around the house where I could earn some money?' " She assigned him some chores, paid him some money, and he went running out of the house to return with a wilted lily for her for an Easter present.

But the offering of flowers would not be enough; nothing would be enough. He would strive to meet all of his mother's rigorously high standards of kindness, generosity, and benevolence. "My grandmother always expected Johnny to do everything for everybody," Nancy said, "and I think there were times when it was hard for him to have that expectation and all of that—responsibility, you know, imposed on him by his mother. . . . Yet he would never let her know, although a few times he would write—he wouldn't say the words 'I resent this,' but he would write in a way where you knew he resented it."

Far from assuaging his mother's grief over the death of his first sister, as Johnny Mercer implied in his autobiography, the birth of Juliana must only have exacerbated Miss Lillian's misery. "There was not something exactly 'right' about my mother. I don't know what was wrong with my mother, but there was something not exactly right about her. And I know she was obsessively compulsive, I know that she was highly emotional, I know that she was not good at school, I know that she did some inappropriate things, like cutting the dining-room tablecloth in pieces." Miss Lillian's grief over her second daughter must have been all the more wrenching because it was never expressed. "There's not a lot written about that in any of my grandmother's writings. There's nothing that—where I have seen where she said, 'I am worried about Juliana.' Or this and that. There's nothing like that. But I know that there was trouble."

Johnny Mercer was as devoted to his sister as he was to his mother, and the pressure must have again fallen upon him to try to make things right. If he could not bring his first sister back to life, perhaps he could protect the second. Because she was an excellent singer, he sent her to the Juilliard School of Music in New York. "But she wasn't able to live independently," her daughter said, "and did not do well. And she was always a little different.

"She never held down a job," she added. "She never really took care of a household, and she never lived independently. She had a very beautiful singing voice, she was a very beautiful, lovely young woman. She was able to play an acceptable hand of bridge and smoke a cigarette and dance. Here, if you had money and you had servants, that was fine. You could probably get away with it."

Juliana married during her year away from home, and she and her husband lived in Detroit, but Juliana was miserable there, so George Mercer brought his daughter back to Savannah, promising his son-in-law a job with the family firm. But soon after they arrived, George Mercer died. Because Juliana was by then nearly nine months pregnant, her husband was told to drive her around Savannah during the funeral for fear that the ceremony would be too upsetting for her. But after the funeral, Nancy said, "My grandmother became the matriarch." Six weeks after Nancy was born, her father left. "Somehow the marriage was ended."

While her mother Juliana could function in her own Savannah social circle, "when it came to the chore of really having a family and raising children and taking care of children, I don't think she was able to do it," Nancy said. "She was not able to do those kinds of things. . . . And that's why I was raised by my grandmother, but she lived in the home with me. But I was raised by my grandmother and my black nanny.

"So you had the stage set," she said. "The tragedy of the little girl, then my mother." Even before these wrenching events, there had been George Mercer's banishment of Johnny's half brother Hugh after George's first wife died giving birth to him. "That little baby lived with Katherine—not my grandmother's sister but my grandfather's, and he did not come back to live with him until my grandfather married my grandmother and had been married a year or so. . . . Hugh never was able to develop well because of it. He was always a sad, melancholy person." Clearly, Johnny Mercer was expected—and expected himself—to make amends for this tragedy as well. "Johnny would come to visit and we'd go to see him off at the train, and Hugh would go, and we'd be standing there at the train and Johnny would say, 'C'mon, Pajuicey— why don't you get in the—why don't you ride with me up to Columbia?' . . . He'd actually end up going all the way to New York, and he'd stay two or three days with Johnny in New York, then Johnny would send him back. And this happened more than once. He was very good to him."

Nancy Gerard believed that her grandfather was also a hypochondriac who so feared disease that he forbade the children to have pets at the house on Gwinnett Street, though he evidently allowed some dogs at the summer home at Vernon View. So another element in Mercer's childhood was a terror of disease. "And then when that little girl died!" she said. "I can't imagine a more horrible tragedy. And they were *away* when she died. They were away when she died. When she became ill and died."

"So you've got this young man, this sensitive young man, feeling he has—all that tragedy going on, and to this young man who had this incredible gift . . . who was trying to make it in show business, who had this talent that was just bursting out of him, coming out, and he ended up living in this show business world, this New York, this Hollywood lifestyle that I think was so against his core . . . being pulled and squished by Ginger, who more or less resented what he did for his family . . . and having all those pressures and all that expectation placed on you by everybody. . . . I think that it was hard for him. And I think he ended up doing things, saying things that he never really meant. But you know you get to a point where you're tired, and you lash out."

As she spoke, I thought of all of the generous things Mercer had done throughout his life: sending two dollars in the mail to help repay his father's business debt, then years later repaying it in full; giving half of his only dollar to a professional beggar during the depression; staying with the B movie producer at RKO who had brought him to Hollywood rather than signing with more prominent figures; starting Capitol Records as a way to help unemployed singers and musicians; working with any songwriter who wanted his talents; moving from Hollywood to Newport Beach when his children threw a "hissy fit"; collaborating with Harold Arlen out of friendship on a Broadway show he knew would be a flop; starting the Songwriters Hall of Fame to help impoverished Tin Pan Alley wordsmiths and tunesmiths. Even his love affair with Judy Garland must have been yet another way for him to help the most desperate person he knew.

Such acts of nobility had been bred into him, gently but terrifyingly, and there were times when he simply could not be the generous, kind, chivalrous southern icon his parents had molded him to be. When he drank, alcohol must have released him from having to be that little boy who felt he had to make everything right for everybody. What came out was probably a very ordinary person—angry, envious, aggressive—but because the pressures that maintained his patrician self would not let such plebian emotions show when he was sober, alcohol unleashed them in sudden, vicious bursts. When its effects wore off, he flagellated himself remorsefully, and, as he had done as a child, gave flowers.

Don't cry, Mutha. Don't cry.

Before I left Savannah, I drove out again to Moon River to look at the landscape he had loved as a boy. It was early evening, the water was darker, and the Spanish moss hanging from the trees gave an eerie feel to the play of dying sunlight and shadows. The astonishing beauty of the spot was still apparent, and the rivulets that curved and twisted in a fluid labyrinth seemed a natural, free pattern that countered the rigid, repressive squares of Savannah's streets. No wonder Mercer loved his summers here as a boy, when he could escape not only the rigors of school but also the strictures and pressures of his family. Playing with friends, away from his parents, day after glorious, lazy day amid a natural world that asked for nothing but aesthetic delight gave him—for a time—a place, a Moon River, that he would try to recapture for the rest of his life.

It was also the place he would draw on for his songs. His lyrics, as his niece said, "are all from here." When he could make people happy with a song, he experienced an ecstatic feeling—"the buzz around the movie set when you've brought in a 'hit' and everyone on the set knows it and is singing it. . . . These are the things that mean even more than the big checks that come rolling in when you've really got a big one—a song that everybody loves—and all the artists can't wait to sing and record. It really is an exciting, stimulating experience, and like having an adventure in love, it does not pale with time, as each adventure is different and the end result is always pleasant, combining as it does, a sense of prideful accomplishment with the happiness of making other people happy."

The happiness of making other people happy. It must have been that happiness that engendered the astonishing love people held for Johnny Mercer and made almost all of them forgive his hideous abusiveness. His lyrics came from that pressure he always felt to be generous, to be kind, to be noble, and he once described the struggle to find the lyric to a melody as a quest for "something you never heard of, the golden fleece. You don't know where it is, it's just up there somewhere and you can tune in on it, and you get a little glimmer and you say, ah—you don't even know if it's a word, and then it begins to—it's like you're tuning into a musical instrument that's miles away, and you say, oh, there's something there if I just dig hard enough." When he got there, for a moment, the song made up for the tragedies of his childhood, made his mother stop crying, made everyone who heard it happy. Whenever Johnny Mercer could do that with a song, his restless, searching heart finally found its home on Moon River.

In the notes below I have used the following abbreviations:

ARI   Archival interview in the Johnny Mercer Oral History Project and Mercer Interview Collections, William Russell Pullen Library, Georgia State University, Atlanta, Georgia. First citation gives name of interviewee, date, and catalog number of interview. Copyright owned by Georgia State University, a unit of the Board of Regents of the University System of Georgia.

AUI   Author's interview, giving name of interviewee and date and place of interview on first citation.

JMA   Typescript of Johnny Mercer's unpublished autobiography in box 1, folders 3–6, of the Johnny Mercer Papers, 1885–1981 (M81-1), Popular Music Collection, Special Collections Department, Pullen Library. Copyright owned by Georgia State University, a unit of the Board of Regents of the University System of Georgia. Citations give chapter and page numbers for each quotation.

JMP   The Johnny Mercer Papers, Popular Music Collection, Special Collections Department, Pullen Library. Copyright owned by Georgia State University, a unit of the Board of Regents of the University System of Georgia. Citations give collection number, archival box and folder numbers, and, where appropriate, page numbers.

NYPL   New York Public Library, Lincoln Center Division, New York. Files for musical shows contain clippings of newspaper reviews, some undated and without attribution.

SPL   The Johnny Mercer file in the Savannah Public Library, consisting primarily of newspaper clippings, some of which are undated and without attribution.

Prologue: Moon River

1 "indoor" . . . "outdoor" Ken Barnes, liner notes, *Johnny Mercer: Singer—Songwriter*, Pye Records NSPL 18443.

2 "the most perfect . . . Pure American" Quoted by Bill Harbach, ARI, March 1, 1996, M96-1, 31.

"one of our great folk poets" Quoted by Deena Rosenberg, "Their Era Has Ended but Their Lyrics Linger On," New York Times, December 4, 1977, sec. 2, p. 6.

"Mercer had an ability . . . from a different base" Quoted in Al Kasha and Joel Hirschhorn, *Notes on Broadway: Conversations with the Great Songwriters* (Chicago: Contemporary Books, 1985), 90.

" 'Good God,' I thought . . . *does* love birds' " SPL, quoted by Tom Buckley, "About New York: A Memorial Accentuating the Positive," *New York Times*, July 24, 1976, 13.

4 "that best portion . . . of love" William Wordsworth, "Lines Composed a Few Miles Above Tintern Abbey on Revisiting the Banks of the Wye During a Tour," lines 32–34.

"sandy spit . . . the day" SPL, n.d.

"beauteous forms . . . the heart" Wordsworth, lines 22–28.

5 "He could seek . . . needle into it" Gene Lees, interview, on *Accentuate the Positive: The Johnny Mercer Story*, BBC 2 series, April 2002.

"I don't want to meet your fucking mother" AUI, Alan Livingston, Los Angeles, Calif., May 21, 2001. In recounting this incident, as well as that of Mercer pouring his drink over Ginger's head, Livingston said, "I won't use his language." I have inserted the profanity based on numerous other interviews where Mercer was quoted directly.

"I always felt . . . didn't have a home" AUI, Ann Mercer Klein, Savannah, Ga., March 10, 2000.

6 "The sadness and lostness . . . I always did" AUI, Ann Mercer Klein.

"I never had . . . really care to" AUI, Ann Mercer Klein

"I don't think . . . It was shabby" AUI, Ann Mercer Klein.

7 "I can get . . . for Christ's sake?' " AUI, André Previn, telephone interview, January 14, 2002.

1. You Must Have Been a Beautiful Baby: 1909–1927

9 "I suppose the reason . . . in Savannah" SPL, *Savannah Morning News*, May 24, 1959.

"Savannah was smaller . . . it so beautiful" JMA, I/1.

"I can remember . . . in various ways" SPL, *Savannah Morning News*, May 24, 1959.

"Although I have never . . . sprang from there" SPL, n.d.

"In sending you away . . . selfabuse" JMP, M81, I/2.

10 "emissions that occur . . . what she will think" JMP, M81, 1/2.

"good deeds in the dark of the night" *Atlanta Journal and Constitution*, June 27, 1976, 10.

"Mr. Mercer Sr. . . . without charge" AUI, Nick Mamalakis, Savannah, Ga., March 10, 2002.

"His father was . . . nobody in that family" AUI, Ann Mercer Klein.

"prospered like Rhett Butler in *Gone With the Wind*" JMP, M81, 31/4.

11 "We had to take . . . 'Blues in the Night' came from" AUI, Nancy and Steve Gerard, Savannah, Ga., March 4, 2002.

"of the most mournful outlook" JMP, M81, 1/11.

"very sensitive . . . Uncle Bubba had" ARI, Nancy Gerard and Steve Gerard, September 28, 2001, M2001-8, 10–11.

12 "I know that a lot of songs . . . off to dreams" JMA, I/10.

"He disappeared . . . resist the music" JMP, M81, 31/14.

"Songs always fascinated me" JMP, 1/15.

13 "rarified airs . . . mountaineer folk songs" JMP, M81, 1/14, 33.

"I'se headed for home . . . done fired me" *Atlanta Journal*, August 14, 1955, 10.

" 'news-wall-papered' shanty . . . on the big road" JMP, M81, 1/7.

"About the time . . . yard boys, cooks, and nursemaids" *Atlanta Journal*, August 14, 1955, 10.

"The roads were still unpaved . . . salt water" JMA, I/1.

14 "They called it . . . from the Ogeechee River" ARI, Nick Mamalakis, May 15, 1997, M97-6, 5.

"He'd just be . . . blow me away" AUI, John Corwin, Palm Desert, Calif., May 25, 2001.

"Buh Dayday . . . on December 31st" JMP M81, 1/7.

"It was quite . . . toward the causeway" SPL, *Savannah Morning News*, May, 1962.

"out on the starlit veranda . . . would grow heavy" JMA, I/10.

"The black boys . . . no one would eat it" Quoted in Bob Bach and Ginger Mercer, eds., *Our Huckleberry Friend: The Life, Times and Song Lyrics of Johnny Mercer* (Secaucus, N.J.: Lyle Stuart, 1982), 16.

15 "A country boy . . . his eyes open" JMP, M81, 14/21.

"there was a colony . . . of Pinpoint" ARI, Nick Mamalakis, M97-6, 7.

"A little boy . . . Sunday evening sermons" JMP, M81, 1/15, 10.

"singing and gospel . . . inside the church" AUI, Nick Mamalakis.

"On what is now . . . down there too." ARI, Nick Mamalakis, M97-6, 7.

"He didn't object . . . to enjoy him" ARI, James W. McIntire, November 11, 1997, M97-9, 7.

16 "The Easter parade . . . with his father" Bob Bach and Ginger Mercer, 6.

"Music was always . . . thirteen or fourteen" ARI, Nancy Gerard and Steve Gerard, M2001-8, 3.

17 "By the time . . . Victor Herbert" JMP, 1/15.

"professional music men . . . they were promoting" JMA, VII/1.

"I was sent . . . I could do it immediately, you see" JMP, M82-10/4.

18 "And, as the shark . . . had to die" JMP, M81, 1/10.

"gave me the confidence . . . to write" JMA, I/4.

19 "He was in our house . . . in the pictures" ARI, Pope McIntire, May 12, 1997, M97-4, 1.

"Big boys inspire respect . . . any competitive sports" JMP, M81, 1/14.

20 "Mistuh Jawnny . . . 'e fire me!" JMP, M81 1/7, 1.

"rather like a purple heart . . . to prove it" JMA, XII/2.

21 "My father never understood . . . 'product of the age' " JMA, I/10.

"He would go . . . black music lover" ARI, Nick Mamalakis, M97-6, 5.

22 "West Broad Street . . . his beat and phrasing" Bob Bach and Ginger Mercer, 16.

"in effect a room . . . balloon tires came in" Frederick Lewis Allen, *Only Yesterday* (New York: Harper & Row, 1931), 83, 134.

23 "careen around . . . from head to foot" JMA, I/2.

"the good Samaritan tradition . . . the terrible swift sword" JMA, II/1.

24 "I suppose today's readers . . . whatever girls wear" JMA, III/5.

"determined to get in on the fun" JMA, III/5.

"one of the greatest . . . of the beat" Will Friedwald, *Jazz Singing: America's Great Voices from Bessie Smith to Bebop and Beyond* (New York: Collier, 1992), 361–62.

"I can remember . . . know she's there" JMA, III/5–6.

"As we really . . . would try anything" JMA, III/6–7.

25 "Mr. Pritchett and Mr. Dick . . . all our lyricists" JMP, M81, 1/15, 10.

"U. R. Goofey . . . vit an instinct" "The Daily Dope," *The Fir Tree* (Woodberry Forest, 1926), 5–6.

26 "Dear Mother Motley . . . you charcoal camel!" "The Sorrycycle," *The Fir Tree* (Woodberry Forest, 1927), 88.

"Among Doo's hobbies . . . is uncanny" *The Fir Tree* (Woodberry Forest, 1927), 34.

27 "at Woodberry Johnny . . . you would swap records" AUI, Peter Ruffin, Wilmington, N.C., April 15, 2002.

"My youth was filled . . . and perhaps longer" JMA, XIII/13.

"many times . . . in his blood" ARI, Nick Mamalakis, M97-6, 8.

"I must have looked . . . favorite male groups" JMA, III/6.

"My relationships were . . . games of post-office" JMP, M81, 1/7.

28 "I can't remember . . . lack of trying" JMP, 1/14, 16.

"everybody does it" Johnny Mercer, interview, *Accentuate the Positive: The Johnny Mercer Story*.

"Sister Susie . . . had been pilfered" JMA, I/4.

29 "can sound like a million" Ira Gershwin, *Lyrics on Several Occasions* (New York: Alfred A. Knopf, 1959), 360.

"all creative artists . . . from your contemporaries" JMA, I/6.

"having tasted . . . to drop a title" JMA, I/5.

"I just had to write . . . or said she did" JMA, II/7.

"my sun on a dark day . . . outside of sex" JMA, I/5.

2. When the World Was Young: 1927–1930

30 "Seventeen was a beautiful age . . . sing harmony" JMA, II/3, 5–6.

"seven times to the body, twice to the head" A. G. Langguth, *Patriots: The Men Who Started the American Revolution* (New York: Simon & Schuster, 1988), 427.

31 "His company never . . . on demand today" JMP, Nick Mamalakis, M97-6, 15–16.

"George Mercer . . . 'where mine is'" AUI, Nick Mamalakis.

"Johnny's two dollars . . . after the liquidation" Nancy Gerard, interview, *Accentuate the Positive: The Johnny Mercer Story*.

32 "dropped by Pop's office . . . 'lose a dime'" JMP, M99, 6/2.

"I had resisted . . . young man do?" JMA, II/3.

"They had a big pavilion . . . things were sparkling" AUI, Georgia Roux, Savannah, Ga., March 9, 2000.

33 "Every time I hear . . . about that age" JMP, M82-8/7.

"The firm was . . . of his services" Worth Gatewood, quoted by Edward Jablonski in liner notes for *An Evening with Johnny Mercer,* DRG Records, 5176, 2.

"We'd give him . . . There they stayed" Quoted by Edward Jablonski, 3.

"one of the few . . . this little colony" ARI, Nick Mamalakis, M97-6, 5.

"He would stroll . . . fascinated by it" AUI, Nick Mamalakis.

"He liked to chat . . . colony of Pinpoint," ARI, Nick Mamalakis, M97-6, 6.

34 "I wouldn't be thrown to the sharks" JMA, III/1.

"No bed was . . . taking it all in" JMA, III/1–2.

35 "The steam coming . . . peasant in Baghdad" JMA, III/4.

"more enchanted and enraptured than ever with the make-believe of the theater" JMA, III/8.

"I found another . . . New York City!" JMA, III/8.

"honked their automobile . . . in those days" JMA, IV/1–2.

36 "I went down . . . burst into tears" ARI, James McIntire, M97-9, 6.

"The sketch contained . . . as the grandson" *New York Times,* May 12, 1928, 9.

"combed stardust out . . . their honest livings" JMA, XIV/9.

"nothing was to . . . from then on" JMA, IV/2.

"I thought acting . . . for a while" *Accentuate the Positive: The Johnny Mercer Story,* BBC-2 series, April 2002.

"Mother is the one . . . Mother for that" ARI, James McIntire, M97-4, 4.

37 "They were very proud . . . make it on Broadway" ARI, Nick Mamalakis, M97-6, 8-9.

38 "The last gasp . . . before the end" JMA, IV/9.

"To come from . . . stars in person" JMA, IV/3.

"Always pay your bills . . . Go back home." JMA, IV/4.

39 "Walking the lake . . . the North Pole" JMA, IV/5.

"too gauche, naive, or plain-looking . . . freed from slavery" JMA, IV/5.

"with a boy . . . the wrong sex" JMA, IV/6.

"He and three . . . in the tub" JMP, M81, 31–14.

40 "I did everything . . . bath-tub gin" JMA, IV/7.

"could do more . . . sugar and oatmeal" JMA, IV/8.

"All I did . . . with tennis rackets" JMA, IV/8.

41 "Anyone who would . . . is affected" Jablonski, 3.

"I think I'll go . . . beautiful redskins" JMA, IV/10–11.

42 "Dear Eddie. Now . . . and ordered dessert" Herbert G. Goldman, *Banjo Eyes: Eddie Cantor and the Birth of Modern Stardom* (New York: Oxford University Press, 1997), 128–32.

"These letters actually . . . encouragement and kindness" JMA, IV/11.

"Mr. Mercer would write . . . immediately read it" ARI, Nick Mamalakis, M97-6, 9.

43 "He is extremely enthusiastic . . . peak of the season" JMP, M81, 31/12.

"While the home-town talk . . . back on oatmeal" JMA, IV/12.

"needing a shave . . . his local debutante" JMA, V/1.

"On warm nights . . . in those days" JMA, V/1–2.

44 "No one really knew . . . my life professionally" JMA, IV-12.

"I had half a song" JMP, M81, 1/15, 7.

46 "The New York papers . . . for favorable mention" JMP, M81, 32/16.

"The *Garrick Gaieties* . . . Tin Pan Alley" JMA, V/4.

3. Jeepers Creepers: 1930–1931

47 "During all this time . . . I just liked them" JMP, M81, 1/14, 17.

"a great big bag . . . raised her three daughters" ARI, Joyce Pelphrey, July 7, 1997, M97-8, 2.

"affordable skill" Machine-made pianos were produced in the late nineteenth century, and some immigrant families, such as the Gershwins, could afford to purchase one, secondhand, for their children.

48 "We all thought . . . they were sisters" ARI, Claire Meltzer, November 7, 1997, M97-10, 6–7.

"Bing could be cantankerous . . . a limitless supply" Gary Giddins, *Bing Crosby: A Pocketful of Dreams* (Boston: Little, Brown, 2001), 176.

"ACCORDING TO US STATISTICS . . . DELORES AND STUFF BING" JMP, M 81, 1/20.

49 "WOULD LIKE TO . . . ELEVEN FIFTEEN BING" Quoted in Giddins, 177.

"WOULD LIKE TO . . . SUE ME BING" JMP, M81, 1/20.

"The story in the family . . . pretty serious" ARI, Joyce Pelphrey, M97-8, 7.

"To Bing . . . he was the fox" Giddins, 182.

"My mother liked him . . . get crushes on him" ARI, Claire Meltzer, M97-10, 9.

"Her uncle told her . . . to Jack Priestley" Quoted in "The Story of *The Good Companions*," notes from "Chappell Vocal Selections, *The Good Companions*" (London: Chappell, 1979).

50 "was interested in every girl in the show *but* me" JMP, M81, 1/15.

"I still don't know . . . in her time off" JMP, M81, 1/9, 5.

"We didn't have . . . whom I admired" JMA, V/2.

"All the kids . . . 'Mean Maybe Now' " JMA, V/6.

"It seemed to me . . . I'd ever heard" Quoted in Giddins, 170.

"Borough Hall! . . . way to Harlem" JMA, V/3.

"Hey, how about you folks . . . too close for comfort" JMA, V/3.

"used to come over . . . stay up with her" ARI, Claire Meltzer, M97-10, 10.

51 "This was again . . . at the time" JMA, IV/10.

"If we were lucky . . . all the while" JMP, M81, 1/9, 3.

"I timidly climbed . . . three dollars to my name" JMP, M81, 1/14, 10.

52 "With a C and an O . . . copies in Colorado" JMP, M81, 1/9, 2.

"a popular resort . . . his week-end companion!" JMA, XIII/10–11.

53 "And work cheap . . . got me the job" JMA, V/5.

"amply apparent" JMP, M81, 1/9, 5.

"I told her . . . him seem small" JMA, V/3.

"the only thing . . . the real feeling" JMP, M81, 1/22, 3.

54 "Ginger, don't ever . . . as you'll let me" JMP, M81, 1/22, 11.
    "I've been around . . . can hardly be that, can they?" JMP, M81, 1/22, 13.
    "It really was a 'Rose Room' . . . a respectable temperature" JMA, VI/1.
    "A favorite joke . . . from the bathtub" JMA, V/5.
    "They showed me . . . the main attraction" JMA, V/5–6.
    "He was very nice . . . was practically bald" JMA, V/6.
    "his youthful peak . . . up the wall" JMA, V/7.

55 "perfect to these old ears . . . the last four weeks" JMP, M81, 1/22, 16.
    "under house arrest . . . let out occasionally" JMA, V/6.
    "Although I don't think . . . in a couple of months" JMP, M81, 1/22, 16.
    "But, I'm slowly writing . . . to replace his" JMP, M81, 1/22, 16.
    "Old Madame Mercer isn't used to operettas" JMP, M81, 1/22, 10.
    "I must sound . . . (for the 50th time)" JMP, M81, 1/22, 10.
    "We must be off . . . the intimate touch dropped" JMP, M81, 1/22, 19.
    "It's pretty awful . . . along behind you" JMP, M81, 1/22, 20.
    "You couldn't manage . . . hear it—from you" JMP, M81, 1/22, 20.
    " 'hair-singing' letters—Hotcha" JMP, M81, 1/22, 45.

56 "The trip has been lousy . . . the Paramount balcony" JMP, M81, 1/22, 7.
    "The land of sunshine! . . . even that excuse" JMP, M81, 1/22, 18.
    "The music is pretty . . . lyrics, of course" JMP, M81, 1/22, 17.
    "done a swell job . . . to the comedy" JMP, M81, 1/22, 21.
    "The story and voices and costuming are grand" JMP, M81, 1/22, 23.
    "Ginger, won't it be marvellous . . . for my own?" JMP, M81, 1/22, 17.
    "I have longed . . . I adore you" JMP, M81, 1/22, 24.
    "I got a wire . . . towards our yacht" JMP, M81, 1/22, 25.
    "So if you've got any dates . . . for The Colonel" JMP, M81, 1/22, 25.

57 "Everything seems to happen . . . from you so long" JMP, M81, 1/22, 27.
    "or something equally as bad . . . whole lousy world" JMP, M81, 1/22, 28.
    "I've gotten to the state . . . called a philosophy" JMP, M81, 1/22, 29.
    "Although I had left Savannah . . . come back to her" JMP, M81, 1/14, 16.
    "Even though we work . . . for *that* illusion?" JMP, M81, 1/14, 16.

58 "The announcement of the marriage . . . spend their honeymoon" *Savannah Morning News*, November 28, 1930.
    "to make her jealous really" JMA, V/7.
    "The picture is one . . . she's getting married" JMP, M81, 1/22, 21.
    "About Miss Cummins . . . candle to you" JMP, M81, 1/22, 23.
    "subconsciously made up my mind . . . say the word?" JMA, V/7.
    "Always be good . . . with you after all" JMP, M81, 1/22, 30–31.
    "I'll certainly have to . . . that night, won't I?" JMP, M81, 1/22, 31.
    "That, of course, stamps me . . . ever happened to me" JMP, M81, 1/22, 31.
    "You're probably a little bored . . . I've felt that all along" JMP, M81, 1/22, 31.

59 "John Mercer has done . . . with American lyrics" *San Francisco Chronicle*, November 12, 1930.
    "The fanfare of trumpets . . . just the same" JMP, M81, 1/22, 24.

"I'm so anxious . . . God help it" JMP, M81, 1/22, 30.

"the best song . . . ever learn it" JMA, V/7.

"As you see . . . 'I idolize you'" JMP, M81, 1/22, 36.

"I saw in *Variety* . . . (a lonely profession—really)" JMP, M81, 1/22, 31–32.

60 "I really think . . . the competition for me" JMP, M81, 1/9.

"Everything seemed so empty . . . leave the place" JMP, M81, 1/22, 37.

"I merely feel . . . roses in your room" JMP, M81, 1/22, 37.

"Really—I'm tired . . . lyric idea there" JMP, M81, 1/22, 38.

"in the most terrible mood . . . about my future" JMP, M81, 1/22, 39.

"The miller is a wreck . . . come what may" JMP, M81, 1/22, 43–44.

61 "All evening I thought of us . . . am I sweet?" JMP, M81, 1/22, 41.

"Do you feel . . . make you happy enough" JMP, M81, 1/22, 41.

"Charlie Miller wants me . . . from the door" JMP, M81, 1/22, 40.

"looked the rosiest . . . on the strength of it" JMA, V/8.

62 "Johnny was getting somewhere" ARI, Claire Meltzer, M97-10, 10.

"She was such a meek little thing" AUI, Margaret Whiting and Jack Wrangler, April 18, 2001.

"I'd have another date . . . for the evening" JMP, M81, 31/13.

"She was very self-centered" AUI, Laurel Howard, Palm Desert, Calif., May 23, 2001.

"She was, quote . . . important to her" ARI, Alan Livingston, October 3, 1996, M96-10, 15–16.

"She was a very polished . . . in the industry" AUI, Jim Corwin, Palm Desert, Calif., May 22, 2001.

"very, very simple . . . few people invited" ARI, Claire Meltzer, M97-10, 11.

"He had tears . . . the time" JMP, 1/9, 5.

"Ginger was in an accident . . . had to do it" AUI, Alan Livingston, Los Angeles, Calif., May 21, 2001. Livingston said he had heard this as a rumor but gave it credence.

4. Lazybones: 1931–1934

63 "I was, in a way, too lucky . . . such a tender age" JMA, V/14A.

"It never came . . . another unproduced smash!" JMA, V/8.

"He had nothing . . . with my grandmother" ARI, Joyce Pelphrey, M97-8, 8.

"I had 25 cents a day . . . Brooklyn for supper" JMA, V/11.

"God knows I was trying . . . be a hit" JMP, M81, 1/9, 5.

64 "Tin Pan Alley in those days . . . with various collaborators" Howard Henderson, interview, *The Best Things in Life: DeSylva, Brown & Henderson*, BBC-2 series, February 2002.

"John is a literary genius . . . these are my convictions" JMP, M81, 2/2.

65 "dream of the skullduggery . . . share of the royalties" JMA, VII/2.

"If Jolie baby . . . an unsuspecting public" JMA, VII/2.

"Then they'd go in . . . but not necessarily" JMA, VII/3.

66 "a dark-eyed, raven-haired lady . . . you ever tasted" JMA, XIII/11.

"After playing softball . . . the smoked sturgeon" JMA, V/9.

"So you see . . . our own strengths" JMA, V/9.

"money that looks like money" George McJimsey, *The Presidency of Franklin Delano Roosevelt* (Lawrence: University Press of Kansas, 2000), 175.

"evidently had faith in me . . . a foreign composer supplied" JMP, M81, 1/9, 5.

67 "Cab drivers, truck drivers, porters . . . the following day" JMP, M81, 1/9, 1.

"the best jazz musicians . . . and even toilets" Giddins, 153.

68 "heard you tonight . . . a big success" JMP, M81, 2/1.

"I had won a Pontiac Youth . . . what good was it?" JMA, V/11. The other two songs in "Sizzling One-Step Medley" were "Dinah" and "Nobody's Sweetheart." On June 23, 1932, shortly after winning the contest, he made another recording, a test-pressing, accompanied by only a piano, of "Watch a Darkie Dance," his own song, and Rodgers and Hart's "You Took Advantage of Me." These rare recordings can be heard on *Johnny Mercer: Pardon My Southern Accent* ("Happy Days" Series, Conifer Records, CDHD 203).

"demurred, hesitating because of the old . . . as had I" JMA, XIII/11–12.

"The theme was the Forgotten Man . . . It wasn't anything" Quoted in Harold Meyerson and Ernie Harburg, *Who Put the Rainbow in the Wizard of Oz?* (Ann Arbor: The University of Michigan Press, 1993), 45.

69 "In making me . . . the muse to strike" JMA, V/8.

"God, he'll sit . . . work that hard" JMP, M81, 1/15.

"I was trying . . . best in the world" JMA, XIII/11.

70 "a young, bouncy butterball . . . he could write" Hoagy Carmichael and Stephen Longstreet, *Sometimes I Wonder* (New York: Farrar, Straus & Giroux, 1965), 239.

"an understanding, sympathetic friend . . . knowledge and experience" JMA, V/12.

"He is such a gifted lyric writer . . . my best work" JMA, XIII/4.

"I gave Johnny . . . but then it stops" Quoted in Lloyd Shearer, "The Man Who Writes the Lyrics," *Cosmopolitan*, April 1946, 181.

"suffered through long months . . . lyrics of 'Thanksgivin'' " JMA, V/12.

71 "We had the first sixteen bars . . . the middle part" JMP, M82-8, 12.

"And then it must have been . . . had the verse" JMP, M82-8, 12.

72 "It took about a year . . . a long time" JMP, M82-8, 12.

" 'Lazybones' is about myself" JMA, XIV/15.

"Have you ever had . . . write with Hoagy" JMA, XIII/4.

"Georgians may be surprised . . . any shiftless countryman" *Atlanta Journal and Constitution Magazine*, April 5, 1964, 37–39.

"Nigger song . . . conform to Nazi ideals" Quoted in Richard M. Sudhalter, *Stardust Melody: The Life and Music of Hoagy Carmichael* (New York: Oxford University Press, 2002), 157.

"for laggardly implementation of various New Deal programs" Sudhalter, 156.

73 "was kind at first meeting . . . and courageous ideas" JMP, M81, 1/14.

"In show business . . . our two weeks' notice" JMA, V/12–13.

"Amos and Andy . . . the right key" JMA, V/14A.

74 "He was cute . . . little colored boy" ARI, Jean Bach, M95-14, 8.

"It was a disappointment . . . didn't handle them gently" Carmichael and Longstreet, 240.

"my helper . . . in the right spirit" Quoted in Sudhalter, 157.

"Ginger and I moved . . . played after hours" JMA, V/14.

"after working all days . . . music was good" JMA, V/10 1/2.

"Most saloons in those . . . babies to me" JMA, V/13.

"utility fielder . . . no matter how faint!" JMA, V/14.

75 "one that could have ridden . . . in movies and shows" JMA, V/10.

"too weak—and too thin! . . . of the public" JMA, V/15.

"Unlike 'show biz' kids . . . to collaborate with" JMA, V/14A.

76 "Pretty soon . . . more than that" AUI, Bob Corwin, Palm Springs, Calif., May 23, 2001.

"Youth and excitement . . . writing, writing, writing" JMA, V/16.

5. Hooray for Hollywood: 1935–1937

77 "I kept my eyes . . . talent might allow" JMA, VI/2.

79 "Can't sing. Can't act . . . bad chin line" John Mueller, *Astaire Dancing: The Musical Films* (New York: Wings Books, 1991), 7.

80 "bring in a brace . . . in nouveaux taste" JMA, VI/2.

"his triple-threat man . . . on my face" JMA, VI/2.

81 "I have seen *Old Man Rhythm* . . . that face of yours" JMP, 2–3.

"The studio gave him . . . movies ever made" JMA, VI/2.

"If he wanted me . . . rat on him" JMA, VI/3.

82 "You could see Carole Lombard . . . club and singing" JMA, VI/3–4.

"And what a thrill . . . the B pictures" JMA, VI/4.

"colored tap dancer . . . in his teeth" JMA, VI/4.

"All the great old writers . . . on those gentlemen" JMA, VII/6.

83 "some big wig . . . we'll have her" ARI, Jean Bach, M95-14, 12.

"He was the kind of person . . . character comes from" AUI, Laurel Howard.

"It was just a reaction . . . joy or comfort" AUI, Alan Livingston.

"Afterward it must . . . taste of drink" ARI, Jean Bach, M95-14, 12.

"The times when . . . it was okay" ARU, Margaret Whiting and Jack Wrangler, M95-7, 35–41.

84 "It was my good fortune . . . and she knew it" Giddins, 416.

"his slang, his ad libs" Johnny Mercer, interview, *Accentuate the Positive: The Johnny Mercer Story*.

85 "The one thing people don't . . . got a whole song down on paper" AUI, Bob Corwin.

"George chose Bessie Wheelus . . . 'Well, don't learn'" ARI, Nancy Gerard and Steve Gerard, M2001-8, 16.

"She didn't consider herself Jewish . . . upset his family" ARI, Barbara Robbins, January 22, 1998, M98-6, 16.

86 "I never heard . . . I heard about it" ARI, Nancy Gerard and Steve Gerard, M2001-8, 17.

"She was so obviously in love . . . enjoy his company" ARI, James McIntire, M97-9, 7–8.

87 "I think that some people . . . for thirty years" ARI, Pope McIntire, M97-4, 13–14.

"She would say, 'She can't even join the Oglethorpe'" AUI, Emma Kelly, Savannah, Ga., March 9, 2000.

"It was because . . . he met her" ARI, Margaret Whiting and Jack Wrangler, M95-7, 41–42.

"I really think . . . more offers after that" Bob Bach and Ginger Mercer, 56.

88 "that damn song" Bob Bach and Ginger Mercer, 54.

"It's a phrase . . . particular approach to it" JMP, M82-8, 26.

"saved me from odious . . . the rainbow's end" JMA, VI/3.

"He was a romantic . . . getting in on the creation" JMA, VII/5.

"a goodhearted man . . . lay on us!" JMA, VII/7.

89 "We would stroll . . . woodcock under glass" JMA, VII/7.

"Not only would his eyes . . . like a caress" JMA, XIII/7.

"was even worse . . . Poetry, okay. Pedantics, no" JMA, XIII/8.

90 "They pitched in . . . enthusiastic opening night" JMA, VII/8.

"There for two or three weeks . . . heather and the gorse" JMA, VII/8.

"one in the front hall, the other wedged in a second-floor window" Quoted in Gene Lees, "The Shaping of Johnny Mercer," *Jazzletter* 18, no. 6 (June 1999), 3.

91 "never work in this town again" ARI, Barbara Robbins, M98-6, 33.

"Listen, Rose, don't worry . . . you can't have" ARI, Barbara Robbins, M98-6, 32.

"I remember . . . living writing songs" SPL, Tom Buckley, "About New York: A Memorial Accentuating the Positive," *New York Times*, July 24, 1976, 13.

"Oh, he writes songs . . . for a *living*?" JMA, XII/4.

6. Too Marvelous for Words: 1937–1938

92 "I have always . . . finds the phrases" JMP, M82-8, 16–17.

"I said, 'I'd rather work with Dick Whiting than anybody'" Max Wilk, *They're Playing Our Song* (New York: Atheneum, 1973), 138.

93 "another of my idols . . . New York writers are" Wilk, 138.

"He generally tried to initiate me into the studio mystique" JMA, XIII/1.

"He had to like the melody . . . a complete collaboration" AUI, Margaret Whiting and Jack Wrangler.

94 "He was working . . . and he said, 'Onward!'" AUI, Margaret Whiting and Jack Wrangler.

95 "secure enough to . . . throw rocks at the blackbirds" JMA, VIII/1.

"Margaret Whiting . . . of the finest kind" JMA, VIII/2.

"I've just got two words . . . —grow up!" Margaret Whiting and Will Holt, *It Might As Well Be Spring: A Musical Autobiography* (New York: William Morrow, 1987), 43.

"The two people . . . fall asleep" ARI, Margaret Whiting and Jack Wrangler, M95-7, 11–13.

96 "I sweat blood . . . the paper, they're notes" Quoted in *Theatre Magazine*, February 1915.

"would wake up . . . through a table" ARI, Margaret Whiting and Jack Wrangler, M95-7, 12–13.

"An order of bacon . . . Fourth of July" Ira Gershwin, *Lyrics on Several Occasions*, 149.

"Hollywood seemed to me . . . fun of it" JMP, M82-8, 6.

97 "Oh, it really was lovely . . . we were home" JMA, VIII/4.

98 "There's old Willis . . . he is nowhere" JMP, 82-8, 18.

"were way ahead of our time, rhythmically" JMP, 82-8, 16.

99 "in one of his most playful . . . middlebrow blandness" Giddins, 516–17.

"I am really surprised . . . one of our own" JMA, IX/8.

"Ginger painted it . . . for the job!" JMA, VIII/5.

"Life in these years . . . jack of all trades" JMA, VIII/7.

"Peck's Bad Boy . . . Gotcha!" ARI, Ervin Drake, December 13, 1996, M96-14, 15–17.

100 "the lowest form of animal life" Wilk, 125.

Brothers . . . you're late . . . And it's shit!" JMA, VIII/2–3.

"always feeling the veins . . . his nitro pills" JMA, VIII/1–2.

"You really stink as a singer" Quoted in Gene Lees, "A Death in the Family: The Rise and Fall of the American Song, Part Two," *Jazzletter* 11, no. 3 (March 1992), 6.

101 "I'll write you a new song . . . from this melody" Roy Hemming, *The Melody Lingers On: The Great Songwriters and Their Movie Musicals* (New York: Newmarket Press, 1986), 272.

102 "an uneasy division of the lyric writing between them" Hemming, 277.

"Al Dubin, unable to cope . . . it was granted" Hemming, 277.

7. Day In—Day Out: 1938–1940

105 "You have to write . . . let it grow" SPL, Bill Gans, "The Mercer Who Shows Mercy," n.d., 3.

"His was not . . . improvising variations" Dave Dexter Jr., liner notes, *Sweet Georgia Brown*, Hindsight Records, HCD-152.

106 "cutouts to display her buttocks" Giddins, 461.

"It was all . . . too well rehearsed" Ginger Mercer, interview, *Accentuate the Positive: The Johnny Mercer Story*.

"Ginger's idol movie star . . . somebody she knew" ARI, Pope McIntire, M97-4, 12–13.

107 "dazzled the audience . . . summer's most amusing ditty" Giddins, 463.

"crepe sole white wooden sneakers . . . with snow" AUI, Howie Richmond, Rancho Mirage, Calif., May 22, 2001.

108 "George Washington surveyed it . . . He WPA-ed it . . ." *Camel Caravan*, CBS Radio Network, March 14, 1939.

"a typewriter . . . ready to do that evening" ARI, Margaret Whiting and Jack Wrangler, M95-7, 21.

"all these little towns . . . in the dark" JMP, M82-8, 27.

109 "easy to write with . . . any idea on him" JMA, XIII/7.

"If you play . . . talk to you again" Johnny Mercer, interview, *Accentuate the Positive: The Johnny Mercer Story*.

110 "kind of a Gershwinesque tune" JMP, M82-8, 28. The melody was based on "Die Stille Bulgar," which was recorded by Harry Candell's Orchestra in 1919 (*Accentuate the Positive: The Johnny Mercer Story*, BBC-2 series, April 2002).

111 "You're Getting Practically Poetic . . . iron is hot" Ginger Mercer and Bob Bach, 68.
"I think it's one . . . kind of tune" JMP, M82-8, 30.
"Imagine that . . . half of the Hit Parade!" JMA, VIII/8.

113 "on the basis . . . as countrywide networks" David Ewen, *All the Years of American Popular Music* (Englewood Cliffs, N.J.: Prentice-Hall, 1978), 303.

114 "We all liked the score . . . songs much exposure" Hoagy Carmichael and Stephen Longstreet, 265.
"Jake Shubert got under . . . did I misspell it?" Hoagy Carmichael and Stephen Longstreet, 265.

115 "hangs around the neck . . . simple and light-hearted" *New York Times*, June 5, 1940.
"He worked on it . . . one-on-one" Giddins, 542.
"Sounds like Johnny Burke" AUI, Bob Corwin.

116 "real, old timey blues . . . top of his head" ARI, Jean Bach, M95-14, 4.
"That just knocked him out . . . into something entertaining" ARI, Jean Bach, M95-14, 5.
"Outside of a few quotes . . . back again to Los Angeles" JMA, VIII/8.
"kind of melancholia . . . where he wanted to get" ARI, Nancy and Steve Gerard, M2001-8, 11.
"I also felt . . . too inarticulate to say" JMP, M81, 1/14, 3–5.
"I had seen . . . to the contrary" JMA, VIII/9.

117 "Amanda was just beautiful . . . a little devil" ARI, Joyce Pelphrey, M97-8, 21.
"would get babies . . . out of jail' " AUI, Joyce Pelphrey, Atlanta, Ga., September 7, 2002.

8. Blues in the Night: 1940–1941

118 "You notice I haven't mentioned . . . I'm a private person" JMA, XII-4.

119 "I'd come into the office . . . rhumba, and fox trot" JMA, XIII/7.

120 "Bing and Johnny . . . mixed with jazz" Ginger Mercer and Bob Bach, 94.
"small but wonderful . . . process of time" JMA, VII/6.

121 "I never cried . . . released that afternoon" JMA, VIII/7.
"in September, 1939 . . . G. A. Mercer, Age 72" Quoted in Bob Bach and Ginger Mercer, 86.
"went off to Palm Springs . . . senior prom corsage" Phil Silvers and Robert Saffron, *This Laugh Is on Me: The Phil Silvers Story* (Englewood Cliffs, N.J.: Prentice-Hall, 1973), 171–72.
" 'I spotted you then . . . falling in love with you for years' " AUI, Jean Bach, New York, December 17, 2001.

123 "And they're dancing . . . like young love" AUI, Jean Bach.
"She was at last in love . . . it was not Rose" David Shipman, *Judy Garland: The Secret Life of an American Legend* (New York: Hyperion, 1992), 118.
"a deep, deep respect . . . integrity of talent" JMP, M81, 1/15, 3.
"Watching you before the mirrors . . . until the next day" JMP, M81, 15/74.

124 "My ear still rings . . . across the sky" JMP, M81, 15/74.

125 "What's going on . . . got to stop" AUI, Jean Bach.

"You marry once . . . stuck with it" AUI, Bob Corwin.

126 "Why do you . . . I might as well drink' " AUI, Jean Bach.

"Harold went off . . . so did I" Harold Meyerson and Ernie Harburg, 163.

"I went home . . . every other blues song" Quoted in William Zinsser, "Harold Arlen: The Secret Music Maker," *Harper's*, May 1960, 44–45.

129 "Johnny took it . . . made it work" *The Fred Astaire Story: His Life, His Films, His Friends* (London: B.B.C., 1975).

"Our working habits . . . with the completed lyrics" SPL, Gans, 3.

130 "only an occasional difference of opinion" JMA, XIII/5.

"I don't understand your music" AUI, Edward Jablonski, New York, December 16, 2001.

"I couldn't write it . . . half an hour" JMP, M82-8, 12.

"I had shown . . . at the telephone and listen" Carmichael and Longstreet, 285.

131 "His heart . . . have a home" AUI, Ann Mercer Klein.

"I wrote it . . . wrote this song" AUI, Quoted from Emma Kelly by Julius Hornstein, Savannah, Ga., March 10, 2000.

9. Ac-cent-tchu-ate the Positive: 1941–1944

133 "Needless to say . . . They really beamed" JMA, IX/7.

"It had finally . . . The first bomb scare!" JMA, IX/6.

134 "he sat down . . . in a couple of minutes" Ginger Mercer and Bob Bach, 131.

135 "I didn't like the serious songs" JMP, M82-8, 32.

"the only thing . . . the morning on Tuesday" ARI, Ginny Mancini, M96-4, 2.

"I wish I had a recording of that" ARI, Ginny Mancini, M96-4, 2.

"I used to ask . . . a radio program" JMP, M81, 1/15.

136 "electrical genius" JMA, IX/1.

"Because he had a liking . . . no record company out in California of note" ARI, Michael Goldsen, January 20, 1998, M98-3, 2.

"there were too many poor arrangements . . . in the business" Maria Cole and Louie Robinson, *Nat King Cole* (New York: William Morrow, 1971), 46.

"So Buddy came in . . . the darn company" ARI, Michael Goldsen, M98-3, 3.

137 " 'How awful!' I said . . . 'it was carrying shellac' " Whiting and Holt, 53.

"Because of Glenn Wallichs' ability . . . augment Johnny's taste" ARI, Michael Goldsen, M98-3, 3.

138 "The number was . . . without being dirty" Ginger Mercer and Bob Bach, 105.

"Oh, the hell . . . No, you can't" Margaret Whiting, interview, *Accentuate the Positive: The Johnny Mercer Story*.

"Capitol had enough things . . . record union musicians" AUI, Fred Grimes, Huntington Beach, Calif., May 20, 2001.

139 "And that's why . . . protected by him" ARI, Bill Harbach, M96-1, 35–36.

"The words don't . . . I don't read music" JMP, M82-8, 33.

"I don't care . . . is the one" ARI, Margaret Whiting and Jack Wrangler, M95-7, 21.

140 "This is where he was brilliant" ARI, Margaret Whiting and Jack Wrangler, M95-7, 28.

"Now describe spring . . . think of the images" Whiting and Holt, 66.

"They really cared . . . a quality audio product" ARI, Billy May, M96-11, 13.

141 "because of the phenomenal sound . . . before the Civil War" Whiting and Holt, 59–60.

"During the war . . . that was so rigorous" AUI, Fred Grimes.

"So I was really kind of proud . . . he started to cry" ARI, Billy May, M96-11, 4.

142 "No man could have had . . . all the more appealing" Dave Dexter Jr., liner notes for *Johnny Mercer: Sweet Georgia Brown*, Hindsight Records, CD-152.

"I thought I could change the world" AUI, Ervin Drake, Great Neck, N.Y., December 16, 2001.

"is a businessman . . . he couldn't do it" ARI, Ervin Drake, M96-14, 5–6.

"In a business . . . insisted on it" Gene Lees, "The Making of Johnny Mercer," *Woodberry Forest Magazine and Journal*, winter-spring 1999, 22.

"He was writing like crazy then" ARI, Ervin Drake, M96-14, 4.

143 "offbeat little rhythm . . . into my mind" JMP, M82-8, 15. According to other accounts, Mercer attributed the title phrase to a sermon by Harlem's Father Divine.

"With a beginning . . . practically wrote itself" *Newsweek*, January 29, 1945, 86.

"It was like getting . . . more or less complete" JMP, M81, 1/15.

"It must have pleased . . . saw him smile" Quoted in David Ewen, *Great Men of American Popular Song* (Englewood Cliffs, N.J.: Prentice-Hall, 1972), 256.

"Harold's melodies are way out . . . the bottom of his feet" Zinsser, 44–45.

144 "quick, probably irascible, and rather conceited" JMA, XIII/14.

"He was a great stickler . . . in the music" *The Fred Astaire Story*, 29.

145 "He gave you . . . to work with" JMA, XIII/7.

"I don't know . . . Latin flavor, the melody" JMP, M82-8, 31.

"And you didn't have to ask" Quoted in Bob Bach and Ginger Mercer, 119.

146 "We were doing . . . unusual for me" Bob Bach and Ginger Mercer, 132.

"cop it . . . with the melody" JMP, M82-8, 8.

"liked the chords" JMP, M82-8, 8.

"Johnny seemed dissatisfied . . . the theme song?" Bob Bach and Ginger Mercer, 132.

147 "I said, 'Gee, Dave' . . . a national—worldwide—hit" ARI, Michael Goldsen, M98-3, 6–7.

"too black" Gene Lees, "The Shaping of Johnny Mercer, Part Five," *Jazzletter* 18, no. 10 (October 1999), 6.

"the most popular colored singer on the radio" Bob Bach and Ginger Mercer, 123.

"the greatest Rhythm . . . I've ever heard" Bob Bach and Ginger Mercer, 179.

" 'Man' more *Spades* love you that you have *no idea*" Bob Bach and Ginger Mercer, 215.

"five nights a week . . . on the second show" ARI, Ray Evans and Jay Livingston, M96-5, 2.

148 "Johnny hated that song . . . didn't record it" ARI, Ray Evans and Jay Livingston, M96-5, 19.

"He had the chutzpah to turn it down" AUI, Ray Evans, Los Angeles, Calif., May 17, 2001.

"We had Johnny . . . make us scrambled eggs" ARI, Ray Evans and Jay Livingston, M96-5, 11–13.

"Why don't you . . . write a song?" AUI, Jay Livingston, Los Angeles, Calif., May 17, 2001.

"I hate your brother's ass!" AUI, Jay Livingston.

"Hey, why don't you play us a medley of your *hit*!" AUI, David Holt, telephone interview, August 20, 2002.

"Johnny was never . . . a memorable, happy period" Quoted by Dave Dexter Jr., liner notes, *Johnny Mercer: Sweet Georgia Brown*.

149 "Well, Irving, you couldn't . . . Good night" AUI, Bill Harbach, telephone interview, July 27, 2002. Harbach did not witness the exchange himself but heard about it from others.

10. Come Rain or Come Shine: 1944–1948

150 "I seem to . . . match the mood" JMP, M81, 1/15.

"DEAR JOHNNY . . . HOP ON IT RIGHT AWAY" Bob Bach and Ginger Mercer, 139. According to Raksin, director Otto Preminger initially wanted to use "Summertime" as the film's theme song, then, when Ira Gershwin refused permission, "Sophisticated Lady," by Mitchell Parish and Duke Ellington. When Raksin asked Preminger why he wanted those songs, the director explained that the film's main character was "a whore." Raksin then pleaded for the opportunity to write his own theme song and was given the weekend to create the melody for "Laura." David Raksin, interview, *Too Marvelous for Words: A Musical Tribute to Johnny Mercer*, KGIU-FM, Los Angeles, California, n.d.

151 "It was an . . . reserve and charm" David Raksin, interview, *Too Marvelous for Words*.

"I hadn't seen . . . atmosphere for me" JMP, M81, 1/15.

152 "I thought Johnny's . . . his little finger" David Raksin, interview, *Too Marvelous for Words*.

"favorite song—among those he didn't write" JMA, XIV/19.

155 "young women of good character . . . described in song" Hugh Fordin, *M-G-M's Greatest Musicals: The Arthur Freed Unit* (New York: Da Capo Press, 1996), 154.

"Cloud Boy . . . Oh, Ginger's fine" JMA, XIII/2.

156 "I thought it had a nice, lyrical quality to it" SPL, *Atlanta Journal*, August 24, 1945.

"like Stephen Vincent Benét says . . . just the right tune for it" JMP, M82-8, 7–8.

"It was an easy one . . . about an hour" SPL, *Atlanta Journal*, August 24, 1945.

"wanted to clarify . . . doing just that" Fordin, 154.

"And when they were . . . I wrote that junk" ARI, Margaret Whiting and Jack Wrangler, M95-7, 14.

157 "It's done . . . It's wonderful" ARI, Hugh Fordin, M95-12/7.

"Italian and everything . . . he is clannish" JMA, XIII/3.

158 "smash story" JMA, X/4.

"It was a fantastic one . . . take the part" Lena Horne and Richard Schickel, *Lena* (Garden City, N.Y.: Doubleday, 1965), 187.

159 "people representing the Negro órganizations . . . in my career" Horne and Schickel, 188.

"Freed insisted that I tell him . . . advising me not to take" Horne and Schickel, 189.

"We sat in the room . . . he sang his heart" Pearl Bailey interview, *Too Marvelous for Words*.

160 "I myself am immodest . . . a colored musical" JMA, X/4.

"Just fine, Mr. Mercer . . . hat is home" Margaret Whiting interview, *Too Marvelous for Words*.

161 "Come hell or high water? . . . I think of that?" Quoted in Ted Mercer, "Johnny Mercer Talks About Songwriting," *Songwriter's Review*, August 1966, 5.

"Exquisite as this lyric is . . . exuberant and spontaneous" Martin Gottfried, *Broadway Musicals* (New York: Harry N. Abrams, 1979), 66, 254.

" 'Come Rain or Come Shine' is beautifully written . . . propulsion on stage" Mark Steyn, *Broadway Babies Say Goodnight: Musicals Then and Now* (New York: Routledge, 1999), 115.

162 "Both Johnny and Harold . . . so it worked" Whiting and Holt, 88–89.

"I had learned it . . . such a thing" Whiting and Holt, 89.

"Everything would be lovely . . . does not do" NYPL, Robert Garland, " 'St. Louis Woman' Opens at Martin Beck Theatre," NYPL, *New York Journal American*, April 1, 1946.

163 "But we can't . . . have anything, can we?' " JMA, X/5.

"John got upset . . . put it out" ARI, Billy May, M96-11, 11.

"he wanted the small little company . . . make it' " ARI, Billy May, M96-11, 22.

"Now, I tried . . . I never met Johnny" AUI, Alan Livingston.

164 "I sat down . . . a smash hit" AUI, Alan Livingston.

"And Johnny still . . . off a bit" AUI, Alan Livingston.

"He worked very, very informally . . . eating a sandwich" ARI, Alan Livingston, M96-10, 8–9.

"That was no problem . . . he *was* Capitol Records, period" ARI, Alan Livingston, M96-10, 10.

165 "Mercer's great talent . . . his contribution was tremendous" ARI, Alan Livingston, M96-10, 5.

"He'd walk in . . . never talk like that" ARI, Alan Livingston, M96-10, 22.

"Johnny brought in Nat Cole . . . one of Capitol's major artists" AUI, Alan Livingston.

"And Johnny said . . . the one that pinpointed it" ARI, M96-10, 7.

"Johnny was an alcoholic . . . and his advice" ARI, Alan Livingston, M96-10, 3.

"he became insulting . . . to *talk* to you" AUI, Alan Livingston.

"used the drinking . . . I know she hurt" ARI, Margaret Whiting and Jack Wrangler, M95-7, 38–39.

"Johnny could be very sweet . . . not very nice to her" ARI, Alan Livingston, M96-10, 15–16.

"There was one occasion . . . which she did" ARI, Alan Livingston, M96-10, 16–17.

166 "'Johnny, before you' . . . And Johnny laughed" ARI, Alan Livingston, M96-10, 3.

"He was very generous . . . badly about it" AUI, Alan Livingston.

"After a while . . . as a writer and a performer" ARI, Michael Goldsen, M98-3, 4.

"When they started the company . . . so Glenn Wallichs became president" AUI, Alan Livingston.

"He was never businesslike . . . no question about that" ARI, Alan Livingston, M96-10.

"Nobody nudged him out. . . . He just wanted this plaything" AUI, Alan Livingston.

167 "John got upset . . . the wrong way" ARI, Billy May, M96-11, 11.

"A couple of times . . . 'in the first place?'" ARI, Billy May, M96-11, 22.

"And when we moved up there . . . sitting in that office" AUI, Alan Livingston.

"He abruptly walked away . . . the company's direction" Dave Dexter Jr., liner notes, *Johnny Mercer: Sweet Georgia Brown.*

"And everybody wanted to know . . . head of the company" ARI, Michael Goldsen, M98-3, 4.

11. Autumn Leaves: 1949–1952

168 "If everything . . . to blow anything" JMA, X/7–8.

"It should have . . . we weren't better known" JMA, X/7.

169 "*Time*style . . . against the English language" *Commonweal*, December 16, 1949, 293.

"Most of the music . . . cheerful-looking show" *New York Times*, November 26, 1949, 10.

"I suggested that we bring in . . . do Uncle Miltie" Silvers and Saffron, 176.

"I knew every flip . . . he found them" Silvers and Saffron, 176–77.

"Milton, it's about . . . guys just like that" Silvers and Saffron, 178.

"I heard a dog . . . high, unearthly *ooooooowwwww*" Silvers and Saffron, 173.

170 "When I'm blue . . . buy a *cat!*" Silvers and Saffron, 179.

"there had to be something good in him if a dog loved him" Silvers and Saffron, 180.

"The whole bit . . . never did it again" Silvers and Saffron, 183.

"pee-in-your-pants funny" AUI, Laurel Howard.

"Phil Silvers finds himself . . . any one thing" NYPL, *New York Journal American*, November 2, 1951.

"The brilliant Johnny Mercer . . . worthy of him last evening" NYPL, *New York Post*, November 2, 1951.

"There is nothing beyond . . . this point of view" NYPL, *New York Times*, November 2, 1951.

"Something about the show . . . he'd say 'Okay'" AUI, Sheldon Harnick, New York, August 13, 2002.

171 "He was mixing . . . drink next to him" AUI, Sheldon Harnick.

"She had come back . . . the same city with Judy" Silvers and Saffron, 182.

"The Palladium experience . . . the terrible, wonderful test" Gerald Clarke, *Get*

Happy: The Life of Judy Garland (New York: Random House, 2000), 294.

"Listen, Judy's opening . . . do some songs" Clarke, 294.

"She sat on the coffee table . . . back to the song" AUI, Jean Bach.

172 "It was a happening" AUI, Bill Harbach.

"This was a funny apartment . . . 'overrides these conditions?'" AUI, Jean Bach.

"I need to lose . . . My feet hurt" Gerold Frank, *Judy* (New York: Harper & Row, 1975), 335.

"She just brushed me off . . . all her life" Clarke, 312.

"My mother's a fucking riveter . . . good for her" Clarke, 312.

173 "How could she . . . broke, angry, and alone?" Clarke, 312.

"Why did you . . . that everyone left" Clarke, 313.

"As the age . . . your market is" AUI, Fred Grimes.

"Eventually it occurs . . . knowledge of that instrument" Steve Allen, unpublished interview. I wish to thank Jan Glazier for providing me with this excerpt of her interview with Steve Allen.

"He had an insecurity . . . didn't feel that way" ARI, Alan Livingston, M96-10, 11–12.

174 "Rock came along . . . no market for them" ARI, M96-10, 12.

"We aren't greedy . . . the 'flip side'" JMA, XIII/6–7.

"Johnny was so easygoing . . . a patsy for composers" AUI, Alan Livingston.

"Paul Weston used to say . . . up in the morning" ARI, Ray Evans and Jay Livingston, M96-5, 18.

"He had a lot of people . . . song for him" ARI, Billy May, M96-11, 8.

"He never inserted himself . . . not his nature" ARI, Alan Livingston, M96-10, 6.

"He was not aggressive . . . anything about it" ARI, Alan Livingston M96-10, 18–21.

"Johnny never lived up to . . . who he was, ever" ARI, Alan Livingston, M96-10, 20–21.

175 "I don't think Johnny . . . had a best friend" ARI, Alan Livingston, M96-10, 20.

"So he got back . . . made a deal" ARI, Michael Goldsen, M98-3, 12.

"So I gave him the lyric . . . hadn't written it" ARI, Michael Goldsen, M98-3, 12.

"So I drove up . . . 'Here it is'" ARI, Michael Goldsen, M98-3, 13.

"And he wrote it . . . so, so Mercerish" ARI, Michael Goldsen, M98-3, 14.

176 "The falling leaves . . . smiles and thanks life" I am grateful to Kathleen Johnson for providing me with this translation.

177 "It's all right . . . it's very original" JMP, M82-8, 13.

"His talent was number one . . . didn't think much of" ARI, Alan Livingston, M96-10, 21–22.

"This was also an Edith Piaf . . . 'I really feel it'" ARI, Michael Goldsen, M98-3, 14–15.

"In other words . . . a girl's lyric" ARI, Michael Goldsen, M98-3, 16.

178 "It seemed to me . . . as a boy" JMP, 82-8, 34.

179 "How do you do it? . . . a lyric in it" AUI, Quoted by Julius Hornstein in author's interview.

"'You know something . . . big the song was" ARI, Michael Goldsen, M98-3, 14.

12. I'm Old Fashioned: 1952–1954

180 "When I lived at the beach . . . especially the ocean" "Johnny Mercer, the Bard from Savannah," *ASCAP Today*, September 1971, 10.

"Johnny got very attached . . . was very unassuming" ARI, Joyce Pelphrey, M97-8, 15.

"The neighbors started selling . . . refused to move" ARI, Joyce Pelphrey, M97-8, 16.

"Finally, I think . . . get that house moved" ARI, Joyce Pelphrey, M97-8, 16.

181 "They sawed it in half . . . ten miles an hour" ARI, Robert Rush, January 20, 1998, M98-2, 29.

"He was the same way . . . 'I like this car'" ARI, Joyce Pelphrey, M97-8, 16.

"What happened was . . . Hollywood setting" ARI, Amanda Néder and Jim Corwin, October 5, 1996, M96-12, 7–8.

"My mother didn't really care for it down there" AUI, Jeff Mercer, telephone interview, July 24, 2002.

"He loved to bodysurf . . . at Huntington Beach" AUI, Jeff Mercer.

"I used to paint . . . the trees and paint" SPL, "Johnny Mercer, the Bard from Savannah," 10.

"He loved to go to the bay . . . with a tire tube" ARI, Michael Goldsen, M98-3, 21.

182 "'You know, Johnny' . . . that kind of guy" ARI, Michael Goldsen, M98-3, 21.

"He was not a good father . . . and loving father" AUI, Laurel Howard.

"'Daddy's asleep.' . . . 'He's writing songs'" AUI, Amanda Néder, Palm Desert, Calif., May 22, 2001.

"What do you think . . . you're my public" AUI, Amanda Néder.

"He pursued it . . . was his life" ARI, Amanda Néder and Jim Corwin, M96-12, 27.

183 "You're famous to . . . famous to me" Amanda Néder, interview, *Accentuate the Positive: The Johnny Mercer Story*.

"He baby-sat me . . . go do his work" AUI, Amanda Mercer Néder.

"I was, I guess . . . in the movies" ARI, Amanda Néder and Jim Corwin, M96-12, 6.

"So he takes me . . . be in it, right?" ARI, Amanda Néder and Jim Corwin, M96-12, 17.

"I'd say, 'Daddy, let's go . . . so you sit down'" ARI, Amanda Néder and Jim Corwin, M98-12, 22–23.

"one of the things . . . at the table except Johnny" AUI, Bob Corwin.

"Of course . . . 'this is what we're doing'" ARI, Amanda Néder and Jim Corwin, M96-12, 27.

184 "my big crush . . . thrilling thing in my life" ARI, Amanda Néder and Jim Corwin, M96-12, 15.

"They would fight . . . 'Didn't you know?'" ARI, Barbara Robbins, M98-6, 16–17.

"He just adored . . . spoiled us all to death" ARI, Amanda Néder and Jim Corwin, M96-12, 38.

"Ginger *thought* she was a very down-to-earth . . . they had *no* car" AUI, Joyce Pelphery, Atlanta, Ga., September 7, 2002.

"I remember all the people . . . have her massage" AUI, Nancy and Steve Gerard.

"sweet and patient spirit . . . drop it on you" AUI, Amanda Néder.

185 "It wasn't anything . . . might have been problematic" AUI, Jim Council, telephone interview, March 30, 2002.

"Mandy did a complete . . . she was just rebelling" ARI, Robert Rush, M98-2, 30.

"Even my mom . . . dedication to marriage" AUI, Nickie Wright, Palm Springs, Calif., May 23, 2001.

"I remember peeking out . . . 'she wasn't mine'" AUI, Nickie Wright.

"Loving. He was . . . my life—his love" Amanda Néder interview, *Accentuate the Positive: The Johnny Mercer Story*, BBC-2 series, April 2002.

186 "I don't like to talk about my mom" AUI Amanda Mercer Néder.

"It was a rough . . . He had a rough one" AUI, Laurel Howard.

"Neither of them . . . only eight years old" AUI, Nancy and Steve Gerard.

"Johnny wasn't sure . . . He cut 'em off" AUI, Nick Mamalakis.

"He was a grandfather . . . sometimes you can't turn it off" AUI, Jeff Mercer.

187 "He played golf . . . just his ego" AUI, Jeff Mercer.

"My father was always pretty . . . freaked out the maids and things" AUI, Jeff Mercer.

"caught Jeff feeding . . . anything like that" ARI, Joyce Pelphrey, M97-8, 27.

"When I got rid of the alligators . . . and was gone" AUI, Jeff Mercer.

"'Can't you imagine' . . . tell them about Hollywood" ARI, Joyce Pelphrey, M97-8, 7.

188 "I found a lion . . . going to have to go" AUI, Jeff Mercer.

"Fred Harvey used to run . . . he'd scribble it down" AUI, Jeff Mercer.

"He was a generous tipper . . . when I was an adult" AUI, Jeff Mercer.

189 "She was totally opposite . . . and a straw hat" ARI, Robert Rush, M98-2, 19.

"Who are these . . . before in my life" ARI, Robert Rush, M98-1, 21.

"They argued and argued . . . 'going to miss him'" ARI, Robert Rush, M98-2, 33.

"she was money-hungry" AUI, Miriam Center, Savannah, Ga., March 9, 2000.

"In a marriage . . . there is anything" AUI, Laurel Howard.

"Ginger began an affair" ARI, Barbara Robbins, quoting Penny Singleton, M98-6, 11.

190 "And so we're having drinks . . . the way Johnny lived" ARI, Michael Goldsen, M98-3, 22.

"Johnny was commuting, which is insane" ARI, Robert Rush, M98-2, 29.

"My father heard the song and loved it" AUI, Frank Capra Jr., Wilmington, N.C. May 1, 2002.

191 "At the time . . . was robbed'" Bob Bach and Ginger Mercer, 98.

"I went one day . . . into the fireplace" ARI, Nancy and Steve Gerard, M2001-8, 7–8.

192 "the Fairy Unit . . . virile of all musicals" Hirschorn, 342.

"*Seven Brides* . . . turned out to be" Jane Powell, interview, *Too Marvelous for Words*.

"He's shy and . . . isn't too prolific" JMP, M81, 1/15.

"There was a . . . such poignant songs" Jane Powell, interview, *Too Marvelous for Words*.

"*Seven Brides* was an enjoyable . . . music to match" JMP, M81, 1/15.

194 "imbued the film with a balletic quality . . . masculine 'feel' of the piece" Hirschorn, 342.

13. Something's Gotta Give: 1954–1956

195 "I never force things . . . twist its arm" JMP, M81, 1/15.

197 "furiously fast and funny" NYPL *New York Daily Mirror*, November 16, 1956.

"The best girlesk . . . Busty, Boy-Bait" JMP, M81, 32/9.

"Whether characters who are full-fashioned . . . a big Broadway show" JMP, M81, 32/9.

"does not have the lightness . . . Kapp's cartoon drawings" NYPL, *New York Times*, November 25, 1956, sec. 2, p. 1.

198 "hated being around . . . of charming things" Quoted in ARI, Margaret Whiting and Jack Wrangler, M95-7, 20–21.

"Would you like . . . I ever saw!" AUI, confidential interview, Santa Monica, Calif., May 21, 2001.

"She always, you know . . . kind of babied him" ARI, Joyce Pelphrey, M97-8, 19.

"Miss Lillian . . . lovefests" ARI, Nick Mamalakis, M97-6, 8.

"When he would come . . . But that was Johnny" AUI, Nick Mamalakis.

199 "the party of the century . . . 'It's *Johnny*' " AUI, Miriam Center.

"He would visit . . . honorable issues of life" ARI, Nick Mamalakis, M97-6, 20–21.

"already behind him . . . into the past" F. Scott Fitzgerald, *The Great Gatsby* (New York: Scribner's, 1925), 182.

200 "I don't know . . . the next day" JMP, M82-8, 13.

201 "Dear Johnny . . . getting the hits" JMP, M81, 2/9.

"Loesser passed me at the turn" AUI, quoted by Ervin Drake, Great Neck, N.Y., December 15, 2001.

"This is Johnny Mercer . . . I love it" ARI, Margaret Whiting and Jack Wrangler, M95-7/16. In other accounts, Mercer said he was driving between his home in Palm Springs and Los Angeles.

202 "I know of no lyric . . . a natural union" Ken Barnes, liner notes, *Johnny Mercer, Singer, Songwriter*.

"It was a jazz tune . . . Rhythmical, you know" JMP, M82-8, 10.

"I've seen Sequoia . . . believe my eyes" JMP, M81, 8/44.

"I don't even know . . . it wasn't used" JMP, M82-8, 9.

"Sounds like Gershwin to me" AUI, Edward Jablonski.

203 "I liked the first version better" AUI, Marilyn and Alan Bergman, Los Angeles, Calif., May 12, 1997.

"You know, this is . . . can compare them" JMP, M82-8, 9–10.

"Johnny not only matched . . . but people" ARI, Ervin Drake, 14.

204 "I'm not going to do any of that crap" Quoted in Will Friedwald, *Sinatra! The Song Is You* (New York: Scribner, 1995), 188.

"Hey, I just fired Columbia" Friedwald, 198.

"You would?" AUI, Alan Livingston.

"A Johnny Mercer lyric . . . love you ever lost" Quoted in Jay Cocks, "Put Your Dreams Away," *Time*, May 25, 1998, 70.

"EMI came along . . . to buy Capitol" AUI, Alan Livingston.

"the oldest record trademark in Europe, dating back to 1898" Russell Sanjek,

American Popular Music and Its Business (New York: Oxford University Press, 1988), 244.

205 "Recordings of American origin . . . of the American market" Sanjek, 377.

"When EMI came along . . . big profit for everybody" AUI, Alan Livingston.

"Mrs. DeSylva had lost Buddy . . . great—great company" JMP, M82-10/4.

"Glenn, I think, retained . . . didn't want it" AUI, Alan Livingston.

"To complete the negotiation . . . companies of $8.5 million" Sanjek, 376.

"This means . . . finish the tower" AUI, Fred Grimes.

206 "He brought it . . . 'It's your money'" ARI, Barbara Robbins, M98-6, 19.

"I was in conference . . . give Johnny the figure" JMP, 99-6, 2.

"From the tone . . . of many individuals" JMP, M81, 2/4.

"I figured he had . . . of the company" *Atlanta Journal*, August 14, 1955, 10.

207 "Shortly thereafter on another . . . forgot to sign it!'" JMP, M99/6, 3.

"That's Johnny," George Hunt reflected. "The best-hearted boy in the world, but absent-minded." Quoted in Jablonski, liner notes, 3.

"After Hunt's departure . . . keeping that letter" JMP, M99/6, 3.

When I looked . . . with the heart" ARI, Nick Mamalakis, M97-6, 16–17.

"I made out . . . other of them" Quoted in Jablonski, liner notes, 3.

"He agreed and told me . . . 'has blinded me'" *Atlanta Journal*, August 14, 1955, 10.

"It's just a family affair . . . my brothers, and myself" JMP, M81, 2/5.

208 "simply the act . . . dark of the night" SPL, n.d.

"No doubt your most . . . one of your tunes" JMP, M81, 2/6.

"You've restored my faith . . . beautiful gesture" ARI, Bill Harbach, M96-1, 22–23.

"'Now, what do you want' . . . write it down" ARI, Nick Mamalakis, M97-6, 17–18.

209 "He asked us . . . in honor of his father" ARI, Nick Mamalakis, M97-6, 18.

"We built a brand-new building . . . Mark it paid'" ARI, Nick Mamalakis, M97-6, 18–19.

14. Midnight Sun: 1957–1962

210 "Music is a life enhancer . . . as the music played" JMA, XVI/3.

211 "through a rather . . . just—wasn't there" ARI, Ginny Mancini, M96-4, 4.

212 "As I understand it . . . act of friendship" AUI, Sheldon Harnick.

"the decision that saves you . . . and labor saved" JMA, X/9-9A.

"if Morton Da Costa . . . you can't write" Quoted in Andrew Velez, liner notes for *Saratoga*, RCA Victor 09026-63690-2.

"John would be there . . . up to that point" AUI, Edward Jablonski.

"the book was twenty years behind . . . and out-of-date book" JMA, X/9.

"bowed out . . . his movie studio" Velez, 8.

213 "With a cast . . . show was unwieldy" Velez, 10.

"Edna Ferber was right there . . . what she says" AUI, Natalie Core, Santa Monica, Calif., May 21, 2001.

"swishiness" AUI, Edward Jablonski.

"It was all for the gays . . . never looked at each other" ARI, Barbara Robbins, M98-6, 31.

"In truth, Morton had never felt . . . to Johnny to make" Velez, 11.

"I'm convinced most hit . . . respect of the others, to decide" JMA, X/2–3.

214 "We opened in Philadelphia . . . You just keep going" Velez, 10.

"because if something . . . 'I like to write'" AUI, Natalie Core.

"He was with *Saratoga* . . . I was working" AUI, Sheldon Harnick.

"Do you want to go . . . prayers of thanksgiving" ARI, Nick Mamalakis, M97-6, 4–5.

215 "The show had a fabulous cast . . . matched upholstery material" Velez, 11–12.

"He asked me . . . drowned his sorrows" ARI, Pope McIntire, M97-4, 2–3.

"Give Mr. Da Costa a script . . . an uninteresting show" NYPL, *New York Times*, December 8, 1959, 59.

"I don't think . . . goes to bat" Velez, 9.

"I thought my work . . . mediocre and unimaginative lyric" JMA, X/9A.

"Though a first-class composer . . . much chance of success" Gottfried, 253–54.

216 "Why don't you invite the whole world?" AUI, Nancy and Steve Gerard.

"Stop it, Johnny, I don't want any more of your fucking roses" Quoted by Gene Lees, interview, *Accentuate the Positive: The Johnny Mercer Story*.

"All of a sudden . . . 'wants me anymore'" AUI, Margaret Whiting and Jack Wrangler.

"background writers . . . work after that" ARI, Ray Evans and Jay Livingston, M96-5, 32–35.

217 "That's how we . . . to Henry Mancini" ARI, Ray Evans and Jay Livingston, M96-5, 32.

"I do believe . . . wonderful lyric to it" ARI, Ginny Mancini, M96-4, 3–4.

"'Hank, who's going' . . . he went home" Henry Mancini with Gene Lees, *Did They Mention the Music?* (Chicago: Contemporary Books, 1989), 99.

218 "I'm Holly . . . Wherever I roam" JMP, M82-8, 8.

219 "Well, you ought to because you're the 'huckleberry friend'" Quoted in Bob Bach and Ginger Mercer, 6.

"Gee, I don't know . . . keep 'huckleberry friend' in" Whiting and Holt, 235–36.

"I don't know . . . song can go" *An Evening with Johnny Mercer*.

220 "Let me see . . . I like those shoes" AUI, Laurel Howard.

"People were looking . . . cracked Johnny up" AUI, Ginny Mancini.

"over the hill . . . more belligerent he got" AUI, Bob Corwin.

"I hate that fucking song" AUI, Miriam Center.

221 "Oh, my God . . . There was a wall" ARI, Margaret Whiting and Jack Wrangler, M95-7, 61.

"Allegorically . . . past that you can't go" JMP, M82-8, 11.

"verbal sensation . . . suggestion of sense" M. H. Abrams et al., *The Norton Anthology of English Literature*, vol. 2 (New York: W. W. Norton, 1968), 1404. Ernest Dowson's poem was based on an ode by the Latin poet Horace.

222 "I think I wrote it . . . at the bar" JMP, M82-8, 11.

"I can't take credit . . . take it down" AUI, Bob Corwin.

"We finally got it . . . in this business" Jack Lemmon, interview, in *Too Marvelous for Words*.

223 "When they were finished . . . And it did" ARI, Ginny Mancini, M94-4, 5.
"I said, 'Now hop' . . . for the message" ARI, Nick Mamalakis, M97-6, 10.

15. When October Goes: 1962–1964

224 "Music can still . . . a matter of course" JMA, III/7.
"had become a derelict shell . . . by the elements" Michael Garrett, "Palace Grand," program notes for *Foxy*.
225 "We decided to . . . came to mind" SPL, "Lyrics by Johnny Mercer," n.d., 42.
"I was only fifteen . . . one dirt road" AUI, Jeff Mercer.
226 "Every time he does . . . to do it!" Quoted in John Lahr, *Notes on a Cowardly Lion: The Biography of Bert Lahr* (New York: Knopf, 1969), 314.
227 "He came up . . . *Foxy* was a sketch" Lahr, 315.
"The rich people . . . on the Yukon River" Quoted in Robert Fishman, "*Foxy:* A Musical Treasure Turned to Fool's Gold," *Show Music* (winter 1988–89), 56.
"The whole show . . . about fourteen thousand" Fishman, 56.
"We had considered . . . be the hit" Fishman, 58.
"he didn't have to . . . any way responsible to" Fishman, 56.
228 "We had a lot . . . to a certain extent, Blyden" Fishman, 56.
"Lahr knew where . . . for a job" Lahr, 319.
"Since the tryout . . . the results closely" SPL, "Lyrics by Johnny Mercer," 42.
"The worst thing . . . money on advertising" Fishman, 57.
"The show, as a show . . . from show to show" NYPL, *New York Herald Tribune*, February 17, 1964.
229 "It's a wonder . . . Merrick gave us" Lahr, 323.
"agreeing with the RCA backers . . . a cast recording" Fishman, 59.
"We could have . . . the producer cared" Lahr, 323.
"He should never . . . the money raising" Fishman, 60.
"*Foxy* I thought . . . unkind word to me" JMA, X/10.
230 "You don't even have . . . that someone yourself!" JMA, X/10.
"When Somebody . . . Songwriter, New York, NY" JMP, M81, 2/9.
"He said he didn't . . . out of show business" JMP, 82–8, 35.
231 "I think one . . . any better than this" ARI, Jean Bach, M95-14, 8–9.
"Blossom was being . . . buddies that weekend" ARI, Jean Bach, M95-14, 9.
"She was recording . . . took all summer" ARI, Jean Bach, M95-14, 10.
232 "There was one . . . 'as it is' or something" ARI, Jean Bach, M95-14, 10.
"He had an American . . . it's just beautiful" Tony Bennett, interview, *Too Marvelous for Words*.
"That was really terrible . . . do it to Seymour" ARI, Jean Bach, M95-14, 12–13.
233 "Oh, you'd go out . . . a lot of sleeping" ARI, Jean Bach, M95-14, 13.
"I was always . . . it was terrific" ARI, Jean Bach, M95-14, 16.
"I just got this idea . . . 'put it together'" Quoted by Jimmy Scalia, "The Dynamic Due," www.jimmyscalia.com.
"I wanted to do . . . That's all" Scalia.
234 "I remember when . . . written with Johnny Mercer" Scalia.
"In those days . . . did three more songs" Scalia.

"They had such a great time . . . stop the band" Scalia.

"As I remember . . . used to hearing" Scalia.

"He is such a pleasure . . . in my pockets" Scalia.

235 "He was afraid Bobby couldn't cut it" AUI, Steve Blauner, telephone interview, July 24, 2002.

"When they were . . . with me again" Scalia.

"The Kennedy assassination . . . as they watched TV" JMA, III/7.

236 "take you for everything you're worth" AUI, Jeff Mercer.

"they were having . . . at the time" AUI, Joyce Pelphrey.

"He had this great regard . . . this world at all" ARI, Jean Bach, M95-14, 10–11.

"You know, I've had . . . 'Yeah, you're right'" ARI, Robert Rush, M98-2, 5.

"old-fashioned and prudish . . . in the house again" AUI, Joyce Pelphrey.

237 "She must have adored him . . . does not buy happiness" AUI, Marsha Hammond, Savannah, Ga., March 3, 2002.

"He was abusive . . . she was saying" AUI, Margaret Whiting and Jack Wrangler.

"He asked Ginger . . . much I know" Rose Gilbert, quoted in Gene Lees, "The Shaping of Johnny Mercer, Part Five," *Jazzletter* 18, no. 10 (January 1999), 7.

"You had to go . . . Very infectious" Lees, 7.

"Will you stay . . . as you live" Lees, 7. Gilbert said she was told of this exchange by her husband, Wolfe Gilbert, a songwriter who was one of Mercer's close friends.

16. Summer Wind: 1963–1969

238 "The lyric gets to so many people . . . and enjoy it" JMP, M81, 1/13, 8–9.

"They didn't want . . . on Gloria's shoes" AUI, Julia Riva, telephone interview, October 26, 2001.

"He liked sex . . . to hear that" ARI, Margaret Whiting and Jack Wrangler, M95-7, 36–37.

"'Charade,' I think . . . to the film" JMP, M81, 1/15.

239 "It was a lovely metaphor . . . and fell apart" ARI, Ginny Mancini, M96-4, 5–6.

240 "As was his habit . . . have you got?" ARI, Ginny Mancini, M96-4, 5.

"especially fond" JMP, M81, 1/15.

"Henry Mancini told me . . . *never* phoned Johnny" ARI, Margaret Whiting and Jack Wrangler, M95-7, 11.

"'Well, there was' . . . all he would say" AUI, Al Jennings, Savannah, Ga., March 8, 2000.

241 "mischievous and sly . . . how he got even" ARI, Ervin Drake, M96-14, 14–15.

"he had a lyric . . . 'Shadow of Your Smile'" ARI, Michael Goldsen, M98-3, 25. According to Barbara Robbins, however, Mercer wrote a "purposely terrible lyric" to Mandel's melody because he thought it derived from one of Harold Arlen's compositions. When Mandel said, "It's not exactly what I'm looking for," Mercer said, "Thank God." "It's a hysterical lyric," said Robbins. "It makes no sense to the picture." ARI, Barbara Robbins, M98-6, 28–29.

242 "You should be . . . bauble is a bomb" Reprinted in Bob Bach and Ginger Mercer, 208.

243 "We were in New York . . . 'whose idea this was'" ARI, Bill Harbach, M96-1, 20–21.

"I still hear . . . into the underbrush" JMP, M81, 1/14.

244 "Jule had always . . . back to New York" ARI, Margaret Whiting and Jack Wrangler, M95-7, 10–11.

"There were always . . . been a racist" AUI, Laurel Howard.

"He asked for some apple pie . . . 'on the train'" ARI, Bill Harbach, M96-1, 5–6.

245 "He would tip . . . wanted to do that" AUI, Jeff Mercer.

"Every black I ever knew . . . to stay mad" JMP, M81, 1/14.

"When he heard . . . 'like Colored People'" AUI, Miriam Center.

"Johnny definitely adhered . . . hurt him deeply" AUI, Al Jennings.

"Johnny, I told you not to use that word" AUI, Ervin Drake.

"darkies" AUI, Jay Livingston, Los Angeles, Calif., May 17, 2001.

246 "'Mama, do you want . . . to the audience'" AUI, Miriam Center.

"I don't like it . . . that down here" ARI, Barbara Robbins, M98-6, 25.

"would hang out . . . practicing racial discrimination" AUI, Jean Bach.

"Oh, just play some colored key" AUI, Jean Bach.

"And up pulls a taxi . . . can you get?" ARI, Robert Rush, M98-2, 20–21.

"I'd like to write . . . need more room" AUI, Ronnell Bright, Kansas City, Kans., April 1, 2000.

"I wanted to sing . . . your beautiful melody" AUI, Ronnell Bright.

247 "sitting at lowly table . . . table number two" AUI, Ronnell Bright.

"Ronnell, what do you want . . . That's just Johnny." AUI, Ronnell Bright.

248 "If it falls apart . . . hard to create" Clarke, 389.

"That beautiful voice . . . toilet to overflowing" Clarke, 390.

"I'm an angry lady . . . and I couldn't" Clarke, 394.

"Everybody was dropping . . . like, never home" Clarke, 398.

"'Who was it?' . . . hide it from her" AUI, James Corwin, Palm Desert, Calif., May 22, 2001.

"Judy would call . . . nice to her" AUI, Nickie Wright.

"I'm worried about Frank . . . while, you know" Clarke, 344.

249 "under the tablecloth . . . perform oral sex" Clarke 399.

"so he could . . . of his semen" Clarke, 381.

"How do you act . . . lost my man" Clarke, 401.

"He told his mother . . . He just cried" AUI, Nancy and Steve Gerard.

"I pulled over . . . like a young boy" JMA, XIII/13.

17. Dream: 1969–1976

250 "I want to tell . . . are that great?" JMA, XI/7.

"The old order . . . they don't dig Mercer's" Quoted by Lee Giffen, "Songwriter Johnny Mercer: Still Going Strong at 64," SPL, *Atlanta Journal*, February 22, 1975, 55.

"They don't want what I do anymore" AUI, Jack Rogers, telephone interview, March 10, 2000.

"Oh God, I should be dead . . . fell into songwriting" Quoted by Lees, "The Making of Johnny Mercer, Part Five," 8.

251 "A songwriter writes . . . and music writers" AUI, Howie Richmond.

"There's Mr. Harburg . . . I don't know" *An Evening with Johnny Mercer*.

"Johnny was *in*" AUI, Margaret Whiting and Jack Wrangler.

"she was getting so bad . . . 'a home there'" ARI, Amanda Néder and Jim Corwin, M96-12, 11.

252 "He was, like, a professional grandfather . . . a very pleasant man" ARI, Amanda Néder and Jim Corwin, M96-12, 33.

"these little teeny . . . in the car" ARI, Amanda Néder and Jim Corwin, M96-12, 34.

"He had a 1971 beige Pinto . . . written the song" ARI, Amanda Néder and Jim Corwin, M96-12, 35–36.

253 "My Little League team . . . and their parents" AUI, Jim Corwin.

"I remember once . . . as he left" AUI, Jim Corwin.

"very polished, very cultured . . . check at Christmas" AUI, Jim Corwin.

"I think the challenge . . . both of them" AUI, Jim Corwin.

"I think he liked . . . songs in him" AUI, Jim Corwin.

"He brought all the boys . . . Ahooo! Ahoooo! Ahooooo!" ARI, Amanda Néder and Jim Corwin, M96-12, 21–22.

254 "I called him 'Beebah' . . . he was 'Bubba'" ARI, Amanda Néder and Jim Corwin, M96-12, 39.

"Here is where . . . but he wasn't" AUI, John Corwin, Los Angeles, Calif., May 25, 2001.

"go back to where . . . say to him now" AUI, John Corwin.

"kind of the rustic . . . wanted to do" AUI, John Corwin.

255 "Yes, I had one . . . hit on Broadway" ARI, Bill Harbach, M96-1, 32–33.

"He twitted . . . 'trying so hard'" ARI, Ervin Drake, M96-14, 8–9.

256 "We've never worked . . . fucks it up" AUI, confidential interview, January 14, 2002. According to other sources, it was Previn who proposed doing a musical based on *Little Women*.

"There's this book . . . bar none" AUI, André Previn.

"He did not . . . in that—in himself" AUI, Ronald Harwood, telephone interview, July 15, 2002.

"I don't think . . . gloom, and smog" JMP, M82, 2/11.

257 "He had a real gift . . . another country" AUI, Ronald Harwood.

"The lyrics kept bursting out of me" Quoted in "The Story of *The Good Companions.*"

"The first time . . . failure in anything" ARI, Hugh Fordin, April 25, 1995, M95-12, 21.

"Okay, so the shows . . . 'didn't write that'" ARI, Hugh Fordin, M95-12, 21.

"didn't matter to a lot . . . Cole Porter?" ARI, Hugh Fordin, M95-12, 22–25.

"was a big hole . . . in his heart" ARI, Hugh Fordin M95-12, 7.

"a little tougher . . . a happy association" ARI, Jean Bach, M95-14, 17–19.

258 "I write quickly . . . 'lyric wasn't finished'" AUI, André Previn.

"I just can't . . . set words to it" AUI, André Previn.

"I'd like to see . . . out of here" AUI, André Previn.

259 "in a pleasant way . . . 'wrong with me'" AUI, André Previn.

"went off into the gentlemen's lavatory . . . thought of it" AUI, Ronald Harwood.

"I think he was one . . . writing the lyric" AUI, Ronald Harwood.

"I couldn't get . . . 'how to phrase something'" AUI, Ronald Harwood.

260 "He was very modest . . . he was right." AUI, Ronald Harwood.

"What do you want . . . why you're here" AUI, André Previn.

"I remember him . . . a happy experience" AUI, Ronald Harwood.

"John said he . . . he needed him" Rose Gilbert, interview, *Accentuate the Positive: The Johnny Mercer Story*.

261 "the audience comes out . . . chime away like bells" NYPL, *London Sunday Times*, July 14, 1974.

"We had a great misfortune . . . to survive" AUI, Ronald Harwood.

"It closed after three performances . . . try another one" AUI, André Previn.

"rather grand . . . never made it" AUI, Ronald Harwood.

"Well, he loved that era . . . closest he ever came" ARI, Amanda Néder and Jim Corwin, M96-12, 42–43.

262 "When I went to visit him . . . for our lives?" JMA, XIV/1.

"a newsboy on a little railway . . . That was a kick" JMA, XVI/1.

"I don't know about you guys, but that's my Joe DiMaggio" JMA, XIV/19.

"When he got sick . . . 'to go home'" ARI, Amanda Néder and Jim Corwin, M96-12, 43.

"He had his arm . . . at the station" AUI, John Corwin.

"That was the last time . . . 'on the air?'" ARI, Nick Mamalakis, M97-6, 11–12.

263 "I can't do it . . . go ahead" AUI, Miriam Center.

"Savannah's still like it used to be . . . loves one another" SPL, Quoted by Sidney Zion, *The Soho Weekly News*, July 1, 1976.

"He didn't have that squeaky . . . on his napkin" ARI, Nancy and Steve Gerard, September 28, 2001, M2001-8, 13–14.

"He had his cousin . . . 'I applaud you'" ARI, Bill Harbach, M96-1, 28.

264 "I was playing this new thing . . . 'go this way?'" ARI, M96-1, 28.

"McCartney has always needed a good lyric writer" AUI, Ronald Harwood.

"You call that a lyric?" AUI, confidential E-mail communication.

"One day his music firm . . . 'do anything now'" AUI, Margaret Whiting.

265 "finally found one doctor that would operate" ARI, Barbara Robbins, M98-6, 6.

"He had safe-deposit boxes . . . the stuff out" AUI, Jeff Mercer.

"very aggressive . . . operating on him" AUI, Dr. Michael Kadin, telephone interview, February 19, 2003.

266 "It was inoperable . . . came down crying" ARI, Barbara Robbins, M98-6, 6.

"The thing that got me . . . are not cancerous" ARI, Bill Harbach, M96-1, 24–27.

"a midline malignant glioma . . . to his surgery" JMP, M95-15/3. I want to thank Dr. Michael Kadin, Dr. Alan Silverstein, and Dr. Terry S. Withers for discussing Mercer's medical condition with me. What I say in the text is my own construction from those discussion and should not be attributed to the physicians.

267 "See, he always wanted to perform . . . 'do any other'" ARI, Amanda Néder and Jim Corwin, M96-12, 30.

"held my hand . . . like a vegetable" AUI, Nickie Wright.

"That would have devastated him . . . just closed up" ARI, Hugh Fordin, M95-12, 18.

"Now, that was a tough time . . . them or anything" ARI, Amanda Néder and Jim Corwin, M96-12, 30–32.

"It was not known . . . thing I saw". ARI, Bill Harbach, M96-1, 26–28.

268 "They made a little hospital room . . . basically a vegetable" AUI, John Corwin.

"Being the 'music' . . . good with words" JMP, M81, 2/11.

"I've been thinking of Johnny . . . talk to him personally" JMP, M-95-15/3.

"she closed herself off . . . took the call" ARI, Barbara Robbins, M98-6, 6.

"My brother . . . getting even with her" AUI, Amanda Néder.

"I'm not sure . . . an interesting couple" ARI, Barbara Robbins, M98-6, 10.

Epilogue: And the Angels Sing

269 "I think I know him . . . with him too" AUI, Nancy and Steve Gerard.

270 "You know, he was always . . . little sister who died" AUI, Nancy and Steve Gerard.

"must have been distressing . . . sister to look after" JMA, XII/2.

"There was not a day . . . 'Don't cry' " AUI, Nancy and Steve Gerard.

271 "Bubba came up . . . 'earn some money?' " ARI, Nancy and Steve Gerard, M2001-8, 2–3.

"My grandmother always . . . he resented it" AUI, Nancy and Steve Gerard.

"There was not . . . there was trouble" AUI, Nancy and Steve Gerard.

272 "But she wasn't . . . get away with it" AUI, Nancy and Steve Gerard.

"My grandmother became . . . marriage was ended" AUI, Nancy and Steve Gerard.

"when it came . . . good to him" AUI, Nancy and Steve Gerard.

273 "And then when that . . . you lash out" AUI, Nancy and Steve Gerard.

274 "are all from here" AUI, Nancy and Steve Gerard.

"the buzz around the movie set . . . other people happy" JMA, XVI/2.

"something you never heard of . . . dig hard enough" *An Evening with Johnny Mercer.*

Books and Essays About Johnny Mercer

Bach, Bob, and Ginger Mercer, eds. *Our Huckleberry Friend: The Life, Times, and Song Lyrics of Johnny Mercer.* Secaucus, N.J.: Lyle Stuart, 1982.

"The Big Fourth." *Time,* 12 May 1947: 90–92.

"Capitol Decade." *Newsweek,* 21 July 1952, 78.

Carrol, Sidney. "Yes, Mr. Mercer." *Esquire,* September 1942, 39, 119–23.

Ewen, David. *American Songwriters.* New York: Wilson, 1987, 279–82.

———. *Great Men of American Popular Song.* Englewood Cliffs, N.J.: Prentice-Hall, 1972, 245–58.

Furia, Philip. *The Poets of Tin Pan Alley: A History of America's Great Lyricists.* New York: Oxford University Press, 1990, 263–82.

———, ed. *American Song Lyricists, 1920–1960.* Detroit: Bruccoli Clark Layman, 2002, 354–74.

Gidlund, Leonora. "Johnny Mercer: Resources for the Study of an American Lyricist." Master's thesis, George State University, 1984.

Giffen, Lee. "Songwriter Johnny Mercer Still Going Strong at 64." *Atlanta Journal,* 22 February 1975, 54–57.

"Johnny Mercer: The Bard from Savannah." *ASCAP Today,* September 1971, 7–10.

Kane, Henry. *How to Write a Song.* New York: Macmillan, 1962, 69–87.

Lees, Gene. "The Shaping of Johnny Mercer." *Jazzletter* 18, nos. 6–10 (June–October 1999).

———. *Singers and the Song II.* New York: Oxford University Press, 1998, 69–89.

Phillips, Joseph. "Johnny Mercer Pays a Debt." *Reader's Digest,* February 1956, 82–86.

Shearer, Lloyd. "The Man Who Writes the Lyrics." *Cosmopolitan,* April 1946, 49, 180–81.

Sheed, Wilfrid. "Bless Yore Beautiful Hide." *Gentleman's Quarterly,* September 1998, 241–50.

"Why Song-Writing Johnny Gave Away $300,000." *Atlanta Journal*, 14 August 1955, 10.

Wilk, Max. *They're Playing Our Song: From Jerome Kern to Stephen Sondheim—the Stories Behind the Words and Music of Two Generations*. New York: Atheneum, 1973, 134–48.

Zinsser, William. *Easy to Remember: The Great American Songwriters and Their Songs*. Jaffrey, N.H.: David Godine, 2000, 157–63.

———. "From Natchez to Mobile, from Memphis to St. Joe." *The American Scholar* 63, no. 2 (spring 1994), 259–66.

Acknowledgments

The writer of a biography incurs more than the usual number of authorial debts to the many people who share their knowledge of his subject. My first and longest-standing thank-you goes to Christine de Catanzaro, Julia Marks, and Chris Paton of the Special Collections Department of the William Russell Pullen Library of Georgia State University. For more than five years, they have guided me through the labyrinth of the Johnny Mercer Papers and shared their insights into Mercer's life and work. I also want to thank Theresa Kidd and Lisa Viall, who helped me navigate the equally rich archive of the Scherer Library of Musical Theatre at the Goodspeed Opera House in East Haddam, Connecticut, and Karen Culbertson, archivist of Woodberry Forest School.

David Oppenheim, president of the Friends of Johnny Mercer organization in Savannah, guided me around the city of Savannah, put me in touch with people who knew Johnny Mercer, and supplied me with a wealth of helpful material, including recordings and radio and television programs. Steve Taksler, who manages a superb Web site devoted to Johnny Mercer, helped me with rare sheet music and other important documents. Similarly, Howard Green, of the Disney organization, shared his extensive collection of Mercer recordings and tapes with me. All three men also shared their appreciation of Mercer in ways that illuminated his achievement for me.

Four of my colleagues at the University of North Carolina at Wilmington—Stanley Colbert, Philip Gerard, Keith Newlin, and Paul Wilkes—read the manuscript of this book at various critical stages. Each an excellent writer in his own right, they took time away from their own books to give mine a thorough and astute reading. I hope that I have been able to incorporate their insights into this final version of the manuscript. Les Block, a former colleague at the University of Minnesota, offered critically important advice at various points, as did Nolan Porterfield, rekindling a friendship that went back to our student days at the Iowa Writers Workshop. William Goldman gave me a wealth of advice in one short meeting at a time when writing about Johnny Mercer seemed an insurmountable enterprise.

A research reassignment from my university provided me with the time to complete the manuscript, and a Cahill Grant enabled me to travel to California, New York, and Savannah to conduct interviews and research. Lorrie Smith, in the Department of Creative Writing, helped me with endless tasks involved in getting this book into print, as did Neil Smith of the department's Publishing Laboratory, Shane Baptista, and my chair, Professor Mark Cox. Dr. Michael Kadin, Dr. Alan Silverstein, and Dr. Terry S. Withers discussed Mercer's medical history with me. Kathleen Johnson graciously lent her professional expertise as a translator of French to help me with Mercer's lyric for "Autumn Leaves."

I also want to thank all of the people who shared their memories of Johnny Mercer with me in interviews: Rita Arlen, Jean Bach, Alan and Marilyn Bergman, Steve Blauner, Ronnell Bright, Frank Capra Jr., Miriam Center, Mike Corda, Natalie Core, Bob Corwin, Jim Corwin, John Corwin, Nickie Corwin, Jim Council, Ervin Drake, Ray Evans, Nancy and Steve Gerard, Fred Grimes, Marsha Hammond, Bill Harbach, Sheldon Harnick, Ronald Harwood, David Holt, Dr. Julius Hornstein, Laurel Howard, Edward Jablonski, Al Jennings, Emma Kelly, Robert Kimball, Ann Mercer Klein, Robert Lissauer, Alan Livingston, Jay Livingston, Nick Mamalakis, Ginny Mancini, Jeff Mercer, Amanda Néder, Polly Ober, Joyce and Gary Pelphrey, André Previn, Ralph Price, Howie Richmond, Julia Riva, Jack Rogers, Georgia Roux, Peter Ruffin, Suzanne Ruffin, Buster White, Margaret Whiting, and Jack Wrangler. I would like to thank all the copyright holders who granted me permission to quote from song lyrics, especially Jack Rosner and Rosemarie Gawelko of Warner Publications.

Finally, I wish to thank my agent, Cullen Stanley, who has believed in this book from the time I first suggested it to her; my editor, Elizabeth Beier, whose warm enthusiasm has always been coupled with trenchant suggestions for improvement; and Adam Goldberger, who copyedited my manuscript with rigor, tact, and imagination. My wife, Laurie Patterson, despite her own doctoral research, her teaching, and her administrative duties, gave me the luxury of seeing her and our daughter, Olivia, off to work and school every morning, then sitting down at my computer to write.

Index

Mercer's songs are designated by an asterisk (*).